Limits to Liberation
after Apartheid

Citizenship, Governance & Culture

Edited by
STEVEN L. ROBINS

James Currey
OXFORD

Ohio University Press
ATHENS

David Philip
CAPE TOWN

James Currey Ltd
73 Botley Road
Oxford OX2 0BS
www.jamescurrey.co.uk

Ohio University Press
The Ridges, Building 19
Athens, Ohio 45701
www.ohioedu.oupress

David Philip Publishers
an imprint of New Africa Books (Pty) Ltd
99 Garfield Road
Claremont 7700, Cape Town
www.newafricabooks.co.za

© James Currey Ltd, 2005
First published 2005
1 2 3 4 5 09 08 07 06 05

ISBN 10: 0-85255-879-1 (James Currey cloth)
ISBN 13: 978-085255-879-9 (James Currey cloth)
ISBN 10: 0-85255-878-3 (James Currey paper)
ISBN 13: 978-085255-878-2 (James Currey paper)
ISBN 0-8214-1665-0 (Ohio University Press cloth)
ISBN 0-8214-1666-9 (Ohio University Press paper)
ISBN 0-86486-674-7 (David Philip paper)

British Library Cataloging in Publication Data
Limits to liberation after apartheid : citizenship,
governance & culture
    1. Citizenship - South Africa. 2. Democracy - South Africa
    3. South Africa - Politics and government - 1994 -
    I. Robins, Steven L.
    320.9'68

Library of Congress Cataloging-in-Publication Data
available on request

Typeset in 10/12 pt Monotype Bodoni
by Long House, Cumbria
Printed and bound in Malaysia

Contents

I

Culture & the Limits of Liberalism

1

2

3

4

II
Rethinking Citizenship & Governance in Urban South Africa

III
Cultural Plurality & Cultural Politics after Apartheid

Notes on Contributors

Ivor Chipkin was a researcher at the Wits Institute for Social and Economic Research (WISER) and is currently based at the University of Oxford. In 2005 he completed his doctoral degree in Political Theory at the Ecole Normale Supérieure de Cachan. His thesis is entitled 'Le sublime objet du Nationalisme'. He has published widely on a number of topics including citizenship, democracy and nationalism in South Africa. He is also actively involved in 'Jewish Voices', a Johannesburg-based organisation that engages with South African Jews about key political issues in Israel and Palestine.

Jean Comaroff is Bernard E. and Ellen C. Sunny Distinguished Professor of Anthropology at the University of Chicago and Director of the Chicago Center for Contemporary Theory. **John Comaroff** is Harold H. Swift Distinguished Professor of Anthropology at the University of Chicago and senior research fellow at the American Bar Foundation. Their publications include *Of Revelation and Revolution*, vol. 1 (1991) and vol. 2 (1997) and several edited collections, such as *Civil Society and the Political Imagination in Africa: Critical Perspectives* (1999) and *Millennial Capitalism and the Culture of Neo-liberalism* (2001). John Comaroff and Jean Comaroff are Honorary Professors in the Department of Social Anthropology at the University of Cape Town.

Shannon Jackson finished her graduate work in Socio-cultural Anthropology at the University of Chicago in 1999. She has been conducting ethnographic fieldwork in Cape Town since 1989, focusing on issues of Coloured identity, urbanisation, and the public sphere. Since 1999 she has been teaching full time at the University of Missouri, Kansas City where she continues her research on issues of identity and the urban environment. She has extended her interests to include embodiment and architectural modernism. She has published articles on education, museums, and the built environment in Cape Town.

Sean Jacobs is a post-doctoral fellow at New York University. He holds a Ph.D. in politics from the University of London. Previously he worked as a senior researcher for the Institute for Democracy in South Africa (IDASA) in Cape Town. Jacobs edited *Thabo Mbeki's World: The Ideology and Politics of the South African President* (Zed Books and University of Natal Press, 2002).

Thomas A. Koelble is Professor of Business Administration in Political Science at the Graduate School of Business, University of Cape Town. He is author of numerous articles and several books including *Democracy and the Global Economy in South Africa* (1998) Rutgers University Press. He is currently working on a book with Edward LiPuma on *The Culture of Democracy in the Post-colony*.

Ron Krabill, Ph.D., is Assistant Professor in the Interdisciplinary Arts & Sciences Program at the University of Washington, Bothell, as well as a Visiting Lecturer at the University of KwaZulu-Natal. His work focuses on comparative media, politics and social movements with a special emphasis on late-apartheid and post-apartheid South Africa; other interests include the history, politics, and ethics of service and broad conceptualisations of peace, conflict, social justice and human rights. He is also a member of the University of Washington's Tri-Campus Human Rights Advisory Board and has extensive experience running service-learning and community action research projects on both the secondary and post-secondary levels.

Edward LiPuma is Professor of Anthropology at the University of Miami. He is author of numerous articles and several books including *Encompassing Others: The Magic of Modernity in Melanesia* (2000), University of Michigan Press and, with Benjamin Lee, *Derivatives and the Globalization of Risk* (2004), Duke University Press. He is currently working on a book with Thomas Koelble on *The Culture of Democracy in the Post-colony*.

Rafael Marks is an architect currently practising in London. Following graduation with an MSc in Urban Development from the Development Planning Unit, London University, he travelled to Zanzibar where he worked on a conservation and development project for the Aga Khan Trust for Culture. In 1995 he moved south to Cape Town where he practised as an architect, taught in the architecture department of the University of Cape Town and carried out several research projects exploring the historical and present urbanism of Cape Town. This included an exhibition entitled 'Texture and Memory: The Urbanism of District Six', later published as a book by the Cape Technikon. *Palaces of Desire* was written in response to the scourge of rampant capitalist development afflicting the post-apartheid city.

Edgar Pieterse is Director of Isandla Institute, an urban development policy NGO based in Cape Town. He is co-editor of: *Democratising Local Government 51; the South African Experiment* (UCT Press, 2002) and *Voices of the Transition: The Politics, Poetics and Practices of Social Change in South Africa* (Heinemann, 2004). He is also a Visiting Lecturer in Urban Studies at the University of Cape Town and the University of Stellenbosch. Current research is focused on urban social movements, the politics of urban integration and insurgent policy responses to differential urbanisation.

Suren Pillay teaches political theory and political philosophy in the Department of Political Studies at the University of the Western Cape, Cape Town. He is currently a doctoral candidate at Colombia University, New York, and researching the relationship between state violence and political identities in South Africa during the late cold war.

Steven L. Robins is Associate Professor of Social Anthropology at the University of Stellenbosch. He has worked on issues of rural development in Matabeleland, Zimbabwe, and the cultural politics of land claims and identity in Namaqualand and the Kalahari

(Northern Cape Province, South Africa). He has also published on Holocaust memory, the Truth & Reconciliation Commission (TRC), and urban governance and citizenship.

Elaine Salo is a feminist anthropologist and lecturer at the African Gender Institute, University of Cape Town, South Africa. Her current research interests include gender and sexuality in African urban contexts.

Clifford Shearing is a Professor at the Regulatory Institutions Network (RegNet) in the Research School of Social Sciences, Australian National University where he is the Co-director of Security 21: International Centre for Security and Justice. His most recent book is *Governing Security* with Les Johnston (Routledge, 2003).

Andrew Spiegel is an Associate Professor and Head of the Department of Social Anthropology, University of Cape Town. His work focuses on southern Africa and has been concerned with kinship and domesticity in contexts of labour migration, urbanisation and housing policy. He has also published on the constructedness of tradition and is presently engaged in an ethnographic study of the expansion of a Europe-based pedagogical movement into southern and east Africa.

Bettina von Lieres is a senior lecturer in the Political Studies Department at the University of the Western Cape in Cape Town, South Africa. She has published articles on issues of citizenship, marginalisation and participation in post-apartheid South Africa. She has also written on problems of democratic theory and inclusion. Her recent research is on new forms of citizen participation and social movement activism amongst the poor in South Africa. She is currently a lead researcher for the Development Research Centre on Citizenship, Participation and Accountability (Citizenship DRC), an international, multi-country research partnership based at the Institute for Development Studies at the University of Sussex, UK. As part of this project she is also working on the politics of inclusion amongst Aboriginal groups in Canada. She is currently living in Toronto with her family.

Jennifer Wood is a Research Fellow at Security 21, RegNet. She is also the General Coordinator of the Argentine Project for Safe and Just Communities that is sponsored by the Canadian International Development Agency and administered by the Centre for International Studies, University of Toronto.

Acknowledgements

I would like to thank CODESRIA for its generous support of the workshops that were the catalyst for this book. I also thank Douglas Johnson, Lynn Taylor and James Currey for their unstinting support. I am grateful to Jonathan Shapiro for granting permission to use his fantastic cartoons. I am also grateful to the contributors for their patience in what has been a long haul to publication. I would also like to thank Jean Comaroff for comments on a draft of the introduction. Special thanks go to Vivienne Ward for her tenacity in finalising the manuscript, and to Kees van der Waal for his support throughout this project. Finally, my appreciation goes to Lauren Miller for her insight and encouragement.

Introduction

STEVEN L. ROBINS

The release of Nelson Mandela in February 1990 was one of the most dramatic political events in South Africa's recent history. Tens of thousands waited patiently in the sun to hear Mandela's speech from the balcony of Cape Town's City Hall overlooking the Grand Parade. Mandela's speech on that day conjured up millenarian visions of national liberation and redemption. Another key moment in the unfolding of the 'political miracle' of the 1990s was the South African Air Force flyover at President Mandela's April 1994 inauguration at the Union Buildings in Pretoria. The massive crowd gasped as fighter jets shot across the Highveld sky, signalling the handing over of state power. This dramatic display of military air power seemed to usher in the new democratic order, one that carried promises that all South Africans would share in post-apartheid's sweet fruits of modernity, progress and prosperity. But it was not long before the expectations of socialist liberation would be tempered with the cold hand of neo-liberal pragmatism and the attendant austerity measures. It also became clear that land restitution and the delivery of housing, jobs, health and education were going to be much more difficult than originally anticipated. Unrealistic targets and time-frames had to be adjusted, and citizens had to come to terms with the limits of liberation.

Whereas the revolutionary rhetoric of national liberation in South Africa envisioned the insurrectionary seizure of state power, the ANC government was rudely reminded of the limits of political power in a country characterised by centuries of inequality and racial domination. During the anti-apartheid struggle, Left scholars had described apartheid as a system of racial capitalism whose overthrow would require more than simply taking racially based legislation off the statute books. Addressing the raw facts of race and class inequality, it was argued, would require nothing less than socialist revolution. However, with the collapse of the Berlin Wall and the breakup of the former Soviet Union, socialism was no longer on the cards for a liberated South Africa. The structural limits of liberation became increasingly visible as the ANC took over the mantle of political power. As the South African economist Sampie Terreblanche put it, the ANC may have won Pretoria, the seat of executive authority, but it did not win Johannesburg, the powerhouse of capital.

A particularly sobering aspect of the South African transition to democracy has been the growing recognition that, while South Africa has one of the most progressive constitutions on the planet, the actual realisation of these constitutional rights has not lived up to expectations. Although there have been considerable gains in terms of 'first generation' human rights – political and civil rights, such as freedom from discrimination on the grounds of race, gender, sexual orientation, religion, etc. – the same cannot be said concerning the realisation of 'second generation' socio-economic rights.[1] Despite these limits, celebrations of South Africa's 'political miracle' continue to focus on, and at times fetishise, 'first generation' rights while glossing over the limited delivery on socio-economic transformation. External and domestic economic and political constraints, as well as capacity problems, have significantly reduced the possibility of extending the scope of socio-economic rights such as rights to housing, to health care and so on. For example, despite international recognition of South Africa's constitutionally enshrined socio-economic rights, recent post-apartheid studies are rude reminders that the poorest 50 per cent of the population are worse off economically than they were under apartheid.[2]

The progressive character of South Africa's Constitution was reinforced following the Treatment Action Campaign's (TAC) successes in pressuring the global pharmaceutical industry to back down after legally challenging initiatives by the South African government to clear the way for importing and manufacturing anti-retroviral generics. The TAC was again in the international limelight following the Constitutional Court ruling compelling the South African government to implement prevention of mother-to-child-transmission (PMTCT) programmes in public health facilities throughout the country.[3] While international commentators continue to laud South Africa's progressive Constitution, less attention has been given to the plethora of problems surrounding the implementation of Constitutional Court rulings. For example, the Constitutional Court order to 'roll out' a national PMTCT programme has been stymied in certain areas by a combination of factors including: a lack of political will from government, social stigma towards HIV/AIDS, socio-cultural barriers to AIDS prevention and treatment (including the disempowerment of women), and logistical, capacity and managerial problems within the public health system. This gap between the rhetoric of rights and the economic and socio-cultural realities is likely to continue to haunt social transformation in post-apartheid South Africa for decades to come.

The chapters in this book suggest that the solutions to many of the problems facing post-apartheid social transformation do not lie in an abstract realm of constitutional law or political philosophy but rather in specific, concrete realities and everyday struggles, negotiations and pragmatic compromises. Acknowledging the limits of South Africa's

---

[1] In the case of cultural rights the outcome has been mixed; the recognition of traditional healers and traditional leaders, as well as traditional marriages, suggests that there have been some gains in the sphere of cultural rights.

[2] The economist Sampie Terreblanche notes that in 1994 the poorest 40 per cent of the South African population was marginalised from the formal economy. By 2003, 50 per cent of the population was marginalised, and unemployment stood at 6.4 million. Terreblanche attributes this dramatic increase in unemployment to the ANC government's free-market and globalisation policies (*Sunday Independent* 15 June 2003).

[3] In December 2001, TAC's legal representatives argued in the High Court of South Africa that the State had a positive obligation, in terms of section 27(2) of the Constitution, to promote access to health care, and that this constitutionally bound obligation could be extended to AIDS drug treatment.

constitutional democracy, the contributors investigate the ways in which citizens and representatives of the state address concrete dilemmas.

The chapter by Koelble and LiPuma addresses the limits on transformation imposed by macro-economic policies adopted by the ANC government. Koelble and LiPuma acknowledge the broad contours of a Left and trade union critique of the ANC's macro-economic policy: the new ruling elite has abandoned the Freedom Charter's brand of socialism and replaced its vision of the interventionist 'Development State' with that of the neo-liberal, rightsized and downsized state. It is these macro-economic policies, Left critics argue, that have led to jobless growth, major cutbacks in government social expenditure, cost recovery measures and privatisation of services such as water, electricity and transport, and the cutting off of essential services for those in arrears. From this perspective, the ANC government has capitulated to the neo-liberal agenda.[4] Despite divergent explanations for why and how this has happened, there is nonetheless consensus amongst these writers that the ANC's GEAR[5] policies and privatisation initiatives have failed to redress inequality. In fact, current macro-economic policies are perceived to be exacerbating historically produced inequalities. This failure to improve the conditions of the bottom 50 per cent of the population has occurred despite moderate rates of inflation, a growing economy, 1.3 million extra telephone connections, clean water for an extra 9 million people, electricity for 1.5 million more, and thousands of new classrooms and clinics. Critics conclude that, despite the benefits of a progressive Constitution and an improvement in the delivery of services, South Africa continues to have one of the most unequal income distribution curves in the world.[6]

This scenario of unrealised expectations of liberation has been told many times before. This book seeks to examine the limits of liberation from a different angle, one that investigates the limits of liberal democracy in relation to questions of 'culture', identity, citizenship and governance. Instead of reiterating political economy critiques of neo-liberalism, or entering the formalistic political science debates on procedural democracy (ballots and political parties), the contributors interrogate the prospects for liberal democracy in relation to questions of cultural diversity, post-apartheid ideas and practices of citizenship and governance.

The chapters in the book fall into three broad areas. Firstly, an investigation of the prospects for liberal democracy in a context of cultural differentiation, marginalisation, and contestation between liberal democracy and cultural claims made on the basis of group rights, custom and 'ethnic' self-determination (von Lieres, John and Jean Comaroff,

---

[4] See Hein Marais, Neville Alexander, Patrick Bond, Sampie Terreblanche to name a few.

[5] GEAR stands for Growth, Equity and Reconstruction Programme.

[6] The broad contours of this strident critique of neo-liberalism go something like this: During the transition process, global and national capital, along with allies within the ANC (the comprador class), conspired to outmanoeuvre the Left within the liberation movement resulting in the shift from the more redistributive Reconstruction and Development Program (RDP) to the neo-liberal orthodoxy of GEAR characterised by rightsizing, downsizing, privatisation and the 'lean and mean' neo-liberal state. This post-apartheid scenario has resulted in the dilution and limitation of the scope of socio-economic rights in ways that have crucial implications for democratic consolidation and civic activism in post-apartheid South Africa. It is precisely because of the failures of the post-apartheid state in the realm of socio-economic transformation that civil society organisations such as NGOs and new social movements have stepped into the breach. The Treatment Action Campaign, the Anti-Eviction Campaign, the Anti-Privatisation Forum, the Soweto Electricity Crisis Committee (SECC) can be seen as militant civil society responses to these perceived failures of the post-apartheid state to address issues of AIDS, job creation and poverty.

Pillay, Koelble and LiPuma). The second cluster of chapters address current debates on neo-liberalism while focusing on issues relating to citizenship and governance in post-apartheid urban spaces (Shearing and Wood, Pieterse, Marks, Jacobs and Krabill, Chipkin; Koelble and LiPuma). Whereas Shearing and Wood's chapter, followed by and Pieterse investigate the 'pro-poor' and progressive possibilities embedded within established neo-liberal modes of governance, the chapters by Marks, Jacobs and Krabill and Chipkin fail to identify any redeeming features of neo-liberalism. The third cluster is less concerned with neo-liberalism than with documenting and analysing the dizzying array of post-apartheid cultural experiences, which include migration/nomadism, gendered identities, constructions of urban 'coloured' identities, and contestations of apartheid and global modernities (Salo, Spiegel and Jackson, Chapters Nine, Ten and Eleven respectively).

Part I
Culture & the limits of liberalism

While there is a growing body of work addressing the socio-economic limits of liberation in post-apartheid South Africa, so far there has been very little reflection on the prospects of liberal democracy given existing conditions of cultural differentiation and contestation. Western debates on multiculturalism offer few insights on these issues, and tend to focus on how to incorporate and assimilate minorities and immigrants into the established democratic order. This has, however, generated an enormous literature on multicultural citizenship and citizenship in diverse societies (see Kymlicka 1995; Kymlicka and Norman 2000). These assimilationist initiatives, with all their homogenising assumptions and 'national culture' imperatives, do not begin to come to grips with the very tangible 'democracy deficits' evident in many Western liberal democracies, including growing public apathy and cynicism about politics, and widening socio-economic inequality and structural unemployment (Luckham 1998: 307). In the developing South, the dis-empowering realities of liberal democracy are considerably more devastating. The countries that underwent democratisation in the 1990s have clearly not met citizens' expectations, and many of these countries have subsequently descended into authoritarian rule, economic decline, civil wars, 'ethnic' violence, famines, political instability and crises of governance and state legitimation. This has in turn contributed to the emergence of an entirely new political science language that uses terms such as 'failed', 'partial', 'kleptocratic', 'criminal', 'rogue' and 'phantom' states and 'limited', 'low-intensity', 'exclusionary' or 'delegative' democracy (Luckham 1998: 307).

This story of the unfinished business of democracy and national liberation is particularly striking in Africa. While the political and economic features of this dire post-colonial predicament are relatively well known, considerably less is known about its socio-cultural dimensions. Relatively little has been written about the growing tensions between the liberal democratic language of rights and the rhetoric of 'culture' in developing countries. Whereas authoritarian ruling elites regularly claim that 'rights talk' in the postcolony is an alien, Western imposition, they have readily appropriated the Western form of the state and neo-liberal macro-economic policies. Such rejections of 'Western' conceptions of rights and liberal democracy also often go with the embrace of the rhetoric of 'culture' and authenticity that promotes exclusivist ethno-nationalisms and the cultural politics of autochthony and xenophobia. This resurgence of ruling elite and popular interest in 'culture' and ethno-nationalism is of course not limited to developing countries in the South.

Reconciling rights and 'culture'
There is a vast literature that takes for granted the purported opposition between culture and rights: rights versus culture. It is becoming increasingly clear, however, that recognising rights does not necessarily mean the denial or dismissal of cultural recognition claims; conversely, recognising cultural difference does not automatically imply rejecting the pursuit of universal individual rights (Cowan, Dembour and Wilson 2001:4; Comaroff and Comaroff, Chapter Two in this volume). This binary opposition between rights and culture fails to acknowledge that both rights and culture talk have to be situated within specific, historically produced social and political struggles. 'Culture' and 'rights' do not exist as givens, but rather they are forged and invoked through historical processes. The chapters in this book draw attention to the complex ways in which 'rights' and 'culture' are being negotiated and contested in ongoing encounters between a liberal democratic post-apartheid state and a highly differentiated 'civil society'.

An interesting recent example of the mutual implication of rights and cultural claims emerged in the late 1990s during the course of the ≠Khomani San land claim in the Kalahari region of Northern Cape Province, South Africa (Robins 2001). With the help of their lawyer, Roger Chennels, and a globally connected NGO (the South African San Institute [SASI]), the ≠Khomani San framed their claim in line with popular conceptions of timeless 'bushman' identity and culture. By stressing cultural continuity and authenticity, the ≠Khomani San were represented as belonging to a bounded, internally coherent and primordial 'bushman culture'. Although the legislative framework of the South African land claims process does not require that cultural authenticity be proved, the success of the ≠Khomani San land claim demonstrated that widespread media dissemination of essentialist narratives of the Kalahari 'bushmen' as Late Stone Age survivors ensured that this particular claim leapfrogged the thousands of others waiting to be processed by the Commission for Restitution and Land Rights. Clearly, from the perspective of the ≠Khomani San and their lawyer and NGO allies, there was no fixed boundary between the rhetoric of land rights and cultural claims.

It clearly made strategic sense, from the ≠Khomani San perspective, to deploy essentialist bushman myths during the land claim process. However, following the land claim settlement, serious intra-community conflicts erupted between 'Westernised' members of the group and 'traditional bushmen'. This conflict was itself the outcome of the contradictory and ambiguous agendas of the donors and NGOs. The latter sought to manufacture *both* modern, rights-bearing citizens, committed to democratic participation and accountability, as well as San peoples committed to indigenous culture and (non-liberal) forms of 'traditional' leadership and governance. In other words, the NGO found itself caught between donors' contradictory desires for both authentic 'bushmen' *and* liberal democratic forms of citizenship and accountability (Robins 2001).

These tensions between liberal democratic principles and the dictates of 'traditional culture' are particularly evident in the ongoing contestations over traditional leadership, customary law, and language and group rights. Given the apartheid state's cynical use and abuse of 'ethnic' and 'tribal' identities as the foundation of the notorious Bantustan system (Boonzaier and Sharp 1988), it is perhaps not surprising that 'culture talk' continues to provoke ambivalent responses from an ANC government. The long history of the ANC as a modern African nationalist movement, coupled with the bitter legacies of the Bantustan system, explains why the ANC generally seems far more comfortable with liberal individualist conceptions of citizenship. It also explains why it has embraced a global, transnational human rights culture that stresses individual rather than group rights. Yet it is possible that the post-apartheid state will increasingly find itself relying on 'traditional' governance structures in response to financial constraints on state expenditure. In other words, the ANC government might well 'outsource' governance and land administration in the former ethnic homeland (Bantustan) areas to traditional leaders.

Koelble and LiPuma (Chapter Four) write about a hierarchy of constraints, including those imposed by global financial institutions, which are undermining the social transformation agendas of the post-apartheid state. This has in turn led to the acceptance of a neo-liberal economic policy paradigm in terms of which the South African state is obliged to 'outsource' many of its core functions, including the governance of rural communal areas, i.e. the former 'homelands' or Bantustans. These developments have strengthened the hand of traditional leadership, at a cost to rural women and the broader objectives of democratic consolidation. While this form of 'indirect rule of a special type' would make strategic sense given the ANC government's commitment to downsizing the Development State, it brings with it significant social costs and democracy deficits. Koelble and LiPuma show how this hierarchy of constraints impacts from the global level of high finance right down to power struggles that constitute national, regional and local politics in the postcolony.

These purportedly contradictory imperatives of neo-liberal pragmatism and democratic consolidation are not easily resolved. It seems as if recognition of the role of traditional authorities in rural governance is taking place despite the ANC's long history of overt antagonism towards traditional leaders, who were seen by many as tribalist, sexist and anti-democratic colonial collaborators and puppets of the apartheid state. Koelble and LiPuma discuss how, in July 2003, calls for a state funeral for former Transkei Paramount Chief, Kaiser Matanzima caused considerable consternation and political ferment, with numerous claims from within the ANC that a state funeral would give legitimacy to an illegitimate former Bantustan leader who had been propped up by the apartheid state. Despite this opposition, President Mbeki and former President Nelson Mandela gave eulogising speeches at the funeral in which they praised the former homeland leader and apartheid collaborator. Koelble and LiPuma discuss the broader implications of this form of post-apartheid historical revisionism, in which a declared 'enemy of the people' during the apartheid period is reinvented as a 'liberator of black people' (see Chapter Four).

Although the ANC government and President Mbeki's ideology of the African Renaissance recognises the significance of African cultural institutions and practices, it remains wary of forms of Zulu and Afrikaner cultural nationalism that could contribute towards reigniting the lethal 'ethnic' conflicts of the recent past. For instance, whereas the

South African government seems to have conceded some ground to traditional leaders, it has rejected white separatist Afrikaner claims to self-determination in a *Volkstaat* (Afrikaner homeland) (see Pillay, Chapter Three). The ANC government has walked a fine line in seeking to reconcile cultural/group rights with a liberal individualist, rights-based Constitution. Post-apartheid state strategies for addressing these cultural claims within the framework of a liberal democratic Constitution are likely to require ongoing processes of negotiation. This suggests that South Africa's liberal democracy will remain an unfinished political project.

The chapters in this book demonstrate that mainstream multicultural theories and political science and policy thinking are an inadequate analytic lens for these perpetually mutating socio-cultural and political processes. The contributors also implode the 'rights versus culture' dichotomy by showing why the mutually implicated concepts of 'rights' and 'culture' have to be understood as historical, fluid and contested. In other words, they cannot be understood through the language of theoretical abstraction and political philosophy, but need to be situated within specific historical contingencies and struggles over meaning.

Democratic dilemmas: recognition versus redistribution?
The ANC government has consistently refused to be taken down the path of group rights and ethnic self-determination. Although this is hardly surprising given the history of apartheid, the rhetoric of Africanisation and the new Constitution have created political and legal space for cultural claims. As a result, the ANC government has been repeatedly forced to renegotiate its positions on traditional leadership, African custom and language rights. For example, political pressures and threats of violence have obliged the government to compromise some of its liberal democratic credentials in order not to alienate and antagonise traditional leaders, a powerful political force within rural South Africa. This has imposed serious constraints on attempts to introduce non-sexist land reforms that provide rural African women with tenure security in circumstances where patriarchal traditional leadership structures have *de facto* control over land allocation and ownership. The contributors draw attention to these tensions. They also draw attention to the strategic compromises and pragmatic manoeuvres that government has devised in order to accommodate these claimants and advocates of cultural and language rights.

A useful theoretical literature for understanding the relationship between liberal democracy and cultural differentiation is outlined by Seyla Benhabib (2002: viii). This study draws attention to the emergence of new forms of identity politics that are exacerbating tensions between 'the universalistic [liberal democratic] principles ushered in by the American and French Revolutions, and the particularities of nationality, ethnicity, religion, gender, "race", and language'. This politics of difference has emerged despite processes of economic, cultural and social homogenisation ushered in by global capital. While McDonalds, Hollywood, CNN and MTV seem to have colonised even the most remote corners of the globe, these cultural forms have encountered resistance, subversion, protest and resignification by those defending their cultural autonomy and 'local' values (ibid.). As Benhabib notes, these world-wide processes have been variously described as 'struggles for recognition' (Charles Taylor, Nancy Fraser, and Axel Honneth), 'identity/difference movements' (Iris Young, William Connolly), or 'movements for cultural rights and multicultural citizenship' (Will Kymlicka). Indigenous rights politics, Afrikaner ethnic separatism, African cultural nationalism, and a growing gay and lesbian movement are all expressions of this globally connected politics of difference (see Robins 2001; Wilmsen and McAllister 1996).

It is widely perceived that post-Cold War popular struggles have shifted focus from class-based social movements and issues of *redistribution* (of economic resources) to identity politics and questions of cultural *recognition*. Nancy Fraser (1997: 5) has argued, however, that redistribution and recognition claims constitute two mutually interconnected but distinct and irreducible paradigms of justice. This book draws attention to the dilemmas and ambiguities of cultural claims in a South African context shaped by colonial legacies of structural inequality. In addressing issues raised by the tensions between universalistic principles and particularistic cultural rights in South Africa, the authors avoid the seduction of cultural reifications and ethnic essentialism. They are acutely aware of the ways in which cultural nationalism and ethnic mobilisation can obscure inequalities along gender, class and other lines. At the same time, they are aware of the limits of forms of economic determinism or class essentialism that treat 'culture' as ideological superstructure.

Clearly questions of cultural difference need to be addressed. Mainstream Euro-American academic and public policy debates on multicultural citizenship are not, however, particularly helpful, as they tend to avoid addressing systemic socio-economic inequalities and focus instead on 'ethnic melting pot' and assimilationist imperatives. Such approaches also presuppose the 'cultural space' of liberal democracy along with liberal individualist notions of citizenship. By contrast, the theoretical reflections and case-studies in this book suggest that the socio-cultural and economic conditions for democracy cannot be assumed or taken for granted in South Africa. The problem is therefore not simply a question of inclusion in the democratic process and the distribution of resources, but rather a question of the fundamental principles of democratic practice and subjectivity. In other words, does the South African situation allow us to presume the existence of citizen-subjects along the lines of the classical Western model of the individual rights-bearing citizen that is deemed necessary for democratic governance, and what is at stake in all this for wider social theory?

Arguing that the politics of post-apartheid South Africa raises important challenges for social theory in general, Bettina von Lieres (Chapter One) considers the relationship between liberal democracy and political and economic marginalisation. The author argues that conventional approaches to the overcoming of marginalisation restrict the question of the incorporation of marginalised groups to two alternatives, assimilation and separatism and, as a result, fail to consider more diverse possibilities for democratic incorporation. Von Lieres proposes a model of democratic incorporation that recognises the fact that political agreements under conditions of extreme marginalisation are highly provisional and open-ended.

John Comaroff and Jean Comaroff take up these issues in their investigation of encounters between African cultural traditionalists and the state's custodians of a universalising liberal Constitution. They illustrate how chiefs, lawyers and judges strive to carve out a space of African custom within the heart of 'Western' modernity. Drawing on a court case about death rituals in North West Province, the authors argue that the contestation between the 'Rule of the Law' (the Constitution) and the 'Kingdom of Custom' is not a zero-sum game; instead, it is an ongoing politics of pragmatism and ceaseless manoeuvring and renegotiation. The contradictions between the 'One Law' of 'The Nation' and the plurality of customary beliefs and practices cannot be resolved but require locally situated 'solutions' and improvised adaptations.

Suren Pillay's chapter on Afrikaner claims to language and minority rights after apartheid focuses on the ANC government's pragmatic manoeuvres in response to Afrikaner recognition claims and Volkstaat aspirations. Pillay is critical of multicultural approaches to minority cultural rights that fail to address the specific contexts and power plays of cultural claims (Kymlicka 1989). For instance, colonialism's legacy of indirect rule and the Separate Development policies of apartheid cannot be ignored when dealing with contemporary Afrikaner claims for ethnic self-determination. The refusal of the South African government to accede to demands by Volkstaters for ethnic self-determination – because it contradicts central tenets of the Constitution – leads Pillay to conclude that liberalism cannot entertain certain claims to difference, which are outside of the differences authorised, for instance, by virtue of being perceived to constitute a threat to individual autonomy, equality and the Bill of Rights.

This case, like the Comaroffs' study, draws attention to liberalism's limits. It leads Pillay to call for more rigorous conceptual labour so that the localness of a universalist argument can be rendered visible in the same way as the voice of the 'local' can be shown to be already situated within an existing (universalist) discourse. In other words, when Afrikaners or African traditional leaders draw on universalistic arguments about 'cultural rights' and 'self-determination' these already exist within a discursive field inhabited by parochial histories of indirect rule and apartheid. This again draws attention to questions of power and the limits of universalising liberal frameworks that do not adequately situate historical constructions of 'culture', 'custom' and 'ethnic' identity. It also draws attention to the limits of the consensus model that animates much writing on South Africa's transition to democracy. These questions clearly have important implications in terms of the limits of citizenship and governance that are addressed in the following section.

Part II
Rethinking citizenship & state governance in urban South Africa

Whereas some observers predicted a systematic process of demobilisation of civil society and the bureaucratisation of political life after advent of majority rule, the post-1994 period has witnessed strong trade union opposition towards the government's neo-liberal macro-economic policies (e.g. privatisation of state assets and the liberalisation of the economy), demands from AIDS activist organisations for state provision of anti-retroviral therapy treatment, calls for more effective land redistribution and other forms of dissent. Depoliticisation is clearly far from complete. In fact, contestation over macro-economic policy has tested the limits of the Tripartite Alliance between the ANC, the South African Communist Party (SACP) and the Congress of South African Trade Unions (COSATU). Vibrant anti-privatisation and anti-globalisation social movements have also animated South African civil society and challenged state hegemony. So what kind of state are we in?

It would seem that the South African state is neither the totalising surveillance state nor the minimalist version of the classical neo-liberal mould. The South African state appears to have a precarious hold on its citizen-subjects, who seem to persistently evade, circumvent and resist state strategies of social control and surveillance. However, this does not imply that we are talking about a weak, 'phantom' state. While the South African government seems to be wary of embarking upon risky and costly ventures, unlike some European states it has not 'outsourced' governance and nation-building projects to 'the market' (Bauman 2001). Instead, it still strives for the modern ideal of the liberal democratic state. Yet private security in the middle-class suburbs and community policing forums in the townships are increasingly being acknowledged by the South African state as a necessary and inevitable response to the predicament of spiralling crime and under-resourced policing departments. This has not, however, led to the government endorsing, or turning a blind eye towards, the violence of anti-crime vigilante groups such as People Against Gangsterism and Drugs (PAGAD) and Mapoga.

While the South African state is, by African standards, a massive and well-resourced apparatus, its capacity to govern and meet the social, economic, health and housing needs of citizens is severely compromised and limited. Like most African colonial and post-colonial states, it is unlikely ever to be in a position to produce the nightmare scenarios conjured up by anti-development critics such as Arturo Escobar. The South Africa state has only had limited success in its deployment of modern bureaucratic techniques for the regulation of the minutiae of everyday life to produce compliant, disciplined subject-citizens (Comaroff 2002: 124).[7] Instead, such state initiatives have often produced violence, resistance, subversion and circumvention. This 'unruly' state of affairs is likely to persist given that the majority of South Africans are still unable to benefit from the freedoms that are meant to belong to rights-bearing citizens.

It would seem that much Foucauldian theorising on the colonial and post-colonial African state has overestimated the reach of the modern bureaucratic state, while underestimating the agency, resistance and 'undisciplined' character of citizen-subjects. These studies have also tended to ignore the spectacular failures of many African states to discipline and order their (un)civil societies and turn their members into compliant citizen-subjects. Recent Foucauldian critiques of the modern surveillance state, including those of Arturo Escobar (1995) and Wolfgang Sachs (1992), unwittingly end up dovetailing neatly with neo-liberal orthodoxy about the need for the downsized post-development state (Robins, 2003). Attacks on the Development State have also been justified on the basis of claims that governments in developing countries are dysfunctional and corrupt. For example, representations of 'criminal' states in Africa (Bayart, Ellis and Hibou 1999), along with accounts of 'vulgar' and ostentatious public spectacles of consumption and rituals of African state power, described as the 'politics of the belly' (Bayart 1993; Mbembe 1992), can be readily appropriated to justify the downsizing of corrupt state bureaucracies and the cutting back of social expenditure and welfare programmes. Similarly, portrayals of Development State disasters in Tanzania (Ujamaa) and the Soviet Union (collectivisation) can be readily deployed to support the arguments

[7] John Comaroff (2002: 121) notes that the more powerful colonial states became 'the less effective they seem to have been over the long run in making "natives" into compliant subjects [and] finally, in surviving the onslaught of anti-colonial forces'.

of neo-liberal ideological warriors. These characterisations and caricatures of the Development State can easily be appropriated to promote and justify a plethora of neo-liberal policies, including decentralisation and programmes that provide loans for micro-enterprises, and those that seek to build 'local capacity', self-reliance and 'social capital'. From this perspective, 'civil society' is valorised as the alternative to intrinsically dysfunctional Development States.

The South African state, it would appear, is caught between its contradictory and ambivalent desires to extend its reach and deliver development (e.g. housing and health care) and the neo-liberal imperatives of the downsizing, rightsizing and outsourcing state. The ANC government is also caught in the middle of a volatile terrain of struggle between its Tripartite Alliance partners (the SACP and COSATU) on the one side, and big business, international finance institutions and investors on the other. These pressures ensure that the South African state is unable to settle into either ideological camp. It is not a classic neo-liberal state and neither is it a textbook modernist social democratic or socialist state. Instead, its policies appear to be the product of perpetual improvisation and pragmatic manoeuvres. Shearing and Wood (Chapter Five) draw attention to the ways in which civil society actors are using similar strategies of improvisation and developing innovative forms of local governance. These community-based innovations are attempting to narrow the 'governance disparity' in South African society.

Narrowing the governance disparity
While political violence and the bloody civil war of the 1980s have all but dissipated, everyday violence and criminal activity continues unchecked. Given this bleak scenario, it is hardly surprising that the South African state is struggling to re-establish governance after apartheid. Neither is it surprising that ordinary citizens have lost faith in the capacity of the police and judicial system to stem the tide of lawlessness and violence that has swept across the country. In many working-class neighbourhoods this loss of faith in policing has led to vigilante violence.[8]

This crisis in governance is particularly evident in South African urban areas, where the efforts by city managers, planners and business entrepreneurs to create globally competitive cities with advanced IT and financial service sectors and world-class hotels and convention centres are regularly undermined by high levels of criminal activity, including violent attacks by heavily armed members of crime syndicates. In response to escalating levels of violent crime, the CBDs and the middle-class suburbs of major South African cities are increasingly characterised by a 'Californianisation' or 'Brazilianisation' of the urban landscape: the creation of fortified enclaves of middle-class gated communities (Caldeira 1996, 2000) with neighbourhood watches, commandos and vigilante

---

[8] In a *Cape Argus* article entitled, 'Kangaroo justice slips past net of law: Arrests change little', it was reported that investigations into the lethal spate of vigilante-style attacks in the Cape Flats townships during the first half of 2002 led to the arrests of dozens of suspects. Nonetheless, the police claimed that they were not any closer in uncovering the vast and efficient network of kangaroo courts operating in the area. Earlier in the year a special unit with 12 investigators was established specifically to deal with vigilantism and kangaroo courts in the Cape Flats (*Cape Argus*, 9 May 2002). On the same day, the *Cape Argus* reported extensively on the case of Harry Joshua, a Cape Flats resident who had killed four Hard Livings gangsters after his wife was held up at knifepoint and his wages were stolen. In his plea to the Supreme Court of Appeal, Joshua's advocate said his client's actions were motivated by his daily experiences of the violent acts of the Hard Livings gangsters that terrorised residents of the Delft area (*Cape Argus*, 9 May 2002).

groups, as well as private security companies, automated surveillance cameras,[9] high barbed-wire fencing and vicious guard dogs. On the other side of the urban divide is the township ghetto characterised by poverty and everyday violence (Davis 1990). The working-class black townships have become ever more disconnected from the historically white middle-class parts of South African cities; white middle-class suburban residents perceive the townships as even more dangerous and 'unruly' than they were under apartheid.

Despite mega-development initiatives aimed at desegregating the apartheid city, the everyday socio-spatial legacies of apartheid continue to be reproduced: middle-class whites seldom venture near the black townships and fears of crime continue to fuel a booming security industry and 'architecture of fear' in the leafy middle-class suburbs and shopping malls (Davis, 1990). While the media and the middle classes attribute the unacceptably high levels of crime and violence to a systemic crisis in governance, Left critics blame global capital and the South African government for neo-liberal economic policies that reproduce the conditions of poverty and structural unemployment conditions that sustain the violent ganglands and drug economies of places such as Manenberg in Cape Town (Robins 2001; see Jacobs and Krabill (Chapter Eight), Chipkin (Chapter Seven) and Salo (Chapter Nine)).

Given limited state resources, the policing of middle-class residential and business districts is increasingly being outsourced to private security companies, resulting in new forms of spatial governance. Sally Merry (2001: 16) writes that whereas 'modern penality is largely structured around the process of retraining the soul rather than corporal punishment [Foucault 1979], recent scholarship has highlighted another regime of governance: control through the management of space'.

Spatial governance and the privatisation of public space seem to emerge in contexts of increasing racial and class polarisation, rising unemployment and poverty. These governance initiatives are also taking place in contexts in which the contracting and retreating neo-liberal state (and its security apparatus) is increasingly helpless in the face of dramatically escalating levels of violent crime and social disorder. This is exacerbated by the fact that large sections of the urban underclass do not seem to buy into the liberal democratic values of virtuous, consumer citizenship. This is hardly surprising given their limited access to economic and political rights in a context of jobless growth and structural unemployment. These developments have placed enormous obstacles in the way of attempts by the South African state to re-establish governance following decades of state violence and systematic race and class inequalities under apartheid.

Attempts at the micro-management of urban space (Merry 2001), including the importation of New York style 'zero-tolerance policing', may be relatively successful in the historically white Central Business Districts (CBDs) but they have proved to be considerably less effective in poor neighbourhoods in which violent underground

---

[9] Cape Town's strategic surveillance unit, which operates the closed circuit television (CCTV) cameras used to fight crime in the city centre and on the N1 highway, has recently begun to expand its operation to include public places and roads in high-crime areas of the Cape Flats such as Manenberg. The CCTV crime unit provides the police and city traffic department with visual information on crime, informal trading, protest marches, advertising billboards and fire hazards. According to Ian Neilson, the Cape Town Unicity's executive councillor for safety and health, the CCTV system would contribute towards the process of developing Cape Town as a model global city (*Cape Times*, 24 January 2002).

economies of drug trafficking, sex work and crime are the only alternatives to unemployment, welfare dependency and chronic poverty (see Robins 2001; Chipkin (Chapter Seven) and Salo (Chapter Nine) in this volume). Where these interventions are successful, for instance in historically white middle-class areas and mega-shopping malls and recreation centres (see Marks, Chapter Twelve in this volume), such attempts at spatial governance usually involve a range of exclusionary measures against 'offensive behaviour' and people, usually the poor and homeless, who look dangerous or disorderly. Meanwhile, in the absence of adequate resources for effective policing or private security, the urban poor continue to be exposed to extraordinary levels of everyday violence. This post-apartheid urban scenario seems to fall far short of the normalising, disciplinary surveillance state that Foucauldian critics are so concerned about!

Much post-apartheid historical and social science literature has endorsed the consensual model of democratic transition, a narrative captured by Archbishop Tutu's image of the 'Rainbow Nation of God'. The chapters in Part II challenge this consensual model by drawing attention to new forms of socio-spatial inequality and what Shearing and Wood refer to as a 'governance disparity'. These inequalities include new types of socio-spatial segregation whereby (predominantly white) middle-class citizens have retreated even further into the privatised public as well as 'safe' private spaces. For the majority of white middle-class South Africans, citizenship generally involves a withdrawal from the public sphere and limited participation in political life. Meanwhile, the black working-class communities often have to resort to community-based vigilante movements after having exhausted attempts to make claims on scarce policing resources.[10]

Focusing on governance after apartheid, Clifford Shearing and Jennifer Wood (Chapter Five) note that established conceptions of governance and citizenship are lagging considerably behind actual governance practices. They employ the term 'nodal governance' to describe a wide range of non-state-centred forms of governance, including the neighbourhood watch committees, shopping mall and airport security procedures and gated communities. Shearing and Wood argue that established understandings of 'citizenship' tend to obscure the changing statuses and affiliations of individuals and collectives *vis-à-vis* multiple governing nodes. They therefore adopt the term 'denizen' to denote the range of expectations and obligations of individuals as they live, work and play within and across new forms of 'communal space'. Their chapter expands on these concepts of 'nodal governance', 'denizenship' and 'communal space' through an analysis of current developments in the governance of security and their normative implications. It also examines the growing 'governance' disparity that is paralleling the growing wealth disparity across the

---

[10] The failure of the state to respond adequately to security, health and housing needs in these poor communities often encourages the strengthening of kinship, clan, village and neighbourhood ties, and religious and occult movements. These can become a serious obstacle to state attempts to transform 'the masses' into autonomous and 'virtuous' citizens of the nation state. These moral communities and parochial institutions and structures are often inaccessible to 'outsiders', and can contribute towards undermining the effectiveness and legitimacy of public/state institutions. The insularity and parochial character of these moral communities also foster evasion, circumvention and overt and subtle forms of opposition to state governance, thereby undermining attempts to manufacture a 'national consensus' based on liberal democratic principles, rules, duties and obligations. Evidence of this breakdown includes land invasions, staggering levels of crime and violence, international drug trafficking, criminal gangs and cartels, vigilantes, and popular boycotts of the payment of municipal service levies, electricity, rent and rates. This inability to assume the prior existence of a cultural space of liberal democracy and citizenship has significant political and theoretical implications for the future of South Africa.

globe. This essay includes an analysis of the authors' own practical engagement with innovations in local governance in poor communities in South Africa and Argentina. It complements Pieterse's chapter (Six), which is based on personal experiences as a key player in developing the new urban governance institutional frameworks for the City of Cape Town.

Edgar Pieterse's study provides an insider perspective on new forms of partnership-based urban governance referred to as 'CDS' (City Development Strategy). Rather than simply dismissing this as yet another neo-liberal incarnation of earlier discourses on 'good governance' and decentralisation, Pieterse explores the implications of the CDS approach for the establishment of a transformative, radical political agenda in urban politics in metropolitan Cape Town. Through a critical review of theoretical debates in the literature on the political efficacy of dialogical planning processes, Pieterse explores the relevance and feasibility of proposals to establish the CDS process in Cape Town, with its widespread informality and deep political cleavages. Pieterse's recognition of the political implications of the 'governance disparity' within Cape Town allows him to provide a theoretically and politically engaged analysis of the limits and possibilities of CDS as a modality of urban governance.

Chipkin's chapter also takes up the challenge of post-apartheid urban governance by analysing an innovative City of Cape Town (CCT) intervention in Manenberg, the predominantly working-class, 'coloured', Afrikaans-speaking township in Cape Town (see Jacobs and Krabill, Chapter Eight). Through a close reading of CCT's planning discourse, he argues that 'development' is not simply about the delivery of a range of social goods or the building of public infrastructure. Instead, it presupposes an ethical norm, a moral register, such that development is about the capture of those being 'developed' to a certain normative conception of the *good and virtuous* citizen. The vehicle for this ethical project is the nuclear family. The chapter describes this ethical imaginary and considers the limits to its realisation. These issues are also addressed in Jacobs and Krabill's investigation how the mass media have represented Manenberg, and the wider 'Cape Flats', as a homogeneous space of pathology and dysfunctionality.

Jacobs and Krabill examine how the media covered the 'Manenberg Tornado', a heavy rainstorm that swept through this township in August 1999, destroying houses and leaving thousands homeless. They show how media coverage of this event, the rescue operation and the subsequent rehabilitation of Manenberg ended up representing this working-class coloured township as a homogeneous space of social pathology. Jacobs and Krabill argue that through these media representations Manenberg came to stand in for a vast and heterogeneous working-class area referred to as the Cape Flats. They also show how residents were represented as 'innocent victims' at the time of the disaster, but later, as they expressed anger and frustration with the slow pace of the rebuilding process, as 'unruly' and 'undeserving'. Like Chipkin's study, this chapter raises important questions concerning the assumptions that underpin notions of the 'virtuous citizen'. Whereas Chipkin and Jacobs and Krabill are concerned with hegemonic representations of social space, Rafael Marks (Chapter Twelve) focuses on the ways in which the socio-spatial grids of the apartheid city are being reproduced by a postmodern architectural dystopia comprising mega-shopping malls and theme parks that destroy public space and possibilities for progressive urban citizenship.

Part III
Cultural plurality & cultural politics after apartheid

This section comprises an interdisciplinary collection of chapters that engage with questions of 'culture', space and identity. The authors draw on an eclectic theoretical toolkit that includes Marxism, post-structuralism, postmodernism and cultural studies. Rather than viewing South Africans as passive victims of an all-encompassing global system of neo-liberal capitalism, they draw attention to the agency, contestations and cultural creativity of ordinary citizens seeking to navigate the complex terrain of the post-apartheid political and cultural landscape.

This engagement with cultural agency goes beyond the deconstructive agenda of the influential apartheid-era anthropology text *South African Keywords* (Boonzaier and Sharp 1988). Whereas *Keywords* systematically debunked the apartheid state's essentialist uses and abuses of concepts such as 'tribe', 'community', tradition, 'culture' and so on, this collection is more concerned with everyday expressions of cultural politics that emanate from sources other than the state. Most of the authors of this volume recognise that ordinary citizens are often the primary authors of post-apartheid forms of cultural expression. This differs markedly from the state-centric approach of *Keywords*. For example, without romanticising individual agency, Elaine Salo shows how urban youth in the working-class 'coloured' neighbourhood of Manenberg, Cape Town, develop their own creolised and highly localised version of global youth culture.

For Marks, the agenda for urban development in post-apartheid Cape Town is being driven by big business and an architectural semiotics of neo-liberal capital. The chapter provides an uncompromising critique of the 'unholy alliance' between a culture of neo-liberalism and 'post-modern' corporate architecture. The object of his fury is Century City, a multi-million Rand mega-development eight kilometres from Cape Town's city centre that combines an office park, a regional shopping centre, entertainment complex, MTN 'Science centre', an adventure park, gated residential complexes and a wetland ecosystem. Marks decries the ways in which the City fathers (sic) allowed Century City to stymie progressive urban development efforts to desegregate the apartheid city. Like Edward Soja and Mike Davis, Marks critiques the nostalgic pastiche that animates Century City's cacophony of styles – ranging from Venetian canalside palazzi to Lost City-meets-Palladio office blocks to Swiss ski resort. He locates this postmodern simulacrum within a global context of market-led urban development. It is also a neo-liberal moment in which all aspects of urban life are rapaciously commodified, and where the privatisation and Disneyfication of public space erode democratic possibilities for urban governance and citizenship. For Marks, Century City represents a dark postmodern architectural dystopia, a monument to commodity fetishism and a global consumer culture that destroys any prospects for instilling a sense of civic pride and for creating meaningful public spaces. Marks's critique of Century City stands in creative tension with the other chapters of Part III, which question whether capital and the culture of neo-liberalism are as homogenising and totalising as some of its most vehement critics suggest. These authors acknowledge structures of inequality but foreground the agency, fluidity and cultural plurality that animate the post-apartheid public sphere.

Unlike Marks's nightmare vision of Century City as an icon of the architectural semiotics of global capitalist consumerism and Disneyfication, Salo provides a far more ambiguous account of the impact of global consumer culture on the racial and gendered identities of young men and women in Manenberg. The chapter shows how male and female youth create local racial and gendered identities in relation to the local histories, repertoires and ideals of masculinity and femininity, as well as in relation to global cultural forces such as soap operas, rap music and international brand name clothes. Young people obtain access to these global features through television, radio or visits to trendy city nightspots and cosmopolitan beachfront neighbourhoods. This ethnographic study challenges the idea that cultural flows from the North necessarily lead to cultural homogenisation in the South. While acknowledging the savvy and creative ways in which young people engage with global consumer culture, Salo also reflects on how young women are often ultimately 'captured', normalised and disciplined through gendered webs of domesticity and parochial forms of social control, including patriarchal and sexist gang cultures. In other words, much like Paul Willis's (1978) seminal ethnographic study of the anti-schooling resistance of working-class 'lads' in English secondary schools in the Midlands, Salo tempers celebrations of 'local' agency and creativity by drawing attention to the limits and paradoxes of youth resistance to parochial forms of social power through the consumption of global signs, music, lifestyles and commodities.

Andrew Spiegel's meditations on the protean meanings of the word '*spaza*'[11] also capture the ambiguities and paradoxes of agency, resistance, emancipation and urban citizenship. Spiegel shows that, since the late 1970s, *spaza* shops have become an increasingly common feature in South Africa. The chapter traces the history of these shops and then proceeds to consider the genealogies of the word *spaza*. Spiegel discusses the process of attempting to derive its etymology and its contemporary meanings. In these discourses he identifies a subtle form of anti-hegemonic resistance that has a long history in the region, and that now reappears in the form of a verbal trope that resonates with ideas about urban citizenship, belonging and respectability. While Spiegel identifies *spaza*-speak as an articulation of an insurgent citizenship, it can also be read as a familiar story of failed expectations of modernity and liberation. Whereas millions of South Africans have dreamt, and continue to dream, of the possibility of owning a 'real' shop and a modern, respectable house, the vast majority have had to reluctantly accept that only a few will be able to become 'truly modern'. Perhaps this is the painful truth of '*spaza* citizenship' in a liberal democracy. Shannon Jackson's chapter (Eleven) takes up similar issues in her examination of the limits and ambiguities of 'coloured'[12] strivings towards (bourgeois) respectability.

---

[11] *Spaza* is a vernacular term that is widely used to refer to informal general stores in South African townships.

[12] The category 'coloured' disguises the cultural heterogeneity and hybridity of people many of whom have European, African, Khoe, San, Indian, Indonesia, Malay and slave backgrounds. The majority of so-called coloureds do not identify themselves as having indigenous Khoe, San, or slave ancestry, largely because of the negative connotations these categories had during apartheid. However, this is changing in the post-apartheid context as a result of the more positive associations now attached to indigenous, slave and African histories, heritage and identities. This could counter the past tendency of coloureds to stress their European background and ancestry.

Jackson traces the genealogy of the category 'coloured' by investigating the historical significance of conceptions of family, moral community, respectability and bodily constraint.[13] She analyses what she refers to as a 'proxemics of constraint', which is captured in the title: Coloureds don't Toyi-Toyi.[14] This finds expression in the refusal of 'respectable coloureds' to participate in 'unruly' public behaviour such as the toyi-toyi, which in turn curtails the possibility for certain forms of African solidarity and resistance. In other words, historically produced bodily comportment and notions of respectability continue to shape 'coloured' notions of belonging and exclusion. This expression of 'practical consciousness' has important implications for understanding the relationship between embodiment, space and identity construction. It is also at the heart of Jackson's critique of instrumental theories of identity formation. Like the chapters by Salo and Spiegel, this ethnographic study highlights the Janus-faced nature and limits of discourses of emancipation.

Concluding reflections on global democratic futures

Writing primarily about 'the North', Nancy Fraser (1997: 2) suggests that the post-1989 period has witnessed a shift from political claims on the grounds of social equality to claims based on group difference. In fact, Fraser identifies this explosion of 'culture/group talk' as 'a defining feature of a post-socialist condition' (ibid.; cited in Cowan, Dembour and Wilson 2001: 2. See also Fraser 1989). This tumultuous post-Cold War period has also witnessed the emergence of globally connected struggles that are simultaneously about 'rights' and 'culture', for instance indigenous peoples and landless peoples movements. It is also a period in which new social movements have emerged on a global scale focusing on AIDS, indigenous rights, Third World debt, trade liberalisation, gay and lesbian rights, the environment, biotechnology, reproductive rights, housing, animal rights and so on. South Africa has of course not been exempt from these new forms of political struggle, which are increasingly taking place simultaneously in the 'local community', the nation-state and global and supra-national institutions and transnational civil society organisations. But what are the implications for citizenship and governance of this growing global public sphere? Can these new globally connected social and political forms address the limits of national liberation in the developing world?

The recent Anti-Racism and AIDS Conferences in Durban and the World Summit on Sustainable Development in Johannesburg revealed the extent of involvement of South African civil society organisations in this emerging global public sphere. The involvement of organisations such as Médecins Sans Frontières (MSF or 'Doctors without Borders') in South African AIDS activist struggles for anti-retroviral treatment is simply one example of a plethora of local–global activist collaborations in the land, housing, health and

---

[13] Such rhetoric privileged the production of particular models of family, which then required particular models of domestic architecture. So, for the ancestors to today's coloureds, this set up the foundations for moral community as well as material frameworks for respectable households.

[14] The toyi-toyi is a dance associated with anti-apartheid resistance. It is usually accompanied by songs of rebellion and defiance.

environment sectors. The formation of internationally connected civil society organisations such as the Anti-Privatisation Forum, the Landless People's Movement (LPM) and the South African Homeless Peoples Federation (Robins 2005), as well as anti-globalisation groups such as Jubilee 2000, has been of particular concern to the ANC government because of the radical and anti-capitalist agendas of some of these global networks.[15] It remains to be seen to what degree these global social movements (Cohen and Rai 2000) are able to overcome the transformational limits of the nation state.

Notwithstanding the media visibility of these global social movements, relatively little reflection has gone into assessing exactly who belongs to this emerging global civil society and what this form of belonging could mean for diverse social classes in different parts of the world. For example, what does all this global connectivity offer in terms of addressing the profound structural limits of liberation in South Africa identified in the chapter by Koelble and LiPuma? Can these new forms of 'grassroots globalisation' transcend the limits of the neo-liberal state, and, if so, how? Or is all this global talk global hype?

Elsewhere I have discussed the limits and possibilities for democratic participation in relation to AIDS activism and the transnational housing activism of the South African Homeless People's Federation (SAHPF), an affiliate of the Slum Dweller's International (SDI) (Robins 2005). The SAHPF case study investigated the degree to which these globally connected organisations have become vehicles for forging progressive forms of cross-border activism, and whether this has indeed resulted in the 'deepening of democracy' (Appadurai 2002). Despite widespread celebrations of the emancipatory possibilities of these civic experiments in 'grassroots globalisation', many of these community-based organisations continue to be characterised by non-democratic forms of local patronage, gate keeping and authoritarian and centralised decision-making (Robins 2003). In addition, it is also clear that many of these globally networked housing organisations have not bypassed the South African state, which continues to dispense development and patronage in the form of millions of housing subsidies and welfare grants. The South African state is likely to remain a key developmental player notwithstanding the emergence of globally connected civil society organisations such as SAHPF.[16] Nowhere is this more evident than in South Africa's 'global cities' such as Cape Town and Johannesburg.

---

[15] This rise in 'global citizen action' has been described in a vast and burgeoning academic literature as cross-border activism (Keck and Sikkink 1998), global social movements (Cohen and Rai 2000); global civil society (Clark and Gaile 1997); global governance (Deacon et al. 1997, Edwards 1999, Scholte 1999) and 'global citizenship' (Gaventa 2001).

[16] While terms such as global civil society conjure up optimistic images of Manuel Castells's networked information societies, it would seem that for the vast majority of poor people in the developing world even the prospect of creating local community networks is often out of reach. Whereas 'community' continues to suggest feelings of comfort, safety and security, it is an increasingly elusive 'paradise', especially for the poor who are in most need of its protection and security. For the poor, the ghetto has become a space that represents 'the impossibility of community', a place of social disintegration, atomisation and anomie' (Wacquant in Bauman 2001: 122); as a document on the SDI website puts it: 'poverty is a relentless isolator'. According to Wacquant, 'Whereas the ghetto in its classical form acted partly as a protective shield against the brutal racial exclusion, the hyper-ghetto has lost its positive role of collective buffer, making it a deadly machinery for naked social regulation' and isolation (Wacquant in Bauman 2001: 122; see also Merry 2001). For the poor trapped in rural and urban ghettoes in South Africa and elsewhere in the world, the Development State remains the most likely source of support and patronage.

Mike Davis (1990) has written eloquently about 'Fortress L.A.' as the archetypical Northern American city – perhaps even the quintessential global city – characterised by middle-class suburban enclaves and gated communities on the one side, and black ghettoes on the other; elsewhere I too have written about post-apartheid Cape Town as 'Fortress L.A. at the tip of Africa' (Robins 2000). The chapters in this volume demonstrate that the post-apartheid period has witnessed heightened socio-spatial segregation between ghettoes and gated *communities*, thereby reproducing the fortified white enclaves and racialised black camps of the apartheid era. What forms of global citizenship, solidarity and activism are possible within and between these highly polarised environments? Given this post-apartheid scenario how can relations of cooperation and exchange, let alone new forms of (post)national citizenship, be forged amongst poor people in South Africa and elsewhere in the South? What relations and connections are possible between the urban poor and the new and old elites living beyond the ghetto walls – i.e., the politicians, bureaucrats and business elite, and the professionals and middle classes barricaded in gated communities? Are the middle classes interested in looking beyond their high walls and electrified barricades? Are the suburbs not attractive to the old and new elites precisely because they appear to allow for a degree of disengagement from the immediacy of urban problems of poverty, crime and violence? What does national *and* global citizenship mean in the face of these stark post-apartheid realities? Given this post-apartheid scenario what kinds of local–global solidarities and forms of citizenship and governance are possible?[17] What could 'grassroots globalisation' and global citizenship look like from the townships and informal settlements at the tip of Africa? How will the post-colonial state respond to the new forms of global apartheid that are highlighted by the authors of this book? These questions, which the contributors to this volume have identified and grappled with, need to be incorporated into future research agendas on the limits and possibilities of liberation in the post-colony.

[17] Community and citizenship are Janus-faced: they may offer the prospect of security and protection, but they can also represent danger, threat and exclusion. For example, while for some the membership of a 'traditional community' offers comfort and security, for others it involves constraints on individuality and freedom. In other words, to belong one has to conform to the dictates and norms of 'community values'. Belonging to a 'traditional community' can also cost you your life, as Gugu Dlamini discovered when she was killed by community members for publicly divulging her HIV-positive status and being perceived to have brought shame and stigma to her rural village. Similarly, male members of tightly knit 'traditional communities' regularly conspire to deprive women of ownership of rural land by drawing on the traditional land tenure system. Witchcraft is another danger that lurks for older women living in 'traditional communities'.

References

Appadurai, A. (2002), 'Deep Democracy: Urban Governmentality and the Horizon of Politics', *Public Culture*, 14(1): 21–47.

Bauman, Z. (2001), *Community: Seeking Safety in an Insecure World*, London: Polity Press.

Bayart, J.P. (1993), *The State in Africa: the Politics of the Belly*, London: Longman.

Bayart, J.P., S. Ellis, B. Hibou, (1999), *The Criminalization of the State in Africa*, London: International African Institute in association with Oxford: James Currey, Bloomington: Indiana University Press.

Benhabib, S. (2002), 'The Claims of Culture: Equality and Diversity in the Global Era', Princeton and Oxford:

Princeton University Press.

Boonzaier, E. and J. Sharp (1994), 'Ethnic Identity and Performance: Lessons from Namaqualand', *Journal of Southern African Studies* 20 (3): 405–15.

Boonzaier, E. amd J. S. Sharp (eds) (1988), *South African Keywords: The Uses and Abuses of Political Concepts*, Cape Town: David Philip.

Caldeira, T. (1996), 'Building Up Walls. The New Pattern of Segregation in São Paulo', *International Social Science Journal* 48(1): 55–65.

—— (2000), *City of Walls: Crime, Segregation, and Citizenship in São Paulo*, Berkeley: University of California Press.

Clarke, J. and G. Gaile (1997), 'Local Politics in a Global Era: Thinking Locally, Acting Globally', *Annals* (The Annals of the American Academy of Political and Social Sciences), No. 551, May.

Cohen, R. and S.M. Rai (eds) (2000), *Global Social Movements*, London and New York: The Athlone Press.

Comaroff, J.L. and J. Comaroff (eds) (1999), *Civil Society and the Political Imagination in Africa: Critical Perspectives*, Chicago: University of Chicago Press.

Comaroff, J. L. (2002), 'Governmentality, Materiality, Legality, Modernity: On the Colonial State in Africa', in J. G. Deutsch, P. Probst and H. Schmidt, *African Modernities*, Portsmouth NH and Oxford: Heinemann and James Currey.

Cowan, J.K., M. Dembour and R. Wilson (eds) (2001), *Culture and Rights: Anthropological Perspectives*, Cambridge: Cambridge University Press.

Davis, M. (1990), *City of Quartz: Excavating the Future of Los Angeles*. London: Verso.

Deacon, B., M. Hulse and P. Stubbs (1997), *Global Social Policy: International Organisations and the Future of Welfare*, London: Sage Publications.

Escobar, A. (1995), *Encountering Development: The Making and Unmaking of the Third World*, Princeton NJ: Princeton University Press.

Foucault, M. (1979), *The History of Sexuality*, London: Allen Lane.

Fraser, N. (1997), *Justice Interruptus: Critical Reflections on the 'Postsocialist' Condition*, London: Routledge.

Fraser, N. (1989), *Unruly Practices: Power, Discourse and Gender in Contemporary Social Theory*, Minneapolis: University of Minnesota Press.

Gaventa, J. (2001), 'Exploring Citizenship Participation and Accountability', *IDS Bulletin*, 33(2): 1–10.

Keck, M.E. and K. Sikkink (eds) (1998), *Activists Beyond Borders: Advocacy Networks in International Politics*, Ithaca, NY: Cornell University Press.

Kymlicka, W. (1989), *Liberalism, Community and Culture*, Oxford: Clarendon.

—— (1995), *Multicultural Citizenship: a Liberal Theory of Minority Rights*, Oxford and New York: Clarendon Press.

Kymlicka, W. and W. Norman (eds) (2000), *Citizenship in Diverse Societies*, Oxford: Oxford University Press.

Luckham, R. (1998), 'Are There Alternatives to Liberal Democracy?' in M. Robinson and G. White (eds), *The Democratic Developmental State. Politics and institutional design*, Oxford: Oxford University Press.

Mbembe, A. (1992), 'The Banality of Power and the Aesthetics of Vulgarity in the Postcolony', *Public Culture*, 4(2) (Spring): 1–30.

Merry, S. E. (1981) *Urban Danger: Life in a Neighbourhood of Strangers*. Philadelphia: Temple University Press.

—— (2001), 'Spatial Governmentality and the New Urban Social Order: Controlling Gender Violence through Law', *American Anthropologist* 103:16–30.

Robins, S. (2000) 'City Sites: Multicultural Planning and the Post-apartheid City', in Sarah Nuttall and Cheryl Ann Michael (eds) *Senses of Cultures: South African Culture Studies*, Cape Town: Oxford University Press.

—— (2001), 'NGOs, "Bushmen" and Double Visions: The Khomani San Land Claim and the Cultural Politics of "Community", and "Development" in the Kalahari', *Journal of Southern African Studies*, 27(4), December.

—— (2003), 'Grounding 'Globalisation from Below: Global Citizens in Local Spaces', in David Chidester, Philip Dexter and Wilmot James (eds), *What Holds Us Together: Social Cohesion in South Africa*, Cape Town: HSRC Publishers.

—— (2005), Robins, S. (2005), 'Housing Activist Networks from Cape Town to Calcutta: A Case Study of the Politics of Trust and Distrust', in Steinar Asvik and Nelle Bak (eds), *Trust in Public Institutions in South Africa*, Burlington, VT: Ashgate.

Sachs, W. (ed.) (1992), *The Development Dictionary: A Guide to Knowledge and Power*, London: Atlantic Highlands.

Willis, P.E. (1978), *Learning to Labour: How Working Class Kids get Working Class Jobs*, Farnborough, Hants: Saxton House.
Wilmsen, E. N. and P. Mcallister (eds) (1996), *The Politics of Difference: Ethnic Premises in a World of Power*, Chicago and London: University of Chicago Press.

I
Culture &
the Limits of Liberalism

1

Marginalisation & Citizenship
in post-Apartheid South Africa

BETTINA VON LIERES

The transition to democracy in South Africa during the 1990s marked an important moment in the development of the global trend towards democratisation. For many, South Africa's negotiations to democracy represented the new post-Cold War age of 'deliberative' consensus and societal integration. However, South Africa's fledgling democracy can also be seen to represent its opposite: the continuation of often violent forms of political contestation and the breakdown of consensus. These realities have resulted in a complex configuration of politics underlying post-apartheid society. At the centre of its political system lies an explosive mixture of liberal and non-liberal politics. The cornerstone of the new democracy, a liberal democratic constitution, is underpinned by a politics with often little or no allegiance to liberal democratic traditions. Indeed, state-driven political discourses are often openly at odds with local political discourses, pitting a politics of juridical liberal individualism against a community-directed politics of collective and cultural rights. These collisions are often framed within a wider juxtaposition of two divergent political discourses: one of political rights, legal proceduralism and social justice and another of cultural rights and customary politics. These clashes occur in local political arenas which have traditionally not been liberal democratic in character. In many local communities associational life was built on political traditions suspicious of pluralist competition. The idea that the will of the citizenry is the subject of a political contest has been rejected. In particular, many communities can be seen to have relied on a form of political life in which the rule of law was absent. The high level of violent antagonism in past political struggles has generated a tradition of political interaction far more reflective of a mode of insulation than a mode of negotiation. In today's post-apartheid era, there is a real possibility that authoritarian political forms may entrench themselves even further. They are likely, at first, ostensibly to appropriate the requisite symbols of liberal democratic principles, while remaining authoritarian in character. In turn they will become so well entrenched that the new government tolerates them for the sake of 'order' and 'stability'.

Far from resulting in a smooth blend of consensual politics, then, post-apartheid politics can be seen to represent a volatile and complex configuration of liberal and non-liberal elements. On the surface, post-apartheid democracy seems to bring together at least three distinct types of liberal projects: a minimalist liberalism aimed primarily at the establishment of the rule of law and minimalist government, a juridical liberalism concerned with rights, justice and obligations, and a communitarian liberalism concerned with cultural pluralism, communal values and group rights (see Connolly 1991: 81–94). At a deeper level each of these liberal strands is criss-crossed by a politics that threatens its very existence: the minimalist liberal strand finds its opponent in a spreading culture of lawlessness, the juridical liberalism finds its foe in social movements demanding more substantive economic equity, and the cultural communitarian strand finds its opposite in marginalised groups demanding various forms of self-determination. As a result of these confrontations, post-apartheid liberalism is continuously undercut by non-liberal discourses which are the effects of identity/difference struggles articulated and attempting to find resonance in contexts other than the ones provided by liberal constitutionalism.

These struggles are bound together by the experience of marginalisation. In contemporary South Africa the introduction of democratic political arrangements has gone hand in hand with the unmasking of widespread marginalisation. While the majority of people's legal status is assured, their experience of citizenship remains ambiguous. They continue to be excluded from economic equality and empowerment and effective, democratic participation in the public sphere. If the South African case is emblematic of anything, it is the intertwining of democracy and marginalisation in contemporary life.

Although there are important differences in the types of challenges faced by more established democracies and those facing South African democracy, the latter, far from representing an irrelevant exception to Western liberal democracy, harbours significant implications for it. In fact, South Africa's transition to democracy raises key challenges for contemporary democratic theory in general. Chief amongst these is the profound challenge of identity/difference politics to the future of liberalism and the value of consensus-based understandings of democracy in complex, culturally diverse societies with few shared 'pre-understandings' amongst their citizens. One of the key political problems facing democracies on a global scale today is the negotiation of cultural diversity and difference, and their accommodation within liberal democracy. While my chapter explores some aspects of these questions, they do not form its principal focus. Instead, I am concerned with exploring a set of problems which has not been the focus of much attention, and one which to me seems to emerge out of the specific political configuration underlying post-apartheid politics. In post-apartheid South Africa, the problem of difference shifts from one of how to accommodate marginalised identities democratically into a society with existing modalities of shared 'pre-understandings' to the very constitution of the politics underlying these modalities. Specifically, the South African case throws into sharp relief the issue of the form of politics underlying the *incorporation* of marginalised groups into the wider polity in contexts where marginality is the rule.

A consideration of the problem of marginalisation potentially challenges some key liberal assumptions about the consensual underpinnings of society, and the conception of politics which underlies them. In post-apartheid South Africa, with its fragmented polity, societal agreements on liberal political values are often episodic and by no means overarching. The language of rights has not always articulated the demands of marginalised groups with ease. As a consequence of widespread alienation from the public sphere, liberal rights-based discourses are not always capable of providing a neutral language for political argument. The South African case demonstrates that there is no reason why a consensus on liberal political values should be more likely than an agreement on comprehensive conceptions of the common good. The problem of marginalisation in post-apartheid South Africa shows how, when competing conceptions of rights are in play, and are themselves in competition with other goods and values, political procedures need to resolve disputes in a manner that takes account of the interests and ideals of those concerned. These procedures involve a shift from the 'ideal' politics of consensual principles and 'public reason', favoured by recent liberal theorists, to the 'real' politics of politically constructed agreements.

Liberal democracy, citizenship and the politics of marginalisation

The last decades of the twentieth century inaugurated the increasing globalisation of liberal democracy. The collapse of the Soviet Union and with it institutionalised communism in the late 1980s paved the way for a series of proclamations about liberal democracy's final triumph. However, while it is today generally accepted that liberal democracy is the dominant political ideology in global terms, it is also possible to argue that liberal democracy's triumph is far from complete. In many parts of the world an increasing number of people are becoming disaffected with its institutions. Extreme right-wing parties are growing stronger in many European countries, and in large parts of Africa people are becoming increasingly cynical about politics in the face of liberal democracy's failure to change their lives. These developments have entailed a loosening of people's adhesion to liberal democratic values. Such dissonances have gone hand in hand with an explosion of non-liberal identity politics. Although there is substantial evidence of a global trend towards democracy, there are also the oppositions and antagonisms asserting themselves against this trend in the name of various forms of difference – ethnic, national, linguistic, religious and cultural. Often these oppositions are positioned on the margins of liberal political systems and are a reminder of the failure of such systems to democratise societies as entities.

Majorities and minorities: basic structures
In the last few years democratic theorists have focused on issues of justice and minority rights.[1] Recently there has been a shift away from the focus on justice to questions of democratic citizenship and democratic practice. While the shift in the debate is to be welcomed in the sense that it refocuses our attention on what Mouffe calls the problem of the 'democratic deficit' (2000: 4), i.e. a growing lack of identification with democratic norms in liberal democracies, it still continues to frame the debate on political marginalisation in terms of questions of ethnicity. Where the focus is on marginalised groups these are construed largely as ethno-cultural minorities.
    This chapter argues for the enlargement of the debate on minority rights and citizen-

---

[1] See, for example, Bauboeck, R. (1994); Canovan (1996); Gilbert (1998); Kymlicka (1995); Miller (1995); Philipps (1995); Spinner (1994); Tamir (1993); Taylor (1992); and Tully (1995).

ship practices to include a consideration of the problem of political marginalisation. We need to include in our considerations a series of wider political questions concerning the politics of incorporation into the body politic. The contemporary debate on minority rights fails to do this. Most contemporary theories of minority rights rely on a specific type of struggle for political incorporation. They focus on minority struggles which are concerned with their incorporation into, and their contestation of, the public sphere of liberal democracies. The dominant assumption is that marginalisation is primarily about minority groups demanding inclusion in the liberal democratic body politic. Minority groups are viewed as being marginal to the dominant political system, and struggles for their recognition are primarily about different forms of inclusion into the body politic. One of the assumptions underpinning this work is the idea that marginalisation entails, above all, an experience of being on the periphery of a political system. What this conception of marginalisation fails to recognise is that most liberal democratic political systems are far more fragmented, hybrid and imbued with differentiation than is often acknowledged. Increasingly, there is evidence of minority groups which are marginal, but do not reside on the periphery of the political system in the way that national minorities which come from a variety of different cultures do. Kymlicka and Norman (2000) refer to these groups as 'sui generis groups', who, unlike national minorities, have a 'homeland that is everywhere and nowhere' (ibid.: 23–4). Examples include groups like African Americans who were previously prevented from integrating into the majority culture. Their specificity lies in the ways in which they cross the boundaries between the margin and the centre of the political system. They cut across the majority/minority schema. These groups often vacillate between demands for their full incorporation into the majoritarian culture, and demands for their separation from it. They reside in the tension between the inside and the outside, and not simply on the outside.

In contemporary societies political life continues to be marked by the exclusion of hybrid identities which reside less on the periphery than interspersed within the dominant constellations of the polity. Claude Forment points out that, compared to marginalised identities in previous times, marginalised identities in today's societies are not found only in rigidly stratified, socially closed hierarchical cast societies on the periphery of the liberal democratic political system (Forment 1996: 315). Instead, they play an integral role and form a vital part of late modern liberal democratic societies. They blur social boundaries and dissolve past political markers. As a result, the liberal democratic polity is far more differentiated and hybrid than most democratic theorists would allow. The conception of marginalisation as primarily an experience of the periphery fails to recognise the possibility that 'democracy and marginalisation have become intertwined in late modernity' (ibid.: 315). It excludes the possibility that marginalisation might be inextricably linked to the development of liberal democracy.

Most conventional analyses of minority politics assume that marginalisation primarily refers to the experience of residing on the periphery of a political system with little or no access to its power structures. This view marks it as a condition external to liberal democracy itself; the political system is not viewed as generating marginalisation. In the conventional literature on minority rights and marginalisation it is assumed that marginalisation in the first sense represents the dominant experience. As a consequence the problem of incorporation is viewed as a problem of 'bringing back into' the system groups marginalised from it. Assimilation in this form comes in different guises. It can involve the idea of liberal assimilation, i.e. the mere extension of established values over an excluded group, or it can involve a more sophisticated version of the same principle. Those who adopt this latter position may develop it in quite radical directions, arguing, for example, that the liberal value of political equality requires considerably more than simply removing the barriers of legality, and that equality depends on major social reforms (such as affirmative action) that will remove the obstacles to equal participation. Even in the latter, more radical position, however, marginalisation and incorporation are presented as antinomies. When groups are excluded from meaningful participation in the political system, their incorporation is viewed as involving their complete inclusion in the liberal polity.

However, the logic of marginalisation can also be used in a different sense. It can refer to a situation in which the political system itself creates marginalisation. This occurs when the system as a principle of organisation is missing. In this case the system itself disorganises communities and spreads fragmentation. This type of marginalisation is often created by the opening up of the system. In situations where the system itself leads to a generalised marginalisation and dislocation, incorporation does not necessarily involve the kind of 'bringing back into' that marginalisation in the first sense involves. If we think of marginalisation as a wider dislocation of the political system, and a generalised unfixity of the polity, then the question of incorporation becomes a question of the political form of the system as a whole. It then becomes important to examine the condition of marginalisation as a political logic affecting the overall structure of the political system.

Marginalisation, politics and citizenship in post-apartheid South Africa

The politics of democratisation emerging out of the experience of citizen movements in liberal capitalist democracies and the politics of democratisation in post-colonial Africa often appear radically different. Whereas the former can be seen to focus on the negotiation, contestation and representation of difference within the public sphere, the politics in post-colonial Africa focuses on the constitution of the public sphere, a redefinition of the constituents of the body politic, and in some cases is aimed at creating new, politically sovereign bodies. In the latter context, forms of grass-roots political participation are often more varied than their Western counterparts. Rights-based discourses of citizenship are often viewed with scepticism by those who were excluded from civic citizenship under colonialism. Instead, a range of discourses emphasising substantive claims to equality have come to symbolise democratic citizenship (see, for example, Shivji, 2000: 37–60). As a result of the disjunction between rights and democracy, forms of grass-roots participation are often different and more varied than their counterparts in the Western liberal context. They go beyond the dominant Western liberal conception of the citizen as an individual bearer of rights, and include a wide range of more substantive contents.

Post-apartheid politics represents an attempt to create a new polity on the basis of two objectives: firstly, the construction of political unity, and with it a stable polity with common 'pre-understandings' as a counterpoint to the widespread dislocation and fragmentation of the polity under apartheid; and, secondly, the establishment of a politics of difference and pluralism. In post-apartheid society there has been no easy link between the extension of rights and the development of an overarching politics of solidarity. While it is true that the extension of rights has facilitated the emergence of marginalised groups, it has not always provided a framework for the articulation of deeper, collective emancipatory aims. Instead, in some areas of society the post-1994 election period has witnessed a dramatic fragmentation of South African political life.

The effect of this has been a loosening of the bonds of political community (to which all other connections are usually seen as secondary). Emerging identities' claims emphasise the specialness of their rootedness, and special rights in a place of birth. The rise of a politics of assertive self-representation has highlighted the difficulties the post-apartheid state has experienced in finding a role for itself. Its attempts to set the terms of national debates often fizzle out as other stakeholders simply retreat into localised terrains of deliberation. The movement away from overarching categories of belonging to connections that seek recourse to the local speaks to the difficulties of institutionalising a consensus based on the idea of a unifying deliberation. National deliberation on key political issues is often episodic and frequently cut short.

Public and private identity
Thus, in a fragmented polity where the language of rights at best produces a periodic enactment of cohesion, consensus-seeking projects are continuously undercut by the need of communities to withdraw from the polity in order to regroup their capacities. Paradoxically, the introduction of a universalising moment (the introduction of universal franchise since 1994) has resulted in the widespread differentiation of the polity. While it is true that the extension of rights has facilitated the emergence of marginalised groups like the Khoi-San, it has not necessarily provided a framework for the articulation of deeper emancipatory aims. Agreement on emancipatory objectives such as justice is often episodic and by no means overarching. This is because it is only after crossing the threshold of identification that a marginalised group can claim to have been treated unjustly. In post-apartheid South Africa most marginalised identities never experience this luxury. For them the enactment of justice takes place in a terrain that is far from settled. Political gains are at best episodic. This is, at least in part, due to ambiguous location of marginalised identities in the public sphere. Contemporary liberal theorists often base their distinction between the public/political and the non-public/non-political on two related factors: the degree to which these are unavoidable and basic, as opposed to voluntary and optional, relationships, and the consequent extent to which reasoning between them must avoid contentious value assumptions. Membership of a state and engagement in an economic activity are said to be inescapable in ways that joining a community or association like a church are not. However, in post-apartheid South Africa, it is unlikely that the two spheres can be entirely distinguished. Not only has the non-public sphere been to some degree publicly defined and regulated through, for example, national debate on the role of civil society in the RDP programme, but, moreover, attitudes and behaviour in the non-public sphere tend to have a spill-over effect with regard to how we act in public. The symbiotic relationship between the two spheres makes any attempt to distinguish them difficult to enact in practice. This is very evident in post-

apartheid South Africa, where debate in the public sphere is often highly divided between different comprehensive conceptions of the good. The 'creaming off' of certain political values from politics is never stable enough to establish an 'overlapping consensus' in the Rawlsian sense (Rawls 1993).

There are many different versions of recent liberal democratic theory's attempt to engage with the question of marginalisation and exclusion. For the most part they are made up of a reaction to a critique of liberal democracy which argues that it offers a limited politics of inclusion, one which proposes only formal legal equality (equal treatment) and full political membership at the price of the renunciation of difference. Recent liberal thought, led by John Rawls, has taken issue with such an interpretation of the liberal principle of neutrality. It affirms that a liberal society needs a form of consensus that is deeper than a simple agreement on procedures. Its 'political liberalism' aims at defining a core morality that specifies the terms under which people with different conceptions of the good can live together in political association. One of its aims is to guarantee stability through a wider societal consensus on constitutional essentials. Its starting point is the standard liberal view of political legitimacy associated above all with the theorists of the contract tradition, that is, that coercive power can only be exercised on grounds that are compatible with the rational consent of its citizens. It insists on the idea that a stable regime requires broad agreement on a core set of substantive values. This core set must have the positive allegiance of a wide range of different comprehensive moral positions, and so become the object of a wider societal consensus. Political liberalism is seen as drawing on a shared pool of basic ideas and principles arising out of the liberal democratic tradition. Political principles are presented as free-standing, forming an essential constituent part of all conceptions of the good.

A new conception of democracy
The South African case, however, demonstrates that, instead, societal agreement involves a deeply political process which does not submerge the politics of becoming under shared 'free-standing' values. This is why William Connolly's (1991) conception of democracy is important as it allows us to conceive of a public sphere whose definition is a matter of deep disagreement, and where societal consensus is more likely to occur around comprehensive conceptions of the good than around overarching political values like political justice.

Connolly argues for 'an operative consensus on the ambivalence of democratic politics as an ambiguous medium of enactment and disturbance'. He is critical of any idea of consensus that grounds its ethics in normal, individual, intrinsic community. He argues for the 'ventilating effects of political disturbance'. In his view the most advanced form such a stance could assume would not conform to the mode of tolerance, where one representative exercises hegemony over another culture and allows others to exist as enclaves within it. Rather, 'it would incline closer to a culture of selective collaboration and agonistic respect in relations between a variety of intersecting and interdependent constituencies' (Connolly 1995: 92).

Connolly argues that the central challenge for democracy is how to reconfigure and renegotiate the constitutive tension between democratic pluralism and 'pluralisation'. He endorses a conception of democracy in which identity is understood as a relational formation laced with contingency. A pluralising democracy is the site of tension or ambivalence between politics as general action to sustain the economic and cultural conditions of existing plurality and the dissonant politics of pluralisation. When this constitutive tension is maintained, a democratic culture thrives. Every constellation of identity/difference relations, because it is established upon human beings not re-designed to coalesce entirely with any particular mode of being, will itself engender surpluses, resistances, intransigencies and protean energies of diversification (ibid.: 97–104). He calls for a non-reducible interaction between two pillars of democracy: one calling for a consensus on economic equalisation and the other calling for a pluralising democracy which must contain and loosen any unified cultural identity that might make a consensus possible.

The crucial issue for us is how this logic of pluralisation would operate in majority/ minority 'assemblages', given that minorities are often not in a position to collaborate selectively with majorities due to their relative lack of empowerment. Connolly argues that two crucial conditions for the formation of majority assemblages in support of economic equality would have to be fostered. Such an assemblage would not take the form of a general consensus, in which each constituency supports the programmes in question for the same reasons as others. Nor would it reflect the will of a nation, organised around a unified language, ethnicity, race or religion. Nor would it amount to a simply coalition of interests. It would be a

> mobile constellation in which some support the programmes in question out of dire economic need, some out of a particular self-interest, some because they are implicated with others who need these programmes, some because they endorse such programmes in exchange for assemblage support for others ethically or materially crucial to them, some because they believe that the negative effects of steep inequality will eventually undermine the good life they now participate in, some because they seek to meet responsibilities flowing from this or that creed, and most out of some mixture of these conditions. (ibid.: 95)

Connolly's politics of 'collective assemblages' is underpinned by a democratic ethos which relies principally on the tension between 'politics as general action to sustain the economic and cultural conditions of existing plurality and the dissonant politics of pluralisation' (ibid.: 97). An assemblage implies many things, amongst others a continual process of intersection and realignment. It involves many possibilities, ranging from a highly consensual (but 'disturbable') assemblage to a highly tension filled, largely non-consensual one. Majorities are not necessarily overtly consensual. They are, as Connolly says, 'closer to food at a potluck supper than to courses at a formal dinner; closer to a diverse set of grasses and bushes spreading over a hillside than to the limbs of an oak tree branching out from a single trunk' (ibid.: 96).

Seen against Connolly's schema, the incorporation of marginalised minorities does not simply imply assimilation. Majorities themselves involve a continual renegotiation and realignment of their identities. The issue of minority incorporation cannot simply be forced in the assimilation/separation matrix which takes for granted the cohesion of the majority. For Connolly, majoritarian politics is made up of the constitutive tension between an already present pluralised terrain and the politics of pluralisation, of becoming. Key to the latter is the moment of the incorporation of new elements into the majoritarian assemblage. New pluralising initiatives are precarious and are easily drawn back into a regulatory discourse. This type of majoritarian politics requires the possibility of a continual renegotiation of root consensus, a permanent openness to new intersections and entry points, and the absence of a fixed matrix. Connolly argues that they cannot be codified or positioned under a matrix such as classical definitions of democracy as rule by a unified people. If you define the root idea of democracy to be rule by a unified people of itself, you bring under arrest the nomadic element circulating through the ethos of democracy. He asks the question: how can a people become unified enough to rule itself? How can rule reproduce the unity of the people? The answer is 'bound to oscillate between the statist (im)possibilities of a general will, a rational consensus, a Schmittean decision-ism, and the arboreal pluralism of Tocqueville, where diversity consists of several limbs stretching out from the civic-territorial trunk that provides them with support and nourishment' (ibid.: 179).

In Connolly's schema, then, democracy is not simply guided by a politics of liberal assimilation. Connolly's schema acknowledges that, on the one hand, we need a social form, a certain measure of commonality to acquire an identity, but, on the other hand, every project of commonality contains the seeds of subjugation and violent exclusion. Politics is the medium through which these ambiguities are confronted. 'It is simultaneously a medium through which common purposes are crystallised and the consummate means by which their transcription into musical harmonies is exposed, contested, disturbed, and unsettled' (Connolly 1991: 94).

In post-apartheid South Africa it would seem on the surface as if the time is ripe for marginalised people to enter the new, post-apartheid South African society as equal citizens. The new (liberal democratic) regime would seem to offer the opportunity to tinker with institutional arrangements in ways that would make it possible to reconcile hybridity with citizenship, culture with liberal democracy. However, in reality the accommodation of marginalised people into public life in post-apartheid South Africa has been fraught. The type of politics required involves a continual unsettling of established political norms and procedures. In a situation where particularity and marginality reign, 'adding on' new claims and identities to the body politic is both disruptive and generative of new possibilities. Such a politics acknowledges the need for societal consensus on key political values, but insists that these need to be politically negotiated and that they are not 'free-standing'.

Conclusion: alternatives

In this chapter I have argued that marginalisation is a decisive feature of the post-apartheid polity. The principal form of marginalisation established under apartheid, the limiting of entire communities to the periphery of the political system, both geographically and politically, has been supplemented with a wider disorganisation of the political system through the introduction of liberal democracy. A noticeable feature of post-apartheid politics is that old forms of marginalisation have not necessarily disappeared. The introduction of rights has not resulted in the greater unification of the political system. In fact, it can be seen to have caused greater fragmentation, as previously marginalised communities have lost their anti-statist focus. Many communities are simply moving further away from the mainstream and into more intense forms of impoverishment. At the same time forms of communal solidarity have becomes less overarching. At the level of local politics, in particular, a myriad of more concealed processes through which society is remaking itself is emerging. These processes are all indicative of the renunciation of manufactured unanimity of consensus imposed on the majority.

Post-apartheid politics betrays its liberalisms in a variety of ways. Firstly, it highlights the paradoxes inherent in the politics of rights. Marginalised communities often have difficulties advancing their interests within the framework of juridical rules. Instead of making use of a rights-based politics, they rely on substantive claims. This highlights the limits of a rights-based politics in providing a framework for overcoming marginalisation. Post-apartheid's 'juridical' liberalism aims at condensing most issues of politics into the juridical categories of rights, justice and obligation. But, because of the specific disjunction of democracy and rights in the South African context, the juridical lacks sufficient credence to attract marginalised protagonists. Emerging marginalised identities are often unable to make use of the new rights offered to them. They retreat into a series of essentialist practices to facilitate their regrouping. The introduction of democracy and a rights-based politics has, thus, not necessarily resulted in a greater societal consensus. This is a consequence, at least in part, of the historical construction of the language of rights in South Africa. In the past the language of rights has not only been anti-statist; it has also lacked the capacity for expressing the demands for justice. As a result of this historical pattern, forms of grass-roots participation are often different and more varied than their counterparts in the Western liberal context. They go beyond the dominant Western liberal conception of the citizen as an individual bearer of rights, and include a wide range of more substantive contents. Secondly, it brings to the fore the limits of the politics of 'consensus' and deliberative forms of democracy in post-apartheid South Africa. One of the principal motivations of the consensus-seeking approach is to bring back into the fold of a unified community those who are excluded. However, any consensus-seeking project that aims to establish a coherent set of standards in the form of a common ethico-political bond in the context of the unifying ideal of harmonious membership and consensus is bound to fail in post-apartheid South Africa. While a common ethico-political bond is crucial in rendering politics a viable social form, in conditions of widespread marginalisation, the strategy of assimilation and 'deliberation' into a single community held together by an ever growing general commitment to the 'common good' is by no means straightforward, and might not necessarily be the most democratic way of organising a highly differentiated and marginalised polity. In post-apartheid South Africa communitarian projects are undercut continuously by the emergence of highly localised identities and forms of struggle which do not rely on a rights-based politics. Marginalised identities need to periodically enter and exit the political system in order to regroup their potential. Any consensus binding them to a wider set of standards must be politically negotiated and constructed. This does not mean that consensus-seeking projects should be de-prioritised. One of the challenges facing post-apartheid South Africa is how to maintain, in conditions of extreme unfixity, a sufficient degree of consensus for the negotiation of public life. Given the high degree of fragmentation of the polity, it is crucial, however, that such a consensus is constructed politically.

References

Bauboeck, R. (1994), 'Changing the Boundaries of Citizenship', in R. Bauboeck (ed.), *From Aliens to Citizens: Redefining the Status of Migrants in Europe*, Aldershot: Avebury, pp. 199–232.

Canovan, M. (1996), *Nationhood and Political Theory*, Cheltenham: Edward Elgar.

Connolly, W. (1991), *Identity/Difference: Democratic Negotiations of Political Paradox*. Ithaca and London: Cornell University Press.

—— (1995), *The Ethos of Pluralization*, Minneapolis and London: University of Minnesota Press.

Forment (1996), 'Peripheral Peoples and Narrative Identities: Arendtian Reflections on Late Modernity' in S. Benhabib (ed.), *Democracy and Difference: Contesting the Boundaries of the Political*, Princeton, NJ: Princeton University Press.

Gilbert, P. (1998), *Philosophy of Nationalism*, Boulder, CO: Westview Press.

Glazer, N. (1983), *Ethnic Dilemmas: 1964–1982*, Cambridge, Mass.: Harvard University Press.

Kymlicka, W. (1995), *Multicultural Citizenship: A Liberal Theory of Minority Rights*, Oxford: Oxford University Press.

Kymlicka, W. and W. Norman (eds) (2000), *Citizenship in Diverse Societies: Issues, Contexts, Concepts*, Oxford: Oxford University Press.

Miller, D. (1995), *On Nationality*, Oxford: Oxford University Press.

Mouffe, C. (2000), *The Democratic Paradox*, London and New York: Verso.

Philipps, A. (1995), *The Politics of Presence: Issues in Democracy and Group Representation*, Oxford: Oxford University Press.

Rawls, J. (1993), *Political Liberalism*, New York: Columbia University Press.

Shivji, I.G. (2000), 'Contradictory Perspectives on Rights and Justice in the Context of Land Tenure Reform', in M. Mamdani (ed.), *Beyond Rights Talk and Culture Talk*, Cape Town: David Philip Publishers, pp. 37–60.

Spinner, J. (1994), *The Boundaries of Citizenship: Race, Ethnicity and Nationality in the Liberal State*, Baltimore: Johns Hopkins University Press.

Tamir, Y. (1993), *Liberal Nationalism*, Princeton, NJ: Princeton University Press.

Taylor, C. (1992), 'The Politics of Recognition' in Gutman, A. (ed.), *Multiculturalism and the 'Politics of Recognition'*, Princeton, NJ: Princeton University Press, pp. 25–73.

Tully, J. (1995), *Strange Multiplicities: Constitutionalism in an Age of Diversity*, Cambridge: Cambridge University Press.

2
Reflections on Liberalism, Policulturalism & ID-ology
Citizenship & Difference in South Africa

JOHN COMAROFF & JEAN COMAROFF

Prolegomenon

Herewith two fragments from the discourses of the recent South African past.

'...we Blacks (most of us) execrate ethnicity with all our being.'
Desmond Tutu, 1981[1]

For the Archbishop, in short, 'native' cultural identities were little more than an excrescence of colonial racism.

'Our duty is to identify and define the main currents of [African] tradition and to incorporate [them] in the modern, technically advanced political entities that we are seeking to construct.'
Penuell Maduna, 1999[2]

For the Minister of Justice and Constitutional Development, the products of those very identities are a necessary element in the making of the post-colonial nation-state.

The difference? Twenty years or so in the history of difference.

If Kymlicka and Norman (2000: 1) are right, recent debate in political philosophy has been preoccupied by two, typically unconnected, issues: 'minority rights–multiculturalism' and the nature of democratic citizenship. This seems unsurprising in an intellectual endeavour devoted largely to the study of Western polities; after all, the triumphal rise of neo-liberal capitalism, new patterns of mass migration, and emergent ethnic and religious movements have all put pressure on the nation-state in its modernist form. But how salient are these issues outside EuroAmerica? How significant are they in everyday *realpolitik* across the planet? On the face of it, they might appear *not* to be especially pressing in post-apartheid South Africa. Why not? Because this country, lately freed from the ethnically coded rule

---

[1] The statement, first made in an article written for the African-American Institute, is published in Tutu (1984), p. 121. It has been much quoted; for just two recent examples, see Lijphart (1995: 281) and Oomen (2002: 6).

[2] '"Revisit Cultural Values"', Zandile Nkutha, *Sowetan*, 17 November 1999, p. 2. Maduna made the statement in an address to a conference on constitutionalism; his audience included leaders of the South African Development Community (SADC).

of a racist colonial state, has fashioned for itself a Constitution founded on the most comprehensive, most liberal, most enlightened notions of democratic pluralism. Not only is that Constitution unusually attentive to universal enfranchisement and human rights. It is also quite explicit in its accommodation of the cultural claims of minorities. Indeed, if its own rhetorical construction were a description of its political sociology, South Africa – deeply committed to the rule of law, to the monopoly of the state over the legitimate means of violence, to a conception of citizenship that both transcends and tolerates diversity – would seem to inhabit the very ideal of the Euro-nation in its twenty-first century guise. On one hand, it embodies all the principles on which that nation was founded (cf. Hobsbawm 1992: 3–4); on the other, it has set about confronting the realities of difference in precisely the manner that many philosophers of 'minority-rights multiculturalism' have proposed.

And yet, almost from the start, a 'crisis of culture', a counter-politics of ethnic assertion *against* the jurisdiction of the state, has rumbled beneath the surface of the new polity, threatening to disrupt the founding premises of its Bill of Rights. This has entailed more than just a quest for the recognition of distinctive identities, languages and life-ways, a quest that has become familiar elsewhere in recent years (Taylor 1992). It has also raised fundamental questions of sovereignty: the sovereignty of African traditional governance and the kingdom of custom, in which ethnic subjects claim, and are claimed by, another species of authority. This authority, as we shall see, does not live easily with the hegemony of the liberal modernist state. It sanctions alternative orders of law and justice, of the use of force, of responsibilities and entitlements, even of tribute and taxation. The generic citizen of post-colonial South Africa may be the rights-bearing individual inscribed in the new Constitution; also the rights-bearing individual – typically urban, cosmopolitan – presumed in much mass-mediated discourse. By contrast, ethno-polities and traditional leadership[3] speak the language of subjects and collective being (cf. Mamdani 1996). For many – perhaps most – South Africans, it is the *coexistence* of the two tropes, of citizen and subject, that configures the *practical* terms of national belonging. But that coexistence, despite the Bill of Rights, does not always reduce to an easy, 'flexible' accommodation (cf. Ong 1999): life as national citizen and life as ethnic subject are as likely to run up against one another – often in contradictory ways – thus making political personhood a fractured, fractal experience. It is when they do that the *real*sociology of citizenship in the 'new' South Africa is most put to the test of democratic pluralism: citizenship *not* as it is envisaged in a political philosophy of the normative future, but citizenship in the concrete politics of a lived present.

The question of the post-colonial political subject, then, is not merely *relevant* to the construction of the 'new' South Africa. It is crucial. But what light might this history-in-the-making shed on philosophical debates about citizenship and difference? How might it inflect a discourse that is heavily prescriptive and, as a matter of course, continues to frame the problem of political personhood, *tout court*, in Euromodernist terms? True, it has become a progressive commonplace to insist that 'multiculturalism' has to be interrogated in its *empirical* particularity, that it takes diverse, labile forms, that liberal

---

[3] Elsewhere (e.g. 1997a) we have sought to problematise the concept of tradition and, by extension, of 'traditional' leadership; we deploy the term here strictly to refer to vernacular usage. 'Traditional leadership' has become a generic label in South Africa for all forms of indigenous African rule.

democracies ought to – some would say, can – be capacious enough to accommodate it (Kymlicka and Norman 2000; Levy 2000; Modood 2000). Still, while this may complicate matters productively, it leaves *untheorized* the most critical issue of all. What happens when a liberal democracy encounters a politics of difference that it cannot embrace ethically or ideologically within its definition of the commonweal, a politics of difference that is *not* satisfied with recognition, tolerance, or even a measure of entitlement – a - politics of difference that appeals to the law or to violence to pursue its ends, among them the very terms of its citizenship? Which, to be sure, is occurring more and more across the world in the early years of the new century.

This last question presupposes others: Why *has* citizenship come to capture the imagination, popular as well as academic, at this particular time, a time when the modernist nation-state and the modes of representational politics that it has long presumed are profoundly in question? Like 'civil society' (cf. Comaroff and Comaroff 1999b), which has enjoyed a similar renaissance of attention since the late 1980s, the manner in which the concept is deployed is often as vacuous as it is appealing; indeed, there seems to be a more or less proportional relationship between its vacuity and its mass appeal. Why, more and more, are contests over fractal identities and the terms of national belonging fought out by means of legalities? Might it be here, and in other sites of contestation, rather than in the realm of theory-making or policy prescription, that we may discern the emergence of *pragmatic* resolutions to the paradoxes of citizenship in polities founded on endemic, irreducible difference?

It is these concerns, these questions, that frame our narrative here. Also the argument we seek to make. Briefly stated, it is that, in postcolonies, which are *endemically* heterogeneous, citizenship *always* exists in an immanent tension with *poli*culturalism; note the term, we shall explain it below. As a result, it is a terrain on which increasingly irreconcilable, fractal forms of political being, embodied in self-defined aggregates of persons, may seek to open up possibilities for themselves, possibilities in pursuit of their passions, principles, ideals, interests. Indeed, it is on this terrain that the modernist sense of ideology gives way to ID-ology, the quest for a collective good, and sometimes goods, sanctioned by, and in the name of, a shared identity. And, in the process, *both* the liberal modernist polity and the kingdom of custom are transformed. The term, ID-ology, note, is not ours: it derives from public discourse in South Africa itself. Argue Rapule Tabane and Ferial Haffajee, in a newspaper report,[4] the Age of Ideology, 'of genuinely competing ideas', is over, killed off by a mix of world-historical and local conditions. In its place has arisen a depoliticising kind of 'mongrel politics' in which party platforms tend to converge, in which charismatics crystallise their popularity into 'customised' political brands, in which differences are confined largely to the implementation of policy and the distribution of material advantage (cf. Comaroff and Comaroff 2000). One might add that, in the upshot, political belonging and the contradictions implicit in it become – above all else – a site of ID-ology, in which various sorts of identity struggle to express themselves in the politics of everyday life.

A final note here. While we phrase our argument with respect to South Africa – and, more generally, to postcolonies – what we shall have to say applies, increasingly, to the

---

[4] 'Ideology is Dead, Long Live ID-ology', Rapule Tabane and Ferial Haffajee, *Mail & Guardian*, 27 June– 3 July 2003, p. 6.

nation-state *form*. Why? Because one of the effects of neo-liberal capitalism, and of the kinds of human flow that it generates, is to make polities, with few exceptions, ever more diverse, ever more prone to a politics of difference that, in the end, is likely to run up against the limits of liberal citizenship. Not all in the same ways, of course. But in some or other way. Which is why the postcolony is so often a harbinger of histories yet to happen.

First, though, to histories that have happened. And are happening.

Constituting the problem, problematising the constitution

The rule of law and dangerous cultural practices
The post-colonial state in South Africa, under the African National Congress, has had no option but to take cultural difference – and especially cultural practices deemed 'dangerous' – very seriously indeed. This, as we have intimated, is because it has been confronted, repeatedly, by social practices that fly in the face of its Constitution. Thus the police have been called upon to deal with, among other things, urban vigilante activities conducted in the name of Muslim morality,[5] 'alternative' justice ostensibly exercised under the terms of African customary law,[6] bloody culture wars in the countryside, and witchcraft-related killings, of which there have been many since the early 1990s;[7] to wit, the 'new' South African Police Service has an Occult-Related Crimes Unit that, not long ago, instituted programmes to teach officers how to handle the forensics of crime scenes involving arcane practices.[8] For its part, the Constitutional Court has had to deliberate, for example, on a claim, made in the name of Rastafarian belief, to recognise the use of prohibited drugs for ritual purposes;[9] it may well, in future, have to address such things as indigenous norms of patrilineal inheritance (see below). And the executive has had to respond to constant demands to permit 'traditional' practices now deemed illicit. What is more, a number of Witchcraft Summits have been held since 1994 to discuss rural unrest, and the lethal forms of cultural policing occasioned by it, arising out of an alleged epidemic of *muti* (medicine) murders (Comaroff and Comaroff 1999a); one such meeting, in September 1999, was attended by prominent politicians, lawyers and public

---

[5] For just one recent account in the print media, see 'Boeremag, Pagad Still Threaten SA Security', Jeremy Michaels, *Cape Times*, 18 June 2003, p. 4. Pagad, 'People Against Guns and Drugs', a Muslim organization, arose in Cape Town in the 1990s to deal with rising levels of violence and alleged police neglect. It has, in turn, been accused of promoting a reign of urban terror.

[6] The most notable case is that of Mapogo a Mathamaga, a large organisation led by Monhle Magolego, about whom much has been written (see Comaroff and Comaroff n.d.: Chapter 9). In an interview with us at Acornhoek on 11 March 2000, Magolego, who has been indicted several times, insisted that the justice carried out by his cadres was 'the African way of stopping crime' and was inflicted 'with the cooperation of local chiefs'.

[7] See Ralushai *et al* (1996: 31) for figures on the early 1990s in the Northern Province, now Limpopo, where witch-burnings were most prevalent. In the first half of 1996 in that province, 676 people were killed; see 'Northern Province Targets "Witch" Killers', *Weekly Mail & Guardian*, 27 September–3 October 1996, electronic edition.

[8] Questions have been raised about the constitutional status of the Unit and its training programs: they appear to presume the *il*legality, and Satanic inspiration, of the cultural convictions of many citizens. See, e.g. 'Occult-Related Killings on the Rise', *Cape Argus*, 9 September 1998, p. 9; 'Police Devil Busters Under Threat', *Daily Mail & Guardian*, 28 March 1999.

[9] Prince v. The President of the Law Society of the Cape of Good Hope and others, CCT 36/00.

intellectuals, including the then Deputy President, Thabo Mbeki.[10] This high level of attention to the issue is unsurprising. Not only do violent witch-purgings call into question the terms of national law and order. They do so by means taken to be irrational, even savage, by the canons of enlightenment reason. As colonial rulers long ago realised, to condone them, even tacitly, is to grant them a measure of legitimacy.

But herein lies a paradox, *the* paradox, for the liberal modernist state in post-colonial, poli-ethnic times. In an epoch in which cultural rights have come increasingly to substitute for political and economic enfranchisement, no government – least of all one representing African empowerment – can afford to ignore the passions that inflame such forms of collective action, especially on the part of the majority that it strives to represent.[11] In this respect, dramatic acts like witch-burning are merely an extreme instance of the challenge posed everywhere to the sovereignty of the state, and to the laws of the nation, under the sign of ethnic particularity, of religion or regionalism, of the primordial politics of tradition. The African National Congress, to be sure, has been unable to resist, remove or repudiate the affective appeal of cultural difference. Not only is it invoked in the name of ethno-nationalism, most assertively by the Congress of Traditional Leaders of South Africa (CONTRALESA), the Zulu-centric Inkatha Freedom Party, and separatist fractions of the Afrikaner right. It is keenly felt by many ordinary South Africans, for whom 'customary' attachments remain strong. As a result, its mass following notwithstanding, the ANC has had to revise the 'post-ethnic' universalism to which most[12] of its leadership was once fervently committed. Always ambivalent, at best, towards anything associated with 'tribalism', the liberation movements tended, during the struggle years and after (cf. Lijphart 1995: 281), to dismiss culture and custom as instruments of colonial overrule – and to see chieftaincy as highly autocratic.[13] This even as they sought to recruit sympathetic chiefs to their cause. Recall here Desmond Tutu's outburst against ethnicity. Some senior ANC cadres were still openly dismissive of indigenous authority in the late 1990s, Barbara Oomen (2002: 29) reminds us; President Thabo Mbeki's support for it, she adds, continues to seem more strategic than intrinsic. As that support suggests, however, the regime has made audible its public recognition of the Kingdom of Custom as part of the country's 'unique mode of governance', citing Section 12 of the Constitution as proof of its commitment; all of which follows what Kymlicka and Norman (2000: 4) term 'the clear trend throughout the Western democracies towards greater recognition of minority rights'. This *volte face* was particularly noticeable before the 1999 election. Since then, party representatives have taken every opportunity – at events such as royal funerals in the countryside, for instance – to persuade powerful chiefs that they, and the cultural bases of their authority, have a secure future in government.

But the ambiguity persists. When the Local Government Municipal Structures Act

---

[10] 'Top Politicians for Witchcraft Summit', *Cape Argus*, 7 September 1999, p. 9.

[11] Of course, it *is* easier, politically, for the state to ignore the 'minority' cultural claims of Khoi-San, Coloureds, and Afrikaners.

[12] But not all. Nelson Mandela, for one, has – famously – always shown great respect for traditional leadership and for the political processes associated with it; see his autobiography (Mandela 1994).

[13] Govan Mbeki (1964) once said that, 'when a people have developed to a stage which discards chieftainship ... then to force it on them is ... enslavement'. This statement has been widely quoted; see, e.g. 'The Chieftancy System is Rooted in Apartheid', Lungisile Ntsebeza and Fred Hendricks, Crossfire, *Mail & Guardian*, 18–24 February 2000, p. 33.

(no.117) was passed in 1999, it made provision for the division of the entire country, including chiefly domains, into municipalities. Where their realms fell into these municipalities, traditional leaders were permitted only 10 per cent representation; the Act has been amended and a White Paper on the topic has been drafted,[14] but the role of the chiefs remains tightly restricted. Said to be 'above party politics', they are expected to confine themselves to, among other things, ceremonial activities of various kinds, the administration of customary law, and the coordination of cultural activities, including first fruits, rainmaking, and other ancestral rites. In addition, they are expected to 'perform such functions as may be delegated ... by a municipal council', to 'carry out all orders given... by competent authorities', and to facilitate things like 'the gathering of firewood'.[15] Hardly the stuff, this, of plenipotentiaries. In fact, as critics have been quick to say, there is now 'considerable confusion as to what exactly the[ir] constitutional recognition implies'.[16] Predictably, many of these rulers, seeing themselves as all powerful in their realms, feel betrayed. This was dramatically evident at a conference, organised by the Ministry of Provincial and Local Government in August 2000,[17] to discuss 'traditional leadership and institutions' with a view to producing a White Paper.[18] Assembled royals, led by prominent members of CONTRALESA, declined to take part. Demanding that the Constitution be amended to recognise their sovereignty, they refused to talk to anyone other than the state president. Since then they have ridden a roller coaster. There have been times when they were sure that government had been persuaded to do their bidding. And there have been other times when they have declared – perhaps tactically, in order to rally their followers – that they had 'reached the end of the road', that 'there was never an intention to accommodate [their authority in] the making of the new South Africa'.[19] Such statements typically draw denials from the ANC – which, in turn, adds fuel to the ongoing battle over the future of the Kingdom of Custom.

In playing the heady game of cultural politics, then, the ANC has drummed up a force that it is unable fully to control, a force that vitiates the very conception of nationhood on which the authority of the state rests. In theory, of course, it is just such contradictions that the Constitution – tacking, as it does, between an emphasis on universal human rights, vested in individuals, and the recognition of cultural pluralism – was designed to mediate. Public debate in South Africa, however, has already drawn attention to 'major tensions' between those of its provisions that structure a system of democratically elected

---

[14] *Traditional Leadership and Governance Draft White Paper* (Gazette 23984, Notice 2103), 29 October 2002. The document can be read at www.gov.za/gazette/whitepaper/2002/23894.pdf.

[15] This is a virtual paraphrase of the Local Government: Municipal Structures Amendment Bill, 2000. It may be read at www.pmg.org.za/bills/municipalstructures2ndamd.htm.

[16] 'The Chieftancy System is Rooted in Apartheid', Lungisile Ntsebeza and Fred Hendricks, Crossfire, *Mail & Guardian*, 18–24 February 2000, p. 33.

[17] *A National Conference on Traditional Leadership*, Eskom Conference Centre, Midrand, 17–18 August 2000, Department of Provincial and Local Government. We attended the conference on the formal invitation of the Minister for Provincial and Local Government, the Hon. F.S. Mufamadi, and wish to thank him and the staff of his Ministry for making our presence possible.

[18] The conference was preceded by, and organised around, a *Draft Discussion Document Towards a White Paper on Traditional Leadership and Institutions* issued by the Department of Provincial and Local Government on 11 April 2000.

[19] These were the words of Mangosuthu Buthelezi, leader of the Inkatha Freedom Party, in a speech made to rally Zulu support in the 'fight for autonomy of the[ir] kingdom'; see 'Unite Against ANC Treachery – Buthelezi', Mawande Jubasi and Thabo Mkhize, *Sunday Times*, 4 August 2002, p. 4.

representatives and those that ascribe legitimacy to the Kingdom of Custom.[20] Let us pause briefly to take a look at how the Constitution itself treats the matter. This, in turn, will provide a frame for what we have to say about the pragmatics of citizenship as a terrain on which political subjects construct various sorts of ID-ology.

The Constitution of Dissent

The Constitution of the Republic of South Africa, adopted in 1996,[21] has been accorded hallowed status in the formation of the post-colonial polity. Translated into all official languages under the legend 'One *law* for One *nation*' – the italics are in the original – the text is shelved, in many homes, alongside the family bible and books of prayer. Yet, almost from the start, there have been doubts about its ability to constitute either *One* Nation or *One* Law; these italics are ours. Even its comprehensibility has been questioned: a mass-circulation black newspaper in Johannesburg, for example, has referred to it as a Tower of Babel, pointing out that its vernacular versions are utterly opaque – and, hence, babble to those whom it was meant to enfranchise.[22]

Culture is dealt with primarily in two sections of Chapter 2 of the Constitution, its Bill of Rights. Section 30, *Language and Culture*, states that 'everyone has the right to use the language and to participate in the cultural life of their choice'; Section 31, *Cultural, Religious, and Linguistic Communities*, adds that nobody belonging to any such community may 'be denied the right, with other members of that community, (a) to enjoy their culture, practise their religion and use their language; and (b) to form, join and maintain cultural, religious and linguistic associations and other organs of civil society'. But, in both cases, there is a clear constraint: these rights 'may not be exercised in a manner inconsistent with any [other] provision of the Bill of Rights'; in other words, precedence is given to those provisions that protect the dignity, equality and freedoms – of which a very broad range is stipulated – of all persons, without prejudice or discrimination. Even when the Constitution, in Section 36, acknowledges that some limitations on those freedoms are 'reasonable and justifiable in an open and democratic society', it stresses that any such limitation is to remain bound by the Bill of Rights; as we shall see, protagonists of the sovereignty of popular tradition and traditional authority have sought support for their arguments in this 'justifiable' and 'democratic' limitation of the universal rights of citizenship. Customary authority, note, is *not* embraced in Chapter 2 itself. It appears in Chapter 12, which states, in rather bland, summary terms, that the Constitution recognises 'the institution, status and role of traditional leadership, according to customary law' – but, again, subject to the Bill of Rights and any relevant legislation. In sum, the subservience of cultural particularity and the Kingdom of Custom to the 'One *law* for One *nation*' seems unambiguous.

But is it? After all, the South African Bill of Rights has been lauded, as we have said, precisely because it *does* seem to acknowledge, within appropriate limits, the entitlement of persons bound by culture, religion and language to be governed by their own customs. True, the collective subject invoked here is not a group *per se;* the Constitution is famously

---

[20] 'The Chieftancy System is Rooted in Apartheid', Lungisile Ntsebeza and Fred Hendricks, Crossfire, *Mail & Guardian*, 18–24 February 2000, p. 33.
[21] Act 108 of 1996 as adopted on 8 May and amended on 11 October by the Constitutional Assembly.
[22] 'Constitutional Tower of Babel', Goloa Moiloa, *Sunday World*, 31 October 1999, p. 16.

silent on group rights. That subject is an aggregate of 'persons.' Nonetheless, the Spirit of the Law, especially Sections 30 and 31, has justified claims to the effect that, in traditional communities where individual rights are alien, customary practice should prevail over the Eurocentric liberalism of the Law, in the upper case; that, when a custom is backed by popular consensus and a clear and present collective interest, the *cultural* subject should take precedence over the *national* citizen. The Supreme Court of Appeal recently made a similar argument: in Mthembu v. Letsela, it decided, in May 2000, that women married under African customary law were subject to the rule of male primogeniture – and, thereby, excluded from inheritance of matrimonial property.[23] The court declared that the 'interests of the community', as expressed in its 'mores and fundamental assumptions', were of paramount importance in the case. Here, in short, one of the highest tribunals in the land found *against* the Bill of Rights, as conventionally interpreted. Or, rather, it found that there *are* situations in which culture ought to limit its provisions. The judgment drew criticism from some quarters, notably feminist. Not only did it prove that 'the idea of equality before the law, regardless of sex or gender, is ... incompatible with certain aspects of customary law', wrote Khadija Magardie in a widely read national newspaper, but it was an 'alarming precedent' for the triumph of 'cultural relativism' over the Constitution.

Magardie was correct: in this decision, the judiciary *had* given culture, and the 'interests' of an ethnic community, priority over other provisions of the Constitution.[24] But did it *really* mean that, thenceforth, cultural difference would amount to a limitation on the Bill of Rights? And what did it *really* prove about the [in]compatibility of custom with those other provisions? The evidence is inconclusive. In June 2003, for instance, application was made to Judge President John Hlophe on behalf of two orphaned girls, whose grandfather had inherited their father's home in Khayelitsha, on the outskirts of Cape Town, under the terms of customary law. He promptly stated his intention to sell the place and evict the children and their mother. Lawyers for the girls sought an order to the effect that primogeniture under African Law and Custom, in this case, be 'interpreted and developed in line with the constitution, particularly the right to dignity and the right to equality', or, if not, that it be declared unconstitutional.[25] Clearly, they doubted that tradition could be rendered compatible with the Bill of Rights – and, if it could not, wished to establish the priority of the latter over the former. The defence, by contrast, asserted baldly that 'customary law was recognized in South African law and protected by the constitution'. Hlophe reserved judgment. In doing so, he repeated the vague and vacuous ANC mantra that tradition could, and should, be suitably updated. 'We promise to develop the law as it should be developed in 2003,' he said.

In 2000, three years before, we had put the question of compatibility to two constitutional court justices and received revealingly different answers. Albie Sachs, legal theorist of the liberation movement and a significant judicial force in the new dispensation, saw no necessary conflict between the Constitution and custom. The first always takes precedence over the second, he said. It provides the frame within which customary

[23] Transcript is from the Supreme Court of Appeal, Mildred Hleziphi Mthembu v. Henryk Letsela, 30 May 2000 (Case No: 71/98), as downloaded from <www.law.wits.ac.za/sca/scadate.html, p. 31–32.
[24] See 'Customary Law Undermines Constitutional Rights', Khadija Magardie, *Mail & Guardian*, 15–22 June 2000, p. 33.
[25] 'Customary Law in the Dock', Fatima Schroeder, *Cape Times*, 19 June 2003, p. 5. Judgment on the case was still pending at the time of writing.

law, to the degree that it remains relevant to everyday life, might sustain itself in a liberal democracy. If conflict *were* to arise – as it did on the question of, say, the traditional right of males to inflict punitive beatings on members of their family – it was to be addressed by means of statutory law; *vide*, in this respect, the Domestic Violence Act of 1999. In a public speech on the topic, Sachs (n.d.: 15–16) put the question in a more nuanced light. The Constitutional Court, he said, had left the 'ever-developing specifics' of customary law to future deliberation and interpretation. This implied that its 'liberation and transfiguration' would occur in 'organic connection with the community'. But its jurisdiction ought never to go far beyond the resolution of family and neighbourhood disputes; even then, traditional authorities would have to act within the limits of the Bill of Rights. In short, there never was, nor is there now, a contradiction between culture and the Constitution. Ethnic subject and national citizen are one and the same legal person.

By contrast, Yvonne Mokgoro, formerly of the law faculty at the University of Bophuthatswana, saw a palpable tension between the terms of the Constitution and the kind of law implemented in traditional tribunals, most notably in such matters as inheritance, succession and domestic relations. In her view, the Constitutional Court operated at a great distance from law-as-lived – and from the policing of everyday life in the countryside. A good deal of local practice continued in defiance of the Bill of Rights, she observed; it was merely a matter of time before cases emerged that contested its Eurocentrism in the name of cultural difference. Meanwhile, these tensions were managed, day in and day out, in variously pragmatic ways, rendering real law in the new South Africa more complex and diverse than most jurists acknowledged.[26]

Just how complex we shall soon see.

Before we address the real-life, pragmatically wrought tensions between the Constitution and the Kingdom of Custom in the 'new' South Africa, however, it is necessary to offer a few general observations about 'the' post-colonial nation-state. For it is only by means of a counterpoint between the general and the particular that we might make sense of the ways in which – here as elsewhere – the law of the land and the cultural lives of its inhabitants vex each other in arguments over sovereignty, citizenship, and the limits of liberal democracy.

Reflections on the postcolony

It became something of a commonplace in the early 1990s to observe that 'postcoloniality' means disparate things to different people (cf. Darian-Smith 1996; McClintock 1992): that, while it denotes temporality, it refers to more than just the time 'after colonialism' (Prakash 1995); that, in its positive voice, it evokes subaltern, 'oppositional consciousness' (Klor De Alva 1995: 245); that it 'foregrounds a politics of … struggle' (Mishra and Hodge 1991: 399). These sorts of statements have drawn their own criticism, but that is another matter. What is of concern here is that, in all the efforts to stress a *kind* of sensibility built into 'the' post-colonial perspective, there has been a tendency to treat the post-colonial nation-state as something of a theoretical cipher on whose ground arguments about the past, about identity, citizenship, consciousness and other things, may proceed

---

[26] Justice Mokgoro has written on the topic as well; see Mokgoro (1994) for her early views.

unencumbered by the facts of actual histories, economies or societies. Clearly, this is not the place in which to 'theorise' post-coloniality, *sui generis*, even if it were possible to do so in the abstract. But, if sense is to be made of the emerging forms of government, politics and popular subjectivity in post-apartheid South Africa, or anywhere else, a few general observations are in order.

They have to do, by and large, with hyphe-nation, with the link between nation and state, state and nation. Some of them, perforce, reprise things we have discussed more fully in other places (e.g. 2000, 2001).

The modernist nation – as Benedict Anderson (1983), among others, has pointed out – was an imagined community defined, putatively, by its cultural homogeneity and its deep sense of 'horizontal fraternity'. This imagining, it is often noted, was more aspiration than achievement. The European polity, after Westphalia, was always a work-in-progress: never a singular, definite article, it evinced a great deal of variation across time and space. Further, for all the idea that it was composed of rights-bearing persons equal before the law, it excluded many from its politics and its commonweal – and was, typically, inhospitable to difference. Nonetheless, the fiction of a unity of essence, affect and interest, of common purpose and *civitas*, mandated the legitimacy of the state as sole guarantor of the individual entitlements and collective well-being of its citizens. Hence the hyphe-nation, the indivisibility of nation from state.

Much has been said in recent times of the so-called 'crisis' of the modernist polity under the impact of global capitalism: of its shrinking sovereignty; of its loss of control over economic policy, cultural production and the flow of people, currencies and commodities; of a growing *dis*junction between nation and state (cf. Appadurai 1990). Whether or not 'the' nation-state is alive and well, ailing or metamorphosing – we prefer the third alternative ourselves – one thing is patent. The received notion of polities based on cultural homogeneity and a sense of horizontal fraternity, real or fictive, is rapidly giving way to imagined communities of difference, of multiculturalism, of ID-ology. This is true even in places as long antithetical to heterogeneity as the United Kingdom, which, despite recent race wars on the streets of its northern towns, now projects itself, with apologies to Benetton, as United in its tolerance of Colour and Culture. And in ones like Botswana, long regarded, if not altogether accurately, as relatively homogeneous. To be sure, the rising incidence of cultural struggles and ethnopolitics since 1989 has called forth a torrent of scholarly argument. There is no need to retrace that argument here. For present purposes, we merely need to register the fact.

For most post-colonial nation-states the politics of difference is not new. (Mark, here, the plural: *the* postcolony is not a singular article either; it is a variegated species of historical formation-under-construction.) Heterogeneity has been there from the first. Born of long histories of colonisation, these polities typically entered the new world order with legacies of ethnic diversity invented or exacerbated in the cause of imperial governance. Colonial regimes, intent on the management of racial capitalism, never constituted nations in the Euromodernist sense of the term, even where they gave their 'possessions' many of the ceremonial trappings of nationhood. In their wake, they tended to leave behind them not just an absence of infrastructure, but a heritage of fractious difference. This has been further attenuated, since *fin de siècle*, by some of the cultural and material corollaries of neo-liberalism: the movement across the planet of ever more people in search of work and opportunities to trade; the transnational mass-mediation of signs, styles and information; the rise of an electronic commons; the growing hegemony of the market and, with it, the distillation of culture into intellectual property, a commodity to be possessed, patented, exchanged-for-profit. In this world, freedom is reduced to choice: choice of commodities, of life-ways and, most of all, of identities. In the upshot, the great irony, the great existential contradiction of our times is that we seem to have entered an age in which identity has become, *simultaneously*, a matter of volition and self-production through consumption *and* a matter of ineluctable essence, of genetics and biology.

As this suggests, postcolonies evince many features common to the modernist polities on which they have had, to a large degree, to model themselves. In coming to terms with the implications of global neo-liberalism, they appear, in fact, to exaggerate – or, more accurately, hyper-extend – those features; all of which makes it seem as if, in their temporal aspect, they are running slightly ahead of the unfolding history of the Euromodern nation-state. Perhaps they are harbingers of the postmodern future. But that is a topic for another time. Our focus here is on two corollaries of the founding of postcolonies, not on homogeneity but on difference, not on deep horizontal fraternity but on a social contract among persons who are at once right-bearing individuals and identity-bearing subjects.

The first corollary has directly to do with the refiguration of citizenship. The explosion of identity politics after 1989, especially in postcolonies, has manifested itself in more than just ethnicity. Difference is also vested, increasingly, in gender, sexuality, generation, race, religion, lifestyle and social class, and in constellations of these things, sometimes deployed in highly contingent, strategic ways. While most human beings continue to live as citizens *in* nation-states, they tend only to be conditionally citizens *of* nation-states: their composite personae may include elements that disregard political borders and/or mandate claims against the commonweal within them. In consequence, identity struggles of one kind or another appear immanent almost everywhere as selfhood is immersed into collective essence, innate substance and primordial destiny (Comaroff and Comaroff 2001). What is more, the assertion of autochthony – which elevates to a first principle the interests, 'natural' rights and moral connectedness that arise from rootedness in a place of birth – has become an ever more significant mode of *e*xclusion with*in* national polities; this, as Americans learned after 9/11, in proportion to the extent to which outsiders are held to undermine the Wealth or Security of Homeland and Nation. It is, putatively, in the name of the latter that the state is becoming a metamanagement enterprise in the neo-liberal world (ibid.):[27] of subjects who, even as they seek to be global citizens in a planetary economy of commodities and cultural flows, demand also to be shareholders in the polity-as-corporation. Herein, then, lies the complexity: the fractal nature of contemporary political personhood, the fact that it is overlaid and·undercut by a politics of difference and identity, does not necessarily involve the *negation* of national belonging. Merely its uneasy, unresolved, ambiguous coexistence with other modes of being-in-the-world. It is this inherent ambiguity, we suggest, that makes the ostensible concreteness of concepts like 'citizenship' and 'community' so alluring.

---

[27] Much the same point was made just before the UK parliamentary elections of 2001: '[W]ith a basically pre-set macroeconomic framework, government becomes a matter...ultimately of microeconomic management. [Labour] is set to be elected as managers of Her Majesty's Public Sector, plc.' See 'Whatever Happened to Big Economics', Faisal Islam, *The Observer* (London), 3 June 2001, Business Section, p. 3.

Of the modes of being that constitute the twenty-first century political subject, cultural attachments are often taken, popularly, to run deepest. In many postcolonies, they are also the most marked. As we have said, ethnicity, like all ascribed identities, represents itself as grounded at once in blood and sentiment, in a commonality of interest, and, by extension, in 'natural' right. Add to this the fact that culture has increasingly come to be seen, and to be legally protected, as intellectual property (above, p. 43; cf. Coombe 1998) – even more, as a 'naturally' copyrighted collective possession – and what is the result? The dawn of the Age of Ethnicity, Inc. Observe, in this regard, that several ethnic groups have been formally incorporated as limited companies; that a large number of others have established themselves as businesses to market their heritage, their landscape, their knowledge, their religious practices, their artefacts; that yet others have successfully sued for the unremunerated reproduction of their symbols, sacred and secular. Thus it is that identity, in the age of partible, conditional citizenship, is defined, ever more, by the capacity to possess and to consume;[28] that politics is treated, ever more, as a matter of individual or collective entitlement; that social being in general, and social wrongs in particular, are translated, ever more, into the language of 'rights'.

Self-evidently, in this light, the term 'multicultural(ism)' is insufficient to describe the fractious heterogeneity of postcolonies. Rendered banal in popular usage, it evokes images of Disney's 'Small World', of compendia of the *Family of Man*, of ritual calendars respectful of human diversity, and the like; in short, of benign *in*difference to difference. Neither as noun nor as adjective does it make clear the critical limits of liberal pluralism: that notwithstanding the utopian visions of some humanist philosophers, the tolerance afforded to culture in modernist polities falls well short of allowing claims to autonomous political power or legal sovereignty. In postcolonies, in which ethnic assertion plays on the simultaneity of primordial connectedness, natural right and corporate interest, the nation-state is less multicultural than it is *poli*cultural. The prefix, spelled 'poli-', marks two things at once: plurality *and* its politicisation. It does not denote merely appreciation on the part of the national majority for the customs, costumes and cuisine of one or another minority from one or another elsewhere. It is a strong statement, an argument grounded in a cultural ontology, about the very nature of the pluri-nation, about its constitution and the terms of citizenship within it; about the spirit of its laws, about its governance and its hyphe-nation. As we have already seen, in South Africa this takes the form of an ongoing confrontation between Euromodern liberalism and variously expressed, variously formulated notions of 'traditional' authority.

Talk of rights, of culture as intellectual property, of citizenship, constitutions and contestation brings us to the second corollary that flows from the heterogeneous social infrastructure of postcolonies. Whether weak or strong, intrusive or recessive, autocratic or populist, the regimes that rule them share one thing: they speak incessantly of and for themselves in the name of 'the' state. Like those born of Euromodernity, post-colonial African states are *state*ments (cf. Corrigan and Sayer 1985: 30). They give voice to more or less authoritative worldviews, sometimes backed by military might, sometimes by

---

[28] *Vide*, in this respect, McMichael's (1998: 113) suggestion that the 'citizen state' has been replaced by the 'consumer state'. See also Hegeman (1991: 72), who argues that identity, at all levels, has come to be defined by consumption (see also Vanderbilt 1997: 141); not merely by the consumption of objects, but also by the consumption of the past.

carnivalesque ritual (Mbembe 1992), sometimes by mass-mediated shows of rhetorical force. But their language is not arbitrary.[29] It is the language of the law. The modernist polity, of course, has always been rooted in a culture of legality. Its subject, as Charles Taylor (1989: 11–12) reminds us, was, from the first, an individual whose humanity and dignity were formulated in the argot of rights and legal privilege. The global spread of neo-liberal capitalism has intensified the grounding of citizenship in the jural: this because of its contractarian conception of all relations, its celebration of 'free' markets, and its commodification of virtually everything, much of it heavily inscribed in the language of the law. It has also required that received modes of regulation be redesigned to deal with new forms of property, possession, consumption, exchange and jurisdictional boundaries (cf. Jacobson 1996; Salacuse 1991; Shapiro 1993).

All of this reaches its apotheosis in postcolonies, precisely because their hyphenation is so highly attenuated, because they are built on a foundation of irreducible difference, because they are endemically policultural. In them, the ways and means of the law – constitutions and contracts, rights and remedies, statutory enactments and procedural rituals – are attributed an almost magical capacity to accomplish order, civility, justice and empowerment. And to remove inequities of all kinds. Note, in this respect, how many new national constitutions have been promulgated since 1989. Note also the explosion across the planet of law-related NGOs – Legal Resource Centres, Lawyers for Human Rights, and the like – whose offices are now to be found in the most remote of African villages. In South Africa, the language of legality has become so ubiquitous, the Constitution (in the upper case) so biblical, that virtually every organisation has its own (lower case) analogue. There is even a Law Train that travels around the countryside offering free legal advice; its volunteer lawyers take pains to encourage *all* citizens to pursue their rights, and to address wrongs, by legal means.[30]

But *why* this fetishism of the law? In policultural nation-states, the language of legality affords an ostensibly neutral medium for people of difference to make claims on each other and on the state, to enter into contractual relations, to transact unlike values and to deal with their conflicts. In so doing, it produces an impression of consonance amidst contrast: of the existence of universal standards which, like money, facilitate the negotiation of incommensurables across otherwise intransitive boundaries. Hence its capacity, especially under conditions of social and ethical disarticulation, to make one thing out of many, to carve concrete realities out of fragile fictions. Hence, too, its hegemony, despite the fact that it is hardly a guarantor of equity. As an instrument of governance, it allows the state to represent itself as the custodian of civility against disorder – and, therefore, as mandated to conjure moral community by exercising a monopoly over the construction of a commonweal out of inimical diversities of interest (Harvey 1990: 108). It is this, to return to our point of a moment ago, that is made manifest in the rash of new constitutions written over the past decade or so. Each domesticates the global-speak of universal human rights, an idiom that individuates the citizen and, by treating cultural identity as a private asset rather than a collective possession, seeks to transmute difference into likeness.

---

[29] The argument summarised in this paragraph was first developed, and is more extensively stated, in Comaroff (1998); it is also to be found, in refined form, in Comaroff and Comaroff (2000).

[30] The train is operated by Legal i, a Section 21 (i.e. a non-profit) Company with a Board of Directors representative of the Law Societies, the Black Lawyers Association, the National Association of Democratic Lawyers and Consumer Agencies.

It is an open question whether or not these constitutions, this obsession with human rights – indeed, the language of legality itself – yield empowerment to those who previously lacked it. They do not, after all, guarantee the right to a living, only to possess, to signify, to consume, to choose. Nonetheless, the alchemy of the law, like all fetishes, lies in an enchanted displacement, one that resists easy demystification: the notion, *not* altogether unfounded, that legal instruments have the wherewithal to orchestrate social harmony and, thus, to manufacture something that was not there before. Its charm also lies in the fact that it *obscures* the most brutal of truths: that power produces rights, not rights power; that law is itself a product of the political, not a prime mover in constructing social worlds; that it, alone, is not what separates order from chaos or an equitable society from a state of savagery.

Put together the fetishism of the law and the policulturalism of the postcolony, and the product seems overdetermined: a polity in which struggles over difference – in particular, struggles over the authority to police everyday life – tend to find their way into the legal domain. Often, indeed, into the dramaturgical setting of the courtroom. But here, surely, there ought to be a rude end to our South African story. To the extent that contestations over the right to police everyday life end up in the realm of the juridical, and to the extent that this realm is dominated by institutions of the state, what chance have claims made under the sign of culture and in the spirit of policulturalism against the hegemony of the Constitution, against the Laws of the Nation, against the ideological dominance of the universal right-bearing citizen? This rephrases, in more general terms, a question we asked earlier. In a world regulated by Eurocentric jurisprudence, should we not expect that any assertion of Afromodernity, any argument for the sovereignty of the Kingdom of Custom, would have little prospect of prevailing? Would not the latter simply fade away of its own accord – or under the pressure of the former? American critical legal theory would probably concur, given its tendency to align the law with the power of the state. Others, like those who contend that multiculturalism is inimical to democracy, would hope that they were correct.[31] As we have implied, however, the matter is not so straightforward. For one thing, phrased thus, it presumes that law and culture – or, more accurately, European liberal legal universalism and appeals to Africanity – exist in a zero-sum equation. This Manichean opposition, it is true, may describe the way the issue is framed in South African popular discourse. But reality is much more complicated. The challenge is to make sense of the ways in which the forces of tradition and those of liberal democracy are confronting one another at the present moment; how, in ongoing, often strident struggles, *both* are being transformed – thereby altering the very shape and substance of post-colonial politics, of citizenship, of democracy.

In order to do so, we appeal to a venerable anthropological device: an extended case. This case is paradigmatic of encounters, in the interstices of post-colonial constitutionalism, between the Rule of Law and the Kingdom of Custom. It concerns a battle, in the North West Province, over the alleged wrongs of a burial rite.

---

[31] Such critics span the political spectrum from radical (e.g. Dirlik 1990) to conservative. One British 'View from the right', Minette Marrin, *The Guardian* (UK), 29 May 2001, p. 7, puts it thus: '[W]hat we must have to live together in harmony is a tolerant, over-arching common culture.' But the very idea of such a culture is 'denounced by multiculturalists as supremacist and racist'.

From customs of death to the death of custom

Mogaga *meets the Human Rights Commission*
What happens when, as an anonymous local reporter wrote, there is a 'head-on collision between the new South African Constitution and [the] age-old traditions, customs and cultures observed by millions of Blacks'?[32] The answer, in the case between Mrs Kedibone Elizabeth Tumane, of the remote village of Mononono in the North West Province, and Chief Nyalala Pilane of the Bgakgatla-Ba-Kgafela, under whose Tribal Authority the village falls, was a lengthy legal tussle, notable for the complex strategies – and the appeals to culture, the constitution, democracy and rights – on both sides. The dispute centred on Tumane's refusal to perform a burial rite. At issue was a Tswana convention that requires a newly bereaved spouse to sprinkle a herb, *mogaga*, on her path when she walks abroad in communal space. In theory, death pollution (*sefifi*) afflicts men as well as women (Comaroff 1980: 643–4). But ritual prophylaxis is more stringently mandated for females, who are thought to be more open to contamination. In the past, the rite was usually observed for a year; in recent times, some Tribal Authorities[33] have insisted on regulating its performance in the cause of communal well-being. Mrs Tumane, a staunch member of the Watchtower Movement, saw *mogaga* as contrary to the dictates of her faith. She claimed that when she tried to leave home, she was prevented from doing so by the Tribal Authority. What was more, members of the local community, deeming her behavior a deliberate breach of tradition, called for her banishment. After various efforts to settle the matter had failed, Mrs Tumane endeavoured to take Chief Pilane and his Tribal Authority to court. With the support of the South African Human Rights Commission (SAHRC), she complained that her human rights had been violated.

Some background here. Mortuary ritual has been a contentious issue among Tswana since time immemorial; early missionaries were quick to recognise that the space of death was a site of singular sensitivity (Comaroff and Comaroff 1997b: 358; see also Durham and Klaits 2000). It still is. A survey in 2000 of chiefly court records in the North West revealed a score of cases brought against local people, mostly immigrants from other regions, who had refused to perform the proper mourning routines. These are matters of great moment because bereavement rites – the initial seclusion of surviving spouses, then the sprinkling of *mogaga* to cool their polluting footprints – are held to prevent the contagion of death from escaping abroad (Comaroff 1974: 124f). In her affidavit to the High Court,[34] Mrs Tumane affirmed that this *is* a widely shared belief; its breach is said to threaten the lives of local cattle or to withhold the rain. The growing impact of HIV/AIDS in the countryside has heightened such ritual anxieties: inadequately observed mourning practices are thought to play a role in rising mortality rates.

From this vantage, then, the performance of prescribed burial rites is not just a question of personal choice, or even of respect for custom: it is a matter, literally, of life and death for the community at large – and, therefore, the responsibility of its traditional authorities. But not everyone in the rural North West agrees. There has been opposition

[32] 'Clash of Custom, Constitution', *The Mail*, 31 July 1998, p. 17.
[33] Tribal Authorities are officially recognised administrative bodies made up of chiefs and chiefly advisers. Instituted by the apartheid regime as part of the system of 'homeland' governance, they were explicitly modelled on an African political institution that endures in many rural areas.
[34] Case No. 618/98, in the High Court of South Africa (Bophuthatswana Provincial Division), p. 3.

to these ritual demands, most often mounted by women in the name of their right to freedom of belief. Thus, in June 1995, a group of 'concerned' female cadres of the ANC and Pan-African Congress presented a memorandum to the Bafokeng chief, Lebone Motlotlegi. It protested against 'the enforcement of traditional laws' in respect of burial which 'deprived South Africans of their rights to full citizenship'.[35] Citizenship, here, denotes a specific sort of political subjectivity: equal, rights-endowed membership within the liberal nation-state, not subjection to the Kingdom of Custom. There was precedent, in short, for Elizabeth Tumane's application for an interdict to the High Court in Mafikeng in June 1998. She claimed that, because of her refusal to observe *mogaga*, a representative of the Bakgatla-Ba-Kgafela Tribal Authority had ordered her to confine herself to her house and yard, forcing her to 'live ... the life of an outcast'.[36]

Tumane emerges from the story as a woman of uncommon resolve; our informants confirmed that prior religious tensions had sharpened local sensitivities to her ritual infringements and had heightened antagonism towards her.[37] Her eldest son, also a Jehovah's Witness – another son in Mononono is not[38] – had initially taken his mother's grievance to the regional Ombudsman, whose staff tried in vain to intervene with the Tribal Authority. The Human Rights Commission[39] was the next resort. Advocate Pansy Tlakula, a Tswana-speaking commissioner with special responsibility for the North West Province, duly accompanied the complainant to a meeting with Chief Pilane. Tlakula had brought veteran politician Helen Suzman and a senior male colleague with her, suspecting that gender tensions might also be at work in the dispute. The battle between custom and human rights has often been reduced, in the heat of political argument, to a stand-off between self-identifying 'traditional' senior men and constitutionally empowered women and youth; that is, between 'subjects' and 'citizens'.

In an affidavit sworn at Mononono, Tumane notes that, at the meeting in June 1998, Pilane had agreed to end her confinement. By then, six months of seclusion had already elapsed; this, she added, was the prescribed length of time, according to a prior Tribal Authority ruling, for which the sprinkling of *mogaga* was compulsory. The chief had consented then to call a gathering of the community, at which he undertook both to announce his decision to free her and to permit the HRC to inform people of existing constitutional provisions 'relating to customary laws and practices'.[40]

The promised gathering was duly held, although the HRC was *not* invited. But, rather than end Tumane's confinement, the 'tribe' resolved that, because of her transgression, she should be banished from the village and the chiefdom. Pilane kept a low profile, allowing

---

[35] 'Women Present Memo to the Chief', *The Mail*, 30 June 1995, p. 3.
[36] Case No. 618/98, in the High Court of South Africa (Bophuthatswana Provincial Division), Founding Affidavit, p. 3.
[37] Interviews with Advocate Pansy Tlakula (Human Rights Commission), 19 July 2000; Simon Ruthwane (Department of Traditional Affairs, North West Province), 20 July 2000; Reginald Mpame (Registrar, High Court, Mmabatho), 10 July 2000; and Elizabeth Tlhoaele (House of Traditional Leaders, North West Province), 24 July 2000.
[38] Answering Affidavit, Nyalala Molefe John Pilane, 13 November 1998, Case No. 618/98, in the High Court of South Africa (Bophuthatswana Provincial Division), p. 28.
[39] The HRC is an independent commission set up under the terms of the Constitution to investigate possible violations of its terms.
[40] Case No. 618/98, in the High Court of South Africa (Bophuthatswana Provincial Division), Founding Affidavit, pp. 5–6.

the ruler of a senior branch of the Bakgatla in Botswana[41] to make a strong statement about the perils posed to tradition by the South African Constitution.[42] In challenging the sovereignty of the State and its *One* Law, customary authorities here presumed a political map that transcends national borders. For her part, Tumane said that she was threatened with assault, the volatile crowd vowing that they were ready to expel her by force. 'I really feared for my safety and that of my family,' she attested.[43] Efforts by the HRC to remind the chief and the Tribal Authority of their earlier agreement elicited a letter from Pilane. He was not, he insisted, in a position to end the confinement. Tumane was 'confined by her own custom', he wrote; this could not be changed without the 'consent of the tribe',[44] of which she herself was a member.[45] Her rights had been respected, he went on, save where they were in conflict with Section 36 of the Constitution, 'which [wa]s applicable in all black South African communities'. Section 36, recall, is the clause covering the limitation of rights. Here it was invoked to justify the suspension of a constitutional entitlement where it conflicted with a collectively endorsed custom.

Tumane and the HRC countered that Pilane and the Tribal Authority *had* violated Tumane's constitutional rights: her right to equality (Section 9), dignity (Section 10), security of person (Section 12[1]), freedom of religion, belief and opinion (Section 15), freedom of movement and residence (Section 21), choice of language and culture (Section 30) and just administrative action (Section 33). While the Kgatla were entitled to promote the religion and culture of their community, went the argument, they could do so only in a manner consistent with the Bill of Rights. An urgent court application was made and, on 20 July 1998, the Mmabatho High Court ruled it a violation of the Constitution to compel performance of the *mogaga* rite. Pilane was ordered to lift Tumane's confinement immediately, and to desist from threatening her in any way.

The order was an interim measure, pending a court hearing in November of that year. According to Advocate Tlakula, who litigated on behalf of the HRC, it had no appreciable effect on Tumane's predicament. Meanwhile, the dispute became a *cause célèbre* in the North West. Reporters who travelled to Mononono to interview Tumane wrote that she was relieved at the prospect of being released from 'house arrest'.[46] The case was also debated in the provincial House of Traditional Leaders, where the chiefs came into bitter confrontation with both the MEC[47] for Local Government, a senior ANC politician, and representatives of the HRC; they argued that the challenge to Chief Pilane was part of a general campaign to 'violate' tradition in the name of the Constitution. Why were the

[41] The speaker was introduced as Paramount Chief of the Kgatla; this despite the fact that, while Tswana chiefdoms recognise an order of ritual seniority among their rulers, they have never had paramount chiefs *per se*. Paramountcy has been claimed from time to time, however, for political purposes.

[42] Advocate Pansy Tlakula (personal communication).

[43] Case No. 618/98, in the High Court of South Africa (Bophuthatswana Provincial Division), Founding Affidavit, p. 6.

[44] Pilane's communication, here, is multiply resonant. At this point in his reply, Pilane invoked a hallowed aphorism: *kgosi ke kgosi ka morafe*, a chief is chief by [with] the people.

[45] Letter from Kgosi Nyalala M.J. Pilane to M.C. Moodliar, Human Rights Commission, 29 June 1998. Item B4 attached to the case record of the Bophuthatswana High Court.

[46] 'Clash of Custom, Constitution', *The Mail*, 31 July 1998, p. 17. Other resonances are at work here. House arrest was commonly used by the apartheid government to silence its opponents; its invocation by Mrs Tumane associates the actions of the Tribal Authority with the tactics of the *ancien régime*.

[47] Member of the Executive Council of the House of Representatives of the North West Province. MECs are the heads of provincial government departments.

customary rights of tribes not protected by that Constitution? Why were the rights of individuals put above those of groups? Why was it that this case was being debated in the High Court rather than in the House of Traditional Leaders?[48]

In November, Pilane submitted a long answering affidavit.[49] The text, which repeats some of his earlier arguments, begins with a history of the Bakgatla-Ba-Kgafela, seeking to establish that its leader 'owed [his] position entirely to the support [he] had within [the tribe], inspired by its history, culture and traditions'. Significant among these traditions were rituals of birth, marriage and death; rituals, like the use of *mogaga*, that enjoyed 'almost complete' observance among the Kgatla, irrespective of education or status. In words that might have been written by structural-functionalist anthropologists of the British School, the ruler declared: 'Tradition is the glue that holds the tribe together, gives it a purpose, sustains its identity and allows for co-ordination and co-operation in ... efforts [towards upliftment].' While virtually all Kgatla regarded themselves as Christians, he went on, only a few, notably Jehovah's Witnesses, objected to performing the *mogaga* rite. Efforts to ascertain precisely *which* biblical injunction forbad the custom, so that 'some compromise' could be reached, had been unsuccessful. So had attempts to get those churches that opposed it to produce their constitutions; a clear example, this, of the power of constitutionalism, in the lower case (see above).[50] Pilane, here, gestures towards an accommodation between the Constitution and culture, an accommodation actively encouraged by the HRC, which advocates the 'modernisation and amendment' of traditional practices in line with the Bill of Rights. But, again, the gesture remains entirely rhetorical: what a 'compromise' might actually have meant, in this case, seems not to have been seriously considered by any of the parties.[51]

In addressing Tumane's claims in particular, however, Pilane's affidavit abruptly changed direction, asserting that she had never been threatened or intimidated by his Authority. *Mogaga*, he now insisted, was a 'ritual voluntarily followed ... [T]here has been no compulsion.' The complainant had, by her own choice, dissociated herself from the life of the village. This was her right. But, to the degree that she showed 'contempt for tradition in the language of religious fervor and self-righteous indignation', her actions were 'calculated to cause an affront to [local] dignity'.[52] Tumane was an 'eccentric' who had chosen to marginalise herself; she was now feeling the hostility of 'the tribe as a community' – not least for dragging them into expensive litigation. What is more, the effort of the HRC to turn a 'non-issue' into a 'human rights' case had backfired. The complainants had sought to demonise an unobjectionable rite in the hope of forcing it to 'adapt' under the pretext that it infringed the Constitution. In joining the dispute, the HRC had made

---

[48] 'Clash of Custom, Constitution', *The Mail*, 31 July 1998, p. 17.

[49] Answering Affidavit, Nyalala Molefe John Pilane, 13 November 1998, Case No. 618/98, in the High Court of South Africa (Bophuthatswana Division); all our citations in this paragraph are from pp. 7–10.

[50] Constitutionalism has been a feature of independent African churches from their inception (Comaroff 1974; Sundkler 1961). But its centrality in the new South Africa to popular notions of organizational legitimacy has given church constitutions new salience.

[51] See the statement made to this effect by Advocate Tlakula during the debate on the case in the North West House of Traditional Leaders; 'Clash of Custom, Constitution', *The Mail*, 31 July 1998, p. 17. According to Tlakula (personal communication), she told the chiefs that the matter rested with them: either they would reform their traditions or the matter would be taken out of their hands.

[52] Answering Affidavit, Nyalala Molefe John Pilane, 13 November 1998, Case No. 618/98, in the High Court of South Africa (Bophuthatswana Division), p. 19.

clear its contempt for the Kgatla and their customs.

Although the thrust of this affidavit was to deny that the *mogaga* rite was binding – or that Mrs Tumane had actually been confined by it – Pilane's conclusions suggested otherwise. For, in closing, he reiterated that he was merely 'chief by virtue of the decision ... of the tribe' and was, therefore, powerless to impose decisions that ran counter to the democratic voice of popular opinion. That opinion, he did not have to repeat, had been strongly in favour of punishing Elizabeth Tumane. Rulers who had defied their people in the past, he reminded the court, had usually come to grief.

This was the last salvo fired by Chief Pilane in the conflict. It was definitive. On 25 February 1999, the High Court dismissed its *decree nisi* of the previous July on the ground that the disputed practice had been declared voluntary. By this time, anyway, the required period of mourning had long elapsed.

Advocate Tlakula told us that the HRC had indeed been interested in the constitutional issues raised by Mrs Tumane's suit. In fact, the Commission regretted that Pilane had *not* stuck to his guns: that he had *not* made the strongest case for the sovereign cultural rights – or prescribed customary rites – of ethnic communities. Tlakula had anticipated an argument to the effect that Tumane lived voluntarily among Bagkgatla and was thus bound by their life-ways. As she noted, there *is* precedent for the judiciary favouring tradition over human rights; the Supreme Court, remember, was to give priority to culture over gender equality in Mthembu v. Letsela. Tlakula said that she had even toyed with the idea of passing on the record of an earlier case of this sort to Pilane's lawyers in the hope that they would mount the most forceful defence possible, thereby ensuring that the matter would be thrashed out in court. The HRC wanted very much to win a landmark ruling that would render it unconstitutional to force anyone to abide by a sectarian cultural practice. To be sure, even this would have been a limited victory: Tlakula had planned to base her counter-argument on Tumane's right to freedom of association rather than her freedom of belief; she sought to avoid pitting 'religion' against 'culture', with all the complexities that this would inevitably have introduced. Above all – and here is clear evidence of how the politics of difference challenges the liberal rule of law – the Commission was anxious not to assert that 'African culture was unconstitutional'. It is one thing to outlaw *compulsion*, quite another to criminalise custom.

But the HRC lost its chance. Rightly or not, the chief's lawyers had told him that – in view of the weight accorded to the Bill of Rights in the 'new' South Africa – he was bound to lose unless he declared that the *mogaga* rite was voluntary; a strategic retreat would, in any case, leave the legal status of custom advantageously murky. This tactical caution might have been justified, albeit for different reasons: Tlakula believed that Kgatla opinion was more divided than Pilane had allowed. Journalists, who interviewed local people, concurred:[53] Tumane had been quietly abetted by many of her neighbours.

As is common in such cases, the public was invoked on all sides, most notably by the chief. Pilane had asserted, early on, that Mrs Tumane was confined by 'her own custom', that it was beyond his power to release her from her duty to follow a popularly mandated tradition. While his disavowal of authority was somewhat disingenuous, the ruler's testimony rested on two broadly endorsed claims: first, that neglect of rites like *mogaga*

---

[53] 'Clash of Custom, Constitution', *The Mail*, 31 July 1998, p. 17.

is regarded by the majority of rural people as a clear and present danger to their physical and moral well-being; and, second, that the obligation to perform this particular rite had been legitimately affirmed by a *democratic* process, the Kgatla nation (*setshaba*) having voiced unanimous support for it in a public setting. In its discussion of the case, the House of Traditional Leaders in the North West Province had explicitly demanded more recognition for the legitimacy of collectively affirmed traditions and modes of governance. In so doing, it echoed a widespread sentiment in the countryside about the need to 'Africanise' democracy by rescuing it from Eurocentric preoccupations with electoral processes and individual rights.

As we have seen, the chief opted for strategic compromise in his final affidavit. But, in his substantive statements, he returned repeatedly to the affront implied by cases like this to the integrity of Kgatla culture. Tellingly, his argument for the sovereignty – some would say fetishism – of custom reproduced the language of the Constitution: it was framed in terms of rights, freedom, dignity and democracy. However, this language was used to evoke a very different vision of persons, polities and politics, one that distinguishes ethnic subjects from national citizens; this in spite, or maybe because, of the fact that the two visions serve to define and limit one another – and that, in practice, neither is as distinct from the other as is often made out in the heat of dispute.

Little wonder, then, that the '*mogaga* case', as it is now known in the North West, has become exemplary of the entrenched contradiction between the One Law of the Nation and the Kingdom of Custom. Significantly, the conflict had no decisive outcome. The antinomy to which it spoke remains unresolved. And unresolvable. Mrs Tumane lives on in Mononono – released, in the end, not by the court but by the passage of time. Other widows since have either performed the rite or desist less visibly. The dispute to which it gave rise and many others like it make three things clear. The first is the growing relevance, in this post-colonial democracy, of ethnically based arguments about rights and entitlements, arguments that frame local struggles against the authority of the state not merely in cultural terms, but with reference to a form of policulturalism that is making itself felt ever more globally. The second is the likelihood that, whatever pragmatic outcomes might be reached, these arguments will persist in pitting individual against collective rights, liberal universalism against culture, citizens against subjects; if anything, *pace* the utopian impulses of liberal multiculturalism, they are liable to reproduce rather than resolve the paradox of pluralism endemic to *neo*-liberal nationhood. The third is the mounting tendency for stand-offs between the Kingdom of Custom and the Constitution to be pursued by legal means, whether in quarrels over rights among groups or in challenges to the sovereignty of the nation-state and *One* Law (cf. Lazarus-Black and Hirsch 1994).[54]

---

[54] In this regard it seems clear that, while they have increasingly been drawn into such litigation, traditional rulers feel relatively disadvantaged by its terms. Pilane and other royals publicly expressed the view that the *mogaga* case should have been conducted elsewhere than in the High Court. In their view, African authority, metonymically enshrined in the chiefship and chiefly courts, ought to be constitutionally recognised. Hence the insistence, at the Midrand Conference on Traditional Leadership and Institutions (see above), that the Constitution be amended to recognise their sovereignty.

Inclusions, exclusions, conclusions

The *mogaga* case, in sum, is not in the least exceptional. It is paradigmatic of the way in which a politics of difference runs up against the limits of liberalism. Similar conflicts are occurring more and more frequently across South Africa over initiation ritual and occult beliefs, inheritance and succession, corporal punishment, landholding, and many things besides. Taken together, they point to the fact that a vernacular praxis is beginning to emerge: in the face of the confrontation between the Constitution and Culture, and the values for which they stand, those who seek to assert the sovereignty of things African have arrived at a series of strategic positions. These are founded on the conviction that, in spite of a rhetoric of recognition for 'tradition', in spite of talk about its 'liberation' by accommodation to the common law, the post-colonial state, even more than its colonial forebear, means to reduce the Kingdom of Custom to a shadow of its former self: in the argot of neo-liberal social management, to make chiefs into lower order managers in the dispute processing and rural development sectors. Also in the sphere of ceremonial, although – as revealed by the *mogaga* case, which was concerned with the *limitation* of chiefly rights in the rites business – 'ceremony' tends to be treated nowadays as little more than powerless pomp. The counter-tactics to which this has given rise range from a politics of avoidance, through open confrontation, to overt hybridisation.[55] The first was the strategy used, in the end, by Pilane in order to prevent the court from outlawing *mogaga*, thus, tacitly, allowing 'his people' to insist on its performance in the future; the second, less common, has been resorted to by some traditional leaders in the effort to force the HRC to prosecute them for making cultural conventions compulsory, or for otherwise flouting the law of the land, thereby to challenge the ANC to put its tolerance to the test. The third has involved exertions on the part of other rulers to alter those conventions by 'tribal' legislation, just enough to render them acceptable under the Constitution.[56] This tactic is less of a departure from the past than it may seem. African traditional codes have never been unchanging. Rather, as in the Euro-American sense of 'customary law', they have grown out of an evanescent history of practice – much in the manner espoused for the future by Justice Sachs (above, p. 41).

Elsewhere (Comaroff and Comaroff n.d.) we explore the implications of these and other means of acting on the conflict between liberal governance and the call of custom. What concern us here are the implications for citizenship, political being and democracy that flow from contradictions inherent in the scaffolding of post-colonial polities at this historical moment – contradictions observable in nation-states everywhere, if in locally modulated form. For these contradictions stem, we argue, from disjunctures of hyphe-nation in the Age of Neo-liberalism: from the ever more problematic relation between the liberal modernist state and the policultural nation. It is this relation, patently, that has not

---

[55] Contrary to some formulations (cf. Modood 2000: 177), we use 'hybridisation' not as an analytic concept but as a descriptive term for one among many self-conscious strategies deployed to address the paradox of difference here. We do not see the concept, conventionally understood, as providing an adequately theorised account of processes of this nature.

[56] There are, of course, 'traditional' practices that chiefs have themselves banished, on grounds of one or another principle, in order to address social and political transformations. Nor is this a purely post-colonial phenomenon. Schapera (1943, 1970) has documented the history of vernacular legislation and legal innovation among various Tswana groupings; see also Comaroff and Roberts (1977).

been adequately addressed or redressed in contemporary normative philosophy or social policy.

Our objective, by contrast, is to explain why, despite strenuous and thoughtful efforts to resolve it, the antinomy persists, why it resists even the best-intentioned, most capacious politics of tolerance. We have sought, therefore, to make sense of the way in which struggles over culture in post-apartheid South Africa have emerged from a *concrete*, ongoing history of difference, a history that has edged uneasily from Tutu's excoriation of ethnicity to Maduna's plea for the necessity of its recognition. It is a history that sheds light on the generic vicissitudes of the life and times of the nation-state at the turn of the new century. For, as they face the forces of global capital, post-colonial societies like this one have come to replicate features of 'late' liberal polities elsewhere, especially in respect of the challenge posed to democratic rule by activism in the name of identity. But the postcolony also makes evident critical differences in the politics of difference, in struggles that do not merely strive for inclusion *within* state institutions, but contest the very sovereignty of those institutions: their constituent forms of politics, citizenship and democracy, their monopoly over the law and the means of violence. Because of this, these struggles are inadequately grasped by liberal terms like 'minority rights' or 'multicultural-ism'. For the policultural activity they embody is born of, and sustained by, the *limits* of liberalism: the limited ability, in South Africa, of the newly democratic state to produce a unified nation amidst the intensifying flow of signs, goods and people across its borders; the limited capacity of its hegemonic discourse to frame an ideology to counter ID-ology and the centrifugal claims of diversity; the limited power of its Constitution to make actual the entitlements it guarantees; the limited capability of its instruments of governance to reconcile the equality it promises its citizens with the stark disparities of life in an increasingly deregulated economy.

It is these limits that reproduce the tensions between the philosophical tenets of universalism and the practical realities of difference, between the abstract language of individual rights and the vernacular sentiments of collective identity, between the truth-claims of citizenship and the true-life experience of ethnic subjecthood; the tensions, that is, which shape the everyday politics of culture, and which erupt intermittently into dramatic confrontations like the one between Elizabeth Tumane and the Kgatla Tribal Authority. The fact that such conflicts are litigated, and that the case brought against the Kingdom of Custom was framed in terms of the plaintiff's rights to citizenship, is no accident. The growing salience of the law – in fact, the legalisation of politics *tout court* – is, for reasons that we have made plain, an integral feature of the neo-liberal moment. Even in contesting the sovereignty of the state, traditional authorities have no choice but to engage it in jural terms: in the idiom of rights, constitutionalism and due process. But, in arguing both with and through the law, advocates of difference are having an impact on its ways and meanings – by, among other things, forcing it to fashion a jurisprudence that can deal with culture without criminalising it.

It is in such cases, too, that the shape of a new popular politics is discernible, a politics that is catching flame as older struggles – under the signs of class, race and partisan ideology – fade away. This may not be the kind of politics, the sort of dialectic, that critical theorists might have chosen; it does not, after all, address some of the more profound moral and material forces shaping the lives of contemporary South Africans. Or others elsewhere. But it is a politics nonetheless, a politics that is yielding new styles of activism, new forms of subjectivity and new sites of history-in-the-making. In postcolonies and in the world at large.

Acknowledgements

We should like to thank Advocate Pansy Tlakula, of the Human Rights Commission, for generously sharing her insights into the *mogaga* case and, more generally, into the politics of culture and traditional leadership in South Africa. We are also indebted to Constitutional Court Justices Albie Sachs and Yvonne Mokgoro, to Henry Giroux and Susan Searls, and to our editor, Steven Robins, for their thoughtful comments on the topic of the essay. Our research assistant, Maureen Anderson, abetted the project with her usual energy and imagination. This essay began life as one in our series of Jensen Lectures at the University of Frankfurt in May–July 2001; we express our gratitude to our hosts there, the Frobenius Institute and its Director, Professor Karl-Heinz Kohl. The research on which it is based was generously supported by the American Bar Foundation and the Lichtstern Fund for Anthropological Research at the University of Chicago.

References

Anderson, Benedict (1983), *Imagined Communities: Reflections on the Origin and Spread of Nationalism*, London: Verso.
Appadurai, Arjun (1990), 'Disjuncture and Difference in the Global Cultural Economy', *Public Culture*, 2: 1–24.
Comaroff, Jean (1974), 'Barolong Cosmology: A Study of Religious Pluralism in a Tswana Town', Phd. dissertation, University of London.
—— (1980), 'Healing and the Cultural Order', *American Ethnologist*, 7(4):637–57.
Comaroff, Jean and John L. Comaroff, (1999a), 'Occult Economies and the Violence of Abstraction: Notes from the South African Postcolony', *American Ethnologist*, 26 (3): 279–301.
—— (2000), 'Millennial Capitalism: First Thoughts on a Second Coming', in J. Comaroff and J.L. Comaroff (eds), *Millennial Capitalism and the Culture of Neoliberalism*, Special Edition of *Public Culture*, 12 (2): 291–343.
—— (2001), 'Naturing the Nation: Aliens, Apocalypse and the Postcolonial State', *Journal of Southern African Studies*, 27(3): 627–51.
—— (n.d.) *Policing the Postcolony: Crime, the State, and the Metaphysics of Disorder in South Africa*. [In preparation.]
Comaroff, John L. (1998), 'Reflections on the Colonial State, in South Africa and Elsewhere: Fragments, Factions, Facts and Fictions', *Social Identities*, 4(3): 321–61 (1998).
Comaroff, John L. and Jean Comaroff (1997a), 'Postcolonial Politics and Discourses of Democracy in Southern Africa: An Anthropological Reflection on African Political Modernities', *Journal of Anthropological Research*, 53(2): 123–46.
—— (1997b), *Of Revelation and Revolution*, Volume II, *The Dialectics of Modernity on a South African Frontier* Chicago: University of Chicago Press.
—— (1999b), 'Introduction', in J.L. Comaroff and J. Comaroff (eds), *Civil Society and the Political Imagination in Africa*, Chicago: University of Chicago Press.
Comaroff, John L. and Simon A. Roberts, (1977), 'Marriage and Extramarital Sexuality: The Dialectics of Legal Change amongst the Kgatla', *Journal of African Law*, 21: 97–123.
Coombe, Rosemary J. (1998), *The Cultural Life of Intellectual Properties: Authorship, Appropriation and the Law*, Durham: Duke University Press.
Corrigan, Philip and Derek Sayer (1985), *The Great Arch: English State Formation as Cultural Revolution*, Oxford: Blackwell.
Darian-Smith, Eve (1996), 'Postcolonialism: A Brief Introduction', *Social and Legal Studies*, 5(3): 291–9.
Dirlik, Arif (1990), 'Culturalism as Hegemonic Ideology and Liberating Practice', in J. Mohamed and D. Lloyd (eds) *The Nature and Context of Minority Discourse*, New York: Oxford University Press.
Durham, Deborah and Fred Klaits (2000), 'Funerals and the Public Space of Mutuality in Botswana', *Journal of Southern African Studies*, 28(4): 777–95.
Harvey, David (1990), *The Condition of Postmodernity: An Enquiry into the Origins of Cultural Change*, Oxford: Blackwell.

Hegeman, Susan (1991), 'Shopping for Identities: A Nation of Nations and the Weak Ethnicity of Objects', *Public Culture*, 3(2): 71–92.

Hobsbawm, Eric J. (1992), 'Ethnicity and Nationalism in Europe Today', *Anthropology Today*, 8: 3–8.

Jacobson, David (1996), *Rights Across Borders*, Baltimore: Johns Hopkins University Press.

Klor De Alva, J. Jorge (1995), 'The Postcolonization of the (Latin) American Experience: A Reconsideration of "Colonialism", "Postcolonialism", and "'Mestizaje"'', in G. Prakash (ed.), *After Colonialism: Imperial Histories and Postcolonial Displacements*, Princeton: Princeton University Press.

Kymlicka, Will and Wayne Norman (2000), 'Introduction', in W. Kymlicka and W. Norman (eds), *Citizenship in Diverse Societies*, Oxford: Oxford University Press.

Lazarus-Black, Mindie and Susan F. Hirsch, (eds) (1994), *Contested States: Law, Hegemony, and Resistance*, New York: Routledge.

Levy, Jacob T. (2000), *The Multiculturalism of Fear*, Oxford: Oxford University Press.

Lijphart, Arend (1995), 'Self-Determination Versus Pre-Determination of Ethnic Minorities in Power-Sharing Systems', in W. Kymlicka (ed.), *The Rights of Minority Cultures*, Oxford: Oxford University Press.

McClintock, Anne (1992), 'The Angel of Progress: Pitfalls of the Term "Post-Colonialism"', *Social Text*, 31/32: 84–98.

Mcmichael, Philip (1998), 'Development and Structural Adjustment', in J.G. Carrier and D. Miller (eds), *Virtualism: A New Political Economy*, Oxford: Berg.

Mamdani, Mahmood (1996), *Citizen and Subject: Contemporary Africa and the Legacy of Late Colonialism*, Princeton: Princeton University Press.

Mandela, Nelson (1994), *Long Walk to Freedom: The Autobiography of Nelson Mandela*, Boston: Little, Brown & Co.

Mbeki, Govan (1964), *South Africa: The Peasant's Revolt*, Harmondsworth: Penguin.

Mbembe, Achille (1992), 'Provisional Notes on the Postcolony', *Africa*, 62(1): 3–37.

Mishra, Vijay and Bob Hodge (1991), 'What is Post(-)colonialism?' *Textual Practice*, 5(3): 399–414.

Modood, Tariq (2000), 'Anti-Essentialism, Multiculturalism, and the "Recognition" of Religious Groups', in W. Kymlicka and W. Norman (eds), *Citizenship in Diverse Societies*, Oxford: Oxford University Press.

Mokgoro, Yvonne (1994), 'The Role and Place of Lay Participation, Customary and Community Courts in a Restructured Future Judiciary', in *Reshaping the Structures of Justice for a Democratic South Africa*, papers of a conference of the National Association of Democratic Lawyers, Pretoria, October 1993 (Ms.).

Ong, Aiwa (1999), *Flexible Citizenship: The Cultural Logics of Transnationality*, Durham: Duke University Press.

Oomen, Barbara M. (2002), 'Chiefs! Law, Power and Culture in Contemporary South Africa'. Ph.D. dissertation, University of Leiden. Published as *Chiefs in South Africa: Law, Power and Culture in the Post-Apartheid Era* (Oxford: James Currey, 2005).

Prakash, Gyan (1995), 'Introduction: After Colonialism', in G. Prakash (ed.), *After Colonialism: Imperial Histories and Postcolonial Displacements*, Princeton: Princeton University Press.

Ralushai, N.V., M. G.Masingi, D.M.M. Madiba *et al.* (1996), *Report of the Commission of Inquiry into Witchcraft Violence and Ritual Murders in the Northern Province of the Republic of South Africa* (To: His Excellency The Honourable Member of the Executive Council for Safety and Security, Northern Province). No publisher given.

Sachs, Albie (n.d.), 'Towards the Liberation and Revitalization of Customary Law', Address to the Southern African Society of Legal Historians, Pretoria, 13–15 January 1999. Ms.

Salacuse, Jeswald W. (1991), *Making Global Deals: Negotiating in the International Marketplace*. Boston: Houghton Mifflin.

Schapera, Isaac (1943), *Tribal Legislation among the Tswana of the Bechuanaland Protectorate*, London: London School of Economics.

—— (1970), *Tribal Innovators: Tswana Chiefs and Social Change, 1795–1940*, London School of Economics Monographs, no. 43, London: Athlone Press.

Shapiro, Martin (1993), 'The Globalization of Law', *Indiana Journal of Global Legal Studies*, 1(Fall): 37–64.

Sundkler, Bengt G.M. (1961), *Bantu Prophets in South Africa*, London: Oxford University Press for the International African Institute, Second Edition.

Taylor, Charles (1989), *Sources of the Self: The Making of Modern Identity*, Cambridge: Harvard University Press.

—— (1992), 'The Politics of Recognition', in A. Gutman (ed.), *Multiculturalism and the 'Politics of Recognition'*, Princeton: Princeton University Press.

Tutu, Desmond Mpilo (1984), *Hope and Suffering: Sermons and Speeches*, Grand Rapids: Eerdmans.

Vanderbilt, Tom (1997), 'The Advertised Life', in T. Frank and M. Weiland (eds), *Commodify Your Dissent: Salvos from* The Baffler, New York and London: W.W. Norton.

3

The Demands of Recognition & the Ambivalence of Difference
Race, Culture & Afrikanerness in post-Apartheid South Africa

SUREN PILLAY

Was Apartheid the product of some horrific shortcoming in Afrikaner culture?... How do we live with the fact that all the words used to humiliate, all the orders given to kill, belonged to the language of my heart?

Antjie Krog[1]

These were the anguished thoughts of the South African poet as she wrote about the Truth and Reconciliation Commission as a journalist. Whilst my chapter does not seek to answer her questions it does inhabit the same political moment – the moment of thinking about being 'post' apartheid, about making and remaking in a time which is also about taking and retaking. The chapter seeks to engage two discussions being conducted in different places, both in the sense of a locality, but also epistemically The one is about minority rights and liberalism; the other is about minority rights claims of Afrikaners in post-apartheid South Africa. The one claims a conceptual globality as its terrain, the other a pragmatic locality. The one speaks from the universal to the specific. The other speaks from the specific to the universal.

Yet it seems that to separate them, both in terms of their sites of engagement and the stakes involved, is not useful. Rather, it may be worth thinking about them as mutually determining but open-ended zones with the conditions of possibility of the one being the conditions of possibility of the other. In my engagement with the conceptual-global debate I wish to make the following argument: we need to problematise the theoretical universalisation of a particular normative view about the relationship between nation, state, minority rights and the right to self-determination. I want to suggest that we question the assumption, implicit and explicit, in some contemporary discussions on minority cultural rights within multiculturalist discourses that take them as an *a priori* 'good'. In relation to the 'pragmatic-local' debate I want to argue that claims emanating from sections of the

---

[1] The excerpt is taken from her book on the Truth and Reconciliation Commission, *Country of My Skull* (1998: 238).

Afrikaner community[2] in South Africa demonstrate a complex shift from racialised claims of 'supremacy' to ethnicised claims to 'protection', in so doing deracialising 'whiteness' and reinscribing difference through the language of 'culture' in the form of the 'volk'. Both arguments enable me to suggest that we locate discussions about the relationship between culture, politics and ethics within particular politico-historic formations, shaped by the play of time and power.

In order to suggest the saliency of an approach which neither denies nor accepts *a priori* recognition claims I therefore turn to minority rights claims being made by sections of the Afrikaner community in post-apartheid South Africa. My entry point into the wider debates will be primarily through the Canadian political theorist Will Kymlicka's influential argument put forward in *Liberalism, Community and Culture* (1989). I then discuss contemporary claims to a Volkstaat in the hope that a discussion of these claims will suggest a set of experiences that too should dialogue at the table of debates around liberalism, difference and minority rights.

I have chosen Kymlicka in particular because he has specifically addressed himself to the counter-argumentative possibility that the South African scenario represents for his desire to suggest that liberalism is the most useful philosophical framework within which both group and individual autonomy can be accommodated. One can find the tendency to universalise a particular way of receiving minority rights claims in a diverse body of contemporary work, from those who are partial to liberalism, or an amended version of it (e.g. Kukathas 1992; Kymlicka 1989; Taylor *et al.*, 1994), to those who suggest that liberalism may have reached its sell-by date in our post-imperial, post-colonial age (Connolly 1995). As an instance of the latter view I briefly engage the work of James Tully (1995). I would suggest that, even though there are indeed substantively diverse views articulated by these authors, there is a shared premise, in my view, in their thinking about the status that a cultural minority claim to self-determination should enjoy *vis-à-vis* institutional recognition. That said, I think each of the arguments presented by the authors mentioned above do indeed merit consideration on their own terms, a project beyond the more modest intentions of this chapter. I think Kymlicka is also useful because in some ways the current constitutional scenario in South Africa seem to resemble his 'model' rather closely, and its current impasses, I hope to show, are revealing of tensions in his argument.

Kymlicka's South Africa

The context of Kymlicka's intervention is of course the debate between what was posited as atomistic liberalism (Rawls) on the one hand, and communitarianism (e.g. Sandel, Taylor) on the other. Kymlicka attempts to suggest that there is a liberalism that can

---

[2] By referring to an 'Afrikaner community' I am referring to a wide range of heterogeneous individuals who self-identify as belonging to a distinct grouping which may be defined as either linguistic, racial or cultural, or a combination of these. Not all Afrikaans-speakers or those of Afrikaner descent may seek to entrench a separate Afrikaner identity. The 'dissident' Afrikaner writer Breyten Breytenbach, for example, argues that 'reconciliation is hybridization' (1996: 35). Secondly, I am referring to communities-in-the-making inasmuch as *singularity* may be the horizon of their historically constructed desires. Thirdly, I am referring to multiple projects which seek to establish a hegemonic notion of Afrikaner community, culture and practice, within a wide range of interpretations about what it means to be an Afrikaner in post-apartheid South Africa.

accommodate both the deontological concerns of the 'agents of justice' and the teleological concerns for the 'good', raised by communitarians. This is a debate, crudely put, between those who see the good of a political community as a set of procedural values which enable undetermined outcomes to unfold – Right *over* Good, and those who suggest the good of the political community is to be located in the outcomes to which it should normatively move towards – Good *over* Right. While there are a range of provocative issues raised by Kymlicka's arguments with both liberals and communitarians, I will, for the purposes of this essay, confine my attention to his argument about the relationship between 'minority cultures and liberalism', in as far as they apply to South Africa.

Key to Kymlicka's argument is his view of culture as 'structure', that 'the cultural structure is … recognized as a context of choice' (1989: 166). He goes on to suggest that '[c]oncern for the cultural structure as a context of choice, on the other hand, accords with, rather than conflicts with, the liberal concern for our ability and freedom to judge the value of our life-plans' (1989: 167). By viewing culture as structure, as form rather than content, Kymlicka suggests that liberals should not view it as a threat to individual autonomy. On the contrary, culture as the context of choice enables and frames the basis on which we judge what is important to us and what is not. Hence the individual remains in some ways prior to the group, as opposed to strong communitarian conceptions of the Self. Culture as structure leads to 'self respect', for Kymlicka, formed within and through a historical community (1989: 192, 197–8). Culture may be viewed as that which mediates between the choices the Self makes and the larger political community.

Kymlicka's argument it seems is motivated by the desire to communicate to a liberal political community that the 'recognition' of cultural minorities does not fundamentally alter the substantive values underpinning that political community. This is exemplified in his arguments with communitarians. The gist of his disagreements is that they make a 'bad case', presumably to a jury of assumed Rawlsian liberals. In his assessment of Waltzer he remarks that '[d]efending minority rights requires that we find an adequate account of the value of cultural membership, an account which can justify minority claims to both the goodwill and the social resources of people outside that culture' (1989: 233). In order to 'justify' minority rights claims Kymlicka posits a non-particularist general claim, not a claim embedded in a notion of 'culture as shared meaning' but of 'culture as structure'. At the same time we should, he argues, retain certain 'safety valves', for 'we must be on guard' for those who might want to 'protect their particular preferred vision of what sort of character the community should have', and, he suggests, we should be willing to use 'temporary illiberal measures', for 'easing the shock which can result from too rapid a change in the character of the culture, helping the culture more carefully toward a fully liberal society' (1989: 170). The latter comment places Kymlicka very close to a position he might be uncomfortable with – that of Richard Rorty, who suggests that the work of liberal democrats is divided between 'agents of love' and 'agents of justice'. Agents of love are the 'connoisseurs of diversity' who 'shepherd into the light' those who have been unrecognised from whence the agents of justice, the 'guardians of universality' will ensure that they are 'treated just like all the rest of us'.[3]

Kymlicka's views on South Africa can be divided into two parts. Firstly, he attempts to show that petty apartheid, the minute forms of segregation which governed public and

---

[3] Richard Rorty (1991: 203–10).

private spaces, from public amenities like benches and toilets, to recreation spaces like beaches, is not equatable with white 'cultural membership'. It follows therefore, for Kymlicka, that '[w]e can't deny the prima-facie applicability of minority rights to white South Africans' (1989: 246). The second aspect of Kymlicka's argument relates to what is called grand apartheid – the structural-institutional aspects of the system. It is his contention that sections of the 'international community', the United Nations and others, had misread the South African situation by suggesting that the struggle was one for self-determination 'by a single people'. But, asks Kymlicka, '[w]hy should the blacks be viewed as a single people, when they in fact are members of different nations, each with its own language and political traditions?' (1989: 248). He goes on to argue that there 'is nothing in principle wrong with a system of distinct homelands in a single country' (1989: 250), but the way it is enforced, the disparities in social service resource allocation, and the 'lack of civil liberties', reflects racist attitudes and '[t]hat is why apartheid is unjust'.

In taking up Kymlicka's views on South Africa, my concern is not to merely make visible inaccuracies, but partly also to suggest the value of historicisation and the implications of its *lack* for our analytical conclusions. If we accept a constructivist view of cultural identities we would need to explore the processes through which particular identities have come to be the taken-for-granted ways in which and through which people come to see their world and others in it. In that sense the first thicket of thorns Kymlicka would run into in much of post-colonial Africa, and South Africa in particular, are the remnants of the edifice of Indirect Rule, which will problematise the ontological 'facticity' of his different 'nations'. His characterisation of black South Africans as being made up of many 'nations' will prompt queries from those who have shown that cultural, ethnic and linguistic communities were consciously fashioned by colonial powers into political identities.[4] By the 1900s, for example, the debate between physical and cultural anthropologists in South Africa was to bring to the fore a debate around how to define 'Bantu'. Bantu was to shift from being used to define physical features (which set them apart from descendents of Ham to the North, in the Hamitic hypothesis, and Bushmen and Hottentot to the South) to linguistic characteristics. This shift was also to be a shift from Bantu as racialised to Bantu as ethnicised, or tribalised.

The racialised view offered the possibility of assimilation, or its opposite, 'swamping' as it came to be known, given the demographic disparities that obtain. With the ethnicisation of 'Bantu' as a cultural identity linguistic communities were mapped onto and fixed into cultural communities. The permanence of difference, rather than the possibility of sameness, was the mantra of this view. Afrikaner nationalists could articulate apartheid and the homeland system as a way of allowing the different 'tribes' or 'nations' to govern themselves and to protect their 'way of life', which was supposedly pastoral, in the language of cultural relativism when it suited them. Indirect rule and the bantustan system was to be its institutional form. That which is called 'customary law' and its concomitant 'traditions' are thus deeply implicated in apartheid state formation, in as far as they authorised particular aspects of 'custom' and invented others to establish 'decentralised despotisms' (cf. Chanock 1998; Costa 2000; Mamdani 1996).

---

[4] See Saul Dubow (1989), Shula Marks and Stanley Trapido (1987), Leonard Thompson (1985), A.A. Costa (2000) and Mahmood Mamdani (1996) for various analyses which explore the ways in which 'tribal' identity became fashioned in the service of domination and separated from the realm of citizenship.

A compelling case can also be made against Kymlicka's analysis by showing the weakness in his argument as it pertains to the notion of 'black self-determination' and the lack of recognition on his part of the language of national liberation as being a contested one, with the dominant one becoming, over time, through contestation, a language which spoke about 'non-racial' citizenship and self-determination on a national territorial basis, rather than 'black' self-determination, i.e. a racialised self-determination.

What I wish to do, however, is to suggest that we approach Kymlicka's argument not through contesting his 'nations', or his views on black identity, as useful a project as that may be, but explore its implications for post-apartheid South Africa by looking at claims emanating from sections of the Afrikaner community for cultural minority rights. In that spirit, notwithstanding the doubts about his characterisation of the South African case, I wish to suggest that we use Kymlicka to look at the current scenario in South Africa as one where a liberal democratic conception of citizenship has been inaugurated which protects both individualised autonomy and group autonomy and minority rights, entrenched through constitutionality.

The current situation

During the tenuous period of negotiations towards a political settlement in South Africa, thirty-four Constitutional Principles were agreed upon in 1994 by all parties to the process. These Constitutional Principles had then to be structured and fleshed out to form a document that would be adopted as the final constitution – ultimately the document agreed upon in 1996. Principle 34 of those thirty-four principles was an agreement which recognised that the possibility of an Afrikaner homeland would be entertained by the party which would win the first democratic elections. It recognised that the 'general right to self-determination' did not 'exclude the right to self-determination of any community sharing a common cultural and language tradition' (Alexander 2002: 161; Norval 1998: 95). Following the constitutional agreement, the Freedom Front, an umbrella organisation of various right-wing organisations under the leadership of ex-Defence Force head, General Constand Viljoen, the National Party, and the ANC, signed an accord in April 1994, which committed the various parties to the following:

1. The parties agree to address, through a process of negotiations, the idea of Afrikaner self-determination, including the concept of a Volkstaat.
2. The parties further agree that in the consideration of these matters, they shall not exclude the possibility of local and/or regional and other forms of expression of self-determination.

The third clause of the agreement spelt out that points one and two agreed upon above would need to be subject to and consistent with the final Constitution and would take into consideration 'such matters as the principles of democracy, non-racialism and fundamental rights; and the promotion of peace and national reconciliation'.[5]

The parties agreed to the formation of a Volkstaatraad (the volk's state council) which would be mandated to investigate the practicalities of setting up an Afrikaner homeland and which was to report to Parliament. The Volkstaatraad's task was eventually subsumed

---

[5] <http://www.vryheidsfront.co.za/minderheidsregte.htm>

by another constitutionally mandated body, the 'Commission For the Promotion and Protection of the Rights of Cultural, Religious and Linguistic Communities', which itself has not been fully operationalised yet,[6] and which was to report to Parliament on this matter in April 2001. A report has been submitted but has not been made available to the public as yet. Yet this may all be void now, since on 3 September 2001 brief newspaper reports told the public of the intention of the government to pass a 'Repeal of Volkstaat Council Provisions Bill' which would be retroactive from 30 April 2001. One newspaper carried the report under the telling headline of 'Death knell for the Volkstaat dream'.[7]

As Norval points out, the demands for a Volkstaat involved the formation of institutions which 'ensure language right ... mother tongue education, the right to autonomy in matters affecting cultural identity ... the right to separate organizations and associations, and the right to territorial autonomy in negotiated areas where majority occupation by Afrikaners could be established' (Norval 1998: 96).

Many of the agreements prior to the negotiations involved concessions by various parties to demands that they had hitherto regarded as 'non-negotiable'. Amongst the concessions made by the ANC was an agreement to recognise Traditional Authorities and customary law administered by chiefs,[8] and to discuss the possibility of an Afrikaner homeland, as stated above.[9] Freedom Front leaders were told by Thabo Mbeki that they should go ahead and *de facto* establish a homeland and then seek *de jure* recognition from the newly elected ANC led government.[10] In that spirit in early 1991 a group led by ex-Professor of Theology and chairman of the Broederbond, Carel Boshoff, literally 'bought' the town of Orania in the semi-arid Karoo region. This small country town on the fringes of the Northern Cape and the old Orange Free State has since become home to about 600 families, and it is hoped that it will provide the *de facto* centre for a delimited territory under Afrikaner control. The early secessionist language of its founders has since given way, though, to a desire for some form of semi-autonomy from the central government (Vestergaard 2001: 32–3).

Afrikaner self-determination: from race to ethnicity

To Afrikanerdom belong only those who by virtue of blood, soil, culture, tradition, belief, and calling form an organic unitary society. This nation is by nature an organic wearer of an authority with the patriarchal leader as chief bearer of authority of the nation, and with the members of

---

[6] A draft Bill was announced in August 2001, outlining the functions and parameters of this Commission. For the full text establishing the commission see Alexander (2002: 191–2)

[7] See <http://www.sundaytimes.co.za/zones/sundaytimes/newsst/newsst999525911.asp>

[8] This recognition is also subject to the Bill of Rights. I have not included it in this discussion because the relationship between customary law and 'civic law' requires a study on its own.

[9] Both demands, the ANC argued, were accepted partly under duress and partly for strategic reasons. In the case of the Volkstaat demand, the potential conflict that could result from armed action by the various right-wing paramilitary groups, and the level of support they enjoyed in the army and police force meant that it was tactically more important to have them participate in the fashioning of a new constitution than to have them remain outside the process.

[10] 'Mr Mbeki said to us: "that Afrikaners with such aspirations must create a reality 'de facto' on the ground and then put it before the government for 'de jure' recognition",' Dr Pieter Mulder, Freedom Front chairperson, 4/23/01 <http://www.vryheidsfront.co.za/minderhiedsregte.htm>

the nation as active and cooperative workers. The national Afrikaner state is in this sense also a medium of Afrikanerdom to protect and promote its own fulfillment and calling.

Piet Meyer[11]

Whiteness is as much a constructed, even if underproblematised, identity. Whiteness in South Africa signifies not only an Afrikaner identity. Since European presence established itself in South Africa from 1652 onwards there has been profound and violent contestation between various colonial powers, particularly Dutch and British, for dominance. It is an identity forged in and through war, both literally and metaphorically. The descendants of Dutch, Portuguese and French settlers, as well as of slaves, Khoi, San and others, are today largely known as 'Afrikaners'. The historical narrative of Afrikanerness, and broader 'whiteness', has of course purged itself of any recognition of 'blood' relations to blacks through an intense emphasis on 'purity'. It is an identity made through harsh contestation, both in the present, and in the past, vis-à-vis internal others, Dutch, the black population, and most significantly in relation to what was perceived as British political and cultural imperialism. Isabel Hofmeyr (1987), Achmat Davids (1990) and Hein Willemse (1991), amongst others, have persuasively shown how Afrikaans as a language initially associated with 'lower classes', slaves and 'coloureds' displaced Dutch, to become an important constitutive component in the iteration of an Afrikaner identity, particularly against English dominance between 1902 and 1924. By appropriating it from its slave origins and elevating its status institutionally, Afrikaans was reinscribed culturally as the lingua franca of Afrikanerness.

There will of course continue to be contestations, but the identity had come to be relatively stabilised by the 1960s around language (Afrikaans), a common historical narrative,[12] marked by 'events' of triumph and suffering (the Battle of Blood River, the Anglo-Boer War, the Great Trek et al.), religion (Christian, Calvinist, Dutch Reformed Church)[13] and race (white, European descent, Voortrekkers). And of course control over a state apparatus and its attendant institutions. Race became a primary marker of fear in a series of elections in which apartheid was defended by the National Party as a way in which to prevent racial 'swamping' (oorheesing and verkaffering) by blacks (O'Meara 1997: 12–13). Invoking this demographic terror, the leader of the Blanke Bevrydings Beweging (White Freedom Movement), Johan Schabort, remarked, 'We believe in the genetic superiority of the white race, and we believe it is the duty of the white race to stop the natural increase and the decadence of the black races from destroying this planet' (The Argus, 12 November 1989). Responding to the repeal of the Group Areas Act in 1991 a Conservative Party councillor for the town of Port Elizabeth lamented that '[i]t does not

---

[11] Piet Meyer, quoted in de Klerk (1975: 214), was chairman of the Afrikaner Broederbond (1958–1972). The Broederbond (Brotherhood) is a secret society of influential Afrikaner males, formed in 1918, from whose ranks came successive government leaders, Prime Ministers and State Presidents, Church leaders, academics and businessmen. It changed its name in the mid-1990s to 'Die Bond', to allow female members.

[12] For a recent revisionist account of this history, which still takes 'Afrikaner' as an ontological fact, see Herman Giliomee's (2003) 'The Afrikaners: Biography of a People'.

[13] Afrikaner religious belief has been described as follows: 'The divine agent of the Afrikaner civil faith is Christian and Calvinist – an active sovereign God, who the calls the elect, who promises and punishes, who brings forth life from death in the course of history. The object of His saving activity – the Afrikaner people – is not a church ... but a nation with its distinct language and culture, its history and destiny.' Moodie quoted in Van Rooyen (1994: 38).

matter if a black person is a doctor, policeman, or priest – the issue is the protection of our own identity and the protection of the character of our suburb – if you allow one black in, where do you draw the line?' (Van Rooyen 1994: 53). Tropes of biological superiority of the Afrikaner Self have often become entwined with recourse to a cultural racism which asserts the cultural inferiority of Other. Both arguments were 'acceptable' to the Afrikaner political establishment. They never energetically attempted to police the discursive borders upon which 'difference' was inscribed, provided that there was recognition of the 'differences',[14] in relation to their various Others.

By the mid-1980s sections of the Afrikaner community began to earnestly contemplate the possibility of a 'volkstaat'. This debate took place in the context of shifting alignments within the National Party around the viability of apartheid prompted by a range of domestic, regional and international motivations. Although perceived as a conservative member of the National Party, P.W. Botha, when elected in 1978, hinted that constitutional changes were to be made to include 'population groups' which were excluded at that time. Apartheid, in the sense of the creation of ethnically defined 'independent' homeland states, neighbouring a 'white South Africa' in which people came to work and went back 'home' never really existed other than as a racialised Utopia-on-paper. The almost enduring presence, and, for apartheid planners, 'problem', of black people in urban Locations or townships, was eventually officially recognised as 'permanent' when the Influx control laws and Pass Laws were scrapped, almost after the fact, in the mid-1980s.

White South African politics by the 1980s comprised small liberal parties like the Progressive Federal Party (PFP), the National Party as the ruling Afrikaner party, and various smaller Afrikaner parties to the right of it. There was intense debate at that time about the future of 'whites', in the sense of both those of 'English' descent and Afrikaners. Some Afrikaners felt that unlike Europeans in other settler states, like Algeria, they had no 'homeland' to go back to.[15] The dominant fissure amongst Afrikaners on the right was between those who demanded a return to implementing apartheid as H.F. Verwoerd envisioned it in the 1960s, and those 'more pragmatic' who began to talk about the formation of a smaller area which would be under Afrikaner control (Van Rooyen 1994: 160).

The moment also saw the birth of a number of political and extra-parliamentary Afrikaner groups, who hurriedly worked out 'defence' plans, and various maps which outlined the borders of a possible Afrikaner homeland, proportionally scaled to political ambition. When negotiations between the freshly unbanned organisations, like the ANC, and the Government began in the early 1990s there were disputes between the right-wing Afrikaner groups about whether to participate in the process. Some contended that they would not negotiate with 'terrorists and communists' while others held the view that they would only speak to leaders of 'nations' (Van Rooyen 1994: 82). 'Nations' here signified homeland leaders, whom they felt spoke a language of 'ethno-nationalism' as opposed to the 'civic-nationalist' discourse of the ANC, with its 'unacceptable liberal' demands for

---

[14] It is worth remembering that Verwoerd briefly sought to call the department of Native Affairs the Department of Plural Affairs, before it became Bantu Affairs.

[15] 'No white community in Africa has so far been able to tolerate being a powerless minority under a revolutionary black government; most of them have fled. Our people, on the other hand, have no boat waiting at the harbour. We cannot flee. Nor will we flee. We will not submit ourselves to this type of domination.' Conservative Party statement, *Cape Argus* (March 1991).

one person, one vote.[16] Most homeland leaders, like Brigadier Oupa Gqozo of the Ciskei, had taken strong repressive measures against the liberation movements and other dissenting voices in the 1980s. Right-wing Afrikaner nationalists recognised in them leaders of similarly ethnicised 'nations' with whom they would find empathy. Homeland leaders were of course largely financed by the South African state and represented the institutional face of indirect rule. In the course of events some Afrikaner groups participated whilst others remained outside, convinced that the process was 'illegitimate'.

The section of the right wing that cohered around the Freedom Front and that participated in the negotiations process, under the leadership of former army general Constand Viljoen, had secured the constitutional recognition mentioned above. However, the language in which their claims were being made had gone through significant shifts over the years. At the outset an important part of Afrikaner nationalism was a notion of white superiority (Norval 1996, 1998; Reddy 2000; Van Rooyen 1994; Vestergaard 2000). Yet the 'official' leaders of Afrikaners have since, in public, marginalised prominent figures like *enfant terrible* Eugene Terreblanche of the Afrikaner Weerstands Beweging (AWB), who continued to sermonise about difference in overtly racialised terms. Viljoen and others who spoke a language purged of racial claims increasingly saw themselves – and were accepted by the state, the ANC and interested external parties – as speaking for conservative Afrikaner nationalists.

In 1992 the Afrikaner Volks Unie (Afrikaner People's Union) was formed by a break-away of 'moderates' in the Conservative Party. Led by Andries Beyers, the AVU, which was to join with the Freedom Front, was part of a trend signifying a shift in the language of Afrikaner claims. While those in parliament representing the Conservative Party demanded a return to apartheid, and emphasised racialised separation, Beyers, of the new AVU, explained to followers during a break in the constitutional negotiations: 'We are bargaining on behalf of the Afrikaans-speaking South Africans. If we are bargaining on behalf of a race we would be accused of racism and we are not doing that' (*Patriot*, 5 March 1989). The AVU had shifted to speaking about an Afrikaner 'ethno-linguistic' group' rather than a white 'race group'.

It is significant that the AVU, together with the Freedom Front, which articulated Afrikaner claims in terms of an 'ethnic minority', began to do so during the negotiations process. Policy papers, emanating from right-wing aligned think-tanks imbued the new discourse with the social capital of academic authority. One such paper, by Dr P.W. Liebenberg from the 'Foundation for National Minorities in South Africa', argued that '[t]he fact that South Africa has a heterogeneous population consisting of different ethno-cultural groups, languages and religions, as well as numerous local communities with specific needs, indicate a high conflict potential.' Without a hint of irony Liebenberg went on to lament that

> [t]his rich diversity of ethnic groups, peoples, tribes, as well as linguistic and religious groups is unfortunately overshadowed by an increasing emphasis on race – black against white – that is the result of the unbalanced way affirmative action is being applied. The effective way to

---

[16] National Party leaders and those on the Afrikaner right have always insisted that 'liberal' democracy, with individualised representation was inadequate as it created 'majorities which dominate minorities'. Apartheid was a system which created, in their view, multiple minorities, with no majoritarianism, and thus was a basis for 'peaceful co-existence of different races and ethnic groups' (see Thompson, 1985).

counter that is to recognise the ethnic, cultural and community differences. This is something that will not disappear.[17]

This is a view that seeks to emphasise the *permanence* of cultural difference. The rationale on which the native's once permanent inability to become civilised stood has since given way to a rationale in which the terrain of 'culture' becomes the site of an almost primordial foundationalism that needs difference to be translated institutionally, and permanently: 'something that will not disappear'. Since 'Volkstaaters', like those in the Freedom Front, have, however, committed themselves to an agreement which binds them to a set of rights underpinning the South African constitution and particularly the Bill of Rights, they no longer articulate their desire for a homeland in racialised terms.

Two further trends are worth noting. One is in the realm of education. An endeavour of sections of the Afrikaner nationalist movement, in accordance with constitutional protection, is to set up independent schools based on 'Calvinist principles' for the 'Boer' nation. According to a spokesman for the 60 schools around the country,

> We place a very strong emphasis on symbols, not as state symbols, but symbols as cultural symbols.... Our role is to educate our peoples to become good Christians and become members of our cultural group. We want them to speak Afrikaans, we want to teach them our history.... Our movement has nothing to do with apartheid.... We turn away white pupils and we turn away black pupils – we don't have anything [sic] on a racist basis. We are very strict on the ethnic principle, which is that we allow into our schools those who qualify as members of the Boer nation.[18]

The second is in the realm of language. Newly baptised 'moderate' Afrikaners, like those in the New National Party, have been defining Afrikaner along linguistic rather than racial lines, thereby including many 'coloured' Afrikaans speakers and thus absolving themselves of charges of racism when defending minority rights for Afrikaners. This is sometimes also the notion of Afrikanerness evoked by the Oranje founders.

In both cases we see an illuminating shift from an emphasis on state symbols to an emphasis on cultural symbols. This is revealing of the shifted terrain of power in South Africa: these 'cultural' symbols were not too long ago also the 'symbols' of state and political power. Control over governance of the nation-state has retreated to a domain of governance over the 'nation' since dominant political control over the state apparatus now resides elsewhere.

Yet it is in these attempts of Afrikanerness to remake itself, to re-enunciate its being-ness, that slippages reveal themselves. In analysing both the rhetoric and the practice, there is constant slippage of signification with regard to the 'Afrikaner' being made reference to (Norval 1998: 101; Verstergaard 2000: 31). Just as there are no blacks in the embryonic Afrikaner homeland, Oranje, so too no black student has yet been admitted to the independent schools. My point, though, is not simply that right-wing Afrikaner nationalists have made a calculated conversion to mask their class or racist motivations, even if this argument may have more than a whisper of force. This is a view of the change in Afrikaner political discourse articulated by the noted scholar of Afrikaner nationalism,

---

[17] Dr P.W. Liebenberg, Foundation for National Minorities in South Africa, Media Statement, <http://vryheidsfront.co.za/minderheidsregte.htm>

[18] 'A Volk unto themselves', *The Teacher*, <http://teacher.co.za/200104/05-cvo.html>

Dan O'Meara, who views Afrikaner nationalism as a purely 'ideological construct' (1997: 7). I remain hesitant, however, to embrace the suggestion that political identities are always instrumentalised invocations of submerged interests. The task such a view leaves us with is to chip away at the social veneer in order to expose the nefarious 'reality' always lurking beneath it. Analysis, to put it bluntly, is thus reduced to a competition in which the rewards accrue to the one that wields the most effective pick-axe. Identities as relational constructions positioned within temporal and spatial topographies of power may be more demanding in the analytical labour they require.

What we may be engaging in when analysing Afrikaner volk claims are shifts induced at three interlocking levels of discourse. One is the discursive level at which, to borrow Homi Bhabha's apt phrase, the 'nation is narrated': who speaks for Afrikaners and simultaneously decentres other voices who speak as 'Afrikaners' in order to speak as '*The* Afrikaners'. The second is the shifting discourse which conditions the relationship between cultural and political identity, fashioned by post-apartheid changes in constitutional discourse in South Africa. And the third is the way in which the 'global' discourse of subjection and domination has shifted from ideology to 'culture' and the effects on local ways-of-being seduced by these.

I have already attempted to outline the terms of the first tension between various groupings which seek to articulate 'Afrikanerness'. Let me turn briefly to the latter two shifts. It may be that the diverse Afrikaner claims to 'cultural protection' may not all self-consciously be made in 'bad faith'. They may be indicative of more complex processes in which the language of the space of 'the political' has altered. It may be that permanent racialised difference has become reinscribed as permanent cultural difference as a way of 'speaking' to a post-apartheid state in a language that is constitutionally acceptable, in as far as I am suggesting that the Constitution is what Talal Asad has called an 'authoritative discourse' (1979: 626). Drawing on Wittgenstein's observation that the 'limits of our world are the limits of our language', James Tully has argued that one of the first limits modern liberal constitutionalism places on demands for constitutional recognition is the limit of language: 'When, for example, Aboriginal peoples strive for recognition, they are constrained to present their demands in the normative vocabulary available to them. That is, they seek recognition as "peoples" and "nations", with "sovereignty" or a "right to self-determination", even though these terms may distort or misdescribe the claim they would wish to make if it were expressed in their own languages' (Tully 1995: 39).

Tully thus suggests that the grammatical rules available for recognition claims require the reconfiguration of the vocabulary of self and community on the part of those who see themselves as the 'claimants'. This is obligatory in order to make them commensurable with those that are the invisible cultural foundations upon which the secular-modern turns. He thus draws our attention to the ways in which modern constitutionalism is always already permeated with relations of power which pre-configure the terms of political discourse and the terms of inclusion and exclusion. Unlike Kymlicka, Tully therefore suggests that liberal constitutionalism is not designed to address minority recognition claims substantively since they are a challenge 'to the basic assumptions of modern constitutionalism' (1995: 43). For him the three schools of thought on modern constitutionalism – liberalism, nationalism and communitarianism – presuppose what he calls a 'comprehensive language' which *a priori* acts to determine, shape and limit the ways in which recognition can occur: 'the post imperial injunction to listen to the voices of others must involve listening to not only what they say, but also the language in which it is said, if the imperial habit of imposing our traditions and institutions on others is to be abjured'. The way out of this impasse is to find a form of dialogue 'in which the interlocutors participate in their diverse cultural forms, and a form of intercultural understanding which does not presuppose a comprehensive language'.[19]

The third discursive terrain to consider is the way in which the acceptable global idiom of relations of domination and subjection in the post-Cold War world are increasingly framed in cultural terms. In one corner are the growing sets of conventions and movements, mobilised through the United Nations and often against governments, which seek to articulate the causes and interests of 'indigenous' and 'first-nation' peoples. San peoples have already had successful recourse to these discourses in land-claims cases in post-apartheid South Africa (see Robins 2001). At the other end of the neighbourhood, buoyed by Samuel P. Huntington's 'Clash of Civilizations' (1993), it has reached a frenzy in the recent attempts to understand 'terror' through Islamic 'culture', resurrecting the Orientalist Bernard Lewis as 'a best selling author' and consultant to the United States government on 'all things Middle East' (Geertz 2003: 1, 4).

Afrikaner nationalists have thus sought to mobilise support internationally by inserting themselves into the narrative of a global-conceptual story, by making the case that the struggles of Afrikaners are homologous to the struggles of ethnic minorities in Eastern Europe and those elsewhere in Africa. Notably, only one South African opposition party set up a stall at the United Nations sponsored '*World Conference on Racism*' hosted by South Africa in August 2001 – the Freedom Front. Opening the stall, which was located alongside movements for self-determination from Tibet and North America, Dr Pieter Mulder, the party's then newly elected leader, noted that 'self-determination and minority rights, also for Afrikaners, have nothing to do with racism but is not afraid to recognize the realities of ethno-cultural diversity [sic]'.[20]

We have seen that there is a constitutional commitment in South Africa to recognise claims to self-determination and special rights for cultural minorities. In that sense the state has taken Kymlicka's advice. Yet those claims and concomitant practices are subject ultimately to the Bill of Rights. Again, one could say that the State has taken Kymlicka's advice, since the Bill of Rights prohibits discrimination, particularly, but not only, on racial, religious, gender and sexual grounds, and guarantees freedom of association and other key liberal rights as foundational cornerstones to which all other rights are subject. The 'safety valve' feature is thus operative – the one set of rights authorises, the other prohibits.

The impasse the ANC-led government currently faces with regard to cultural minority rights claims is precisely the one that I think shows that Kymlicka's liberal democratic conception of citizenship cannot deal in 'good faith' with substantive claims to difference, in situations where we think of culture as 'shared meaning' rather than 'structure'.[21] For

---

[19] Quotes are from Tully (1995: 57). Tully's argument is challenged by the South African case, in addition to the reason I put forward in the text, by two more reasons. Firstly, there is a tendency in his argument to take post-colonial minority identities as fashioned outside of colonial influence, as found (aboriginal) rather than made. This does not adequately address in my view the effects of indirect rule. Secondly, he largely avoids the problematic of power and its relationship to privilege in the solutions he offers.

[20] < http://www.vryheidsvront.co.za/media%202001.htm>

[21] An example of this impasse was Constitutional Court case no. 2960/98, which involved another group of

example, if the schools that some members of the Afrikaner community have set up, which operate under certification from the South African Department of Education, are challenged legally, the claims of 'culture' will have to square off with the state's discourse of 'rights'. In this case, where rights are seen as a 'fundamental' liberal good of the society and is counterposed to 'culture', culture may end up the bruised party.

The state had dragged its feet on discussing the modality of a Volkstaat to the extent that leaders, like Constand Viljoen, have lost some legitimacy amongst their constituencies for participating in the elections.[22] There is growing angst amongst sections of the Afrikaner leadership that they were dealt with in bad faith.[23] If the concession to recognise a Volkstaat was made for security reasons, then it may be that the ANC, once it was more ensconced in state power, had little inclination to pursue the matter further, and in fact changed its position on being receptive to discussing the formation of a Volkstaat. After a period of relative calm, there was a spate of bombings in black neighbourhoods in December 2002, threats of future violence, and the arrest of individuals involved in 'coup-plots' by newly formed right-wing Afrikaner groups. These events may, amongst other things, also be the ominous fallout of the ANC's misrecognition of the impasse it finds itself in as it navigates the brittle path between 'nation-building' and recognition.[24]

An Afrikaner community, if mobilised as such, and which seeks to practise its 'culture', will have to do so within the confines of the rights constitutionally authorised, which define the 'good' of the 'political' community, as things stand. I have drawn attention to the complexity of an *a priori* assumption of the 'goodness' of this cultural recognition claim within a liberal framework through a reading of Kymlicka's South Africa. I have also alluded to an alternative reading which critiques liberalism whilst also making an *a priori* argument for cultural recognition, and indeed makes the argument that cultural recognition claims bring liberalism to a limit – which we can overcome by reworking the very assumptions we base our understanding of political community on. For Tully 'the politics of cultural recognition is a continuation of the anti-imperialism of modern constitutionalism, and thus the expression of a genuinely post-imperial age' (1995: 17).

In my view, Tully's enthusiasm to embrace minority cultural recognition claims are also restrained by Afrikaner recognition claims. Tully is motivated by a serious ethical

[21] (cont.) white faith-based private schools which petitioned the Minister of Education in 1999 to set aside a prohibition on corporal punishment at their schools. They argued on appeal, after dismissal at the regional court of Port Elizabeth, that the Constitutional Court consider their case on the grounds that it violated their right to practise their religious and cultural beliefs, as protected by the Constitution. The Constitutional Court dismissed the case, on the grounds that that the case did not qualify, on a number of technicalities, to be heard by it; see *Die Burger*, 13 August 1997, or <http://concourt.gov.za> For a sense of a growing debate around religion in schools prompted by some Afrikaner nationalists see 'Religion at schools in a holy mess', *Mail and Guardian*, 7 May 2003.

[22] Ravi Nessman, 'Afrikaners feeling marginalized, disillusioned', *Associated Press*, Thursday, 14 November 2002; see also Christopher Hope, 'Afrikaners want judicial protection', *Guardian*, 5 May 2003; and Alexander (2002: 96).

[23] Connie Mulder, Chairman of the Freedom Front, remarked in Parliament on 13 June 2000 that 'The honourable President started off reaching out to Afrikaners. We applauded it. Fifteen months ago he promised a special unit in his Department...nothing happened. Mr President I personally wrote to you to be our guest and open the most modern dairy facility in the Southern Hemisphere, built by Afrikaners. I did not receive an answer.' <http://www.vryheidsfront.co.za/minderheidsregte.htm>

[24] Anthony C. LobBaido, 'Right Wing rising in Pretoria? Anti-ANC Afrikaners charged with trying to over-throw government', 17 November 2002, *WorldNetDaily.com*; 'South Africa: Explosions rock Soweto – right wing blamed', *Southern Africa Documentation and Cooperation Center*, 31 October 2002 <http://www.sadocc.at/news2002/2002-325.shtml>

concern: 'How can the proponents of recognition bring forth their claims in a public forum in which their cultures have been excluded or demeaned for centuries' (1995: 56). Afrikaners, however, in as much as they have cohered as a politically fragmented cultural identity, have enjoyed a degree of domination and privilege which interrupts his linear conception of an increasingly inclusive horizon towards which a modern political community sails. 'Afrikaner' is an identity, as we have seen, not without problems. It has been forged through conquest, through various negative conceptions of 'Englishness', of 'Jewishness', especially of 'blackness' – through various Others, so to speak, viewed as inferior 'races' or inferior 'cultures'. It has been this common conception of the Otherness and of blackness that has to some extent also moulded the significatory character of whiteness as an identity of domination which has enabled privilege and is, one could argue, important to its constitution. Whether one can think 'Afrikanerness' without 'whiteness' and 'privilege' is the challenge certain Afrikaners face today. If they cannot successfully unhinge this trinity of significations they will be subjected to charges of racism, as they already are when the racial Afrikaner and the cultural Afrikaner seem to inhabit the same schizophrenic Self, albeit a more policed self. And both seem to have a hard time getting along with the the the linguistic Afrikaner – the 'coloured' Afrikaner. It is not all that apparent, therefore, that they have a *prima facie* case for special rights by virtue of 'white cultural membership', as Kymlicka suggests, when one considers the specificity and heterogeneity of the identity and the values that underpin it, that is, when one takes the identity as *made*, not *given*. It is precisely its significatory past – its association with apartheid, with continued racial privilege and separation, domination and violence – that renders any 'Afrikaner' claim to special rights problematic in the post-apartheid socio-political space configured by racialised inequality.

This space is saturated at present by desires to cultivate 'nation-building' and the refashioning of 'South Africaness' into an inclusive identity which also recognises diversity hitherto suppressed by the apartheid state. This seemed to be a part of the ethos guiding the formation of the previously referred to constitutional commission for the protection of cultural rights. But inscribing the language of recognition as a universal one means making it available to all citizens. Afrikaner nationalists therefore also see themselves as representing an eligible group to which this language applies. This places the newly de-racialised liberal democratic state in the awkward position of having to distinguish between the diversity suppressed and the diversity cultivated and crafted by the old apartheid state, each carrying its own historical normativity written into the status of the composition of their recognition claims. The astute South African activist-intellectual, Neville Alexander, has noted this tension, pointing to what he calls the 'separatist dangers' in making constitutional concessions to right-wing Afrikaner nationalists. But he also counsels that 'it is of extreme importance that the question of the rights of disempowered privileged (or former ruling) minorities be considered in detail' as this will be 'crucial for the character of the transitional South African state'.[25]

Whilst Afrikaner nationalists face the considerable challenge of disentangling whiteness, privilege and being an Afrikaner, it may also be productive if the state were to develop a more nuanced reading of Afrikaner recognition claims. This would be a reading

---

[25] See Alexander (2002: 186, 65, 99–102, 185).

that distinguishes between claims which can be addressed within a nation-building project and in fact help shape the 'nation' and dialogically reshape Afrikanerness in turn, and claims which may, whether as cause or effect, further entrench, rather than redress, white privilege. The position of the Group of 63, an organisation established by primarily Afrikaans-speaking intellectuals, is a case in point. The organisation was set up to protect and further the interests of the Afrikaans language. Its reference point is thus the 'linguistic-Afrikaner'. It sees itself as a 'democratic and moderate interpreter of Afrikaner interests', committed to 'liberal democratic values'.[26] Its concern, according to its founders, is the fate of Afrikaans, since the language has lost its pre-eminent status as one of two official state languages and has since become merely one of eleven other constitutionally recognised languages. The organisation has amongst its founding members Afrikaner intellectuals who had advocated negotiations with the ANC in exile and had initiated talks with them. They were therefore not considered part of the Afrikaner right wing, or part of those calling for a Volkstaat, or for a return to apartheid.

The Mbeki government seems to have been confounded by the impasse it finds itself in and has tended to treat all Afrikaner recognition claims, whether about language or a Volkstaat, as threatening to the sovereignty of its nation-building project. An unintended effect may have been to make Afrikaans-speaking 'moderates', who might hitherto have been unpalatable to those on the right wing of the Afrikaner nationalist movement, now seem more appealing. It emerged from documents detailing a planned coup by the recently formed paramilitary grouping, the Boeremag (Farmers Force), somewhat it seems to the embarrassment of the Group of 63, that they (the Boeremag) had reserved government positions for some members of the Group of 63 in a *post*-post-apartheid government.[27] When the Group of 63 issued a statement condemning the spate of bomb blasts in December 2002, and vigorously disassociated themselves from the Boeremag, whilst also noting that the violence was the result of 'alienation' that should be addressed politically, they were lambasted by some pro-ANC groupings for 'polarising' the country and being 'counter-productive to the nation-building process'.[28] One analyst, however, noted that there was an attempt on the part of some in the government to tarnish the Group of 63 by allowing the National Intelligence Agency (NIA) to leak the confiscated Boeremag plans to members of the press. He goes on to note that subsequent newspaper reports 'quoted an unidentified security official' who described the relationship between the 'Group of 63 and the Boeremag as the link between Sinn Fein and the IRA', a somewhat far-fetched conclusion according to many analysts.[29]

I raise this not to endorse, or denigrate, the claims of the Group of 63, but to indicate differences within Afrikaner recognition claims that could be debated differently. In effect, in pursuing the present strategy, which more or less seems to draw a line through all claims identified as 'Afrikaner' as being hostile to the 'nation-building' project, the

[26] Patrick Laurence, 'ANC should heed the Group of 63's Warning', <http://www.hsf.org.za/ focus29laurence.html>, pp. 2, 3.
[27] Ranjeni Munusamy, 'Right Wing Plotters have plans for top Academics', *Sunday Times*, 17 November 2002.
[28] 'Group of 63 slammed for "polarisation"', Wed., 13 November, <http://iafrica.com/ news/sa/185579.htm>
[29] Patrick Laurence, 'ANC should heed the Group of 63's Warning', <http://www.hsf.org.za/ focus29laurence.html>, p. 2; see also the assessment of retired South African National Defense Force Col. Henri Boshoff in Jim Fisher Thompson, 'Despite Terrorism, Analyst discounts "right wing" coup in South Africa', *Washington File*, 9 December 2002, <http://www.globalsecurity.org/wmd/ library/news/safrica/saf-0212>

state could be inadvertently helping to demarcate a circle in which right-wing Afrikaner nationalists could be the political beneficiaries of the us/them binary it entrenches between the 'new nation' and those who increasingly see themselves as standing in new-found alterity to it.

(In)Conclusion

The colonial experience of indirect rule, and the experience of apartheid in particular, suggests that we need to do more conceptual labour with regard to how we engage discussions about minority rights claims and about how a 'dialogue' around new forms of political community unfolds. The South African case requires us to think about forms of political community which privilege a notion of justice that can address *both* claims for recognition, and equally, if not more compellingly, claims for redistribution – in this case two poles of a complex and bitter relationship which seem to be pulling in opposite directions. By reading Kymlicka and others through the South African case, by interrupting an almost self-evident conceptual-global normative lens with the fog of a pragmatic-local discussion, I think we can reach two conclusions, both of which I would like to suggest in the spirit of reading 'conclusions' as being openings to other questions, rather than endings.

We have seen that despite recognition of an 'Afrikaner community's' right to special rights, even if we set aside any lingering reservations, they would still *have to* reconcile cultural practices to the Bill of Rights, or their cultural practices will become criminalised. I am inclined therefore to agree with those who suggest that liberalism, despite claims to the contrary, cannot entertain certain claims to difference which are outside the differences authorised. Those claims bring it to its 'limit', as James Tully (1995) and others persuasively argue (Connolly, 1995; Scott, 1999). That is the first 'conclusion'.

The second is that recognition of the inadequacy of a liberal framework to deal with difference does not translate into the argument that claims to difference should not be contextually considered and historicised through some ethical prism. Afrikaner claims bring an *a priori* or *prima facie* defence of minority rights to its own conceptual limit, and reveal the problematic nature of generalising from a specific case, compelling as those arguments might appear at first blush. It may be worth pursuing a line of enquiry that asks whether contemporary rights claims are discursively articulated within what has become an 'acceptable' grid that authorises that we speak about 'injustice' in terms of 'culture' and 'self-determination', consistent with 'international conventions', in a post-Cold War world. We need to probe a little beyond, between and within the language. This seems to me to be a productive site at which the global-conceptual and the local-pragmatic reveal themselves to be mutual determinations which cannot be separated. In other words, the localness of a universalist argument needs to be made visible in the same way that the voice of the local can be shown to be inhabiting a discourse already there, already prior *to that which* it articulates (in the dual sense of the word), and simultaneously becomes visible to itself, rather than a pristine place *from which* it speaks. This as we have seen always also involves a silencing. This is not to suggest that all claims for minority rights or group recognition conceal sinister interests and are presented in bad faith by what some would call 'ethnic entrepreneurs', but it is to suggest that we need to find a way to wed a scepticism of recognition claims to our scepticism of liberal claims. It also prods us to keep that wily old fox, power, resolutely in our field of vision – if only to remind us, as we ponder the sprawling vistas of infinite conceptual possibilities available to us, that we inhabit a political moment always already thick with competing hopes, fears and interests, all in search of horizons of elusive contentment too.

References

Alexander, N. (2002), *An Ordinary Country: Issues in the Transition from Apartheid to Democracy in South Africa*, Pietermaritzburg: University of Natal Press.

Asad, T. (1979) 'Anthropology and the Analysis of Ideology', *Man*, 14(4), pp. 607–27.

Breytenbach, B. (1996), *The Memory of Birds in Times of Revolutions*, New York: Harcourt Brace and Co.

Chanock, M. (1998), *Law, Custom and Social Order: The Colonial Experience in Malawi and Zambia*, Portsmouth: Heinemann.

Connolly, W.E. (1995), *The Ethos of Pluralization*, Minnesota: University of Minnesota Press.

Costa, A.A. (2000), 'Chieftaincy and Civilization: African Structures of Government and Colonial Administration in South Africa', *African Studies*, 59(1), July, pp. 13–43.

Davids, A. (1990), 'Words the Cape Slaves Made: A Socio-historical-linguistic Study', *South African Journal of Linguistics*, 8(1), pp, 1–24.

de Klerk, W.A. (1975), *The Puritans in Africa: A Story of Afrikanerdom*, London: Rex Collings.

Dubow, S. (1989), *Racial Segregation and the Origins of Apartheid in South Africa, 1919–1936*, New York: St Martin's Press.

Geertz, C. (2003), 'Which Way to Mecca?', *The New York Review of Books*, 50(10), 12 June, pp. 1-4.

Giliomee, H. (2003), *The Afrikaners: Biography of a People*, Cape Town: Tafelberg.

Hofmeyr, I. (1987), 'Building the Nation from Words: Afrikaans Language, Literature and Ethnicity, 1902–1924', in S. Marks and S. Trapido (eds), *The Politics of Race, Class and Nationalism in Twentieth Century South Africa*, London: Longman Publishers.

Huntington, S. (1993), 'The Clash of Civilizations', *Foreign Affairs*, 22(3).

Krog, A. (1998), *Country of My Skull*, Johannesburg: Random House.

Kukathas, C. (1992), 'Are There any Cultural Rights?', *Political Theory*, 20(1) (February), pp. 105–9.

Kymlicka, W. (1989), *Liberalism, Community and Culture*, New York and Oxford: Clarendon Press.

Mamdani, M. (1996), *Citizen and Subject, Contemporary Africa and the Legacy of Late Colonialism*, Princeton, NJ: Princeton University Press.

Marks, S. and S. Trapido (1987), *The Politics of Race, Class and Nationalism in 20th Century South Africa*, London, Longman.

Norval, A. (1996), *Deconstructing Apartheid Discourse*, New York: Verso.

—— (1998), 'Reinventing the Politics of Cultural Recognition: The Freedom Front and the Demand for a Volkstaat', in D. Howarth and A. Norval (eds), *South Africa in Transition*, New York: St Martin's Press.

O'Meara, D. (1997), 'Thinking Theoretically: Afrikaner Nationalism and the Comparative Theory of the Politics of Identity', paper presented to the Inaugural Conference of the Harold Wolpe Memorial Trust, University of the Western Cape, South Africa.

Reddy, T. (2000), *Hegemony and Resistance: Contesting Identities in South Africa*, London: Ashgate.

Robins, S. (2001), 'NGOs, "Bushmen" and Double Vision: The Khomani San Land Claim and the Cultural Politics of "Community", and "Development" in the Kalahari', *Journal of Southern African Studies*, 27(4), December, pp. 833–53.

Rorty, R. (1991), 'On Ethnocentrism: a Reply to Clifford Geertz', in R. Rorty (ed.), *Objectivity, Relativism and Truth*, Cambridge: Cambridge University Press.

Scott, D. (1999), *Refashioning Futures, Criticism after Postcoloniality*, Princeton, NJ: Princeton University Press.

Taylor, C., A. Gutman, S. Woolf, S. Rockfeller, M. Walzer, J. Habermas and A. Appiah (eds) (1994), *Multiculturalism – Examining the Politics of Recognition*, Princeton, NJ: Princeton University Press.

Thompson, L. (1985), *The Political Mythology of Apartheid*, New Haven: Yale University Press.

Tully, J. (1995), *Strange Multiplicity, Constitutionalism in an Age of Diversity*, Cambridge: Cambridge University Press.

Van Rooyen, J. (1994), *Hard Right: The New White Power in South Africa*, New York: Tauris Publishers.

Vestergaard, M. (2000), 'Who's Got the Map? The Negotiation of Afrikaner Identities in Post-Apartheid South Africa', *Daedalus*, 130(1) (Winter), pp. 19–44.

Willemse, H. (1991), 'Securing the Myth: The Representation of the Origins of Afrikaans in School Language Textbooks', in J. Jansen (ed.), *Knowledge and Power in South Africa*, Johannesburg: Skotaville Publishers.

4
Traditional Leaders & Democracy
Cultural Politics in the Age of Globalisation

THOMAS A. KOELBLE & ED LIPUMA

Introduction: the comeback of the chiefs

In June of 2003, Chief Kaizer Matanzima passed away at the ripe old age of 88. Matanzima had been the first premier or chief minister of the Transkei, the first of the homelands fabricated by the apartheid regime in its aborted efforts to give substance to the doctrine of separate development. Matanzima went on to become a key ally of the apartheid regime in its efforts to establish the Bantu Authorities and the various land consolidation and agricultural betterment programmes that are today seen as major causes of black impoverishment in the rural areas of South Africa. Matanzima did everything in his power to ensure that the Transkei did not become a hotbed of political activity during his reign and had a hand in the silencing of numerous opponents to the regime. Moreover, his dealings with several key industrialists and entrepreneurs, among them Sol Kerzner, the hotel magnate, earned him a reputation as being easily swayed and corruptible. In a one-line review, this was not a comrade in the struggle against apartheid. Quite the contrary: Matanzima was an important black collaborator in the establishment and functioning of apartheid and certainly one of its few black beneficiaries.

What is remarkable about the chief's passing away is the politics of events that followed his demise. An appeal was made by Chief Mwelo Nonkonyana, ANC MP, member of the Eastern Cape House of Traditional Leaders and provincial chairperson of the Congress of Traditional Leaders in South Africa (CONTRALESA), to the provincial government of the Eastern Cape to provide for an official state funeral for the King of the Emigrant Thembu (AbaThembu baseRhode). The Premier of the Eastern Cape, Makhenkhezi Stofile, then requested that central government covered the costs of a state funeral. There is no doubt that the Matanzima family, which includes several high-ranking members of the ANC including Pathekile Holomisa, the current national chairperson of CONTRALESA and Nelson Mandela, the former President of the Republic, could afford to shoulder the funeral costs. The issue of a state burial came up as a result of Matanzima having been a monarch and 'head of state', and, while the status of the Transkei as an independent country was certainly not undisputed, he could qualify for a state funeral as a result of the royal position he had held for some forty years.[1] President Thabo Mbeki vetoed the granting of a state funeral. Yet the Eastern Cape government, itself in receivership as a result of gross mismanagement of funds rooted in the malpractice of the Matanzima regime, took it upon itself to provide a portion of the costs for what became a rather lavish affair. But the really surprising development of the funeral was that several eminent statesmen who had fought against apartheid and everything Matanzima stood for, and who had been the architects of the new, democratic South African dispensation, hailed the chief as if he had been a member of the freedom struggle and had joined his life to the fight for a better South Africa. Overturning his own veto, President Mbeki appeared at the funeral and praised the chief for his tireless efforts to provide a better life for his 'subjects'. No less a figure than Nelson Mandela provided a praise song for the man who at one point offered to take him into his 'protective care' while imprisoned on Robben Island. Matanzima's gesture was not friendly towards Mandela as the obvious implication was that Mandela would no longer represent a threat to the apartheid regime if handed over to the Transkei authorities. In his speech, Mandela referred to the chief as a victim of the former regime and as a person worthy of respect and honour. The aforementioned MP Nonkonyana even referred to Matanzima as a 'liberator of black people' and 'a statesman among statesmen'. Given the role Matanzima had in providing some semblance of legitimacy to apartheid, these sentiments and statements were the reversal of the history being unearthed by the Truth and Reconciliation Commission (TRC) and the public redemption of a figure who once epitomised the many smaller acts of black self-interested betrayal that wounded the ANC and no doubt retarded the overthrow of apartheid. One observer, voicing the view of many, asked why the ANC leadership had stooped to the 'sanctification of an evil man'.[2] Why had it chosen to cauterise the wounds of the past through a publicly orchestrated act of forgetting? And why now?

The eulogising of Chief Kaizer Matanzima is only a fractional part of a surprising story about the comeback the traditional authorities so fundamental to the apartheid regime and the rural misfortunes of the majority of South African citizens are making. In several parts of the country – mostly in the four former Bantustans of Bophuthatswana, Venda, Ciskei and Transkei but also in other rural areas in the Limpopo, Mpumalanga and KwaZulu-Natal provinces – the traditional leaders are staging an important political comeback, armed with the blessing of several pieces of recent legislation and in contradistinction to the once more pronounced professions by leading ANC politicians that traditional authority is a thing of the past. While during the 1990s the ANC voiced its opposition to traditional leaders and authorities and reinforced its commitments to the weakening of these institutions through the introduction of a municipal government meant to replace them, by 2000 the governing party appeared to dramatically, pragmatically shift its position to one of accommodation with the traditional leaders and, some might argue, outright collusion.

---

[1] The manner in which Matanzima became premier of the Transkei is usually described as one of 'title grabbing' since the apartheid regime had a very heavy hand in the selection of Matanzima and promoted their protégé over several other, more entitled yet less pliable, candidates for the succession of King Sabata Dalindyebo, who was closely associated with the ANC and its leading members. See Tom Lodge (1983).

[2] See Editorial Comment, 'The Sanctification of Evil Men', *Mail and Guardian*, Johannesburg, 30 June 2003.

The long-awaited and much-anticipated Municipal Structures Act of 2000 went well beyond the deliberately vague and delimited role given to traditional leaders in the 1996 Constitution by providing them with representation in the municipalities where 20 per cent of the seats are reserved for traditional leaders. There are several clauses in the new legislation on land and tenure rights that provide for exceptions to general rules regarding land usage in areas controlled by traditional authorities. And certainly the fact that in a state in which there is reluctance, even outright opposition to providing a general policy on HIV/AIDS medication due to its costs, it must be seen as surprising that the state coughs up some Rand 50 million a month to support an institution long seen as an anachronism and a vestige of the colonial and apartheid past.

How can we explain this surprising and unexpected turn of events? Some observers suggest that the politics surrounding Matanzima's funeral were simply prompted by electoral considerations. The funeral was attended by Bantu Holomisa, the leader of the United Democratic Movement (UDM) that has its core electorate in the central parts of the Transkei, and Mangosuthu Buthelezi, leader of the Inkatha Freedom Party (IFP) based in the rural areas of KwaZulu-Natal. Both Holomisa, a former general in Matanzima's army, and Buthelezi, a fellow homeland leader, eulogised Matanzima. Yet the direct electoral explanation, while providing a straightforward line of reasoning and motivation insofar as it considers only the political and the present, does not carry much weight. There are, first of all, the empirical facts. As a result of the recent floor-crossing legislation that allowed minority party members to cross over to the ANC camp, the United Democratic Movement (UDM) is a much reduced force in the Eastern Cape and with a paltry electoral following of just over 3 per cent nationally it does not represent a threat to the ANC. In fact, in almost all constituencies of the Eastern Cape the ANC enjoys a commanding electoral majority of between 70 and 80 per cent of the vote. While there are indeed elections looming in 2004, and considerable cynicism amongst the population about that, there appears to be no apparent need for ANC leaders to alienate their core urban and activist constituencies with praise-songs for what they know to be (and on other earlier occasions have referred to as) apartheid stooges because of the impending elections.[3]

There is, we suggest, more than the politics of the immediate at work. The explanation of why the present ANC regime is treating Chief Kaizer Matanzima personally and traditional authority generally with kid gloves is an implication of a more global economic context and an emblem of a deeper political history that, lying in the background and easily misrecognized, are constituting the 'limits of liberation' that the ANC has had to confront since ascending to power – to political power – in 1994. The following essay, which is a first down payment on a more comprehensive analysis, begins to specify a hierarchy of limits and a theory of constraints on post-colonial democracy. We see these limits operate from the very global level of transnational circulations down to the local where the chances of affecting major change grow slimmer by the day and political alliances are being made in order to minimise the consequences of the state's incapacity to function as a transformative agent in the rural hinterlands. Our principal argument is that it is possible to evaluate the prospects and success of a democratic regime only if its

---

[3] The joke circulating in the Eastern Cape is that 'earth-moving equipment can be seen to be moving in several parts of the province to upgrade the pot-holed roads. This was indeed a sign that elections were near. The trucks were sure to disappear again a day after the event'.

forms of action and inertia, pronouncements and silences, are framed within a theory of constraints that thematises the force field of global processes and the now deeply embedded dislocations generated by its colonial/apartheid past.

A hierarchy of constraints

Transformative movements, not least the advent of democracy, make two promises: to periodise and encapsulate the lack of freedoms of the past by adopting transparently different and more democratic policies, and by implementing institutions that remedy the injustices inherited from that past. Especially the national state, in respect of the views circulating within the public political sphere, is supposed to realise these promises, and indeed the perceived success of the transformation and the consolidation of democracy turn on their realisation. On the one hand in the foreground, this depends on the admixture of policies, the correct weighting of priorities and the successful implementation of these promise-keeping policies. On the other hand in the background, this greatly depends on the capacity of the state to raise the necessary revenues, determine its policies domestically and extend its reach into those areas, such as the Transkei, that were wilfully marginalised by the apartheid government. As other accounts in this volume testify, the limits of liberation and dispensation depend on what lies in the foreground. But they also arise from this abstract and easily misrecognised background – which is the subject of our analysis.

So, to grasp the limits of liberation, we seek to contextualise both the post-colonial state and its democratic project within the multiple and imbricated processes of circulation (Lee and LiPuma 2002) defining the present. Though it is sometimes thought otherwise, there is simply no way to begin or sustain this discussion without situating the postcolony in respect of the constraints imposed by the cultural, political and economic dislocations of its past and the powerful reorganisation of the global political economy, especially the technologically amplified flows of capital and the globally saturating discourse of neo-liberal democracy (Comaroff and Comaroff 2000: 300–1). By constraint, we mean the absence of self-determination and the state's necessity to author and advance policies that deflect or mute the imminent violence of globalising forces (e.g. financial markets) by suppressing the most immediate, palpable and pressing concerns of its citizen-subjects (e.g. creating jobs). By constraint, we mean not only the objective limitations imposed by neo-liberal economics in conjunction with metro-centred politics, but the subjective limitations that become deeply embedded in the trajectories, dispositions and visions of post-colonial institutions and agents. Our objective is to provide in a preliminary way a basis for grasping the limits of liberation that goes beyond traditional critiques of the difference between what the ruling elite say and what they accomplish, or the disparity between constitutional political equality and the presence of manifest socio-economic inequalities. What must also be grasped are the limits to liberation imposed by abstract transnational forces and the sociostructures laid down by the long-term imbrication of colonial/apartheid and indigenous worlds. This is significant because the way the present conjuncture inserts the postcolony into the reorganisation of production in concert with the new circuits of capital determines the economic viability of the democratising state, and thus the extent to which it can realise the substantive objectives demanded by its citizens in the name of democracy. In short, if the state is to mediate the relationship between the citizen-subjects of a nation and their visions of the future – such as enhanced social justice and welfare – it must have the economic resources and monetary control to fulfil its promises and pursue those visions. Narrowing the frame, the analysis then attempts to define the post-colonial state, not in terms of sovereign powers or capacities, but rather as a mediating agent, temporally caught between a past founded on forms of disenfranchisement and a present progressive aiming at inclusivity, and spatially between circulations, one that involves the perpetual circulation of people, money and everything captured in the notion of culture from a plurality of rural regions to a few urban areas (exemplified by Johannesburg) and then back again, and the other that involves the constant circulation of commodities, capital, social imaginaries, mass media images and much more among global, urbanised and variously rural spaces. Based on experience as well as research, we also take it as axiomatic that democratising states mediate these circulations through an ensemble of quasi-coordinated, sometimes competing and usually underfunded institutions. Though South Africa allows us to ethnographically ground this theorisation, we take it as emblematic of a more general condition confronting the postcolony.

It is important to be clear about the argument. The colonial past and the globalising processes of the present do not determine the character of democracy in South Africa or the postcolony generally, but they do create an overarching and frequently unmovable set of constraints and limits to liberation that analysis must account for. For these reasons, an understanding of democracy outside the walls of the metropole must begin with a theorisation and description of the constraints imposed on the political culture. A founding tenet of our account is that, while constraints are never in and of themselves determinative, there can be no adequate theory of democratic governance in the postcolony without an account of the limitations and shackling created by the ascendance of globalising cultures of circulation and by the way in which the social consequences of colonialism and apartheid inflect the processes of national and regional circulations and also the domestic reception of transnational forms.

The culture of financial circulation

More specifically, our viewpoint, reinforced by every theoretical and experiential moment of our ongoing field research, is that it is possible to talk about transitions to democracy only in the contextualisation of the simultaneous, intrinsically connected, transitions in the world economy. Although such an account must necessarily be schematic, without it there is no way to grasp the forms of asymmetry and power now in circulation, or the seeds of disenchantment and discontent that seem to be nourished by, of all things, people's education in its processes and prospects that globalisation brings about. We thus conceptualise the globalising culture of financial circulation now in train less as a new stage in the history of the modern, than as a way of problematising the linkages that these forms of circulation have created with the social institutions, sectors and imaginaries that they attempt to subsume and pre-empt in constituting themselves. This is critical because most approaches to democratic theory, as well as standard accounts of liberation, however else they may differ, continue to invoke a separation between economy, politics and culture – the extremely ideological nature of which globalisation is forcing us to recognise. The money markets have two critical, but interrelated, dimensions: debt and currencies, both of which are subject to global markets through interest rate and currency derivatives respectively. On the one side, world lending institutions (e.g. World Bank and IMF) have nationalised the debt incurred by post-colonial regimes, however authoritarian and corrupt, 'technically by inserting cross default clauses in rescheduling packages' and ideologically and institutionally by propping up the fictions of national sovereignty and of a national currency even as they instigated programmes (e.g. financial market liberalisation) that sought to 'denationalise the economy' (Hoogvelt 1997: 168–9). Though massive debt repayment has been a critical constraint across most of the postcolony, and especially Africa, it has not figured centrally in South Africa because of the internal generation of capital and foreign exchange, until recently because of its manufacturing exports and now principally through its technology and finance sectors, and the export of dollar denominated commodities (e.g. gold).

However, for this very same reason, the currency markets, particularly the global circulation of currency derivatives, are creating a dominant, though hidden, constraint. The ascent of these financial markets and instruments, this symbolic economy that specialises in the jet streams of capital, signals a reorganisation of the global relationship between production and circulation. It has become increasingly clear that, since the early 1970s, the cultures of circulation, especially that defined by speculative capital and the risk-based financial derivative, have unceremoniously begun to displace production as the leading edge of capital. Capitalism appears to be transforming from a production-centred nation-based political economy to a much more cosmopolitan structure in which production not only shares the stage with circulation, but circulation appears to be subsuming production. This is a process that seeks to simultaneously amplify global productive output while it encompasses and reorganises the social geography of the existing regime of production.

At least in its basic outline, it is important to begin by clarifying what is happening in the sphere of production. Many of the world's nation-states, especially in Africa, Latin America, the non-petroleum producing states of the Islamic Mediterranean, and huge swathes of South-east Asia are being simultaneously detached from the global structure of production even as they are reattached via the chains of circulation. There is, more, an intrinsic connection between their disenfranchisement from the global realm of production and their absorption into a transformative circulatory system. The metropole's contemporary economic condition, characterised by industrial overcapacity and capital over-accumulation, is leading to what may turn out to be a politically if not economically toxic triangulation, especially because Euro-American capitalism and the politics intermeshed with it envisages its best immediate economic prospects in using its resources to advance this triangulation.

In the metropole, this appears as the much-written-about slow dissolve of industry and manufacturing, and a resulting restructuring in which the circulatory enterprises of finance, media/internet services and logistics come to the fore, coupled with the shift in production to technologies of circulation and the use of technology/software platforms to design products manufactured (in whole or part) elsewhere. We could enlist an extraordinary amount of statistical evidence to support this point, although it is sufficient to observe that, in the OECD countries, manufacturing jobs and the relative contribution of industrial production to their overall national product have declined every year for the past decade (OECD 2002). This reformation of production underpins the post-Fordist metropolitan economy of outsourcing coupled with the compulsory, out- and relocation of entire sectors of production (e.g. textiles, children's toys, footwear and component assembly) to various points along the multipolar periphery, though this is registered through the use of subsidiaries. It is this horizontal reconfiguration and also multi-territorialisation of industrial production within the frame of the differences and distances produced by national politics that are engendering the conditions of connectivity enabling a culture of financial circulation.

From another viewpoint, both outsourcing and the relocation of industrial production are benefiting certain countries and regions and all but excluding others. Much of South-east Asia, the eastern half of China, itself huge and densely populated, selected enclaves within the Indian subcontinent, plus a few other areas are the main beneficiaries of this new geography and functional rescaling of global capitalism. Especially noteworthy is the florescence of eastern China as the epicentre of production while its near neighbour competitor, Japan, struggles to wean itself from what was once its way to wealth but is now an economically suffocating regime of state-steered, production-monocentric capitalism. This is exemplified by a banking system that is yoked to what was once a very prosperous regime of industrialised production and the real estate values it supported. According to a World Bank assessment of globalisation, only twenty-four nations, led by China, have benefited from the reorganisation of global industrial production, though some of those are now beginning to slip behind (2001). What the report says, and possibly underestimates, is that the metropole in concert with the new national centres of industrial production and the oil exporters are doing well economically, whereas much of the remainder of the world is suffering a decline in personal incomes, product per capita, standard of living and practically every other measure of economic prosperity.

Though the forces of circulation affect the lives of all nations, they do so unevenly according to the way in which various regions are inserted into global capitalism. The situation is as clear in its large form as it is lapidary in its detail. In order to transcend the limits of economies that are still deeply dependent on minimally skilled labour, unfinished goods and tourism, the smaller but more advanced nations of the periphery, such as Thailand, South Africa and Malaysia, have sought to invest in value-adding sectors, such as manufacturing communications technology. Less advanced economies (e.g. Mexico and Ghana) are aware that there is a steady decline in the value added of simple production, making it all but impossible for their expanding populations to maintain, much less increase, their product per capita. The hitch is that, in order to accomplish the goal of making manufacturing more technologically directed, they need to attract capital from Euro-American investors. But to attract such capital, even now from the World Bank, requires the borrowing country to liberalise its internal financial controls on the assumption that the free market makes better long-term economic decisions than the political system. The process of liberalisation, as enunciated by the IMF for example (1996), calls for the privatisation of state-held banks, the deregulation of local money markets, the elimination of foreign exchange controls (letting the currency float) and the introduction of more accessible records and more transparent (read standardised) accounting. However, such liberalisation opens the borders not only to manufacturing capital but to its speculative cousin. Indeed, the record indicates that, while net private capital inflows to many countries have remained stagnant for a decade (Institute for International Finance 2000), there has been an astronomical increase in the circulation of speculative capital. What should give pause is that nations (e.g. the Ivory Coast) that only a decade ago were on the verge of development now appear to be slipping backward into an economic chaos that is causing instabilities of many types.

The third leg of the triangulation is an increasing number of nations and soon perhaps continents that are being progressively excluded from the global structure of production. Due to the character of a global reshaping of production in which outsourcing is narrowly channelled, increasingly the enrichment of China and other privileged regions of the multipolar periphery is coming at the expense of others. A large number of developing and transitional countries are internally fractured into a few industries, such as textiles and tourism, which are, at best, marginally integrated into global capitalist production. For these nations, the real issue is not the functional rescaling of capitalism (illustrated by the rising importance of global cities) or the restructuring of production inputs (outsourcing), but being decoupled from the global economic system on which they are dependent for the critical resources (especially but not only petroleum, medical supplies/ pharmaceuticals, technology and capital) that would form the foundation for sustainable development.

Within the reordering of production, South Africa has a markedly split economy. On the one hand, it is becoming the major player in the rising cultures of circulation within the southern cone of Africa, with its technology, informational infrastructure, logistic expertise, mass media productions, high-end tourism and financial sophistication. And there is every indication that this dimension of the national economy has continued to expand since the new dispensation. It has added knowledge-based jobs, in the process promoting narrowly focused growth in gross domestic product. On the other hand, and in line with the trajectory of other countries, such as Mexico (Ferero 2003), there has been a constant erosion of manufacturing, mining and other related industrial-based jobs. Euro-American imports from China are accelerating by 20 per cent annually and falling by a similar amount from other countries and continents. The result of these counter-vailing forces is modest economic growth without increased employment, especially at the low end, and without a broadening of the tax base on which the government relies in order to finance the substantive objectives promised in the constitution itself.

But the global economy now in train is creating an even more important constraint at the level of circulation. In the metropole, a critical dimension of this reorganisation is a fragmentation of the production process at the level of primary inputs (Jones 2000). The proliferation and institutionalisation of contractual outsourcing (i.e. an agreement to supply a product over some delimited time period) created new and larger risks for Euro-American corporations. To hedge these risks, financial institutions began to develop derivatives and their markets for their corporate clientele. In order for these financial derivatives to be effective, their markets needed to be liquid, principals able to buy and sell securities as their needs demanded. The demand for liquidity and the self-expansive character of these markets also furnished a new avenue for absorbing the over-accumulation of capital in the metropole (Brenner 2002: chap. 1), spawning new institutions, such as hedge funds and new banking divisions that specialise in managing speculative capital (Eatwell and Taylor 2000). The derivative is the functional form that speculative capital assumes in the global financial markets because the derivative unifies in a single instrument the objectification and amalgamation of many types of risk (e.g. political risk, counterparty risk, etc.), the leveraging of those risks and the possibility of being used for hedging and/or speculation (Saber 1999: 128).[4] Furthermore, as the pools of capital expanded, as financial technicians fabricated new derivative contracts to expand the reach and maximise the leverage of speculative capital, and as new technologies permitted instantaneous round-the-clock global trading, the economic clout and political implications of speculative capital grew exponentially. The numbers are truly staggering: for example, the data posted on the US Treasury Department website show that the banking conglomerate JP Morgan Chase presently (the first six months of 2003) maintain derivative positions that control over two *trillion* dollars in foreign currency. That is not a misprint, though it is certainly more than the gross national product of all but a handful of nations. It is equally clear that JP Morgan Chase has the financial strength alone, never mind in concert with other major players (e.g. Bankers Trust and Goldman Sacks), to overpower the central banks of even the largest and most developed developing nations, such as Brazil, which, in 2002, had its currency devalued by some 30 per cent as the global financial market responded to the election of a presumably socialist-leaning president.

Though financial derivatives are complex, virtual, and circulate almost exclusively in the cloistered world of investment banks, hedge funds,[5] transnational corporations and specialised global trading firms, it is impossible to grasp the institution and influence of global flows of capital without knowledge of how they operate within a culture of financial circulation. Derivatives have come to the foreground because they constitute the chosen instruments of a speculative and opportunistic finance capital that circulates globally, thereby producing worldwide implications, but is controlled by a rather small coterie of socially interconnected, mutually aware Euro-American agents and institutions. The heart of globalisation – or, better perhaps, 'glocalisation', which captures the fact that its processes are simultaneously large and intimate – lies in the ways the financial community organises the money markets to pump capital through the global circulatory system. Essentially, a derivative is a particular species of transactable contract in which there is no exchange of capital until settlement and in which the change in the price of the underlying asset determines the value of the contract at some specified time in the

---

[4] A derivative is the generic name for any security whose value is tied to an underlier; there are as many kinds of derivatives as there are forms of connectivity. Leverage means that an investment position is subject to the multiplier effect, in which a small change in the value of the underlier has a relatively large effect on profits or losses. The financial markets recognise many kinds of risk, such as what is commonly and somewhat euphemistically called country risk, meaning the risk that attaches to a financial instrument when the investor's country is different from that of the country in which the instrument was issued.

[5] To hedge is to reduce risk by taking a position in futures equal and opposite to outstanding or anticipated cash position or by shorting a security similar to the one in which a long position has been taken. This is commonly done by large corporations whose profits are denominated in one currency but who obtain earnings from many. Hedge funds are private investment pools that invest, usually by increasing the level of risk, in numerous types of markets. Despite their name, hedge funds rarely hedge.

future. What are in fact an extraordinary assortment of financial instruments are called derivatives because their value derives exclusively from an underlying relationship (e.g. cross currency or interest rates) rather than from any intrinsic economic value.

Although speculative capital's use of risk-bearing derivatives capitalises on the long history of international finance, it also spawns an economic technology whose reach and powers are greater than anything that has come before – captured in the statement by John K. Galbraith that 'no economic development of our time is so threatening as to its effect and so little understood as the great and unpredicted movements of financial capital between countries' (2001: 191). Galbraith is alluding to the reality that the ascension of circulatory capital generates a double movement in which new forms of financial progress and freedom, as defined by the West, are inseparable from the rise of a new form of domination and disenfranchisement, generally and most visibly visited on others. Perhaps the most arcane and thus least understood and yet the most crucial dimension of the derivatives market is the way in which it tilts the world economy in favour of the metropole (Soros 2002). This leads the economist Joseph Stiglitz to observe that anyone who thought that 'money would flow from the rich countries to the poor', that the metropole would assume 'the lion's share' of the deep systemic risks associated with currency and interest rate volatility, or even that 'the global markets were efficient' would be sadly mistaken (2002: 24). There is an expanding body of evidence that the culture of financial circulation is more than incidentally instrumental and responsible for the expanding disparities in wealth between rich and poor and that understanding its global dynamics is essential to comprehending the underlying causes of immiseration and conflict, which, in turn, shape the conditions for the rise of non-state, militia-like fundamentalisms and war machines in the postcolony.

To appreciate why this is the case it is necessary to understand what happens when speculative capital, geometrically exaggerating the effects of corporate hedging strategies, uses its stores of capital in conjunction with the power of leverage to devalue the currency of countries such as Turkey, South Africa, Indonesia or Argentina (to cite recent examples). The telling question is what happens when speculative capital uses the power afforded by leverage to sell or short a given currency on a significant scale. The net effect of these cumulative sales is to dramatically reduce or cancel the demand for that currency in respect of its supply. So, as momentum builds and more capital speculates on the short side, thus betting against the currency, a precipitous, and occasionally enduring, devaluation of that currency occurs. Almost overnight the cost of repaying dollar/euro denominated debt spirals upward as does the cost of oil, technology and new capital, igniting inflation, draining the nation's exchange reserves, and, a short while later, causing numerous businesses to fail, unemployment to escalate and the standard of living to fall. This is not an imaginary or overwritten scenario. It is simply the Western logic of a globalising culture of circulation that maintains that in a competitive capitalist world there will be those people who triumph and those who suffer. For example, numerous studies now indicate that, in 1997, the world currency markets depressed the Thai baht by 30 per cent with the result that its banks stopped lending, interest rates became exorbitant for those who could borrow while bankruptcy consumed those who could not, unemployment climbed to its highest level in twenty years and workers took to the streets of Bangkok to protest their plight. As a result, an IMF agenda forced Thailand to replace its constitution with one more adapted to global flows of transnational capital (Noble and Ravenhill 2000). The 'reformed' constitution dramatically deregulated the national capital markets, opening them up to foreign speculation. The economic debacle in Thailand and the recent currency crises in Turkey, Argentina and Brazil have confirmed what many already suspected: that circulatory capital has already gone a substantial way towards subjugating production and manufacturing capital to its dynamic.

The most demonstrative and visible effect of the new financial circuitry centres on the ways in which a derivatives market of this magnitude influences exchange rates between floating hard and soft currencies and therefore the global purchasing power of a country's currency, a relation that becomes especially crucial when its economy is struggling, its democracy is yet to fully consolidate and the state is weakened. However, the threat of devaluation is perhaps even more important, because it is more general than actual instances of precipitous devaluation. Especially across the postcolony, the persistent reality that a nation's currency may suddenly come under attack all but compels these nations to maintain substantial dollar reserves, often amounting to a significant proportion of total national assets. Holding these liquid reserves is inherently deflationary and anti-growth not only because they represent money not deployed to stimulate the economy, but also because they prevent those nations from reinvesting in programmes such as education and business loans that would serve to boost future economic output. Global circumstances, over which they exercise no control, compel these governments to remove local capital from food making, manufacturing and other commercial activities in order to appease the gods of circulation. This creates a ripple effect through the economy because depressed economic activity frequently leads to overwhelming numbers of under-employed, directionless youths who, in many of the already large and swelling cities of the post-colonial world, gravitate toward violent crime. The threat of violence, in turn, motivates local owners of capital to direct their expenditures to guarding existing output, such as hiring a private police force to protect their businesses and homes, rather than investing in new output. More, the investment by the periphery in the currencies of the metropole also has the effect of underwriting the valuation and stability of the dollar and euro. For the postcolony, the negative effects of highly valued metropolitan currencies are more numerous and more widespread than the benefits because the governments of the United States and European Union offset the advantage that peripheral economies might gain due to their low cost of labour as measured in US dollars and euros by subsidising their domestic producers and by erecting trade barriers on especially agricultural goods,[6] textiles, as well as other contested sectors (e.g. steel).

For the postcolony, there is a deeply disturbing quality to the directional dynamic engendered by the structure of financial circulation. To guard against a downdraught in

---

[6] Jacques Diouf, an agricultural economist and the director of the United Nations Food and Agriculture Organisation, has made it clear that 'in the last 15 years, as rich countries increased their subsidies to their farmers and slashed aid to the world's poorest farmers, poor countries have gone from net exporters of food to net importers of food' (Becker 2003: 5). And, sadly, the total aid supplied by the metropole to help farmers grow enough to feed their own people has actually fallen during this time span. The irony of the current demolition of the laissez-faire doctrine is that subsidised Italian tomatoes and other European agricultural products have obliterated the agricultural sector of large parts of Africa. While Italian tomatoes can be found on Ghanaian shop floors, Ghanaian tomato producers have had to declare bankruptcy and find themselves on the streets. See Pendleton (2003).

the value of their currency, the world's marginal economies must maintain reserves in metropolitan currencies, particularly the dollar. This is in effect a transfer of wealth or subsidy from nations that are southern, struggling and peripheral to the metropole. There is little doubt that the funding of these reserves added to the cost of debt service generates net capital outflows that exceed direct external assistance by some $50 billion per year (Held 1995: 256). More, the metropole does not distribute this inflow of wealth equally to all its own income classes; quite the contrary, the wealthiest 1 per cent receives a disproportionate share. Then, seeing a dearth of economic opportunities either in the expansion of manufacturing or, save for technology, in the local equity markets, this group increasingly turns around and reinvests its new capital in hedge funds, made attractive partly because of their success in speculative trading of financial derivatives (Edwards 1999). A hidden cycle is now in train – a form of abstract violence – in which the world's poorest countries are compelled to finance the institutions that destabilise them both economically and politically. The general metropolitan view – the 'Washington Consensus' as it is called – is that this directional dynamic is simply the logical unfolding of a globalising culture of circulation, a competitive capitalist world in which there are those who triumph and those who suffer.[7]

There is thus no way to get around the reality that the sociostructure of financial circulation reproduces existing forms of global asymmetry and, more importantly perhaps, introduces a new form of structural and structuring asymmetry that owes its coherence to a set of ideologically impregnated conceptual schemes. The Western capitalist conception of risk becomes the only empowered and empowering notion. It is imposed by the transnational banking system, by multilateral monetary agencies and also by metropolitan governments when extending foreign aid. This concept of risk fosters asymmetry because it inscribes Western ideology, specifically an acultural notion of modernity as a set of enhancing transformations that every nation-state can, should and no doubt will be forced to undergo. On this view, which appears implicitly or explicitly in every account of global money markets, modernity issues from the growth of rationality and the rationalisation of society and economy.

The upshot is that markets are seen as able to assess economically any nation or culture based on the extent to which it has become the input of this general function. Accordingly, then, the market presumes that forms of national economic, political or social policy that stray too far from this model engender risk. The market routinely applies terms such as non-market, socialist, state controlled, excessively bureaucratic – terms that it considers to be pejorative – to decisions by governments to regulate trade or foreign investment, provide job relief by hiring more state employees than functionally necessary,

---

[7] Former U.S. Treasury official, Robert Altman, in a passage that has drawn a considerable amount of attention, argues that derivatives are the economic equivalent of nuclear weapons because they are 'capable of obliterating governments almost overnight' (1998: 34). To make matters even worse, when currency devaluations in countries such as Indonesia and Argentina drag them into a financial quicksand, the structural adjustments demanded by the IMF in exchange for an infusion of capital, particularly the elimination of barriers to the movement of monetary flows and adoption of Euro-American accounting standards, makes them even more vulnerable to future devaluations. The general manager of the European Investment Bank articulates the Euro-American view, noting that the risk of rapid currency devaluation, even for 'countries with sound [economic] fundamentals', is 'the price to pay for reaping the benefits of globalisation' (Steinherr 1998: 180).

or extend economic emancipation via social welfare programmes such as state-sponsored housing projects. The agents of the global money market perceive policies such as these as magnifying the level of objective risk and thus placing a quantifiable strain on their interest rate and currency models. Such added risk motivates a contraction of finance capital, which, in conjunction with increasing monetary volatility, can precipitate a devaluation of a nation's currency. What is more, many in the academic world, apparently blind to the power of speculative capital and derivatives markets, think that such problems come about because those on the periphery lack the statecraft to create and use institutions that channel the efforts of interest groups and political forces in directions that encourage free trade and open markets. The end result is a form of encompassment and domination that is nearly absolute because the very determination of these systems of circulation is founded on Western forms of intellectual and technological capital.

South Africa and the financial markets

Recently, the director of South Africa's bureau for economic research observed that something appears to have completely uncoupled the state of the nation's manufacturing and productivity from the exchange rate of its currency (Cauvin 2001). The result is what might be called a permanent state of monetary emergency because the central bank can no longer modulate the price of money to advance citizens' interests, such as stimulating the economy by lowering interest rates. In a previous work, Koelble (1998) has shown how the global economy influences the course of democracy in South Africa. He shows that the notion of democracy articulated by global agencies such as the World Bank fixates on institutional arrangements and ontologically saturated Western concepts such as electoral procedures, the freedoms of speech and association, and human (read individual) rights even as it pays little attention to the content of emancipation and socio-economic redistribution that are critical if not determinative aspects of the popular local concepts of what democracy means. In particular, much of the local populace associates democracy with education and housing programmes, especially important in that many areas have squatter settlements, substandard housing and too few schools. There is a general consensus across South Africa that the nation requires a democracy that incorporates critical measures of social justice. The understanding is that the formerly disenfranchised portions of the population cannot forge interest groups, evaluate their elected officials, develop a sense of nationness or national solidarity, etc. if they do not possess the income, education and basic standards of living to do so. Moreover, a notion of democracy that incorporates the social and economic – presently manifested as a desire for emancipation, reconciliation and redistribution – is much closer to an African vision of how collectivities work, a point underscored by Koelble (1998: 174–8) and illustrated in Halisi's (1999) exposition of black political thought on democracy in South Africa.

Despite popular and intellectual support for this broader concept of democracy, the government is reluctant to pursue emancipatory and redistributive goals on the under-standing that such 'socialism' would offend transnational corporations located in South

Africa, scare away the financial capital needed to grow the economy, and run foul of the budgetary spending limits mandated by the IMF. Indeed, it has been made clear that the unrestrained pursuit of emancipatory aims would exaggerate the perceived level of risk, which would, in turn, lead to a contraction in foreign funding, higher interest rates and a devaluation of the rand. Accordingly, the government has to walk a fine if not impossible line: it must embrace a social justice notion of democracy in order to provide enough housing, education, employment and medical services to meet the expectations of its constituency even as it must accede to a EuroAmerican conception of neo-liberal democracy in order to maintain access to the economic resources that fund emancipatory and redistributive programmes – the absence of which would lead to social upheaval. So, although the end of apartheid and the advent of democracy have exponentially increased people's subjective freedom, globalisation, here in the form of the derivatives markets, has, if anything, increased their state of objective dependence.

In the latter half of 2001, the culture of financial circulation began to wreak havoc on the South African economy. At first, the South African rand, which had been losing ground to the dollar and euro for several years, began to slide at a more precipitous pace. Given that the domestic economy had grown during this period, there appeared to be no economically fundamental reasons for the decline. Several economists noted, however, that the rand's prolonged slippage was a result of the failure of the government to privatise state-owned companies rapidly enough. The state's decision to do so in ways that did not aggravate an already socially injurious unemployment rate did not, according to the financial markets, conform to its ideology of the inherent primacy of economic over social and political factors.

A second reason cited for the rand's decline was that the political problems in Zimbabwe shook the market's confidence that black Africans were capable of governing a sophisticated economy. Conventional theory predicts, of course, that an economy characterised by increasing growth coupled to declining inflation, as in the South African case, should attract the over-accumulated EuroAmerican capital, such inflows leading to a certain rise in the rand's value as foreign investors exchanged dollars and euros for South African assets, such as equities and property. Beyond the limits of this logic, impoverished by its lack of culture – most conspicuously, the absence of any semblance of a concept of representational processes – very few EuroAmerican investors redirected capital towards South Africa. Quite the contrary: figures assembled by the Bureau for Economic Research at Stellenbosch University for this period indicate that not only was there little direct foreign investment but instead a diet of disinvestment. A dissembling dialectic was in play in which the currency markets assigned South Africa an abstract risk premium based on its quest for social justice and its racial complexion. Accordingly, the forward currency contracts predicted a continuing decline in the value of the rand, the seemingly unending depreciation discouraging foreign investment, which, in succession, pressured the rand ever lower despite improving economic fundamentals. Then, in December 2001, seeing the absence of foreign investment, the rising tide of economic turmoil incited by the rand's decline and the market's cascading downward momentum, torrents of speculative capital attacked the rand leading to a further 12 per cent devaluation for that month. By year's end, the currency markets had generated extraordinary volatility in the cross-currency exchange rates and, on average, taken the rand down by between 30 and 50 per cent on a year-to-year basis against the euro and dollar.[8]

In a kind of self-fulfilling prophecy, the repercussions from the rand's devaluation – predicated on a social objectification of abstract risk (that is, the risks caused by a failure to privatise, the counterparty risk posed by a black African government on a continent where government failure is endemic, the risk that the AIDS epidemic would siphon off too much government funds, etc.) began to cause the economy to falter. Once under control and declining, inflation accelerated as domestic producers shipped goods abroad to capture the exchange rate differential and the cost of necessary imported goods became prohibitively expensive in rand. However, their profit margins expanded much more slowly due to the rise in petroleum prices, the cost of imported capital goods and high interest rates as expressed in the central bank's reluctance to reduce rates in order to protect the vulnerable rand. One of the important factors in understanding the effects of devaluation is that the temporality of production is glacial with respect to that of circulation. Though currency depreciation almost instantaneously increases export competitiveness, the expansion of production operates on a much longer temporal string and in some cases is relatively inelastic (e.g. wine production). Insofar as global markets decouple the value of the rand from South Africa's economic fundamentals – meaning the state of labour-based production – they also detach the temporality of the currency from that of production. And, since the currency and economy are disconnected, there exists no reason why, just as local producers have increased production capacity to meet surging export demand, the rand could not suddenly turn around and appreciate equally rapidly against the metropolitan currencies, thereby eroding the competitive advantage domestic producers briefly enjoyed. Indeed, observing the trading in the South African money market it is all but certain that beginning in mid-2003 those who had shorted the rand are now unwinding their positions by selling dollars to buy rand denominated bonds. This helps spur an appreciation of the rand as against the dollar, allowed the SA central bank to progressively lower interest rates, which it subsequently began to do. However, this also has the effect of generating enormous new profits in rand for holders of speculative capital as the bonds increase in value due to the lowering of interest rates, meaning that the Euro-American owners of such speculative capital are now being vaulted into an even more powerful position to depreciate the rand in the future. Should some unforeseeable event, such as the death of Nelson Mandela, trigger the wholesale dumping of these bonds combined with a swift increase in short derivative positions, the rand could easily slide by anywhere from 20 to 40 per cent in a matter of a few weeks (to give some idea of how dramatic devaluations can be, recall that in 2002 the Turkish lira fell nearly 50 per cent in just *three days*).

---

[8] A potentially disastrous impact is that dollar- and euro-poor nations cannot afford to buy the medical equipment, surgical instruments, supplies and pharmaceuticals necessary to maintain, let alone improve, their health care systems. What is more, the metropolitan nations are now using their exchange rate advantage as a financial lure to recruit the best health personnel, especially experienced nurses, from the advanced developing nations. An example: according to the US Immigration and Naturalisation Service, American hospitals recruited over two hundred South African nurses in 2001 despite the fact that South African already suffers a serious shortage of experienced nurses, especially in face of the AIDS pandemic (INS Statistical Yearbook for 2001). So, while it is certainly true that the current administration has taken a benighted policy towards AIDS, which should be corrected, this is only a part of the story.

The increasing power of circulation is eating away at the techno-economic functions of the state, particularly its attempt to regulate money, credit, international commerce and, especially in the postcolony, the influence of alien interests on its internal relations of production. But, more, the cultures of financial circulation now in motion also immediately, deeply inform the political functions of the state – its policies of taxation, privatisation, legislative oversight, welfare practices and indeed any projects that may affect the economic interests of global markets. The collective agency of the market, driven by the logic and laws of profit, and shaped by a view of state governance that conceives it as minimal and procedural, can and does forcefully punish states whose politics aim at other objectives. It likewise follows from this logic that national states should involve themselves directly in political cultural projects – such as those aimed at building national solidarity, ensuring dignity and affirming social identities – only insofar as they do not compromise the profitability of the markets. For the citizens of South Africa and the postcolony generally, few things are as much on the inside of social life as money: for money is a social relationship that is a connectivity; money can take on forms and functions that encompass but also go beyond the economic. The circulation of money is certainly the connective medium that facilitates the circulation of goods and services, but it is also part of the moral economy that citizens use politically to assess the quality of governance. In this respect, people throughout South Africa and the world seem to interpret the instability or volatility of their national currency as an index and aspect of the instability of the state that issues, and presumably guarantees the value of, that currency. That many post-colonial states (most more than South Africa) exist in a permanent state of monetary emergency ignites a chain reaction that begins in the economy but influences many dimensions of political life, such as the level of trust and confidence that the citizen-subjects have in their government.

Though any particular crisis may have its local factors (ranging from bad decision-making to mismanagement of public funds, as the story of the Transkei underlines) the reality is that, because the South African state has only a minimal control over currency and interest rates, it has only a limited control over the domestic economy. The globalising culture of financial circulation acts as a powerful non-democratic constraint on the possibility and prospects for liberation. We have in this section articulated three related reasons. First, the central bank has little control over the domestic price of money, currency and interest rates rising and falling mostly with respect to external realities that lie outside of any form of governmentality. Second, there is little or no relationship between the success of the domestic economy of production and the value and/or volatility of the currency on the transnational markets. Even in an expanding and increasingly productive economy, an externally motivated, precipitous and thus unanticipated decline in the value of the currency may compel the central bank to defend the rand by increasing interest rates and tightening access to credit, moves that slow an economy that hardly needs to be slowed. Finally, violent swings or volatility in exchange and interest rates make it difficult if not impossible to coordinate the circulation of capital with the capital investments required to augment production. So, in both speech and report, the president of the SA central bank parrots the words of the neo-liberal ideology of Alan Greenspan and his European counterpart, not, as is sometimes said, because he has forgotten that once upon a history he was a left labour leader, but because he has no discretionary power. He knows that, if he pursued an independent, domestically oriented, monetary policy aimed at redistributing wealth, bolstering the national economy (e.g. employment) or instituting genuine capital controls, the global markets would certainly and unmercifully punish South Africa. In a critical sense, it makes only a relatively marginal difference who controls domestic monetary policy because the South African state does not control the rand's value or volatility.

Substantive freedom and the national state

It is useful to conceptualise the nation-state as a set of overlapping topological spaces – economic, political, religious, etc.– that must be continually brought into alignment by commonalities of language, the performativity of engaging in the same roster of everyday practices, and the institutions and policies of the state. In this respect, a fundamental premise of democratic governance as a critical agent of socio-economic development is the capacity of the elected to regulate and oversee the structures and structuring of economic relations. Democracy as we know it has always assumed that the topological space of the economic and the political, while seldom in complete alignment, were sufficiently congruent to provide social goods, such as justice, education, social welfare, health administration, immigration and naturalisation services, a nationwide infra-structure (e.g. national highways) and the creation of governmental institutions and policies that imbricate national and local, urban and rural spaces. To finance such projects requires the nationwide capacities to tax effectively, print money to address domestic needs, and regulate its use, value and circulation (e.g. credit criteria). This is particularly true in South Africa where the state means nothing if not an instrument of dispensation, an institution whose main mission is to realise the twin promises. More, the realisation of a transformative democracy requires a sufficiently sovereign space in which citizens elect leaders responsible and responsive to their interests, in which the state and those who govern regulate the economy as exemplified in its control over money and other financial instruments, in which the state integrates the nation through policies that promote nation-wide economic development, and in which the government pursues the emancipatory objectives, such as social justice, that allow citizens to genuinely participate in the dispensation.

It is here that the constraints imposed at the global level – in the sphere of production and even more so circulation – translate into national constraints on governmentality. How can the government pursue policies that, for example, stimulate job growth and broaden corporate ownership when it knows from experience that the global money markets, interpreting such policies as augmenting financial risk, can not only nullify their potential benefits, but impose monetary penalties that threaten a more general harm? At the global level, the cultures of circulation emanating from the metropole both advocate the installation of a EuroAmerican model of the proactive, progressive state and advance an economic asymmetry that confounds the possibility of realising the form of governmentality that is necessary to produce such a state. This constraint on the empowerment of the state and consolidation of governance also has a historical dimension, rooted in the reality that the policies of the apartheid state had no necessary relationship to the indigenous economy or the political aspirations of its majority. In contrast to the history of the EuroAmerican state, where an organic linkage has developed between the forms and institutions of government and the structures of the global economy – exemplified by the fact that money as an instrument of global interconnectivity is denominated in dollars and euros – South Africa is defined and diminished by the absence of these linkages. So, across the postcolony generally, analyses of attempts by the national state to generate employment, alleviate shortages of food, initiate housing projects, instal rural electrification, control the outflows of capital and supply of money or upgrade the educational system, underline that the state is highly constrained in its efforts to mediate the relationship between the politics and economy of the nation.

Nonetheless, because since the middle of the nineteenth century, the interthreading of this relationship has served as the significant foundation of the production-centred and sovereign EuroAmerican state, it is deeply embedded in its political discourse, appearing as an unquestioned presupposition in its advocacy of democratic governance. In this respect, the contemporary debate in the metropole concerning globalisation represents its own burgeoning self-awareness that the circulatory forces that it set in train are beginning to fracture this relationship – the state decreasingly able to mediate the relationship between the economy and the nation. What is beginning to happen in the metropole (which appears as a rescaling of state functions) was, however, an original and continuing condition of the constitution of nations such as South Africa, even if its split economy of production mitigates the impact more than in other less developed regions of the postcolony. We are arguing that there is a conspiracy between colonial/apartheid history and the globalising process of the contemporary moment that makes it impossible for South Africa to emulate or replicate the EuroAmerican brands of liberation, that, because the capacities of the state to mediate between the global and national economy are nowhere near those of its EuroAmerican counterparts, the character of its liberation may be compelled to take its own, necesssarily different and more restricted course. In a one-line review, the economic constraints imposed by the contemporary restructuring of global markets appear nationally as constraints imposed on government policy, both in terms of having sufficient revenues and economic latitude to carry out its promises of transformation and in light of the reality that global financial markets, oriented by a deep-seated neo-liberal habitus, working in a virtual and abstract space, punish legislative policies (or even the suggestion of these) to redistribute wealth. The burden of the present reality, and a limit of liberation, is that the South African government must demonstrate a perhaps unreasonably high expectation of political intelligence, institution-building and integrity precisely because it is forced to manoeuvre in a restricted economic space not of its own choosing.

Local constraints

Taking special account of its federalist structure, and the way in which globalising forces constrain state policy and practice, a critical question for the government is exactly how much power it has to devolve or externalise to the private sector in order to maintain sovereignty, and in what respect it must do so. Given the relative inability of the state to reach into the hinterlands, and the legacy of opposition between urban and rural as end (or perhaps just stopping) points along a continual circulation of people, commodities and images, how can the state enact and implement policy in regions where its presence is slight, but where the issues are crucially important to the future of the nation. To take Matanzima's homeland as an example, if the state cannot help create un- and semi-skilled jobs for a local population sorely lacking in education and job training, and has only sufficient financial resources to build a rudimentary educational system, how is it possible to initiate development? If neither the state nor the provincial government have the capital or personnel to institute a judicial system, how is it possible to settle local disputes? The constraints imposed on governance are, in other words, leading to a rescaling of the critical functionalities that were, from the twentieth century view of governance, the very definition of the national state.

At the local level, this political vacuum falls in with a politics already in progress, significantly, the longstanding structures of traditional authority. Accordingly, whatever plans the constitutional democracy has for the integration and development of the rural regions must pass through the already situated politics of those who hold power, however undemocratically. Modern political leaders, including the ANC, have come to see chiefdoms as an embedded institution that will allow them to penetrate and integrate the hinterlands into the nation, particularly if the state, lacking resources, is forced to turn the implementation of distributive policies over to the local municipalities. So South Africa's quasi-compulsory (i.e. globally economically rational) adoption of a neo-liberal economic paradigm has led to a situation in which state expenditures through local channels are insufficient to alleviate the pressing socio-economic problems, exemplified by the politically flammable underdevelopment of overcrowded communities.[9] Needs in terms of access to schooling, health facilities, housing, not to mention employment, even the basic services such as electricity and clean water supplies, are beyond the scope of many rural municipalities (Hart 2002: 235–89). As local government is unable to satisfy the demands of a restive population, the ANC-led state has turned to traditional leaders as uncomfortable allies in the pacification of this rural constituency. On every major government initiative – such as AIDS prevention, improving school attendance or better distribution of pension funds to the elderly in remote places – the chiefs are called upon by the leadership of the ANC to help implement the policy.

So the palpable reality is that much of what passes as 'traditional leadership' is a very modern manipulation, despite an ambivalent if not overtly suspect past in which some overly ambitious chiefs, such as Matanzima, collaborated with the apartheid regime. Thus, ignoring a history in which their present-day status emerged from, and was forged in, the crucible of successive colonial administrations, 'traditional' leaders, encapsulated and euphemised in the term *amakhosi*, are now serving as both figure and ground in the representation, rationalities and rhetorics of the rural South African political cultures. In sociostructural terms, hereditary leaders occupy privileged positions because they mediate and organise the circulations of people, goods and services from the hinterlands to urban centres and then back again. Chiefs may be expected to resolve local conflicts,

---

[9] There is now a considerable body of literature that asserts that the economic policies of the government, collectively referred to as GEAR, have failed to achieve their targets on growth, employment, not to speak of redistribution, rather spectacularly (Bond 2000; Marais 2000).

broker incoming development projects and serve as ombudsmen between their communities and state bureaucracies. Simultaneously authorities by tradition and of tradition – both roles now reinforced in response to globalising processes whose effects are to culturally dissemble and deterritorialise locality – chiefs often come to personify the insertion of the community into what appears to be a hostile and incomprehensible space. In this respect, and rarely with a clean line of sight from the local to the global, chiefs domesticate and sometimes dampen the effects of the abstract violence of globalising processes, because they impose, in a very undemocratic manner, the will and interests of the metropole. In other words, our argument begins with the reality that hereditary leaders are, culturally, time-occupying signs so positioned in social space that they have come to mediate the connectivities between rural and urban, community and state, local and global, in ways that are reproducing the institution of chieftainship in very modern, very transformative, forms. To think of chiefs as either traditional or modern is to ignore the very transcendence of their role that is critical to their resurgence.

While some aspects of chieftaincy are incompatible with the Western democratic conceptions of representation, the location of chiefs in semiotic and structural space allows them to assume a number of critical functions, culturally, politically and ideologically, for the ruling party. These functions are difficult to organise, precisely because chiefs stand outside the formalising logic of state governance. Nevertheless, while neo-liberalism, the rise of globalising financial institutions and practices and the internet revolution are washing away the foundations and territoriality of the state, the persistence of indigenous (non-Western?) culture, the realms of family, community and the character of collective agency are becoming increasingly crucial not only in the imaginations of the post-colonial political elite but at the grassroots level. Safeguarding what the present envisions as the treasured parts of its 'past', the cultural autonomy of the 'nation', African 'ways of doing things' all become vital ideological resources in the struggle for authority, self-determination and the legitimacy of the local. When, from this perspective, traditional authority is imagined to be of a pre-modern, pre-capitalist but highly democratic nature – as village democracy in Africa is typically portrayed – it may serve the powerful ideological purpose of building South African agency, collectivity and pride in African cultures.[10] It becomes a useful trope for reversing Western notions of African patriarchy, ungovernability and autocracy. Rhetorical and reflexive images of 'village democracy' – images that reference the wise chief or leader as a unique African contribution to democratic discourse – would not be of great importance in themselves if it were not for their widespread use by political elites across Southern Africa, most often expressed by leading figures such as Nelson Mandela.[11] Mandela's notions of an African version and vision of democracy are of utmost import in the discourses on Southern Africa's modernity and governmentality.

The importance of African democracy, of safeguarding traditional and customary institutions, including traditional leadership, goes well beyond the ideological and

---

[10] There are several examples where the village council, or *kgotla*, is likened to the concept of direct democracy. The village council is seen as a forum of discussion where the chief is advised on policy and in which the opinions of the community are voiced, debated, and in which consensus decisions are reached. See, for instance, Nelson Mandela (1994) on this kind of African direct democracy.

[11] See Nelson Mandela (1965), p. 147. See the very insightful discussion of Mandela's vision of village democracy in Nash (2002), pp. 243–56.

cultural debates on self-worth (what has been called the African renaissance). As globalising processes lead to a rescaling of functions once exclusively under state control, manifest across the postcolony as a decline in the capacity of the state to reach into and directly govern the hinterlands of the rural areas, traditional leaders become an alternative instrument of governance and a potential arm of state government. For the same reasons, however, it would be misguided to think of chiefs along any dichotomy that portrays them as either independent of state politics and governmentality or as simply puppets of the ruling party. They occupy a much more contested and shape-shifting space; their timely role springs out of a reinterpretation and adaptation of culture grounded in an interested (re)vision of the collective past (sometimes cloaked in a self-imposed amnesia). They help to set out an agenda for the future with a definitive envisioning of what society, the proper community, a proper social order, ought to look like.[12] Enterprising chiefs – aware of their semiotic and structural place in the contemporary moment – seize the opportunity invested in them by the new dispensation and the relative impotence of the nation-state to reach into rural countrysides to do in the name of custom what customarily they could not do: reformulate and historicise the concepts, practices and dispositions underpinning their claims to authority and adaptively assume forms of agency that reassert their powers and prerogatives. All this revolves around cultural practices, economic resources such as access to arable land, and the politics of survival in a setting of poverty and underdevelopment. For those still clinging to hope, the very fact that modernisation is failing the rural areas of South Africa, in terms of material improvements, economic prosperity and creation of new opportunities, serves as reason enough for the revitalisation of traditional leadership and the reinvention of 'customary' practices. In different words, one of the critical triangulations of contemporary politics (not only in South Africa) interlinks an urban elite, hereditary tradition-based leaders and immiserated communities whose members (especially but not only youths) circulate between shrivelling hinterlands and impoverished urban townships.

In sum, chiefs have emerged, at a number of different levels, as both a resource for the constitutional democracy and, insofar as (like NGOs) they are non-democratic, a limit on liberation in the modernist sense. The comeback of the chiefs is a response and result of a hierarchy of constraints that imbricates the global and the local. From this perspective, it begins to make sense why the ANC-run government felt it necessary to use the occasion of Matanzima's funeral to make overtures to the chiefs. The verbal pardons or absolution granted to Matanzima, certainly the most publicly visible collaborator, indicate that the view of chiefs once enunciated by the ANC – that they were both politically anachronistic and too closely associated with the apartheid past – had given over to a more sympathetic vision of their place in a constitutional democracy.

It is important not to either overstate or misinterpret our argument. The government can make better decisions regarding the allocation of funds, domestic economic policy, and should ardently pursue its own betterment. The present government can become more accountable and deal more effectively with what corruption exists. Measures can be taken to better deliver necessary services to rural communities through government channels.

---

[12] See Arjun Appadurai (2000, 2002), who argues that a conceptualisation of culture must include both its 'backward-looking' elements in terms of interpretations of the past as well as its 'forward-looking' qualities in which a vision of the 'good society' to come is presented and defended.

Indeed, a good argument can be made that emerging democracies are more vulnerable to miscalculations and malfeasance than richer established ones. But the limits of liberation in South Africa, and the postcolony in general, begin and are strongly inflected by reorganisation of production and the global culture of financial circulation, oriented around the speculative capital, risk-driven use of financial derivatives. This carries through, reinforces and combines with the constraints emergent at the national level in terms of the state's ability to both implement economic policies and create nationally integrative institutions (e.g. a national educational system and health care administration). The result is not, we underline, a determination of political culture or policy in South Africa, but a powerful hierarchy of constraints that limits liberation.

References

Altman, Roger (1998), 'The Nukes of the 90's', *New York Times Magazine*, 1 March: 34–7.

Appadurai, Arjun (2000), 'Grassroots Globalization and the Research Imagination', *Public Culture* 12: 1–19.

—— (2002), 'The Capacity to Aspire: Culture and the Terms of Recognition', Paper given at Yale University.

Becker, Elizabeth (2003), 'U.N. Official Plans to Urge US to Reconsider its Food Policies', *New York Times*, 24 September, p.A5.

Bond, Patrick (2000), *Elite Transition: from Apartheid to Neo-liberalism*, London: Pluto.

Brenner, Robert (2002), *The Boom and the Bubble*, London: Verso.

Cauvin, Henri (2001), 'What's Eroding South Africa's Economy?' *New York Times*, 12 December, pp. W1, 7.

Comaroff, Jean and John Comaroff (2000), 'Millennial Capitalism: First Thoughts on a Second Coming', *Public Culture* 12:291–343.

Eatwell, John and L. Taylor (2000), *Global Finance at Risk*, New York: The New Press.

Edwards, Franklin (1999), 'Hedge Funds and the Collapse of the Long-Term Capital Management', *Journal of Economic Perspectives*, 13:189–210.

Ferero, Juan (2003), 'As China Gallops, Mexico Sees Factory Jobs Slip Away', *New York Times*, 3 September, p. A3.

Galbraith, J.K. (2001), *The Essential Galbraith*, New York: Houghton Mifflin.

Halisi, C.D.W. (1999), *Black Political Thought in the Making of South African Democracy*, Bloomington: Indiana University Press.

Hart, Gillian (2002), *Disabling Globalization: Places of Power in Post-apartheid South Africa*, Pietermaritzburg: University of Natal Press.

Held, David (1995), *Democracy and the Global Order*, Stanford: Stanford University Press.

Hoogvelt, Ankie (1997), *Globalization and the Postcolonial World*, Baltimore: Johns Hopkins University Press.

Immigration and Naturalization Services (2001), *INS Statistical Yearbook*, Washington, D.C.: INS Publications.

Institute for International Finance (2000), *Capital Flows to Emerging Market Economies*, Washington D.C.: Institute for International Finance.

International Monetary Fund (1996), *World Capital Market Report*, Washington, D.C.: IMF Publications.

Jones, Ronald (2000), *Globalization and the Theory of Input Trade*, Cambridge, MA: MIT Press.

Koelble, Thomas (1998), *The Global Economy and Democracy in South Africa*, New Brunswick: Rutgers University Press.

Lee, Benjamin and Edward LiPuma (2002), 'Cultures of Circulation: The Imaginations of Modernity', *Public Culture* 14: 191–214.

Lodge, Tom (1983), *Black Politics in South Africa since 1945*, Johannesburg: Ravan Press.

Mandela, Nelson (1965), *No Easy Walk to Freedom*, London: Heinemann.

—— (1994), *A Long Walk to Freedom*, Randburg: McDonald Parnell.

Marais, Hein (2000), *South Africa: Limits to Change*, Cape Town: Zed Books.

Nash, Andrew (2002), 'Mandela's Democracy', in Sean Jacobs and Richard Calland (eds), *Thabo Mbeki's World: the Politics and Ideology of the South African President*, Pietermaritzburg: University of Natal Press.

Noble, Gregory and John Ravenhill (2000), *The Asian Financial Crisis and the Architecture of Global Finance*, Cambridge: Cambridge University Press.

OECD (2002), *Economic Outlook for OECD Countries*, Paris: OECD.

II
Rethinking Citizenship & Governance in Urban South Africa

5
Nodal Governance, Denizenship & Communal Space
Challenging the Westphalian Ideal [1]

CLIFFORD SHEARING & JENNIFER WOOD
in collaboration with John Cartwright and Madeleine Jenneker

Introduction

Established notions of citizens and citizenship are informed by the Westphalian ideal of autonomous, territorially bounded nation-states.[2] Collective life is defined and explained by reference to 'national' cultures, politics and economic systems. To be a 'citizen' means to be an individual who has rights and responsibilities in relation to these states.

This Westphalian ideal continues to frame our thinking but it is no longer as self-evident as it once was. While the ideal is usually thought of as governing relations between states, it has been central to our thinking of how states do and should operate as authorities who govern state territories through state agencies. These structures have always been layered into, upon and around assemblages of governance that do not fit neatly within this framework (Krasner 2001). However, it is only recently that this West-phalian thinking and its utility as an organising concept has begun to be seriously questioned. Today, as this layering of multiple worlds becomes increasingly visible, the simple elegance of the Westphalian model is no longer as compelling as it once was.

Within our contemporary world, because states continue to exist as important sites of governance and political authority, citizenship remains relevant and most people today continue to be defined as citizens of one or more nation-states. However, as new auspices of governance emerge and reconfigure collective life, people now exist within a host of non-state affiliations and associated expectations. If we are to understand these new statuses and their implications we need to extend our conceptual framework in ways that enable us to home in on them as central objects of analysis. Our conceptions of governance and

---

[1] We would like to thank Michael Kempa, Nicola Piper and Paddy Stamp for their comments and suggestions. An earlier, and substantively similar, version of this chapter is published as 'Nodal Governance, Democracy and the New "Denizens"', *Journal of Law and Society*, 30(3): 400–19.

[2] Stephen Krasner comments that the 'Peace of Westphalia which ended the Thirty Years War in 1648, is taken to mark the beginning of the modern international system as a universe composed of sovereign states, each with exclusive authority within its own geographic boundaries. The Westphalian model, based on the principles of autonomy and territory, offers an arresting, and elegant image. It orders the minds of policymakers' (Krasner, 2001: 124).

citizenship, and the worldview such conceptions support, lag behind our practices (see Hermer *et al.* 2002; Wood and Shearing 1999). The conceptual challenge is to respond to this lag.

In considering how to do this, we begin with a review of transformations in governance. We then propose three new conceptual pillars that we suggest should be employed in coming to terms with these transformations and the new political landscape they have created. These concepts are 'nodal governance', 'denizens' and 'communal space'. We explore them through the empirical window of the governance of security. Following this we examine the normative implications of nodal governance with an emphasis on the 'governance disparity' that is paralleling the 'wealth disparity' across the globe. In response to this disparity, we outline a normative vision and practical programme aimed at deepening democracy in poor areas of South Africa, Argentina and elsewhere. We argue that the main feature of nodal governance, namely, its emphasis on the mobilisation of dispersed capacity and knowledge – that have been so effectively deployed by powerful global players (sometimes termed the 'Washington Consensus' (Bond 2002: 27)) to promote the deep structural inequalities (Bond 2001a, b) – can be refigured in ways that enhance the self-direction of poor communities while strengthening their collective capital (see Bond's 2002 discussion of 'community-based', 'sustainable' and 'pro-poor' visions of local economic development).

From state-centred to nodal governance

For much of the twentieth century, security was seen as an essentially state function. This was true both empirically and normatively. States owned security. While the governance of security had historically been carried out under a range of auspices (Johnston 1992), a narrower view, coupling the function with the apparatus of the state – i.e. the 'police' – became widely entrenched in thought. This state-centred view of the governance of security, privileging the strategies and practices of the three 'c's' (cops, courts and corrections), remains the dominant organising paradigm of 'criminology'.

Within this view, the authority and limits, as well as the defining capacities and resources of the state, are central objects of study. Considerable emphasis is therefore placed on the state's ability to exercise or threaten coercion in ensuring individual compliance in the promotion of the 'social' order. The nature and degree of this authority, and its exercise in practice, have formed a significant part of criminological enquiry. For instance, the bulk of work devoted to accountability for policing is informed by this state-centred view. In liberal democracies, the ideal system of accountability is one that circumscribes this exercise of force by police. At the same time, the criminal justice system, along with other state institutions, is seen as the bastion of 'social' (Rose 1996) expertise, whilst citizens are understood as uninformed and passive recipients of services and programmes (O'Malley and Palmer, 1996). This was not only the way things were in fact. It was also the way we thought things ought to be, and had to be, if the world was to be properly regulated. For many, and perhaps most people, state ownership of the governance of security was simply the way the world worked and had to work.

States continue to govern security and do so through the use of state agencies and agents who use force and the threat of force. Indeed, today these agencies are bigger and more extensive than they ever were. There are more state police, doing more policing, and more courts, doing more adjudication, and more sentencing agents, doing more to enact sentences than ever before. We also have more police stations, courts and prisons than ever. While at one time this would have been regarded as the whole story, it is today increasingly recognised as only one part of a much bigger picture.

Today, there are many agencies and agents involved in the governance of security besides the police. The same is true of adjudication and sentencing agents and agencies. Across the world there are now many more non-state policing agents than there are police officers. In North America, for example, ratios vary between 2 and 3 to 1 (Swol 1998; Rigakos and Greener 2000). In South Africa, estimates vary between 5 and 7 to 1 (Irish 1999; Schönteich 2000). Substantial growth in the private security industry has also occurred in Europe and Asia (Johnston 2000; Jones and Newburn 1998). And these formal agents are only the tip of the iceberg. Policing has become increasingly an activity that agencies and agents outside of the state are engaged in. Perhaps most importantly, state agents no longer claim they can 'do it alone' (see Garland 1996)..

While this 'pluralisation' of governance can be attributed to a deliberate policy by state governments to devolve governance functions to other auspices and agents, much of it was not planned or anticipated. The net result of both the planned devolution and unplanned pluralisation, or what Bayley and Shearing (2001) have termed a 'multi-lateralisation', has been a massive fracturing of the spheres of governance into a wide variety of governmental nodes. Some time ago Macauley (1986) referred to these non-state nodes as 'private governments'.

While these developments have been characterised as 'privatisation' or 'devolution' from within a state-centred framework dominated by Westphalian imagery, this is only one part of the picture (Shearing and Wood 2000). What has been involved is not simply the devolution of state functions motivated by 'neo-liberal appeals to the efficiency of markets, to the importance of accountability; to the liberty, enterprise, responsibility and independence of individuals; and to the virtues of the non-interventionist state' (see O'Malley and Palmer, 1996: 141).[3] Rather, what has occurred is that existing private sector institutions have emerged as sites of governance (Shearing 1997). This growth of non-state governance, both with and without state action, has revealed what Garland (1996) has termed the 'myth of the sovereign state'.

In a recent review of the literature, Hermer and colleagues (2002) have argued that, while, as we have just suggested, state privatisation and devolution policies have only been partly responsible for the pluralisation of the governance of security, state-based legal frameworks have played a major role in enabling these developments. For instance, property law has provided the framework that enables corporations, as 'private' property owners, to assume a role in the governance of security. One conclusion to be drawn from this is the importance of developing a framework of analysis that recognises the linkages that relate state and non-state nodes of governance and the activities they are engaged in.

[3] This Foucauldian understanding of 'neo-liberalism' is wider and more inclusive than the usage common in South Africa that tends to equate it with such things as the structural adjustment programmes of the 'Washington Consensus' (Bond 2001a, 2002).

In order to do so, we adopt a 'nodal' rather than a state-centred conception of governance, as a way of moving beyond a framework founded on Westphalian imagery (see Hermer *et al.* 2002; Johnston and Shearing 2003; Kempa *et al.*, 1999; Shearing 2001; and Shearing and Wood 2000).

Within a nodal conception of governance no set of nodes is given conceptual priority. Rather, the exact nature of governance and the contribution of various nodes to it are regarded as empirically open questions. It is assumed that the specific way in which governmental nodes relate to one another will vary across time and space. While these arrangements might very well become entrenched for considerable periods in many places, they should be regarded as an empirical feature of these times and places, rather than an analytical constant.

We have, for the past several decades, been living in an age where the empirical regularities that we took for granted have changed radically. Today, as studies of the governance of security are making clear, the relationship between nodes of governance is considerably varied and involves both cooperative alliances and various forms of contestation. In exploring these relationships Grabosky (1992; 1994; forthcoming) has examined the ways in which resources flow across nodes, with state nodes supporting non-state nodes and vice versa. Scott (2001) has recently adopted a different approach, exploring the extent to which regulatory activity cuts across the state/non-state distinction by challenging the idea that regulation always flows from state to non-state nodes. His analysis demonstrates the ways in which non-state nodes have become increasingly engaged in regulating state actors.

While we still have a long way to go in adequately mapping different nodal sets it is clear that within the non-state sector both business corporations and voluntary institutions are actively involved in governance (see Bayley and Shearing, 2001; Hermer *et al.* 2002). This has led to distinctions being made between various governmental sectors. Within nodal governance we may now speak of a first (state), a second (corporate or business) and a third (non-governmental organisations) sector (Turner 2001; Fonseka 1999; Ellickson 1991). It might be useful to think of a fourth, informal sector, made up of people who operate outside of the first three sectors. Within each of these sectors action can be seen as either legal or illegal in terms of some set of rules (for example, state law and international law).

Once we stop giving conceptual priority to state nodes it becomes possible to consider what range of governmental nodes exist and how they relate to each other. This would not mean, as we have already suggested, that at certain times and places state governments are not empirically significant and powerful or that they do not sometimes come together with other states to establish new 'supra-state' auspices of governance (see Sheptycki 2000). It would, however, ensure that we are using concepts that do not assume any particular assemblage of auspices, spaces and practices.

It is also important to recognise that every empirical form of governance is a human invention, or, more accurately, a perpetual reinvention. The ongoing reinvention of governance occurs through 'waves' of change rather than dramatic ideological or structural shifts (Wood, 2000). Such waves are the product of the actions of a variety of constituencies in response to perceived challenges and new objectives in their world. Sometimes change is intended, but not always. The effects of change, too, are not the outcome of a linear trajectory, but rather are mediated by resistance and contestation, contingent events and the subtle alignment of interests, motives and agendas (Wood 2000; O'Malley 1992, 1996, 2004; O'Malley *et al.* 1997). While state and non-state nodes operate under different cooperative arrangements (such as contracting out, sponsorship, partnership or hiving off) it is also the case that nodes can operate in benign neglect of one another, or in forms of outright conflict (see, for example, the relationship between state police and vigilante groups in South Africa (Brogden and Shearing 1993; Nina and Russell 1997), Northern Ireland (Hillyard 1993, 1997) and Brazil (Huggins 2000)).

Much is taking place all over the world to shape and reshape the way in which the new assemblages of governance operate and to imagine ways of regulating nodal governance arrangements so that they conform to normative values. Much of this thinking is taking place within the normative frames that are central to liberal and democratic values, including Paul Hirst's thoughts on 'associative democracy' (1994) and Held and his associates' explorations of 'cosmopolitan democracy' (e.g. Archibugi and Held 1995; Falk 1999; Held *et al.* 1999). The normative stance we outline below acknowledges the reality of nodal governance and its challenges – the way it has been utilised to enhance power and wealth differentials (Alexander 2002; Bond 2001a; Terreblanche 2002) as well as possibilities it poses for alternatives that seek to deepen democracy and promote more equal and inclusive relationships (Bond 2002).

From citizens to denizens

As already suggested in our introductory comments our notions of citizens and citizenship are closely tied to the Westphalian ideal of governance. They do not fit well with the expanded notions of membership within the new governance arrangements that now dominate the contemporary period. People now live within a world full of criss-crossing memberships that operate across and through multiple and layered governmental domains. Within such worlds, to think of people's political or governmental status only (or even primarily) as 'a member, native or naturalised, of a (usually specified) State or Commonwealth' (*New Shorter Oxford English Dictionary* 1993) is too limiting. What is to be done? As citizen and citizenship have very well-established meanings and connotations relating to the expectations and responsibilities of state membership, to seek to redefine citizens and citizenship might be a less sensible strategy than looking to an alternative conception that resonates with the ideas central to citizenship but is not state-centred.

One possibility suggested to one of us by Sebastian Scheerer (the German criminologist based in Hamburg) would be to broaden and reshape the definition of 'denizen' as it has a less well-established meaning and to invent the term and concept 'denizenship' (personal communication). What we propose is to broaden 'denizen' beyond 'a habitual visitor to a place' so that it refers to an affiliation with rights and responsibilities that applies to any auspice of governance. One's denizenship might be very temporary, for instance, a denizen of a commercial gated enclave, or more permanent, for example, a denizen of a university or of a virtual collective of Internet users. Our suggestion is that, for purposes of situating people within a framework of nodal governance, the term 'denizen' be defined as a person situated within the regulatory domain of a governmental node and that we think of denizenship as the status of being a denizen.

Within this conceptualisation, persons are recognised as having multiple denizenships depending on the number of domains of governance through which their lives are regulated. Each domain would carry with it expectations and obligations that would define the specific nature of the denizen's status. This conception has links to the literature on 'social capital' (Putnam 2000) that seeks to locate people within networks of trust and obligation. Some of these are very 'thin' while other networks are 'thick'. In relating social capital to denizenship we suggest that one measure of social capital might well be the 'thickness' (Walzer 1994) of denizenships that persons, or groups, have. The more regulatory zones that persons within a collective participate in, the greater the social capital that collectivity is likely to possess. As this understanding of social capital is perhaps more narrowly focused than the way in which the term has come to be used, locating this idea within a nodal governance framework has the advantage of making the meaning clearer than is often the case. To avoid confusion we propose to use the term 'collective capital' to refer to the networks of trust and obligation that link individuals, collectivities and agencies within a regulatory environment. This usage also has the advantage of not using the term 'social', whose analytic history is closely tied to the nation-state (Rose 1996).

We have argued that the Westphalian world of states monopolising governance, in which political affiliations are understood exclusively in terms of citizenship linked to a social space that extends across states, has been replaced by a multi-layered world of governing auspices. This world is best conceived, we have argued, in terms of assemblages of governmental nodes that relate to each other in a variety of ways that shift over time and space. Within this world people operate as denizens of different governmental domains. Their affiliations, depending on the relationship between the nodes with which they are associated, might be congruent with one another but they might just as easily be at odds.

From public to communal spaces

As suggested above, the Westphalian world is associated with a neat distinction between 'public' and 'private' realms. This distinction has distinct Hobbesian roots (Hobbes 1968 [1651]). 'Public spaces', within a Westphalian world, are spaces accessible to all citizens simply by virtue of their citizenship – to be a citizen means in part to be free to wander at will through 'public' spaces within nation-states. 'Public' space by definition is a space open to all citizens (see von Hirsch and Shearing 2000). Within private spaces citizens are thought of as free from unwarranted intrusion by other citizens and state agents. 'Private' spaces are places in which citizens can, by virtue of their ownership/ control of property, put limits on who can use these spaces and the nature of the use that can be made of them (ibid.; Hermer *et al.* 2002). The essence of this distinction is nicely captured in the following passage from a landmark English court case, from which the aphorism the 'Englishman's home is his castle' is derived:

> Our law holds the property of every man so sacred, that no man can set his foot upon his neighbour's close without his leave; if he does he is a trespasser though he does no damage at

all; if he will tread upon his neighbour's grounds he must justify it by law (*Entick* v. *Carrington* 1765).

In 'private' spaces citizens within many states have the right to regulate the use of these spaces and to apply these regulations to the state as well as to fellow citizens. The characteristics of both 'private' and 'public' spaces are guaranteed by these states. The 'public'/'private' distinction is an essential feature of the Westphalian state. A 'public' space is a space that all citizens have access to while 'private' spaces are spaces that citizens can control according to their whims provided these do not violate the law. For centuries this distinction worked simply and elegantly.

Ironically, the emergence, and subsequent development, of nodal governance has been enabled by this distinction and the laws that constitute and support it. Central to this has been the emergence of what Shearing and Stenning have termed 'mass private property' (1983). This refers to private property that has developed features that make it appear very much like a 'public' space. The most obvious examples are shopping malls, industrial parks and mass recreational facilities. While owners retain the right to exclude people from these properties and impose what are typically implicit limits on access to these spaces, they appear to be open to 'the public' in the same way as conventional public spaces are open to all citizens.

These new spaces have now proliferated widely across the globe and are common in almost every developed and relatively affluent developing country. A central feature of these spaces is that property owners (often corporate entities) manage their governance. At times this occurs with the assistance of state officials, who typically operate in them on the invitation of owners and who are sometimes paid for (at least in part) by them (Grabosky, forthcoming). It is the governance of these spaces by 'private' legal entities that provides the most visible examples of private governments.

This new governance and the spaces associated with it have blurred the 'public'/'private' distinction. The 'public' spaces of mass private property are not 'public' in the same way as conventional public spaces are. They are not spaces that all citizens have a right to access provided they comply with state law. They are spaces where access is dependent on an invitation from the private owners of the property on which the spaces exist. These real spaces coexist with 'virtual spaces' that have come into existence on the same basis – for example, the spaces made available by the owners of Internet sites that people are invited to use.

While by no means identical, these spaces have a strong resonance with medieval common spaces legally controlled by feudal authorities to which certain people had rights of access. These spaces were common to persons who lived within feudal estates but not to persons from outside of them. The same sort of situation held with respect to the pre-feudal period where similar 'commons' existed. These spaces were common to some people but not to everyone within a wider kingdom. Today we have within the domains of nodal governance what we suggest should be thought of as new 'communal' spaces (von Hirsch and Shearing 2000; Hermer *et al.*, 2002). These are spaces that different sets of denizens have access to and whose denizenship is, in part, defined in relation to them. These spaces cut across the 'public'/'private' distinction.

While these new communal spaces have emerged in the context of mass private property, they are beginning to proliferate within 'public' spaces. This is seen, for example, in the development of enclosed residential and business communities of various sorts (enclosures may be literally fenced off or simply an effect of 'traffic calming' arrangements such as speed bumps and maze-like streets).

To summarise, we have argued that in order to gain an adequate understanding of new developments in governance, and the new features of the world that these developments reflect, we must shift our focus away from state-centred lines of enquiry. In acknowledging the reality of 'nodal governance', we suggest that the notion of 'denizen' be utilised to capture the affiliations, rights and expectations of those who are governed within and across multiple forms of 'communal space'.

We now turn from the explanatory to the normative, discussing the implications of these nodal developments for democratic reform.

The governance deficit

As indicated earlier, the developments we have just reviewed have occurred alongside a mammoth shift in political sensibilities, institutional arrangements and technologies of governance under the sign of neo-liberalism (whether broadly or narrowly understood). A central feature of neo-liberal sensibilities has been the argument that the 'rowing' of governance is more effective and efficient if it takes place locally and if governmental services are provided through markets and market-like mechanisms. The reinvention of governance that has taken place under the guidance of this sensibility has promoted arrangements that enable the 'steering' of governance to remain within state agencies that are accountable to elected legislatures (Osborne and Gaebler 1992).

This Hayekian normative vision of markets and local mechanisms taking responsibility for the 'rowing' of governance with governments continuing to 'steer' has tended to be conflated with an empirical reality that is often considerably at odds with this vision. While the devolution of governmental services to business enterprises has taken place, there has also been a significant shift as well in the steering of governance away from state agencies. One of the consequences of this has been a massive increase in the political authority of corporate entities that have emerged as significant auspices of governance (Shearing 1995; Shearing and Wood 2000). This authority has not, as we have already suggested, taken place within a legal vacuum. Both state and international law has enabled, and shaped, the way in which this emerging non-state authority is exercised.

All of these developments have complicated the way in which accountability over governmental action is exercised. Alongside the established modes of representative democracy, new market-based mechanisms that depend on consumer choice have emerged for holding governmental authorities accountable. The market-based 'com-modification' of governmental services has enabled consumers to exercise a degree of control over the services provided outside of the established state-based democratic processes (see Bayley and Shearing 1996; Loader 1999). Not only do governments who contract out service provision to business enterprises exercise control through the contract process, but people who consume governmental services from non-state governing auspices (either as part of a devolution process or outside of it) are also able to exercise a degree of control over the services provided by virtue of their status as consumers. Thus, for example, users of shopping malls and purchasers of homes within gated communities as well as people whose medical services are subsidised by state-financed health care are able, through their purchasing power, to express their preferences and shape the way services are provided (Bayley and Shearing 1996).

While it is difficult to obtain systematic data to support the following claim, the evidence suggests that the growing 'wealth' disparity between the rich and the poor is associated with a growing 'governance disparity' (McGrew 2000). One feature of this disparity is the relative inability of those without purchasing power to direct, and hence render accountable, service delivery. This is very obvious in the security sector, where those with purchasing power are able to extend and strengthen their 'security quilt' (Ericson 1994) by engaging, directing and tailoring service delivery. In addition, as many state policing services now provide services on a user-fee basis over and above their general services, wealthier persons and corporate entities can purchase these services in addition to the ones to which they are entitled as 'citizens'. Again, this enables them to extend service provision and to exercise greater direction and control over the way in which these services are provided. Poor people, on the other hand, are for the most part excluded from these market-based arrangements in their capacity as '"flawed consumers" who are unwilling or unable to be seduced by the market' (Loader 1999: 384; also in Huggins 2000: 128). Those 'unwilling or unable' to engage as 'citizen consumers' (Lacey 1994) are thus structurally excluded from opportunities to direct or 'steer' service delivery.

A second feature of the governance deficit is the extent to which poor people are subject to forms of coercion and banishment by a range of agencies that operate in the interests of other collectivities or denizenships. As individuals who are unable or unwilling to live up to the expectations and responsibilities ascribed to certain forms of communal space – such as shopping malls or Business Improvement Districts – poor people are largely unable to gain the status of 'denizen' within such spaces. Having been excluded from such 'bubbles of governance' (Bottoms and Wiles 1995; Rigakos and Greener 2000; Shearing 1997), these individuals are left to live and work in spaces surrounding the bubbles (Shearing 1999), spaces within which increasingly cash-strapped public police tend to devote their resources (see Bayley and Shearing 1996).

Even more, those unable to purchase basic goods and services, like food and shelter, tend to live in spaces surrounding these bubbles, including 'conduit spaces' (Shearing 1999) like parks and roadways, or 'communities of fate' (Sutcliffe 1996) like squatter camp settlements or shanty towns. Such communities are a ubiquitous feature of developing countries like South Africa and Brazil, and their members are routinely subject to brutal forms of violence by a range of governmental agents. Huggins discusses the Brazilian context:

> Wealthier neighborhoods not only have more police...they also hire private security guards to protect their social spaces against 'illegitimate' entry by, or the lingering presence of, those seen as 'noncitizens'. In contrast, while the 'noncitizen' poor are rarely protected by the state's social control system, they have learned to expect violent periodic Militarized Police lightning raids into their shanty towns, punctuated regularly by death squad murders, lone-wolf 'justice-maker' killings, and lynch mob assassinations. This social control structure of formal police, 'rent-a-cops,' death squads, lone-wolf 'justice-maker' killers, and lynch mobs suggests a world no longer neatly divisible between public and private space and public and private property. (2000: 121)

The people who live and work in these underprivileged communities are individuals whose denizenship is shaped 'by fate' more than 'by choice', and this is largely due to their lack of buying power and hence their lack of control over governance budgets (in this case, the budgets for security). As argued previously (Shearing 2001b), ownership of security budgets necessarily determines the nature of governance strategies and technologies and, accordingly, the kind of agents, capacities and resources required for their implementation. For instance, security budgets owned by states are largely allocated to state institutions, and in particular the police and the criminal justice system. As such, it is the central capacities of the police and the criminal justice system – that is, the capacity for coercion and banishment – that are privileged within state-owned forms of communal space.

Furthermore, security budgets that are owned by corporations tend to be allocated to services and products available in the marketplace, ranging from 'rent-a-cops' to surveillance devices. Of note is that these services and products also provide the capacity for coercion and banishment, a capacity that is wielded in particular towards those without denizenship status in these spaces (Huggins 2000). On the other hand, those who are denizens (that is, members of these communities 'of choice') tend to be subject to strategies and technologies of governance that are subtle, embedded, risk-oriented and less explicitly coercive (see Shearing and Stenning 1985). Indeed, it is in the interests of these corporate nodes to seduce members into compliance in order to secure their continuing denizenship (Rose 1989).

What our analysis suggests is that, while markets – and the neo-liberal sensibility that supports them – appear to have hastened and deepened the governance deficit, it is not so much market mechanisms broadly understood as it is access to purchasing power and budget ownership that is the source of the problem. A focus on purchasing power rather than markets provides a basis for distinguishing the features of markets that have proved harmful to poor people from those that they could benefit from if they had access to them. This analysis makes sense within the framework we have outlined. Denizenship is very much a matter of access through purchasing power. To be a denizen of a recreational facility like a gym, a university or a residential gated community depends on one's ability to buy one's way into these communal spaces unless they are completely publicly supported, in which case one gains access as a matter of right but not by virtue of purchasing power.

This focus on purchasing power rather than markets as a basis for accessing auspices of governance and communal spaces as a denizen suggests a normative stance that can be taken in addressing the governance deficit. This stance seeks to blend features of market-based governing mechanisms with a feature of Keynesian economics – namely, the use of tax resources to promote economies for enhancing self-direction and 'thickening' collective capital. The specific strategy we will outline seeks to utilise tax resources to promote economic activity within the informal or fourth sectors in ways that will provide poor communities with purchasing power, and hence choice and self-direction in service delivery. What we have in mind here resonates with Bond's (2002: 9) advocacy of a local economic development strategy that seeks to ensure that 'the most needy' are 'active partici-pants in new developments with the capacity to plan, monitor and enforce wider benefits' through 'institutions such as community development trusts and worker or community-controlled enterprises such as local credit unions or development corporations'.

A programme for deepening democracy

Katherine Rankin (2001: 33) has recently called for a similar response that would move governance research beyond a descriptive account of the consequences of neo-liberalism and associated trends in governance towards the development of a normative stance with programmatic proposals for deepening democratic values (see also O'Malley, Weir and Shearing 1997; O'Malley, forthcoming). In thinking about how to go about developing such a stance it is important to respond in a manner that moves beyond a 'simple dismissal' (see especially Rose 1996: 353) of the mentality associated with neo-liberalism we have outlined to one that recognises that what this mentality means in practice can, and does, vary significantly. If this normative stance is adopted it requires looking anew at the Hayekian claim that governance is best exercised when it relies on local direction, knowledges and capacities and recognising that this is not the same as saying that governance can and must be exercised through 'free market mechanisms' (which of course are never free – Shearing 1993) as these are understood by institutions such as the World Bank and the International Monetary Fund. Such markets may mobilise and focus dispersed knowledges and capacities but these are not typical of those found in poor communities. Indeed, as so many commentators have made clear, they tend to do precisely the opposite (Alexander 2002). This is Bond's (2002) point when he contrasts orthodox local economic development with what he terms a 'developmental' approach to LED. It is also Terreblanche's (2002: 446) point when he argues that while the South African Reconstruction and Development Programme was based on sound principles (ones that required a thriving private sector to be integrated with the 'active involvement of all sectors of civil society') the government 'made a huge mistake' when it allowed a 'powerful corporate sector to co-opt it in implementing a liberal capitalist version of democratic capitalism' in which the economy is 'entrusted to "free market mechanisms"'.

Because this distinction between values and implementation strategies is seldom developed in critiques of neo-liberal sensibilities and associated modes of governance, critics have too often thrown the baby out with the bathwater in rejecting not only the particular ways in which these Hayekian ideas have been realised, but in rejecting the ideas themselves. This is nicely illustrated in the movement to 'reinvent government' associated with Osborne and Gaebler's book by the same name (1993) which claims to be grounded in Hayekian ideals. In considering these and similar developments it is important to recognise the obvious, but all too often neglected, point that such proposals do not flow from the Hayekian principles in the same way as Euclidean theorems are derived from their axioms. There are many different ways in which to interpret these and similar ideas about how to focus and mobilise local knowledge and capacity. Some of these ways can and sometimes do enhance the self-direction of poor communities. When implemented through processes that are not controlled by poor communities, it is not surprising to find that they seldom do.

It does not take much scrutiny to realise that Osborne and Gaebler's proposals, along with those of others who have promoted the devolution and privatisation of governance functions, are not designed to enhance the self-direction of local, and more especially poor, collectivities in a significant way. In their insistence that the 'rowing', but not the 'steering', of governance be devolved, it is quite clear that they seek to enhance the centralisation of control and the influence of those who dominate central processes, while devolving implementation. While this might be seen as maintaining existing democratic controls over governmental functions – and reasserting the ideal of representative democracy – it can hardly be seen as deepening democracy through the enhancement of local self-direction.

It is vital not to conflate what most disadvantaged communities, in our experience, regard as sensible general values (in particular the importance of local steering and capacity) with particular programmes that claim to implement them that promote inequality and are not pro-poor. This leads to a situation in which sound values are rejected because they can be, and often are, used to justify programmes that either do not realise them or do so in ways that violate other equally important values (Shearing 1997).

In what follows we will briefly outline an attempt to develop a programme of 'local capacity governance' that seeks to uncouple the general values that support governance that mobilises diverse knowledges and capacities, from particular applications that are associated with the sorts of deficits we have identified – what a South African writer (Alexander 2002: 171) identifies as the 'barbaric effects of neo-liberal economic policies and practices'. This programme was developed in South Africa in a black 'township' called Zwelethemba (a Xhosa word that means 'place of hope') on the outskirts of a country town about a two-hour drive from Cape Town. The model of local capacity governance developed in Zwelethemba by 2000 has since been 'rolled out' to some twenty communities (mostly in informal housing settlements) in three provinces.[4] Its transferability to Argentina is now being explored in two pilot sites in Rosario (one primarily made up of informal housing, the other with a mixture of formal and informal housing).[5] The Zwelethemba model embraces the values of democracy as well as selected features of what O'Malley (1996, above) identified as neo-liberal governing sensibilities such as the importance of local knowledges and capacities to the governing processes, market-related approaches to service delivery and a risk focus that looks to the future rather than the past in resolving problems. These elements are mixed with a Keynesian sensibility that seeks to direct tax resources into local collectivities to promote a demand that local entrepreneurs can be encouraged to fulfil (see Braithwaite (2000) generally on the need to retrieve Keynesian virtues).

Very briefly, the model creates Peace Committees, made up of local persons, to whom local community members bring interpersonal disputes. After meeting with disputants, members of Peace Committees invite members of the community who they believe have the knowledge and capacity to contribute towards a resolution of the dispute to a Gathering in which a future-focused, non-coercive solution is agreed upon. Gatherings operate in accordance with a set of procedures and a Code of Good Practice that centres on respect for human rights and lawful conduct (see Shearing 2000).

For every gathering held in accordance with procedures and according to the Code of Good Practice a sum of money (at present Rand 200[6]) is provided to the Peace Committee

[4] The development of the model was supported by the Swedish Government through the Raoul Wallenberg Institute, Lund University. The extension phase of the project is supported by the Finnish Government through their embassy in South Africa.
[5] This programme in Argentina is supported by the Canadian International Development Agency through its Transfer of Technology Program.
[6] At the time or writing one US dollar equals approximately 8 Rands.

for the work they have done by local governments – 'in your pocket' monies. This sum is matched by a further R200 that provides for a fund to be spent on community development initiatives that respond to generic developmental issues in the community through the use of future-focused solutions that, where possible, mobilise local entrepreneurs as service providers. Just what generic issues are to be addressed and how they are to be addressed are also decided upon in gatherings to which members of the community thought to have the knowledge and capacity to provide ideas and solutions are invited. The programmes supported by this 'peace-building' range from infrastructural projects, such as building a children's playground, to supporting sports teams. The model favours programmes that utilise the resources of local entrepreneurs.

This model seeks to shift both the steering and the rowing of governance to local persons through a market-like mechanism that channels tax resources to local people for future-focused solutions to governmental issues on an outcome-oriented basis. This outcome-based payment system is an important distinguishing feature of this model. As the peace-building money is earned along with the 'in your pocket' money, it is spent with considerable caution and frugality as these monies 'belong' to the Committees.

Although this model, in its dispute resolution aspect, bears a family resemblance to other dispute resolution processes such as mediation and restorative justice, its future emphasis and lack of professional involvement give it a distinctive character (Roche 2002). In addition, while the model operates through the window of security, as a convenient way of mobilising local capacity and knowledge, it is designed and operates as a generic programme of local capacity governance.

Just as the model differs in significant ways from other dispute resolution approaches, to which it bears a family resemblance, so too does it differ from other mechanisms, such as the micro-lending models associated with institutions such as the Grameen Bank (Todd 1996; Rankin 2001). Whereas such conventional loans approaches provide capital in the form of micro-loans, the Zwelethemba model seeks to use tax resources to promote micro-markets in ways that will enable local entrepreneurs to build and manage their businesses. This resonates with Bond's (2002: 9–11) support for local economic development strategies that 'make a commitment to supporting': 'community-based development' in which 'municipal assistance is directed at the grassroots'; the 'development and maintenance of infrastructure and services'; mechanisms that 'stem the outflow of money from poor areas by encouraging people to buy local, supporting and building periodic markets, funding special events and festivals, providing infrastructure using local labour' and 'networking enterprises … in the local area'; and 'the retention and expansion of existing businesses'.

Conclusion

The three conceptual pillars of nodal governance, denizens and communal spaces form an integral part of the Zwelethemba model and its rationale. Each Peace Committee constitutes a governmental node that operates to mobilise denizens of local collectivities to govern the communal spaces common to them. The locally based explorations that led to the development of the Zwelethemba model seek, in Rankin's (2001: 33) words, a 'foundation for articulating a political rationality from the standpoint of the oppressed and for challenging the reigning neo-liberal ideology'. It does so in a way that does not treat this 'ideology' as something to be taken or discarded as a whole but rather as a complex assemblage of ideas and practices that should be disassembled and then drawn upon in creating new assemblages that seek to respond to the concerns and objectives of the 'oppressed'.

The central task of this chapter has been to articulate a normative vision and practical plan that recognises the key features of contemporary developments in governance. In doing so it recognises that alongside the reinvention of state governance new governing auspices and technologies within non-state sectors have emerged. We have argued that in order to understand, and where necessary, to reshape these developments it is necessary to move beyond a state-based conception of governance and to move beyond the conceptual blindness that this has induced.

Much work remains to be done in understanding the implications of nodal governance for the promotion of democratic values and outcomes, particularly for marginalised communities. We have begun to identify some of these implications and to develop a normative response to them. Our central focus in this regard was the growing governance disparity that is paralleling the growing wealth disparity across the globe. A prominent feature of this governance disparity is the lack of self-direction on the part of poor denizens in the promotion of collective security and well-being. In response to this, we argue for an agenda that redirects tax resources directly into the hands of poor people so that they may mobilise the local capacities and resources required to improve the quality of their denizenship.

References

Alexander, Neville (2002), *An Ordinary Country*, Durban: University of Natal Press.

Archibugi, Daniele and David Held (1995), *Cosmopolitan Democracy: an Agenda for a New World Order*, Cambridge, MA: Polity Press.

Bayley, David and Clifford Shearing (1996), 'The Future of Policing', *Law and Society Review*, 30(3): 585–606.

Bayley, David and Clifford Shearing (2001), *The New Structure of Policing: Description, Conceptualization, Agenda*, National Institute of Justice.

Bond, Patrick (2001a), 'Reflections from South Africa: Breaking the Chains of Global Apartheid.' *International Socialist Review* 19 (July–August). http://www.internationalsocialist.org/publications.shtml

—— (2001b), *Against Global Apartheid*, Cape Town, South Africa: University of Cape Town Press.

—— (2002), 'Local Economic Development Debates in South Africa', Municipal Services Project, Occasional Papers 6: 1–27.

Bottoms, Anthony and Paul Wiles (1995), 'Crime and Insecurity in the City', in Cyrille Finjaut, Johan Goethals, Tony Peters and Lode Walgrave (eds), *Changes in Society, Crime and Criminal Justice in Europe*, The Hague: Kluwer Law International, Vol. 1.

Braithwaite, John (2000), 'The New Regulatory State and the Transformation of Criminology', *British Journal of Criminology*, 40: 222–38.

Brogden, Mike and Clifford Shearing (1993), *Policing For a New South Africa*, London: Routledge.

Ellickson, R. (1991), *Order Without Law*, Cambridge, MA: Harvard University Press.

Ericson, Richard (1994), 'The Division of Expert Knowledge in Policing and Security', *British Journal of Sociology*, 45: 149–75.

Falk, Richard (1999), *Predatory Globalisation: A Critique*, Cambridge: Polity Press.

Fonseka, Leo (1999), Good Urban Governance (Draft Document: 1 August), mimeo.

Garland, David (1996), 'The Limits of the Sovereign State: Strategies of Crime Control in Contemporary Society', *British Journal of Criminology*, 36(4): 445–71.

Grabosky, Peter N. (1992), 'Law Enforcement and the Citizen: Non-Governmental Participants in Crime Prevention and Control', *Policing and Society*, 2: 249–71.

—— (1994), 'Beyond the Regulatory State', *The Australian and New Zealand Journal of Criminology*, 27: 192–7.

—— (forthcoming) 'Private Sponsorship of Public Policing' (author's draft, cited with permission).

Held, David, Anthony McGrew, David Goldblatt and Jonathan Perraton (1999), *Global Transformations: Politics, Economics and Culture*, Stanford, CA: Stanford University Press.

Hermer, Joe, Michael Kempa, Clifford Shearing, Philip Stenning, and Jennifer Wood (2002), *Policing in Canada in the 21st Century: Directions for Law Reform: A Socio-Legal Analysis*, Ottawa: Law Commission of Canada.

Hillyard, Paddy (1993), 'Paramilitary Policing and Popular Justice in Northern Ireland', in M. Findlay and U. Zvekic (eds), *Alternative Policing Styles: Cross Cultural Perspectives*, Deventer/Boston: Kluwer Law and Taxation Publishers, pp. 139–56.

—— (1997) 'Policing Divided Societies: Trends and Prospects in Northern Ireland and Britain,' in Peter Francis, Pamela Davies and Victor Jupp (eds), *Policing Futures: The Police, Law Enforcement and the Twenty-First Century*, London: Macmillan; New York: St. Martin's Press, pp. 163–85.

Hirst, Paul (1994), *Associative Democracy: New Forms of Economic and Social Governance*, Amherst: The University of Massachusetts Press.

Hobbes, Thomas (1968 [1651]), *Leviathan*, edited with an introduction by Crawford Brough Macpherson. Harmondsworth: Penguin.

Huggins, Martha K. (2000), 'Urban Violence and Police Privatization in Brazil: Blended Invisibility', *Social Justice*, 27(2): 113–34.

Irish, Jenny (1999), *Policing For Profit: The Future of South Africa's Private Security Industry*, Halfway House South Africa: Institute for Security Studies (Institute for Security Studies Monograph Series No. 39).

Johnston, Les (1992), *The Re-Birth of Private Policing*, London: Routledge.

—— (2000), *Policing Britiain: Risk, Security and Governance*, Harlow: Longman.

Johnston, Les and Clifford Shearing (2003), *Policing Diversity*, London: Routledge.

Jones, Trevor and Tim Newburn (1998), *Private Security and Public Policing*, Oxford: Clarendon Press.

Kempa, Michael, Ryan Carrier, Jennifer Wood and Clifford Shearing (1999), 'Reflections on the Evolving Concept of "Private Policing"', *European Journal on Criminal Policy and Research*, 7(2): 197–224.

Krasner, Stephen D. (ed.) (2001), *Problematic Sovereignty: Contested Rules and Political Possibilities*, New York: Columbia University Press.

Lacey, N. (1994), 'Government as Manager, Citizen as Consumer: The Case of the Criminal Justice Act 1991', *Modern Legal Review*, 57 (July): 534–54.

Loader, Ian (1999), 'Consumer Culture and the Commodification of Policing and Security', *Sociology*, 33(2) 373–92.

Macauley, Stuart (1986), 'Private Government', in L. Lipson and S. Wheeler (eds), *Law and the Social Sciences*, New York: Russell Sage Foundation.

McGrew, Anthony (2000), 'Power Shift: From National Government to Global Governance?' in David Held (ed.), *A Globalizing World? Culture, Economics, Politics*, London and New York: Routledge, pp. 127–66.

New Shorter Oxford English Dictionary Volume 1 (A–M) (1993), Oxford: Clarendon Press.

Nina, D. and S. Russell (1997), 'Policing "By Any Means Necessary": Reflections on Privatisation, Human Rights and Police Issues – Considerations for Australia and South Africa', *Australian Journal of Human Rights* 3(2) available online: http://www.austlii.edu.au/au/journals/AJHR/#52.

O'Malley, Pat (1992), 'Risk, Power and Crime Prevention', *Economy and Society*, 21(3): 252–75.

O'Malley, Pat and Darren Palmer (1996), 'Post-Keynesian Policing', *Economy and Society*, 25(2): 137–55.

—— (1996), 'Indigenous Governance', *Economy and Society*, 25(3): 310–26.

O'Malley, Pat, Lorna Weir and Clifford Shearing (1997), 'Governmentality, Criticism, Politics', *Economy and Society*, 26(4): 501–17.

—— (2004) 'The Uncertain Promise of Risk', *The Australian and New Zealand Journal of Criminology*, 37: 323–43.

Osborne, David and Thomas Gaebler (1993), *Reinventing Government*, New York: Plume.

Putnam, Robert D. (2000), *Bowling Alone: The Collapse and Revival of American Community*, New York: Simon and Schuster.

Rankin, Katherine N. (2001), 'Governing Development: Neoliberaism, Microcredit, and the Rational Economic Woman', *Economy and Society*, 30(1): 18–37.

Rigakos, George and David Greener (2000), 'Bubbles of Governance: Private Policing and the Law in Canada', *Canadian Journal of Law and Society*, 15(1): 145–84.

Roche, Declan (2002), 'Restorative Justice and the Regulatory State in South African Townships', *British Journal of Criminology*, 42(30): 514–33.

Rose, Nikolas (1989), *Governing the Soul*, London and New York: Free Association Books.

—— (1996), 'The Death of the Social? Refiguring the Territory of Government', *Economy and Society*, 25(3): 327–56.

Schönteich, M. (2000), 'Fighting Crime With Private Muscle: The Private Sector and Crime Prevention', *African*

Security Review, 8(5), available online: http://www.iss.co.za/Pubs/ASR/8No5/ Contents.html

Scott, Colin (2001), 'Analysing Regulatory Space: Fragmented Resources and Institutional Design', Public Law, Summer: 329–53.

Shearing, Clifford (1993), 'A Constitutive Conception of Regulation' in P. Grabosky and J. Braithwaite (eds), Business Regulation and Australia's Future, Canberra: Australian Institute of Criminology.

—— (1995), 'Reinventing Policing: Policing As Governance', in Privatisierung staatlicher kontrolle: Betunde, konzepte, tendenzen, Baden Baden: Nomos Verlagsgesellschaft.

—— (1997), 'Unrecognized Origins of the New Policing: Linkage Between Private and Public Policing', in Marcus Felson and Ronald V. Clarke (eds), Business and Crime Prevention, Monsey, NY: Criminal Justice Press, pp. 219–30.

—— (1999), 'Remarks of Professor Clifford Shearing' [on Zero Tolerance Policing], Criminal Law Buelletin, 35(4): 378–83.

—— (2000), 'Transforming Security: A South African Experiment', John Braithwaite and Heather Strang (eds), Restorative Justice and Civil Society, Cambridge: Cambridge University Press, pp. 14–34.

—— (2001a), 'A Nodal Conception of Governance: Thoughts on a Policing Commission', Policing and Society 11:259-72.

—— (2001b), 'The Most Critical Unresolved Issue Associated With Contemporary Democratic Policing', in S. Einstein and M. Amir (eds), Policing, Security and Democracy: Special Aspects of 'Democratic policing', Huntsville, TX: Office of International Criminal Justice.

Shearing, Clifford and Philip Stenning (1983), 'Private Security: Implications for Social Control', Social Problems, 30(5): 493–506.

Shearing, Clifford and Philip Stenning (1985), 'From the Panopticon to Disney World: The Development of Discipline', in A.N. Doob and E.L. Greenspan (eds), Perspectives in Criminal law: Essays in honour of John Ll.J. Edwards, Toronto: Canada Law Book Inc., pp. 335–49.

Shearing, Clifford and Jennifer Wood (2000), 'Reflections on the Governance of Security: A Normative Inquiry.' Police Practice 1(4): 457–76.

Sheptycki, J.W.E. (ed.) (2000), Issues in Transnational Policing, London: Routledge.

Sutcliffe, Michael (1996), 'The Fragmented City: Durban, South Africa', International Social Science Journal 147: 67–72.

Swol, Karen (1998), 'Private Security and Public Policing in Canada', Juristat 18(3) (Ottawa: Statistics Canada, Canadian Centre for Justice Statistics).

Terreblanche, Sampie (2002), A History of South Africa 1652–2002, Durban: Natal University Press.

Todd, Helen (1996), Cloning the Grameen Bank: Replicating a Poverty Reduction Model in India, Nepal and Vietnam, London: IT Publications.

Turner, Bryan S (2001), 'The Erosion of Citizen', British Journal of Sociology, 52 (2 June): 189–209.

von Hirsch, Andrew and Clifford Shearing (2000), 'Exclusion from Public Space', in Andrew von Hirsch, David Garland and Alison Wakefield (eds), Ethical and Social Perspectives on Situational Crime Prevention, Oxford: Hart, pp. 77–96.

Walzer, Michael (1994), Thick and Thin: Moral Argument at Home and Abroad, Notre Dame, Indiana: Notre Dame.

Wood, Jennifer (2000), Reinventing Governance: A Case Study of Transformations in the Ontario Provincial Police, Toronto: Centre of Criminology, University of Toronto.

Wood, Jennifer and Clifford Shearing (1999), 'Reinventing Intellectuals', Canadian Journal of Criminology, April: 311–20.

Legal Case Cited

Entick v. Carrington (1765) 19 St. Tr. 1029, at 1029.

6

Political Inventions & Interventions
A Critical Review of the Proposed
City Development Strategy Partnership in Cape Town

EDGAR PIETERSE[1]

Today we face two problems, related to one another in complex ways, often difficult to separate from one another: how to get away from certain utopian or transgressive images of thought – or the 'future' of thought – and envisage other modes of critical intervention and critical analysis; and how to develop a new conception or image of cities, their shapes, their distinctive problems, the ways in which they figure in our being and being-together, the manner in which they acquire their identities within and among us – an image that would still allow for the play of critical invention and intervention. (John Rachman 1998: 108–9)

A new wave of reform on partnership-based urban governance is currently dominating the urban development landscape and unleashing a world-wide programme of policy intervention. The discourse is captured by the new buzzword in policy circles – CDS, which is an acronym for City Development Strategy. This discourse is a continuation and extension of earlier discourses – good urban governance and decentralisation (Carley *et al.* 2001). The CDS discourse reflects the increasing importance attached to city-wide economic planning and management by public agencies (in conjunction with the private sector and civil society) and the rise of strategic planning as an organisational development tool to improve the managerial and political management capability of local authorities. Significantly, the CDS discourse featured centrally in the reform plans of Cape Town as the city moved from a two-tier local government system to a single, unitary metropolitan authority after the municipal elections in December 2000. In this chapter I explore the thinking behind this new policy refrain, CDS, and in particular explore the implications of the approach for the establishment of a transformative, radical political agenda in urban politics in metropolitan Cape Town.

The new local government dispensation in South Africa heralded by the December 2000 municipal elections represents a qualitatively different and important political opportunity. New political spaces can be constructed in South African cities through strategic engagement across a plurality of fronts, cohering coalitions of progressive actors.

[1] I want to acknowledge the generous and supportive input I received from Mirjam van Donk, Kirsten Harrison, Sue Parnell, Steven Robins, Jenny Robinson and Samantha Yates in preparing the chapter. I remain solely responsible for the argument.

This unprecedented opportunity is inscribed in the legislative framework that underpins municipal government in South Africa. It is further embedded in the recent policy reforms promoted by the Unicity Commission in Cape Town. However, translating these 'policy opportunities' into material and symbolic constructs will require a very different political strategy from that currently the norm amongst actors that seek to fundamentally alter the nature of the city. Past political strategies, weak organisational capability and pessimistic readings of urban futures add up to a reactive, visionless politics that is incapable of challenging powerful vested interests that are by design and default shaping the futures (and histories) of Cape Town. Advancing a new progressive politics requires: a) a strategic appreciation of new governance opportunities (and pitfalls); b) new alliances across class and cultural boundaries; c) seizing or, at least, destabilising those arenas where discourses about the future are produced; and d) building a political culture and sensibility that is fundamentally pluralistic, non-essentialist, outward-looking and open-ended (Pieterse 1997 and forthcoming). The transition to the establishment of the single city, embodied in the Cape Town Unicity Municipality (hereafter Unicity), presents a unique opportunity to construct a new politics simultaneously at the city and neighbourhood scale, despite the coalition of vested interests that won the elections through the Democratic Alliance[2] machinery.

One entry point for building a new politics in Cape Town is the proposed CDS Partnership that will entail a municipal driven initiative to establish a city development partnership along the lines currently being promoted by the World Bank, United Nations Council on Human Settlements (UNCHS) and the Cities Alliance (GHK 2000). Significantly, this proposed dialogical forum – the CDS Partnership – can be a force for entrenching vested interests or a platform to advance a redistributive agenda in the city. Through appreciating the malleability of this forum I argue that it can become a site of transformation. Such progressive potential is contingent on the mobilisation of various other political energies – direct action, development politics and discursive interventions.

To ground the essay, I explore the emergence of the CDS discourse in the context of the Unicity Commission recommendations prepared for the elected Unicity of Cape Town. Thus, in the first section of the chapter I briefly explain the origins, mandate, recommendations and significance of the Unicity Commission. This political body was charged with formulating detailed recommendations before the elections for consideration and adoption by the elected Unicity. The second section explains what the CDS is in general and how it emerged in Cape Town in order to lay the basis for exploring the significance of the CDS methodology as a process of visioning and planning.[3]

[2] The Democratic Alliance is a new political party that is an alliance between three national political parties: the Democratic Party, the New National Party (NNP) and the Federal Alliance. All three are traditionally white parties that reflect, respectively, a right-of-centre liberal orientation, a religious right-of-centre orientation and a right-wing conservative approach. It was formed after the last general election in 1999 to constitute a more substantial opposition block to the ruling party, the African National Congress (ANC). The move has generally consolidated race-based divisions in South African society and politics (Nijzink and Jabobs 2000). However, in November 2001 the NNP decided to withdraw from the alliance and explore a cooperative arrangement with the ANC. As a result, the NNP and the ANC now govern the Western Cape Province under a cooperative agreement and this formula was repeated at the Unicity level after 'floor-crossing' legislation came into effect in September 2002.

[3] This chapter focuses on policy discourses of the Unicity Commission, which functioned during 2000. In the first two years of terms of office (2001/2) of the elected City of Cape Town municipality, the CDS discourse was not taken up by the new municipality as part of a political decision to jettison most of the recommendations

The third section moves in a more theoretical direction by drawing mainly on urban planning debates between the communicative and political economy schools of thought to explore the potential political 'use-value' of the CDS methodology as a participative process. These ongoing debates in the planning literature are relevant because they are centrally concerned with the modalities of creating favourable conditions in democratic systems to engender social justice through urban planning interventions. However, the imaginary and reference points of these debates have mainly been first world cities and their material basis that makes rational intervention viable. In working with this literature it is crucial to recognise that those third world cities, such as Cape Town, where the CDS approach will be promoted are not so easily manageable are capable of being planned. In cities of the South, urban productivity and dynamism tend to function through multiple registers of governance, economy and sociality that can be summarised, somewhat clumsily, as informal (Halfani 1996; Werna 2001). I therefore take care to foreground the constitutive nature of informality in Cape Town in teasing out the political relevance of CDS. This is done in the fourth section of the chapter.

The chapter culminates in section five in a discussion on what a radical political agenda and approach may add up to under the new local government dispensation in South Africa and similar contexts. Since CDSs are of growing importance in cities throughout the world (Freire and Stren 2001), this study also seeks to add to an ongoing debate about using multi-actor institutional forums to animate and transform urban politics. These linkages are not drawn explicitly but the location of the analysis in a broader urban planning literature facilitates such cross-fertilisation.

New times, new politics?[4]

New political times arrived with the complete eradication of racially based local government after the municipal elections in December 2000. Prior to the first democratic local government elections held in May 1996, the Cape Metropolitan Area (CMA) was governed by forty appointed local authorities that worked through nineteen separate administrations. The 1996 local government elections saw the establishment of a two-tier metropolitan government system with six autonomous local authorities and a 'weak' (policy and co-ordinative) metropolitan authority (Cameron 2000). The same CMA region became the juridical territory of the Unicity after the local government elections on 5 December 2000. The Unicity Commission was a statutory body charged with the responsibility of preparing detailed recommendations for the incoming Unicity to ensure a smooth transition process from seven distinct municipalities to one municipality for the CMA. The previous seven municipal councils combined comprised 26,000 staff and a cumulative annual budget of R8.5 billion (U$1.2 billion in rand value of 2000) in 1999/2000, of

[3] (cont.) of the Unicity Commission. This changed dramatically towards the middle of 2002 when a CDS Task Team was established towards the implementation of a participatory process to define a CDS for Cape Town. With the uncertainty after the floor-crossing legislation came into effect, this process was delayed again. The CDS planning process remains rudimentary at the time of writing.

[4] This section draws heavily on a paper in *Urban Forum* that sets out the national context that framed the emergence of Unicities in South Africa and the various recommendations made by the Unicity Commission, with a special emphasis on the prospects of new governance mechanisms (Pieterse 2002).

which approximately 22 per cent was allocated for capital expenditure to address mainly the severe backlogs in African and Coloured residential areas. Working out the logistics of amalgamating these seven organisations, sustaining service delivery and rolling out a substantial capital investment programme in a highly charged labour relations environment has proven to be a massively complex undertaking and inevitably riven with conflict. Nonetheless, it was agreed that the Unicity Commission would not restrict itself to preparing transition plans to ensure uninterrupted provision of services, but would also develop a five-year service delivery and financial plan to enable the new council to 'hit the ground running' as quickly as possible. According to the independent chairperson of the Commission, the transition had to be about *transformation* as opposed to transition. This referred to a strategic perspective of the Unicity Commission that new policies, systems and strategies had to be implemented as rapidly as possible to avoid staff becoming complacent and resistant to radical change (interview with N. McLachlan, 2 February 2001).

Legally, the Unicity Commission was mandated to fulfil six tasks:

- Advise the Provincial Minister on the transition to a Unicity, including: a) disestablishment of the seven councils; and b) establishment of the Unicity;
- Protect the integrity of the Unicity, especially with regard to financial management and maintenance of assets;
- Design a five-year term-of-office plan (an integrated development plan (IDP)), including budgets and service delivery strategies for the Unicity;
- Design arrangements to ensure initial smooth functioning of the Unicity, especially uninterrupted delivery of municipal services;
- Consult and negotiate with employees and unions;
- Communicate with all stakeholders (internal and external), including municipal employees (www.unicomcapetown.gov.za).

The most salient aspect of this agenda was the design of the 'term-of-office IDP'. It required that the Unicity Commission prepared detailed proposals around four policy themes: a) the provisional city development strategy; b) a metropolitan governance model; c) a service delivery strategy; and d) a medium-term (five-year) income and expenditure model. The policy proposals of the Unicity Commission were premised on a very general consensus amongst decision-makers, advisers and key stakeholder groupings that the long-term vision and plans for Cape Town were required to address: global competitiveness, eradication of poverty, sustainability (financial and environmental) and good governance (www.unicomcapetown.gov.za). The precise meanings of these notions were never clearly spelt out.

The proposals contained in the Unicity Commission's final report to the Unicity presented a range of opportunities for civil society organisations (CSOs) to influence and shape the agenda of the transformation process. One set of opportunities revolved around democratic participation in the public and political spheres to influence the content of the political agenda of the newly elected Unicity and a second set pertains to opportunities to become involved in different types of service delivery partnerships at neighbourhood and locality levels. These two dimensions were conceptualised as fundamentally interrelated and mutually reinforcing in order to feed a transformative agenda (White and Robinson

1998). It is beyond the scope of this chapter to unpack and explore the range of specific participation and partnership opportunities available to civil society organisations (see Pieterse 2002). Suffice to say, the CDS is one aspect of a much larger governance framework aimed at stimulating participatory democracy and responsive local government. However, as the vast literature on participatory local governance and decentralisation suggests, the multitude of 'new' governance techniques turn on the quality and capacity of agency within civil society, and especially amongst the poor (Cooke and Kothari 2001; Edmunds and Wollenberg 2001; White and Robinson 1998). Now that I have briefly sketched the emerging political matrix of municipal reform in Cape Town, I want to delve deeper into the political significance of the proposed CDS process.

Dialogical forums: cul-de-sac or strategic path?

Stakeholder-based urban governance and dialogical forums
The Unicity Commission decided at the outset that it wanted to use the transition process as an opportunity to put long-term strategic planning on the agenda of municipal government in order to expunge the short-term mentality in local government (interview with N. McLachlan, 2 February 2001). The 'short-termism' that characterises municipal government in South Africa is related to the legal–institutional legacy of municipal reform since the Act of Union in 1910 (Cameron 1995) and, more recently, to the profound uncertainty in local government during the last ten years due to perpetual, even if essential, restructuring processes (Cameron 1999). The Unicity Commission identified this deeply ingrained institutional culture as detrimental to the strategic political management function of the incoming Unicity in its pursuance of global competitiveness, poverty reduction, sustainability and good governance. After a delegation of the Unicity Commission attended the 'Second World Competitive Cities Congress' (organised by the World Bank) in Washington DC, it was agreed that the CDS methodology would be explored as a mechanism to shift the short-term institutional culture and lay the basis for institutionalising strategic planning into municipal governance and urban planning.[5]

The Unicity Commission embraced this new policy approach in its own deliberations and recommendations. However, since the central tenet of a CDS process is a carefully designed and protracted process of stakeholder and community consultation/participation, it was inopportune to initiate a CDS process proper (see GHK Group 2000). Instead, the Unicity Commission decided to make the CDS a central recommendation and proceeded to recommend an institutional mechanism to drive the process after the elections, if the incoming Unicity accepted the approach. Specifically, the Unicity Commission recommended to the democratically elected Unicity Council the following:

> 1.3.1 That the council agrees to initiate a city development strategy/partnership process to enable the development and implementation of a shared agenda for the city.

[5] The delegates were impressed by the debates at the conference on CDS as a methodology to involve a broader range of stakeholders in urban governance and proceeded to invite one of the leading experts on CDS processes, who spoke at the conference, to come to Cape Town. The expert, Dr Nicholas Miles (based in London), presented the findings of international experiences to the Unicity Commission and other politicians and officials participating in the Unicity Commission process. I facilitated this workshop on 21 July 2000.

1.3.2 The CDS process be co-owned by the Council, other government agencies, parastatals, the private sector, the academic sector, labour and civil society. To this end, that mechanisms to ensure such co-ownership be established and that a single ownership structure must be created to act as custodian of the process on behalf of the city (Unicity Commission 2000: 19).

These recommendations amount to a proposal to involve all the stakeholders in the city in a comprehensive city visioning exercise, similar to metropolitan strategic planning initiatives such as the iGoli 2010 partnership initiative in Johannesburg (GJMC 2000) and earlier efforts in cities such as Barcelona, Toronto, and so on (GHK Group 2000; Landry 2000). The focus and medium-term planning echoes recent policy ideals of the World Bank, UNCHS and the Cities Alliance (Freire and Stren 2001). Thus far, the World Bank is clearly setting the pace in terms of policy definition on the issue. According to their most recent policy framework on urban development and local government, a CDS involves:

> a strategy that reflects a broadly shared understanding of the city's socio-economic structure, constraints, and prospects (the analytical assessment) and a shared vision of goals, priorities, and requirements (the strategic plan of action). This city development strategy is both a process and a product that identify ways of creating the conditions for urban sustainability along the dimensions of livability, competitiveness, good management and governance, and bankability. ... Each city development strategy exercise would be unique, but all would generally involve three broad phases. A first, 'scoping out' phase would provide a quick assessment of the readiness of the city, the chief concerns of its officials, and the industrial, commercial, and banking interests. These findings would form the basis for a second, more in-depth analysis of the local economic structure and trends, the potential obstacles – institutional, financial, environmental, and social – and the strategic options. A third phase would focus on outside assistance, particularly on how the Bank and other agencies could help the city achieve its goals (World Bank 2000a: 64).[6]

This description of a typical CDS process, along with more recent guidelines (Campbell and Mehta 2000) rest on the following three assumptions, amongst others:

- A shared vision of the future is definable through deliberation and negotiation between various, preferably all, stakeholders and such a 'consensus vision' can serve as a basis to inform choices about trade-offs, alignment and investment of scarce public and private resources;
- A well-structured process (inclusive and rigorous) of dialogue will lead to an outcome that is the sum total of the best possible 'rational consensus' about the nature of problems and what needs to be done to address them;
- The diverse and wide-ranging challenges facing the city are knowable, intelligible and can be broken down into discrete parcels of knowledge to inform targeted inter-ventions.

It is crucial to interrogate these assumptions more closely in analysing the pros and cons of CDSs. Even though a number of (poorly cross-referenced) literatures present

---

[6] There are so many issues in this short statement that warrant critical commentary but it will have to wait for another opportunity. Suffice it to say that I think the blatant elitism, economic determinism and instrumental assumptions are profoundly problematic.

themselves for the task (e.g. Borja and Castells 1997; Edmunds and Wollenberg 2001; Fung and Wright 2001), I will restrict my analysis to the planning literature (Healey 1997; Fainstein 2000; Sandercock 1998; Watson 1998; Huxley and Yiftachel 2000). However, the limitation of the planning and strategic planning literature is that it does not adequately factor in the constitutive nature of informality in the third world city. I address this by taking a detour into a brief discussion on the 'informal city' because it represents a critical part in reaching conclusions about the efficacy of CDS in advancing a transformative political agenda in Cape Town. Central to my analysis are certain assumptions about the link between CDS approaches and urban planning. It is important to tease these assumptions out because my conclusions rest on them.

Precursors in urban planning to CDSS

The wave of democratisation and decentralisation across most parts of the world during the 1980s–1990s has effectively displaced, in theory at least, top-down, elite-driven urban governance (Carley et al. 2001). In its wake there has been a prolific experimentation with various participatory planning and decision-making systems and structures (Fung and Wright 2001; Pieterse 2000; Plummer 2000). This wave of democratisation struck at the heart of traditional modernist planning, characterised by master planning and rigid land zoning systems. Strategic planning has emerged as the successor to master planning because of its participatory elements and its ability to combine the continued need for regulation along with an acknowledgement that various uncontrollable forces shape the urban territory (Devas and Rakodi 1993). Thus, the 'state of the art' in current planning thinking is defined in the following terms by the Urban 21 Commission:

> The overall strategy is to develop *flexible* planning strategies at different spatial scales, from the strategic to the local. The strategic plan for a metropolitan area would set out broad principles of development and would, above all, make clear where infrastructure investments were expected in the short-to-medium term. Within it local design briefs would develop a simultaneous control of environmental standards and planning standards, set out transparently the proposals for infrastructure provision and upgrading, and develop policy solutions to control and land speculation. (Hall and Pfeiffer 2000: 308, emphasis added)

It is also in the context of institutionalising strategic planning that stakeholder-based dialogical forums have come to the fore. For Jorge Borja and Manual Castells strategic planning can only be successful if it involves a wide spectrum of stakeholders from various backgrounds in the city: 'Strategic planning is a way of directing change based on a participatory analysis of a situation and its possible evolution...', and further achieves, beyond everything else, 'the dissemination of strategic thought, the process being more important than the results themselves'. Crucially, the '... participation of the public and private agents is an indispensable condition of strategic planning and distinguishes it from other forms of planning' (Borja and Castells 1997: 154, 155). However, it is the communicative planning school of thought (and their critics) that have gone furthest in theorising the political implications of this approach to urban planning and its reliance on stakeholder-based participation mechanisms.

The rationale for and potential of dialogical forums

According to the communicative planning school of thought, dialogical[7] processes are effectively structured mechanisms to surface and confront the 'dilemmas as regards co-existence in shared spaces' (Healey 1997: 284). The assumption is that the city is comprised of a rich diversity of social actors (with diverse interests and divergent senses of place), rooted in multiple and disjunctive territories, with often divergent claims. This diversity, along with the multiplicity of exogenous and endogenous forces that impinge on urban development produces a profoundly complex array of challenges (Ravetz 2000). Therefore, for Patsy Healey, this approach rests on:

> ... a dynamic relational view of urban life. Its focus is on relations and processes, not objects. It emphasizes dynamics not statics, and the complex interactions between local continuities and 'social capital' and the innovative potential. It 'sees' multiple relations transecting the space of the city, each 'driven' and 'shaped' by different forces, interacting with each other in different ways, bypassing, conflicting, coordinating in complex trajectories. It recognizes that these social relationships, although shaped by powerful forces, often outside the space of a particular urban areas, are actively socially constructed. In the social processes of defining meanings and identities and in the routine ways of living in the city, people make the multiple times and places, its differentiations, cohesions and exclusions, and its power dynamics. (Healey 2000: 526)

In view of this constitutive multiplexity the following rationale underpins the need for dialogical governance and planning mechanisms. By definition such complexity in the city can only be addressed through *synectics* – an approach to solving problems based on creative thinking of a group from different areas of expertise and knowledge. Therefore, it follows that in order to forge sustainable economic, political and social ecologies for cities it is essential that these diverse social actors confront each other with their divergent claims in order to arrive at difficult, politically situated, decisions about whose claims will be addressed, in what sequence and with what resources. Since assent and compliance depend on the legitimacy and inclusivity of the process it is essential that as many stakeholders as possible participate in such dialogical forums. Further, communicative theorists assert that it is impossible to arrive at legitimate, situated agreements without some measure of shared values, which, ideally, can be expressed through a shared vision about the future (Landry 2000). However, in a context of deep social cleavages and structural inequalities it is not that easy to arrive at shared values. This is why structured (dialogical) processes of joint, experience-based, socialisation are required to allow people to relativise their claims in relation to other claims and a broader system of values and principles. In other words, '[i]n these processes of collaborative strategy-making, participants engage in collective efforts in institutional design. Through it, they change themselves and their contexts. They build new systems of meaning, new cultures, new organising routines and styles and new social networks' (Healey 1997: 285).

Patsy Healey (1997) is confident that, in a participatory democratic framework, forums for dialogue are the most effective approach to address structural inequalities in the city,

---

[7] Dialogical is derived from dialogue, which in turn can mean discussion, exchange of ideas, flow of information, and so forth. Theoretically, the dialogical approach draws on the work of Jürgen Habermas on communicative action to democratise the public sphere (see Healey 1997 for a creative adaptation of Habermas's theories to urban politics and planning; and Flyvbjerg 1998 for a systematic critique).

precisely because it operates at the edge of what is politically achievable in policy terms, and then creates, through the creation of new understanding and new cultures, a stepping stone for attempting more ambitious and risky political interventions. Forums for dialogue are essentially processes that engender social learning through direct experience in confronting difference and commonality with 'the other'. One dimension of such political practices is the scope for the production of new, more empowering policy discourses. Since the communicative approach rests on continuous dialogue and reflection about successes and failures, greater confidence is socially constructed to always cut deeper into problems to get the structural bone of issues. In this sense, it is a deeply intimate and strategic politics that works through continual critique and reformulation of dominant discourses by interrogating those discourses and revealing their assumptions and technologies and supplanting them with more empowering ones.

Another dimension of the communicative approach is the institutional reconfigurations within the state that are required to give effect to it. Specifically, the challenge is to create a learning culture within local government which can enable politicians and officials to consciously reflect on the interdependencies and causal links between: i) developmental outcomes and the institutional efficiency and effectiveness of development structures within the state and between the state and other social actors; ii) developmental outcomes and the systems of power–knowledge relations that characterise municipal plans, interventions and assessment criteria; and iii) developmental outcomes and the quality of citizen participation and involvement in the conceptualisation and delivery of municipal services (Flood 1999). The mere acknowledgement of these problems represents an important political opportunity for CSOs and citizens to assert their rights and claims on local government. In this sense, the broader rationale behind the adoption of dialogical political mechanisms – such as a CDS – is that they create unprecedented opportunities for advancing the interests of disadvantaged groups. However, these arguments in favour of dialogical forums are not without their critics.

The potential pitfalls of dialogical forums
Critics point out that with the growing convergence (Atkinson 2000) of various contiguous and overlapping policy debates – poverty reduction, sustainable development, good governance, decentralisation – in mainstream perspectives on urban development (e.g. World Bank 2000b), it is unsurprising that dialogical forums are regarded as the ideal vehicle to achieve 'sustainable urban development'. CDS-type forums bring together ideas about increased stakeholder involvement in urban governance which feed off perspectives arising from participatory development critiques, on the one hand, and reducing the role of the state in the provision and regulation of public goods, on the other. The CDS discourse also reflects the revalorisation of urban economies in a context of intensifying globalisation, which essentially pulses through dispersed but interlocked city-based economic flows (Scott 1998). Such urban economies need to embody tremendous strategic capacity to anticipate the needs and proclivities of potential (foreign) investors and shape their territories accordingly. Deploying such strategic capacity presupposes a high degree of social cohesion between various conflictual interests and political capacity (read decentralised powers) to put in place strategies to construct new 'network infrastructures' (Graham and Marvin 2001). However, since such infrastructure development programmes

invariably have long-term horizons, they are packaged into marketable 'messages' and 'images' about the city (Barke 1999). Such representational imperatives struggle to accommodate difference; are impatient with messy conflicts; and deplore the display of 'dirty linen' for visitors to see. These representational requirements prefer that politics are ordered, predictable and safe. As a consequence, a powerful political and social pressure to stage a 'united front' – a monolithic, non-threatening urban image that is welcoming to the outside world – is created. Planning theorists from the political economy school of thought argue that in contexts of severe inequality and deep social cleavage, multi-stakeholder forums fuel a consensual politics that invariably structure and maintain sharp insider/outsider boundaries (Fainstein 2000).

These lines of critique are akin to past experiences of 'city visioning' and metropolitan planning in Cape Town, as reported by Vanessa Watson (1998) in her analysis of the Metropolitan Development Forum (MDF), which initiated the process towards the formulation of the Metropolitan Spatial Development Framework (MSDF).[8] Her findings demonstrate a serious effort on the part of local government to solicit input from a wide spectrum of civil society organisations and citizens, channelled via the Western Cape Economic Development Forum (WCEDF). Significantly, in early 1995, when the draft MSDF was presented, there was hardly any disagreement about the content of the proposals, suggesting a high degree of consensus about the direction, principles and approach to spatial planning in a post-apartheid city. Watson (1998: 342) captures the reason for this succinctly: 'The fact that the plan was based on a set of unified and well-rationalized ideas which clearly implied a reversal of apartheid planning ideology, at a time when any continuation of apartheid ideas would have been totally unacceptable, probably encouraged most Forum representatives to accept it unhesitatingly.'

More important for my purposes here, she suggests that a 'quick consensus' was possible because of: a) the rational-comprehensive form of deliberation; b) the hierarchical structure of the MDF; c) the prevalence of effective disagreement resolution mechanisms; and d) an accommodating political culture amongst bureaucrats to establish their legitimacy amongst previously excluded (but soon to become the majority) political leaders and their organisations (ibid.: 342–4). In effect, Watson argues, the high level of consensus reflects the divisions amongst disadvantaged groups because shack dwellers were hardly represented and their interests were ill-served by the policies of the plan.[9] It also reflects the demanding pressures on civic and squatter representatives who simply are not equipped to keep pace with the gruelling schedule of meetings and committees that invariably accompany a dialogical process such as the WCEDF. In other words, the WCEDF displayed worrying features described by Edmunds and Wollenberg (2001) as a masking of power and structural inequality. 'In doing so, they [multi-stakeholder forums]

---

[8] Significantly, the MSDF process was characterised by a participatory visioning process which provided the basis for establishing planning principles and priorities similar to the way CDS is conceptualised by the World Bank and others. The final MSDF was formally published by the Cape Metropolitan Council in 1998. The MSDF is noteworthy for its lofty ideals about urban integration and compact city development but steers clear of any controversial political interventions – such as intervening in land markets – that would be required to give effect to its ideals.

[9] Significantly, only one person (from an NGO!) represented civic, labour and community interests in the sub-committee of the Urban Development Strategy Commission of the WCEDF that deliberated the MSDF because civic and labour representatives were simply to widely spread (Watson 1998). In fairness, it is important to point out that the draft MSDF proposals were put to the plenary and forum sessions for input.

are prone to exaggerate the level of consensus reached through negotiations and expose disadvantaged groups to greater manipulation and control by powerful stakeholders' (ibid.: 232). Other participatory exercises undertaken by local government in Cape Town at metropolitan scale in preparation of the 2004 Olympic Bid also reflected half-hearted participatory efforts that were ultimately subsumed by top-down agendas (see Hiller 2000).

In summary, criticisms of stakeholder-based political institutions have tended to turn on one, or a combination, of the following lines of critique:

- They legitimise decisions that are taken by proxies of elite interests and consequently fulfil a function of cooptation through 'corporatist localism' (Ruppert 2000);
- They potentially subvert the emergence of oppositional political discourse and practices by framing such actions as illegitimate and undemocratic because they emanate from outside of the negotiation framework (Fainstein 2000);
- They reinforce divisions within poor and marginalised communities because these forums tend to draw in relatively better-off community associations that crowd out less organised and articulate associations (Cooke and Kothari 2001);
- They undermine informal and non-rational livelihood strategies of the poor through an insistence on working with formal planning frameworks and rationalities (Cleaver 2001).

There is no question that these criticisms are accurate in the context of Cape Town. Before I turn to a discussion on the political implications of this critique of dialogical forums, it is appropriate to explore the salience of informality in the city. As mentioned at the outset, planning debates tend to function on the assumption of first world urban infrastructures that reflect less pronounced relations of informality. The significant level of unemployment (22 per cent), massive informal settlements, well-organised and pervasive criminal syndicates and constant flow of movement into Cape Town underscore the importance of recognising the salience of these factors in redefining metropolitan governance (see Pieterse 2002, 2003). In the next section I briefly explore the theoretical and political significance of the informal city.

Is the city's future knowable, let alone able to be planned?

Mainstream approaches to stakeholder-based urban planning unfold with a quiet confidence that the city is intelligible and consequently able to be planned. This is an entirely reasonable premise if one considers that the planning discipline is founded on the confidence that through rational scientific application the unknown can be tamed and rendered predictable (Sandercock 1998). However, it is becoming common cause in urban theory and policy literatures that such confidence is entirely misplaced and probably counter-productive in the wake of relentless counter-evidence that suggests a stubbornly unpredictable and intractable reality that is clumsily termed informal, illegal or parallel. Marcello Balbo is one of the more perceptive observers on the salience of the informal city, especially in the South:

> The major metropolis in almost every newly-industrialised country is not a single unified city, but, in fact, two quite different cities, physically juxtaposed but architecturally and socially distinct. The truth is even more extreme: the city in the Third World is a city of fragments, where

urbanisation takes place in leaps and bounds, creating a continuously discontinuous pattern. In the fragmented city, physical environment, services, income, cultural values and institutional systems can vary markedly from neighbourhood to neighbourhood, often from street to street. ... Those [pieces] on the periphery are incomplete and more 'fragile', while older areas are well established with clearly-defined boundaries. (Balbo 1993: 24)

Informality is driven along by numerous interrelated features in developing economies, *inter alia*, weak state capacity, slow and/or weak formal economic growth (caused by exogenous or endogenous factors), scarce public infrastructures and resources, rapid urbanisation, intense movement and mobility, and restrictive land tenure systems (Balbo 1993; Simone 1997; Werna 2001). Two implications arise: rethinking the role and utility of urban governance and management instruments, e.g. strategic planning frameworks, and acknowledging that there will always be an outside to formal governance processes that simply cannot be incorporated because its ontology depends on being exterior (Laguerre 1994). To illustrate the first implication I want briefly to explore a recent attempt to address, in particular, the informal city in Cape Town through the Municipal Spatial Development Framework (muni-SDF) of the former City of Cape Town municipality (CCT 1999). I turn to this example because it builds onto the MSDF discussed earlier, but explicitly seeks to extend the thinking of the MSDF by dealing with varied and conflicting dynamics in the city.

Most interesting about the muni-SDF for my purposes here is that it seeks to acknowledge the presence of the informal city through its promotion of: a) a pedestrian principle in location of public infrastructures; b) promotion of market spaces in and around agglomerations of public infrastructure; and c) the provision of dedicated spaces for 'traditional' and religious practices such as circumcision and slaughtering of live animals (CCT 1999). These provisions are ensconced in a more elaborate and compelling argument about how the city can be reintegrated and beautified to improve the quality of life of everyone. As lead consultant David Dewar explains, the muni-SDF 'has as its starting point the recognition that the concept of accessibility is central to the making of a more compact, equitable and integrated city. ... The challenge posed by achieving this is two-fold: to make existing opportunities more accessible to the majority, and to create a hierarchical pattern of agglomerated opportunities and special places' (Dewar 2000: 213–14). The specific design proposals that flow from this approach conform closely with the main tenets of the 'new urbanism' design movement in the US and Europe (Fainstein 2000). New urbanism approaches have been criticised for being overly instrumental with their obsession with urban form rather than process, producing a distinctive environmental determinism (Graham and Marvin 2001). In other words, if planning can simply manage to create the right structure of opportunities through the application of rational planning principles (producing appropriate urban network infrastructures) the 'city that works for all' can be realised (CCT 1999).[10] In contradistinction to the

---

[10] I should stress that I have great sympathy for the underlying objectives of the muni-SDF but fear that, if it is approached as the definitive argument about the role of spatial configuration and achieving sustainable urban development, it fails to grasp the inevitable and necessary contingencies that shape cities. Spatial frameworks are but one aspect in a much larger debate that makes for urban contestation about the future and whose interests will be served and therefore can never succeed in 'establishing a way of thinking that helps decision makers to deal with unexpected development initiatives, problems and opportunities, based on argument and principle, and not opinion' (CCT 1999: 17).

environmental determinism in evidence in the muni-SDF, Rem Koolhaas argues for an urbanism that:

> will not be based on the twin fantasies of order and omnipotence; it will be the staging of uncertainty; it will no longer be concerned with the arrangement of more or less permanent objects but the irrigation of territories with potential; it will no longer aim for stable configurations but for the creation of enabling fields that accommodate processes that refuse to be crystallised into definitive form; it will no longer be about meticulous definition, the imposition of limits, but about expanding notions, denying boundaries; not about separating and identifying entities, but about discovering unnameable hybrids. (Rem Koolhaas quoted in Graham and Marvin 2001: 413–14)

This sense of urbanity seems much more appropriate for engaging with the informal city that Marcelo Balbo (1993) and Ayyun Malik (2001) suggest is constitutive of the urban in post-colonial contexts. However, in the absence of surfacing and concretising the everyday practices of the majority of urban citizens through counter imaginaries and discourses, it is virtually impossible for the insurgent practices and imperatives of the most marginal groups to be addressed by formal governance registers. This is not necessarily a bad thing, especially if the informal activity in question relies on invisibility or obscurity (Simone 2001). However, it is crucial if we are thinking about new governance mechanisms to reconfigure the entire cityscape, as is the aim of the CDS.

What are the implications of accepting the constitutive nature of 'the informal' for thinking about city-wide planning through stakeholder-based dialogical forums? First, it underscores the importance of seeing such political forums as only one instance in a much larger democratic project. Second, it suggests that we need to interrogate fundamentally the assumptions and imaginaries that underpin visions and future plans, especially spatial frameworks for the city. I would contend that quasi-master planning, although framed as strategic spatial planning (e.g. MSDF and muni-SDF), is still seen as the solution to the development challenges facing the city. This is false; provisional, contingent solutions will emerge from time to time in the wake of the contestation between opposing interests. It is such situated and always vulnerable 'solutions' that will effectively shape the multiple futures of the city.

It is of course true that the spatial imaginary of the MSDF and the muni-SDF is driven by concerns about ideal urban forms and the powers of spatial patterning through land-use (re)design to construct ideal cities, whereas the CDS is propelled by an imaginary of economic prosperity that creates the resources to invest in making the city a more equitable and integrated space. These differences lead to divergent assumptions about the role of 'experts', the nature of participation processes (e.g. in relation to spatial maps or open-ended and issue-based), and the hierarchy and sequencing of development investments that are appropriate. Consequently one can argue that a CDS opens up a different approach to spatiality as compared to spatial frameworks such as the MSDF. In the case of the latter, the fluid and complex spaces of the city are often reified whilst the CDS frameworks are much more problem-solving oriented and less fixed in terms of spatial connotations.[11] Arguably, CDS processes could be seen as more amenable to

---

[11] I want to thank the Reviewer for pointing to these differences and suggesting that it be made more explicit in the argument.

address the informal, makeshift spatial practices of the poor in the city. Outside of concrete political struggles, this is not guaranteed, of course. The danger with a CDS is that it will reinforce the confidence of planners that, once an 'inclusive mandate' has been established through a so-called vision for the city, they can go about their professional business of translating the vision into discrete planning systems and processes. This is precisely why it is problematic to over-invest theoretically and politically in the CDS approach. The challenge is to locate the CDS in a broader and more complex radical democratic framework that can continuously emphasise both areas of agreement or commonality and, crucially, areas of contestation and unresolvability. I will now turn to what kind of politics such an approach adds up to.

Dialogical forums and transformative politics

Clearly, the basis, focus and strategies of radical democratic politics must be conceptualised through a sound assessment of the material conditions and symbolic structures that characterise our era. Rethinking the traditional roles of the state, private sector and civil society is undeniably on the agenda with profound consequences for citizenship and collective practices (Amin and Graham 1997; Holston 1998; Isin 2000). As pointed out earlier, these shifts are particularly acute in cities as profound economic restructuring processes are expressed primarily through networks of city economies, precipitating new demands on political and physical infrastructures (Graham 2000) and effecting exaggerated spatial relations of inequality and exclusion (Tajbakhsh 2001).

Treating these shifting dynamics as a given, I want to suggest a strategic approach to urban politics that knits together four types of political action with engagement through dialogical-stakeholder forums (see Figure 1 below).

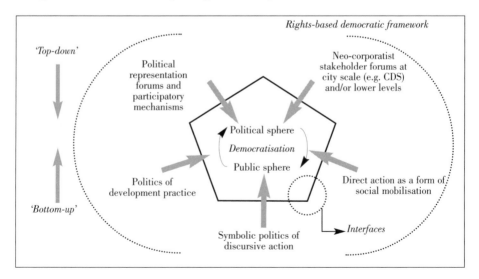

Figure 1: Dimensions of urban political practice

Note: The human rights-based constitution established the values and principles that underpin contestation in each of the five domains.

Political representation refers to the formal political system that characterises municipal government in the city, as set out in the Municipal Structures Act (No. 117 of 1998). In terms of the Act, single-tier metropolitan authorities have been established in the six largest urban areas in the country. Political authority is vested in a single council for the entire area, although the Municipal Structures Act does make provision for metropolitan councils to 'establish decentralised metropolitan substructures as committees of the council, and delegate powers and functions to them' (Wooldridge 2002: 127). The main avenue of political participation in this process is through political parties that are elected on the basis of a combination proportional and ward-based, first-past-the-post, system. The democratic effectiveness of the system depends in large measure on the democratic nature of the respective political parties along with their rootedness in their constituencies (Goetz and Lister 2001; Heller 2001). It also depends on the quality and maturity of the institutional rules and systems that structure the functioning of council and committee meetings and associated mechanisms for transparency, responsiveness and accountability (see Blair 2000).

Direct action involves various forms of collective action by disadvantaged groups aimed at stretching the liberal democratic constitutional framework to its limit. This assertion implies that social movements and looser social formations must claim their rights and entitlements through non-violent social action focused on concrete issues that shape the quality of life of the poor. In South Africa's recent history there are a number of examples where such action has resulted in favourable constitutional judgements on the rights to shelter for children, protection from forced evictions (see Liebenberg 2001) and access to essential drugs and medicines (*The Sunday Independent*, 7 April 2002). Put differently, the South African Constitution (Act No. 108, 1996) creates massive scope for a rights-based approach to social mobilisation that can entrench the accountability of the state to ensure adequate measures to reduce poverty and destitution. At the same time, this rights-based approach reinforces the constitutional democratic framework and commitment to citizen empowerment because the fulfilment of rights, especially socio-economic rights, implies addressing structural inequalities (Pieterse and van Donk 2002).

The *politics of development practice* unfolds at the neighbourhood scale (and beyond) where autonomous and state-dependent projects are undertaken to improve the quality of life and livelihoods, protect against the vicissitudes of crime, violence and other shocks, and deliberate future trajectories for the community in relation to other communities and the larger regional economic-ecological system. However, both direct action and the locality-based politics of development have their limits in the absence of a broader intervention to shift public/popular opinion and popular cultural imaginaries. This point rests on the recognition of the nature and dynamics of disciplinary power in society.[12]

However, formal political representation through council structures, direct action and the locality-based politics of development have their limits in the absence of a broader

---

[12] Disciplinary power refers to the quiet coercions of dominant discourses that shape our use and relationship to our bodies and our understanding/perception of our location in the world – internalised patterns of behaviour rooted in specified patterns of thought. Knowledge does not emancipate (due to the enlightening power of truth) but rather authorises and legitimates the workings of power. Because there are so many competing ideas, institutions and discourses, no single authorised truth ever emerges to dominate society and disciplinary power also inadvertently always produces resistance (Danaher *et al.* 2000: 80). Power therefore is fluid and mobile but also always incomplete in achieving its desires (Flyvbjerg 2001).

intervention to shift public opinion and popular cultural imaginaries. Thus, the fourth type of political action is *symbolic politics through discursive intervention* aimed at achieving political 'ground-clearing' – i.e. to reconstitute the discursive framework of what is considered legitimate, appropriate, sufficient, sustainable, etc. (Flyvbjerg 1998). If participation in stakeholder forums such as the CDS Partnership is not linked to these other forms of political intervention, it is very likely that the pitfalls mentioned above will open wide. Moving from this understanding I want to specify why dialogical forums represent a strategic political opportunity for progressive actors in the city.

In the first instance, CDS processes can contribute to the deepening of democracy. Democracy fundamentally means the articulation of citizen dialogue and action in an unending dialectic. The regulation of public life in South Africa is invariably inscribed in legal and procedural codes which represent vital democratic achievements, unassailably expressed in the abolition of the apartheid legal apparatus. In fact, by broadening the institutional space for as many actors as possible to contribute to the acts of deliberation and action, democracy is enriched and potentially deepened. However, this is not to deny that participation and expression of voice is always circumscribed by unequal and potentially oppressive power inequalities rooted not least in the exploitative impulses of incessant, disjunctive capitalist expansion (Appadurai 1996). However, 'controlling power' to subjugate is never a given and it needs to be asserted, exercised and deployed to have effect. It is in this process that resistances are implicit and fundamental. Therefore, I regard dialogical forums as critical sites for oppositional politics to find coherence and relevance.[13]

In the second instance, CDS forums also create a strategic opportunity to engage and recast dominant discourses about sustainable urban development. I concur with Frug (1999) that an important strategy to engage with the dominant discourses and associated imaginaries about what is 'wrong' and 'right' in our cities needs to be tackled head on and not simply vilified or dismissed as bourgeois values or utopias. In speaking about shifting the intractable problems of consumerist, surveillance architecture and suburbanisation in America, Gerald Frug argues that 'it is important also to speak in the language of privatized self-interest that has become so dominant in our contemporary political discourse'. He continues, 'change has to be built on concerns people have about their daily lives: their fear of crime, their anxiety about the future of public education, the distress they experience when they attempt to combine work with family,' and so forth (ibid.: 221). His point is that these so-called 'middle-class issues' need to be recast as a much broader political and economic problematic that cannot be de-linked from dealing with systemic and structural inequality in the city. This coincides with similar arguments by leftists in other cases of urban politics (Atkinson 2000; Fainstein 1999). Dialogical forums provide an important public opportunity to reframe and recast the dominant discourses that so readily justify and naturalise more gated communities, privatised consumer spaces, private transport infrastructures and so on. Obviously it presupposes astute political leaders, clarity of analysis and message, and rootedness in insurgent spaces.

---

[13] This confidence rests on an understanding that the design, procedures, ground rules and facilitation of dialogical forums are critical to the outcomes that such forums produce. Barnard and Armstrong (1998) set out the details of the procedural and methodological considerations in advancing a progressive approach to implementing dialogical policy forums.

Finally, the imperatives of making CDS processes work can promote the strategic objective of transforming the state and civil society. I accept Sandercock's argument that 'any advances achieved outside of the state will quickly reach material limits' (Sandercock 1998: 178). Scepticism about the transformative potential of dialogical forums often operates on the assumption that (autonomous) civil society is virtuous and the state is villainous. This is simply incorrect and patently dangerous. Radical political ambitions need to acknowledge the political ambiguity of both the state and civil society. Again, Leonie Sandercock's conceptualisation is particularly insightful on this issue:

> We need to think about the complementary as well antagonistic relationship between state and civil society and of the possibility of social transformation as a result of the impact on the state of mobilized groups within civil society. If modernist politics could be defined as the bi-polar struggle between capital and labour, in which the state was allied to capital, a postmodern urban politics is perhaps best understood as a multiplicity of struggles around multiple axes of oppression, in which the role of the state is not a given (not simply 'the executive committee of the bourgeoisie'), but is dependent on the relative strength of the social mobilizations and their specific context in space and time. In other words, there is an unresolved, and unresolvable, tension between the transformative and repressive powers of state-directed planning practices, and their mirror image, the transformative and also repressive potential of the local, the grass-roots, the insurgent. (ibid.: 179–80)

Overall then it is a profound strategic error to dismiss the potential of progressive transformation within the state for at least two reasons. One, the bulk of public resources that can be deployed by the state for redistribution purposes requires a well-defined radical political agenda and, crucially, conducive institutional cultures to ensure a correlation between policy intent and outcomes (Flood 1999; Landry 2000). Preconditions for achieving institutional transformation of this nature are expansive and complex (Evans 2002; Heller 2001). For example, it requires, *inter alia*, incessant struggles within the bureaucracy to create an outcomes orientation, reflexivity, account-ability and transparency in decision-making (Barnard and Armstrong 1998; Perri 6 1997). Second, without a progressive state it is difficult to sustain and grow democratic ambitions within civil society (Johnson and Wilson 2000; Tendler 1997). Evidence from Brazilian, Indian and African cities illustrates that grassroots associations can grow in influence and relevance in occasions where the local state identifies strong associations as a critical bulwark against absolute poverty and marginality (Fung and Wright 2001; Lüdeking and Williams 1999). The state will not act against its own interests, but political discourses can be shaped to reflect the mutual benefits that can derive from of a strong state and strong, autonomous civil society (Evans 2002; Friedmann 2000). Urban politics does not have to be a zero-sum game.[14] The challenge is to pursue 'the best combination of complementary procedures of representative and participatory democracy' (Smith and Blanc 1997: 3).

---

[14] Some of the most insightful research in this vein emerges from literature that deals with partnerships (synergy) between the state and civil society organisations to address service delivery challenges in contexts of dire poverty (see Evans 1996, 2002; Fowler 2000; Johnson and Wilson 2000). The lessons that arise from the literature provide further support for my argument.

In conclusion: politics without guarantees

At the threshold of a new era in urban politics it seems likely that governance will be broadened through participatory processes at a neighbourhood scale and, simultaneously, at a city-wide scale. Both of these political trends will be expressed through stakeholder-based institutional frameworks which are consistent with the democratic imperatives of various national policy frameworks and an international trend towards increased participation and joined-up planning as the state seeks ways of levering in contributions from the private sector and civil society associations. These democratic experiments occur, not incidentally, at the same time as neo-liberal policy frameworks are ascendant with numerous implications for closing-off interventions by the state. However, these democratic innovations can be redeployed in radical ways that provide counter arguments to the strictures of neo-liberal imperatives and provide practical spaces for renewed citizenship, constituted through opposition and reconstruction of alternatives – these are alternatives with a lower-case 'a' since it can hardly be prefigured or imagined outside of situated contexts. However, such a political project cannot be imagined or expressed on essentialist premises about class agency or associated high modern planning solutions, especially in an era of complex and indeterminate processes of localisation/globalisation (Pieterse forthcoming; Robins 2002; Tajbakhsh 2001). By definition, it can only be expressed through multiple, contiguous and, ideally, articulated struggles, along various lines of oppression and exclusion. Such multiplicity of struggle can be distinguished conceptually, as discussed above, as five types of political action: direct action, politics of development, discursive interventions, formal representative politics and participation in dialogical forums. The politics that flow from dialogical forums are fundamentally contingent on a broader, vibrant political and civil sphere. If such a broader politics is absent or anaemic, it is likely that dialogical forums will reflect the worst fears of critics (Fainstein 2000) and promoters (Healey 2000) of collaborative planning.

It is therefore conceivable to construct a new political approach that moves across formal/informal and insider/outsider binaries. In terms of such an approach, CDS forums are a critical site of contestation and conflict between a broad range of stakeholders and classes in the city. Progressive actors can use the forum to keep questions about 'causes, constraints and substantial outcomes' (Fainstein 2000: 456) alive and also spell out the implication of enduring inequality that can only be addressed through a combination of redistributive measures and tangible empowerment of disadvantaged actors (Frug 1999). At the same time, community leaders gain insight into the strategic frameworks that govern the prioritisation and deployment of public resources which can serve as valuable intelligence to target grassroots politics (both direct action and development intervention) more effectively. Crucially, it allows for the coordination of multiple localised struggles across the urban space, counterworking the prospects of pitting community against community in the struggle for scarce resources. In the same vein, it encourages the articulation of localised, city-wide and broader scale political action which is crucial in the current era of disjunctive capitalism (Amin et al. 2000; Comaroff and Comaroff 2000). Thus, the significance of CDS-type dialogical forums is not so much in what they produce in themselves but what they make possible in other, seemingly unrelated, arenas.

Currently, this (personal) political vision of 'invention and intervention' is incipient, but hopefully, by elucidating its faint contours it is somewhat closer to the surface of the city.

References

Amin, A. and S. Graham (1997), 'The Ordinary City', *Transactions of the Royal British Geographic Society*, 22: 411–29.
Amin, A., D. Massey and N. Thrift (2000), *Cities for the Many not the Few*, Bristol: The Policy Press.
Appadurai, A. (1996), *Modernity at Large: Cultural Dimensions of Globalization*, Minneapolis and London: University of Minnesota Press.
Atkinson, A. (2000), 'Promoting Sustainable Human Development in Cities of the South: A Southeast Asian Perspective', *UNRISD Geneva 2000 Occasional Paper* 6: 1–41.
Balbo, M. (1993), 'Urban Planning and the Fragmented City of the Developing World', *Third World Planning Review*, 15(1): 23–35.
Barke, M. (1999), 'City Marketing as a Planning Tool', in M. Pacione (ed.), *Applied Geography: Principles and Practice*, London and New York: Routledge.
Bernard, A. and G. Armstrong (1998), 'Learning and Policy Integration', in J. Schnurr and S. Holtz (eds), *The Cornerstone of Development, Integrating Environmental, Social and Economic Policies*, Boca Raton: Lewis Publishers and IDRC.
Blair, H. (2000), 'Participation and Accountability at the Periphery: Democratic Local Governance in Six Countries', *World Development*, 28(1): 21–39.
Borja, J. and M. Castells. (1997), *Local and Global. The Management of Cities in the Information Age*, London: Earthscan.
Cameron, R. (1995), 'The History of Devolution of Powers to Local Authorities in South Africa: The Shifting Sands of State Control', *Local Government Studies* 21(3): 396–417.
—— (ed.) (1999), *Democratisation of South African Local Government, A Tale of Three Cities*, Pretoria: J.L. van Schaik.
—— (2000), 'Megacities in South Africa: A Solution for the New Millennium?' *Public Administration and Development*, 20(2): 155–65.
Campbell, T. and D. Mehta. (2000), 'City Development Strategies: Taking Stock of Progress – Issues and Policy to Increase Impact', Unpublished Report, Washington and Nairobi: World Bank and UNCHS.
Carley, M., P. Jenkins and H. Smith (eds) (2001), *Urban Development and Civil Society. The Role of Communities in Sustainable Cities*, London: Earthscan.
CCT (City of Cape Town) (1999) *The Municipal Spatial Department Framework*, Cape Town: City of Cape Town.
Cleaver, F. (2001), 'Institutions, Agency and the Limitations of Participatory Approaches to Development', in B. Cooke and U. Kothari (eds), *Participation: The New Tyranny?* London and New York: Zed Books.
Comaroff, J. and J.L. Comaroff (2000), 'Millennial Capitalism: First Thoughts on a Second Coming', *Public Culture*, 12(2): 291–343.
Cooke, B. and U. Kothari (2001), 'The Case for Participation as Tyranny', in B. Cooke and U. Kothari (eds), *Participation: The New Tyranny?* London and New York: Zed Books.
Danaher, G., T. Schirato and J. Webb. (2000), *Understanding Foucault*, London: Sage.
Devas, N. and C. Rakodi (1993), 'Planning and Managing Urban Development', in N. Devas and C. Rakodi (eds) *Managing Fast Growing Cities. New Approaches to Urban Planning in the Developing World*, New York: Longman.
Dewar, D. (2000), 'The Relevance of the Compact City Approach: The Management of Urban Growth in South African Cities', in M. Jenks and R. Burgess (eds), *Compact Cities. Sustainable Urban Forms in Developing Countries*, London: Spon Press.
Edmunds, D. and E. Wollenberg (2001), 'A Strategic Approach to Multistakeholder Negotiations', *Development and Change*, 32(2): 231–53.
Evans, P. (1996), 'Government Action, Social Capital and Development: Reviewing the Evidence on Synergy', *World Development*, 24(6): 1119–32.
—— (ed.) (2002), *Livable Cities? Urban Struggles for Livelihood and Sustainability*. Berkeley: University of California Press.
Fainstein, S. (1999), 'Can We Make the Cities we Want?' in R. Beauregard and S. Body-Gendrot (eds), *The Urban Moment. Cosmopolitan Essays on the Late 20th Century*, London: Sage Publications.
—— (2000), 'New Directions in Planning Theory', *Urban Affairs Review* 35(4): 451–78.

Flood, R.L. (1999), *Rethinking the Fifth Discipline. Learning within the Unknowable*, London and New York: Routledge.

Flyvbjerg, B. (1998), 'Empowering Civil Society: Habermas, Foucault and the Question of Conflict', in M. Douglas and J. Friedmann (eds) *Cities for Citizens. Planning and the Rise of Civil Society in a Global Age*, Chichester: John Wiley and Sons.

—— (2001), *Making Social Science Matter. Why Social Inquiry Fails and How it can Succeed Again*, Cambridge: Cambridge University Press.

Fowler, A. (2000), 'Civil Society, NGDOs and Social Development: Changing the Rules of the Game', *Geneva 2000: Occasional Paper*, No. 1, UNRISD: January.

Freire, M. and R. Stren (eds) (2001), *The Challenge of Urban Government. Policies and Practices*, Washington D.C. and Toronto: World Bank Institute and Centre for Urban and Community Studies.

Friedmann, J. (2000), 'The Good City: In Defence of Utopian Thinking', *International Journal of Urban and Regional Research*, 24(2): 460–72.

Frug, G.E. (1999), *City Making. Building Communities without Building Walls*, Princeton and Oxford: Princeton University Press.

Fung, A. and E.O. Wright. (2001), 'Deepening Democracy: Innovations in Empowered Participatory Governance', *Politics and Society* 29(1): 5–41.

GHK Group. (2000), 'City Development Strategies (CDSs). Taking Stock and Signposting the Way Forward', A Discussion Document for DFID (UK) and the World Bank. London: GHK Group of Companies.

GJMC (Greater Johannesburg Metropolitan Council) (2000), *iGoli 2010*. Johannesburg: GJMC.

Goetz, A.M. and S. Lister (2001), *The Politics of Civil Society Engagement with the State: A Comparative Analysis of South Africa and Uganda*. Brighton: Institute of Development Studies.

Graham, S. (2000), 'Constructing Premium Network Spaces: Reflections on Infrastructure Networks and Contemporary Urban Development', *International Journal of Urban and Regional Research* 24(1): 183–200.

Graham, S. and S. Marvin (2001), *Splintering Urbanism. Networked Infrastructures, Technological Mobilities and the Urban Condition*, London and New York: Routledge.

Halfani, M. (1996), 'Marginality and Dynamism: Prospects for the Sub-Saharan City', in M. Cohen, B. Ruble, J. Tulcin and A. Garland (eds), *Preparing an Urban Future*, Washington, DC: The Woodrow Wilson Centre Press.

Hall, P. and U. Pfeiffer (eds) (2000), *Urban Future 21. A Global Agenda for Twenty-First Century Cities*, London: E. and F.N. Spon.

Healey, P. (1997), *Collaborative Planning. Shaping Places in Fragmented Societies*, London: Macmillan.

—— (2000), 'Planning in Relational Space and Time: Responding to New Urban Realities', in G. Bridge and S. Watson (eds), *A Companion to the City*, Oxford: Blackwell.

Heller, P. (2001), 'Moving the State: The Politics of Democratic Decentralization in Kerala, South Africa, and Porto Alegre', *Politics and Society*, 29(1): 131–63.

Hiller, H. (2000), 'Mega-Events, Urban Boosterism and Growth Strategies: An Analysis of the Objectives and Legitimations of the Cape Town 2004 Olympic Bid', *International Journal of Urban and Regional Research*, 24(2): 439–58.

Holston, J. (1998), 'Spaces of Insurgent Citizenship', in L. Sandercock (ed.), *Making the Invisible Visible. A Multicultural Planning History*, Berkeley: University of California Press.

Huxley, M. and O. Yiftachel (2000), 'New Paradigm or Old Myopia? Unsettling the Communicative Turn in Planning Theory', *Journal of Planning Education and Research*, 19(4): 333–42.

Isin, E.F. (ed.) (2000), *Democracy, Citizenship and the Global City*, London and New York: Routledge.

Johnson, H. and G. Wilson. (2000), 'Biting the Bullet: Civil Society, Social Learning and the Transformation of Local Governance', *World Development* 28(11): 1891–906.

Laguerre, M. (1994), *The Informal City*, London: Macmillan.

Landry, C. (2000), *The Creative City. A Toolkit for Urban Innovators*, London: Comedia and Earthscan.

Liebenberg, S. (2001), *South Africa's Evolving Jurisprudence on Socio-Economic Rights*, Cape Town: The Socio-Economic Rights Project, Community Law Centre (University of the Western Cape).

Lüdeking, G. and C. Williams. (1999), *Poverty, Participation and Government Enablement. A Summary of findings, lessons learned and recommendations of Habitat/ISS evaluation research (1996–1998)*. Nairobi: Habitat.

Malik, A. (2001), 'After Modernity: Contemporary Non-western Cities and Architecture', *Futures*, 33(10): 873–82.

Nijzink, L. and S. Jacobs (2000), 'Provincial elections and government formation in the Western Cape: The politics of polarisation', *Politikon* 27(1): 37–49.

Perri 6 (1997), *Holistic Government*, London: Demos.

Pieterse, E. (1997), 'Urban Social Movements in South Africa in a "Globalising Era"', *Urban Forum*, 8(1): 1–17.

—— (2000), 'Participatory Urban Governance. Practical Approaches, Regional Trends and UMP Experiences', *Urban Management Programme Formal Series*, Vol. 25, Nairobi: Urban Management Programme.

—— (2002), 'From Divided to Integrated City? Critical Overview of the Emerging Metropolitan Governance System in Cape Town', *Urban Forum*, 13(1): 3–37.

—— (2003), 'Problematising and Recasting Vision-driven Politics in Cape Town', in C. Haferburg and J. Oßenbrügge (eds), *Ambiguous Restructurings of Post-Apartheid Cape Town: The Spatial Form*, Münster, Hamburg and London: LIT Verlag.

—— (forthcoming), 'At the limits of possibility: Working Notes on a Relational Model of Urban Politics', in A. Simone and A. Abouhani (eds), *Urban Processes and Change in Africa*, Dakar: CODESRIA; London: Zed Books.

Pieterse, E. and M. van Donk (2002), 'Incomplete Ruptures. The Political Economy of Realising Socio-Economic Rights in South Africa', Paper prepared for Colloquium on the Grootboom Judgement and Socio-Economic Rights, Strand, 15–17 March 2002. Cape Town: Community Law Centre (UWC).

Plummer, J. (2000), *Municipalities and Community Participation. A Sourcebook for Capacity Building*, London: Earthscan.

Rachman, J. (1998), *Constructions*, Cambridge, MA, and London: MIT Press.

Ravetz, J. (2000), *City-Region 2020: Integrated Planning for a Sustainable Environment*, London: Earthscan.

—— (2000b), Local Government: Municipal Systems Act. No 32. Cape Town: Government printers.

Robins, S. (2002), 'Planning "Suburban Bliss" in Joe Slovo Park, Cape Town', Cape Town: Anthropology Dept, UWC, unpublished paper.

Ruppert, E. (2000), 'Who Governs the Global City?', in E. F. Isin (ed.), *Democracy, Citizenship and the Global City*, London and New York: Routledge.

Sandercock, L. (1998), 'The Death of Modernist Planning: Radical Praxis for a Postmodern Age', in M. Douglas and J. Friedmann (eds), *Cities for Citizens. Planning and the Rise of Civil Society in a Global Age*, Chichester: John Wiley and Sons.

Scott, A. (1998), *Regions in the World Economy. The Coming Shape of Global Production, Competition, and Political Order*, Oxford: Oxford University Press.

Simone, A. (1997), *Urban Processes and Change in Africa*, Dakar: CODESRIA.

—— (2001), 'Straddling the Divides: Remaking Associational Life in the Informal African City', *International Journal of Urban and Regional Research*, 25(1): 102–17.

Smith, D.M. and M. Blanc (1997), 'Grass-roots Democracy and Participation: a New Analytical and Practical Approach', *Environment and Planning D: Society and Space*, 15(3): 281–303.

Tajbakhsh, K. (2001), *The Promise of the City. Space, Identity, and Politics in Contemporary Social Thought*, Berkeley: University of California Press.

Tendler, J. (1997), *Good Government in the Tropics*, Baltimore and London: Johns Hopkins University Press.

Unicity Commission (2000), Building a Unified City for the 21st Century. A Summary of the Proposed Service Delivery and Institutional Change Proposals for the Terms of Office of the New City of Cape Town. Cape Town: Unicity Commission.

Watson, V. (1998), 'Planning under Political Transition – Lessons from Cape Town's Metropolitan Planning Forum', *International Planning Studies*, 3(3): 335–50.

Werna, E. (2001), 'Shelter, Employment and the Informal City in the Context of the Present Economic Scene: Implications for Participatory Governance', *Habitat International* 25(2): 209–27.

White, G. and M. Robinson (1998), 'Towards Synergy in Social Provision: Civic Organizations and the State', in M. Minogue, C. Palidano and D. Hulme (eds), *Beyond the New Public Management. Changing Ideas and Practices in Governance*, Cheltenham and Northampton: Edward Elgar.

Wooldridge, D. (2002), 'Metropolitan Government', in S. Parnell, E. Pieterse, M. Swilling, and D. Woodridge (eds), *Democratising Local Government. The South African Experiment*, Cape Town: UCT Press.

World Bank (2000a), *Cities in Transition. World Bank Urban and Local Government Strategy*, Washington, DC: World Bank.

—— (2000b), *Entering the 21 Century. World Development Report 1999/2000*, Oxford: Oxford University Press.

7

'Functional' & 'Dysfunctional' Communities
The Making of Ethical Citizens

IVOR CHIPKIN

Introduction

If we scan government documents, White Papers and reports we will frequently find that the term development is clustered with several other terms. Uppermost amongst these are those of 'rights', the 'citizen' and the 'nation'. Usually, these terms are said to relate in the following way: development is that process whereby citizens are able to realise their rights to services and housing. In this way, it contributes to nation-building. While the meaning of terms like 'rights' and 'citizen' have, at least, been argued and debated in South Africa the same cannot be said for nation-building. Indeed, the term begs the question 'what is a nation?' – a topic sorely neglected in the South African and, indeed, Africanist scholarship. When it is broached, nation-building is deemed an affair of identification (imagination): getting people to identify with certain common symbols, to recognise each other as members of a common political body etc., to identify with state institutions. 'Citizen' and 'nation' are said to speak to different relations: the first to that of democracy and the second to that of community. They are said to articulate to the extent that citizens also identify with the national symbols/institutions. Development, in this regard, is said only to relate to the national project to the extent that it helps foster a sense of national belonging.

Yet, construed simply as a rights-bearing individual, what is neglected about the citizen is precisely the moral-ethical register that citizenship presupposes. In other words, citizenship also assumes a certain kind of behaviour (ethical practice) in the public domain. Unfortunately, this is too frequently overlooked by those interested in civil society. While starting from the Hegelian cue that civil society is a domain between the family and the state, they ignore that it also refers to a 'system of ethical order' (Hegel: *Philosophy of Right*, Section 183).

Understood as a system of ethical practice, the conditions of democracy become different from those normally supposed by political science or political sociology. It is not simply a question of institutions (to exercise rights, etc.). An additional and more fundamental question is necessarily posed: what are the conditions of ethical public behaviour? Or rather: what are the conditions of the public domain?

We shall see, through a case-study of Manenberg, that what is at stake in development is the production of ethical citizens – what the City of Cape Town calls 'functional communities'. Furthermore, the way the municipality deals with this question sheds valuable light onto the specificity of the nation. We shall see that what is at stake for the municipality is the capture of people's souls. The condition of ethical citizenship is deemed to capture Manenberg residents not simply to democratic values. Rather, their capture to such values is deemed contingent on holding them to the nuclear family! At stake is biopolitics *par excellence*. We shall see, therefore, that the nation is less an affair of identities, than it is of biopolitics – producing the people according to an image of the good subject. If in the past this figure was deemed a white male, more and more now it is associated in South Africa with individualisation.

Different notions of development

In his foreword to the *White Paper on Local Government* (henceforth the White Paper) Pravin Gordham, then chair of the political committee overseeing the writing of the document, proposed that the urgency of local government transformation followed from two world-historical processes: globalisation and the redefinition of the nation-state, as well as a new 'emphasis' on decentralisation. Now, his short remarks do not begin to establish the relationship between these processes, although he contrives to use a phrase that is deeply telling. 'The White Paper', he explains, 'is the expression of the belief that our *decentralisation of a special type* can work' (Gordham 1998: viii, emphasis added). What the latter refers to, Gordham tell us, is a unique system of cooperative governance established to mediate relations between the respective spheres of government (national, provincial and local). Yet his choice of adjectival phrase is by no means neutral or merely descriptive. It is resonant with allusions to the theory of National Democratic Revolution (NDR) and more precisely to the theory of Colonialism of a Special Type (CST). But what should we make of its usage in such an unfamiliar context? Here it certainly lacks the political and theoretical weight of its parent phrase. I presume the content of this to be familiar to the reader and hence unnecessary to discuss further. Given, however, that the paper came out in 1998, two years after the adoption by the national government of the Growth, Equity and Redistribution Strategy (GEAR), a strategy that privileges the role of the market and the private sector as the motors of economic growth and development, does Gordham intend by his neologism a nostalgic allusion to anti-capitalist struggle, waged this time through the local state? It seems more likely that his surreptitious reference to NDR and CST is intended as a warning or a refrain. In discussing what is required for the policies discussed in the White Paper to succeed, Gordham remarks: 'It will require our participation and rolling up of sleeves, our acting like citizens, as opposed to mere atomised consumers of municipal services' (ibid.: viii). This is not simply a broadside at GEAR, although it may well be that as well, but a call to vigilance in the face of local government reform. It is a warning, reminiscent of the Reconstruction and Development Programme, but by no means identical, that local government will not realise its developmental role simply by relying on the private sector and the market. But let us note too a certain curiosity of phrase in his remarks. What should we make of the conditional sense in which his words are framed? Certainly for Gordham it may only have been a stylistic preference, but it nonetheless points to what is the potential novelty of the developmental approach discussed in the White Paper: that it demands of 'role players' to act as citizens. It does not assume, in other words, that they already do; indeed Gordham worries that they might not. There is an implicit distinction here between a citizen *in right* and a citizen *in practice*; where the developmental role discussed in the White Paper 'requires' a movement from the one to the other. We might say that Gordham is alerting us to the fact that those with *de jure* rights and duties might not exercise them in practice; and that the success of development will be measured by the extent to which they do. Now, this was, in part, the critique made of 'formal' democracy by the theory of CST; or more precisely it was the critique made by the political and theoretical sources from which it derived. Even if it was not Gordham's intention to pose the problem in these terms, it is nonetheless valuable to discuss the developmental role of local government with the following question in mind: under what conditions does a 'citizen' behave as a *citizen*? We will see that the developmental role of local government defined in the White Paper begs precisely this question and that its ability to realise such a mandate means providing practical, concrete answers to it. It requires, in other words, that realisable measures are taken to assist 'citizens' to act as such in the face of globalisation and the redefined role of the nation-state.

We will see that the White Paper departs radically from hitherto defined notions of development in South Africa in suggesting that the rights of the citizens are not simply those of 'basic needs', where this refers to the provision of a range of social products (a house, a serviced site and so on), but lie in furnishing the conditions for individuals and households to sustain themselves socially and economically.

In considering the work the of the Department of Community Development (Devcom) in the City of Cape Town, what will be evaluated is the way in which such a developmental vision has been implemented, its institutional consequences and the obstacles to its realisation. A distinction shall be made between an administrative and a theoretical limit, where the former refers to managerial, financial and budgeting obstacles to development and where a theoretical limit is one produced by the concept itself. We will see through a case-study of Manenberg on the Cape Flats that the difficulty of intervening in the area has as much to do with the institutional limits of Devcom as with the normative presuppositions inherent in the notion of a developmental local government. At stake is the production of a virtuous community; deemed by Cape Town to be one that reproduces itself in a way that is deemed *'functional'* as opposed to *'dysfunctional'*. Now, the *moral* norm that informs the work of Ahmedi Vawda and his team is not merely contingent on their personalities, their religious and/or political beliefs but follows necessarily from the 'idea' of development they seek to accomplish. We will see, therefore, that the limit of development is the capacity of local government, depending on the circumstances, to transform real communities into *'good'* communities, i.e. communities that reproduce themselves without recourse to crime or any other activity deemed 'inappropriate' by the state.

This is precisely the dilemma in Manenberg. In an area where a gang-controlled drugs-based economy is more and more prevalent, where unemployment affects 42 per cent of men and women older than fifteen, where less than 7 per cent of residents have a matric and/or post-matric qualification, where those sectors from which residents of Manenberg have traditionally found employment are in decline (chiefly manufacturing and the textile industry), what is an appropriate developmental intervention? It is certainly less about providing services and housing stock in an area where most residents have access to formal accommodation, water and electricity. What does it mean, therefore, to assist households to secure their economic and social needs in a sustainable way? In a community more and more precariously linked to the formal economy and where a growing drugs-based sector provides economic and social support for the vast majority of households, does a developmental role for local government, if we take the White Paper at its word, mean assisting residents to participate in crime? The question is rhetorical, given its patent absurdity for government.

This chapter will argue that a developmental role for local government is less a technical, managerial task than a political-moral one. It implies necessarily that local governments grapple with the questions raised in Devcom: what constitutes 'good' sustainability and what municipal interventions are required to provide for it? Development, that is, is driven by a moral aesthetic and as such is necessarily repressive: it implies supporting and consolidating activities deemed 'acceptable', 'honest', 'legal' and negating those deemed not, ultimately to realise a state of community that accords with the image of the 'good society', the 'modern'. Now, in the case of Manenberg it is precisely this moral order that is in question, and it is precisely this 'other' moral[1] order that is being consolidated by trends in the global and the national economy. We will see, therefore, that the limits to development in Manenberg have less to do with 'efficiencies' and 'flexibilities' in the administration of Cape Town, than with the obstacles to realising a certain idea of the 'virtuous'[2] community. This said, we shall see that the citizen is above all an ethical figure and that the precondition for citizenship in a *national* context is the production of moral communities.

The RDP and integrated development

What is at stake in the White Paper is the granting to local governments their proper autonomy as *political* bodies, elected by and responsible to their *citizens*. Now, this marks an important departure from previous conceptions of local government in two respects. Research done for the White Paper dealt with this more fully, but we can summarise some of its conclusions as follows: In the first instance, the Reconstruction and Development Programme cast third tier government as the 'hands and feet' of delivery initiatives; that is, essentially as administrative bodies charged with the execution of tasks mandated from above. In the second instance, development was conceived primarily as a state-institutional task where the ostensibly political role of municipalities was limited to 'change management' or 'transformation' to realign their institutional capacity to the RDP

---

[1] For convenience sake I will discuss this 'other' order as a moral order. Now my reticence here does not derive from the fact that 'immoral' would perhaps be deemed more appropriate, but rather that, in discussing gangs, kinship groups and so on, such a vocabulary is inappropriate for *theoretical* reasons.

[2] My thanks to Firoz Khan for this expression.

tasks at hand. I have considered this more closely elsewhere (Chipkin 1997a), but very briefly we can say the following: it presupposed that residents became citizens when their needs were satisfied, where needs were defined, essentially, as a house and a serviced site. Now the novelty of the White Paper lies in the way that this relationship is reconceptualised. In that section dealing with a *developmental local government* such a role is defined as follows:

> Developmental local government is local government committed to working with citizens[3] and groups within the community to find sustainable ways to meet their social, economic and material needs and improve the quality of their lives. (Gordham 1998: 17)

What is striking about this formulation is what is not said. If we compare it, for example, to the task of local government as it is defined in the Urban Development Strategy, the difference becomes more apparent. The 1995 document states:

> The primary responsibility of local authorities is to ensure the delivery of services at a community level within an agreed planning framework. In support of this, local authorities will be responsible for development and physical planning as well as the preparation of 5-year infrastructure investment programmes.[4]

Now, whereas the UDS is emphatic that the *primary* role of municipalities is that of service delivery, the White Paper does not even mention it. This is not simply because the term 'development' is used as a synonym for service delivery; nor does it mean that the provision of household infrastructure and services is somehow neglected in the document. It does mean, however, that service delivery is no longer judged an end in and of itself but is subordinated to another objective: finding sustainable ways to meet the social, economic and material needs of communities. In other words, 'development' in the White Paper is measured not against how many homes are built or sites are serviced but against the degree to which 'citizens' are able to *sustain* themselves and their households. This implies a radical reworking of how local government works. If, during what is termed the 'interim' phase, municipalities have been chiefly preoccupied with 'deracialising' their institutions and installing effective management and financial systems to deliver services – they have tended to be inward looking – the 'final' stage envisaged by the White Paper implies that local governments will have to grapple not simply with the *'how'* of development but, as importantly, with the *'what'*. In other words, they are asked to address the following question: what public interventions will assist residents in the area under their jurisdiction to sustain and improve their material needs and the quality of their lives? Now, despite a superficial resemblance, this is a different kind of question to that one hitherto posed: how can public services be deployed to meet the needs of communities? Indeed, despite the fact that they employ a common vocabulary – nearly all discussion documents, legislation, White Papers refer to 'community needs', 'citizens', 'participation' *et al.* – they nonetheless imply distinct notions of development. In the first place, the one that is driven by standard indicators is predicated on the assumption that service delivery satisfies local governments' developmental mandate. For convenience sake let us call it the RDP approach; although this is intended with a little irony. It follows

---

[3] Note that the term 'citizens' here simply refers to those residents with *de jure* rights and obligations.
[4] Government of National Unity, *Urban Development Strategy*, Pretoria: Ministry in the Office of the President, 12 October 1995, p. 35.

that institutional design and performance management are undertaken with a view to most effectively delivering a number of products seen as ends in themselves: housing units, serviced sites and so on. In the second instance, I will discuss it as that of Integrated Development (ID). These standard outputs are judged as, at best, *means* of realising development. In other words, for a developmental local government a house is not a product unless it contributes to development. The measure here is a 'sustainable community', where the indicators that follow from this objective are neither self-evident nor knowable in advance. Indeed, what the first calls a developmental product may, according to the second, be either non-developmental or, worse, profoundly anti-developmental. When, that is, a house and/or serviced site does not grant to residents a resource with which they may access further opportunities, or even worse burdens them with a product they cannot afford, the results may be considered ineffectual or even harmful.

Let us note too the institutional consequences that follow from 'RDP' and 'ID' approaches, respectively. In the case of the former what is paramount is the delivery of a range of goods, *discernible in advance*. In the original RDP conception, housing stock and municipal services were intended to be the products of a government-driven programme of investment, where state institutions were cast as the leading agents of implementation. I have already touched on this but very briefly we can say that this privileged the importance of building the capacity of state institutions to execute their RDP-given obligations. Now, following the reassessment of state capacity that informed and followed from the GEAR strategy (see introduction, Chipkin 1997b), what has been strongly muted, especially in the Municipal Structures Bill (MSB), is the role of 'alternative service providers'. At stake is the deployment of a range of agencies, other than the municipality *strictu sensu*, to execute certain functions traditionally performed by local governments themselves.[5] What this reflects is the rise of the New Public Management.

In 1991 and in preparation for a post-apartheid public service, a group of public administration academics and practitioners adopted the so-named Mount Grace Resolution. It called for a break with the Public Administration of the apartheid period and move towards the New Public Administration associated with the American 'Minnowbrook' movement (Fitzgerald 1995: 512). At stake was a critique of the 'wholly outdated' principles and methods that made the South African public services a 'bureaucratic, law-driven, hierarchical, multi-layered, departmentally fragmented, inward-oriented, racial Oligarchy' (ibid.: 514). The starting point for a new paradigm was an adaptation to local circumstances of Osborne and Gaebler's (1992) *Reinventing Government*. Here, the emphasis was on cultivating an 'entrepreneurial spirit' to transform the public service. If the traditional public administration model was premised on the idea of a 'neutral' Weberian bureaucracy, Fitzgerald tells us, the corporate management approach recognised that public service could not plausibly be conceived as obedient and neutral. It accepted, rather, that there would invariably be an important element of bureaucratic discretion in interpreting and implementing policy. What it proposed, as a result, was that 'discretion or influence [was] best safeguarded in the hands of suitably qualified personnel who possess both proven expertise and an appropriate code of professional ethics' (ibid.: 517).

---

[5] Republic of South Africa, *Municipal Services Bill*, as introduced in the National Assembly as a section 75 Bill, Gazette No. 21071, Pretoria: Government, 2000, p. 48.

Allied to this new emphasis on management was an interest in 'commercial con-tracting'. Profoundly suspicious of the quality, quantity and manner in which the public service allocated public goods, 'consumer power' and 'citizen control' were deemed best guaranteed when line departments and the administration were organised into competing delivery units. These divisions operate as stand-alone businesses that compete for market share both internally – with each other – and externally – with other private businesses (ibid.: 518).

We see the influence of the New Public Management in and through the Graduate School of Public and Development Management at the University of the Witwatersrand. Notes prepared for the Urban Governance Elective, for example, discusses these proposals according to the following tripartite division: in-council ring-fenced operations ('corporatised' units, agencies, utilities), contracting out (service contract, management contract, leases, concessions, build-operate-transfer contracts) and full privatisation of services.[6]

More shall be said about this later but for the moment what is important to note is the value such options are thought to bring. 'Conventionally,' the P&DM notes remark,

> a municipality delivers through its various line departments, each organized into much the same institutional layout, each managed by the same hierarchies of officials and each subject to the same organisational wide-systems of financial accountability, staff grading and remuneration, political accountability. Traditionally, the development and service delivery obligations of each line department are funded out of the same municipal budget (albeit from different accounts) decided annually by council. This approach ... creates the basis for a sense of institutional coherence, for integrated planning and for cross-subsidisation of equally important but less financially self-sufficient services by others that easily generate profit. However ... not all service delivery is best managed through the same organisational structure: a health department or civic theatre is not the same as a water department, and to apply the same management hierarchy to each may be inappropriate. ... Most importantly, perhaps, integrated budgets often mean that cross-subsidised services are less efficient and financially self-sufficient than they could be, and cross-subsidising departments often lose hard-won reserves of revenue that could be used internally for development.[7]

As a result, the notes continue, 'South African local government has begun to talk about different service delivery options to address these *inefficiencies*. The challenge in moving from traditional department led service delivery is to introduce new *flexibilities* [*sic*] into the municipal administration without losing the capacity of a council to direct and control integrated development and delivery through its various operations' (emphasis added).[8] Later they add: the general principle is that 'through creative institutional engineering, a very much more *efficient* and *effective* organisation with more stable sources of revenue can be created' (emphasis added).[9] For the moment let us not quibble with the remark that surpluses from certain functions are deservedly 'ring-fenced' because 'hard-won' and note that the benefits of such alternatives are deemed essentially managerial and administrative. They allow for greater 'flexibilities' and 'efficiencies' in the institution to

[6] Salga/Jupmet, Executive Leadership Programme for Local Government: Service Delivery Module (extracts), March 2000, p. 3.
[7] Ibid.: p. 1.
[8] Ibid.: p. 2.
[9] Ibid.: p. 3.

deliver their traditional services. What is not raised here is the value of such services for development. In other words, the value of 'alternative' service delivery providers is measured simply by the extent to which they are able efficiently and cost-effectively to deliver municipal products. Now, the mention in the notes above of the possibility for Integrated Development even within a dispensation using corporatised entities, leases, agencies, etc. is a red herring. It should not deceive us into underestimating the distance between ID and the RDP approach. There it tends to refer to the possibility of co-ordination and cooperation between various departments, enterprises and municipal units. But such a reading reduces ID to little more than an internal administrative problem and hence purges the term of its meaning in the White Paper. We can note too that despite the claim in the Municipal System Bill that the document 'gives effect to the country's vision of 'developmental local government' as envisaged in the Local Government White Paper' there is a definite drift towards conceiving Integrated Development as little more than an exercise in institutional coordination. We have seen, however, that the gauge of ID is not simply the successful delivery of services, but rather the extent to which households can socially and economically sustain themselves. In other words, ID is not merely another managerial device aimed at institutional efficiency. We will see shortly that in the case of the Unicity Commission this is exactly the distinction that is made between, on the one hand, institutional efficiency *vis-à-vis* service delivery and, on the other, development as the social and economic sustainability of households. Ring-fencing certain departments is intended to make possible the most effective provision of basic services (water, electricity) precisely to release municipal resources (human and financial) for development. Let us merely flag for the moment a danger to which I will return in the conclusion: a developmental local government is not simply one that more efficiently and effectively delivers housing stock and municipal services.

We have here two contrasting responses to the question posed earlier: under what conditions does a 'stakeholder' become a citizen? In the first instance, the implied response is: when they are able to exercise their rights to a house and a serviced site and, in the second: when they are able to access resources sustainably to reproduce themselves socially and materially. Of course, these responses are not mutually exclusive, but nor are they necessarily sequential. Now it is precisely the undecidability of this relation *in advance* that grants to local government a new role as the protagonist of '*integrated development*'. What this means concretely is that municipalities are expected not simply to build their institutional capacity to deliver a range of products but to identify, first and foremost, what products would best assist those in need to sustain themselves and their households.

The notion of development as furnished by the White Paper is haunted by a certain imprecision concerning the notion of the citizen. A resident is deemed a citizen to the extent that she is able to exercise her rights to a sustainable livelihood. From the point of view of government, however, it is not enough that people do so by any means (violence, coercion and so on), or that this livelihood takes any form (crime, corruption, illicit activities). Residents are expected to do so in a way becoming of citizens. What this brings to the fore is the following hidden surmise: that the figure of the citizen is also an *ethical* character; it is someone that conducts herself 'rightfully' and sustains herself in and through activities deemed virtuous by the state. Now, if a developmental local government means by the rights of the citizen the right to a sustainable life – and sustainability here implies a definite ethical norm – then development implies necessarily an ethical measure. Citizenship, that is, can never simply refer to a) the granting of rights and b) the establishment of forums through which these rights can be exercised. It necessarily presupposes c) that these rights are exercised 'fairly', 'honestly', 'legally'. And yet it is precisely this dimension of citizenship that is neglected in the academic and policy literature in South Africa.

What have in fact been collapsed into a single term are three distinct qualities: a constitutional *status*, a moral-ethical *disposition* and a political *identity*. The current literature on development in South Africa tends, for the most part, to be cast in a legal/constitutional light, where the citizen is deemed, rather naively, simply to be a certain bearer of rights and duties to the state. As a result, debate and policy proposals are preoccupied with the following concerns: what are the rights of the citizen and how are they realised? Merely the first and last qualities of citizenship mentioned above are discussed. Note, for example the Municipal Structures Bill. It defines a municipality as consisting of both the 'governing structures and administration' of a local government as well as 'the residents and communities' in its demarcated jurisdiction.[10] By this it intends to ensure that public participation is built into the daily working of local government as a *necessary* component of its functioning as an institution. In this way, moreover, the Bill claims to 'elaborate the core principles, mechanisms and processes that are necessary to enable municipalities to move progressively towards the social and economic upliftment of communities ...'.[11] According to the MSB the conditions of citizenship are thus deemed to be the mechanisms and processes through which residents can articulate their needs as citizens.

If we scan the document, however, we will find it replete with ethical provisos. In Chapter One, on the 'Legal Nature and Internal Relationships of Municipalities', we read: 'The council of a municipality and its committees and functionaries have the right – ... to conduct their business without *interference or fear of intimidation and threats* [emphasis added]'.[12] Elsewhere, in discussing the rights of 'communities', it remarks: 'A resident and a community of residents in a municipality has the right ... to proceedings of the municipal council and its committees and functionaries that are ... conducted *impartially and without prejudice* [emphasis added]'.[13] Regarding the duties of such residents it adds, amongst other things, that they are obliged to: '*respect* the municipal rights of other residents [and] to treat councillors and municipal employees with *dignity and respect* [emphasis added]'.[14] Schedule 1 of the Bill discusses a 'Code of Conduct for Municipal Officials'. It mentions, amongst many clauses discussing undue influence, declaration of assets and so on, that: 'An employee of a municipality must at all times *loyally* execute the *lawful* policies of the municipal council [and] perform the functions of office in *good faith, diligently, honestly* and in a transparent manner [emphasis added]'.[15] Now, these are merely a few scattered examples to demonstrate the extent to which the document presupposes a standard of moral or ethical conduct for national citizens and officials. If

[10] Republic of South Africa, *Municipal Systems Bill*, as introduced in the National Assembly as a section 75 Bill, Pretoria: Government Gazette No. 21071, 2000, p. 15.
[11] Ibid.: p. 6.
[12] Ibid.: p. 17
[13] Ibid.: p. 18.
[14] Ibid.: p. 21.
[15] Ibid.: p. 163.

this is the case then a developmental practice that is concerned with the citizen can never simply be a matter of 'efficiencies' and 'effectiveness'. This is precisely what the role of Devcom brings to the fore: that development, as a practice for and on citizens, is principally about making 'virtuous' subjects. In Cape Town, this is called producing 'functional' communities.

Manenberg

There are today two distinct moral registers that inform, on the one hand, social relations in Manenberg and, on the other, political relations. The first is a notion of social *respectability* amongst residents in Manenberg, allied to a conception of 'proper living' and, at the same time, a notion of rightfully/honourably meeting one's needs. The former is an aesthetic that is contingent on local factors, whatever these might be (religion, media, etc.). The second is a state norm, defined in and through the Constitution, legislation about crime, judicial precedent and so on. What is happening in Manenberg, following shifts in the capitalist economy, is that the capacity to live *respectably* through *honourable* means is declining. Indeed, this relationship is in profound crisis,

The Coloured Labour Preference Policy of 1953 sought both to prevent the influx of Africans into the Western Cape and to assist Coloureds to enter the labour market. The legislation, the brainchild of the infamous apartheid ethnologist Dr Eiselen, was intended to prevent Africans becoming a majority in the region so that one day it could become a predominantly 'white' homeland! If, notes Salo, the 'Coloured Labour Preference Policy racialised labour preference in the Western Cape, the nature of the local Cape Town economy gendered it'.[16] The clothing, textiles and leather sectors have traditionally relied on female labour, drawn especially from Manenberg. As a result, the 'work-force placed employed, coloured, working class women in a powerful economic position as breadwinners of households'. Their privileged economic status was further consolidated by the fact that men were mostly confined to casual labour in the docks or in the construction industry. Now the value of Salo's work lies in her analysis of the social power this gave to employed women. Until the 1990s, that is, access to work was mediated by such women through a process referred to as '*ingebring*' (to be brought in). What this designated was not simply an exercise whereby older women assisted those younger than themselves to find a job. More importantly, it referred to the initiation of work-seekers into *womanhood*. By controlling access to jobs, older women were in a position to define what constituted eligibility to be '*ingebring*' and, therefore, to define also the properties of a *good* woman. Elaine Salo claims, therefore, that:

> [A]s Apartheid legislation was implemented in the context of Manenberg township, [it] inscribed particular roles, namely women as mothers with particular local moral and material meanings that ultimately constitute personhood for Manenberg residents. In this context motherhood refers to the act of biological and social parenting of one's own offspring. Moreover, it refers to women's

---

[16] I am drawing here on a draft chapter of Elaine Salo's doctoral thesis. The chapter in question was presented to a seminar at the University of the Cape Town (29 August 2000) and subsequently sent to me with her permission. In referring to her work, the reader should note that it is ongoing and her conclusions are in no way final. I would like to record my thanks to her.

social parenting of their wider community. Herein lies the essence of personhood in Manenberg. In short, a gendered ideology of personhood exists which is embodied in the identity of the adult female household head, as the 'moeder' (mother). It is through their identities as mothers women are able to exercise agency and to confer personhood on other residents.[17]

For our purposes let us say that a 'respectable' life was to a certain degree possible until the 1990s through 'honourable' means, deemed 'appropriate' by the state. There was some scope for women that qualified as *decent* to fulfil their roles as *good* mothers (both to their children and to the 'community' at large) through formal economy jobs. Moreover, and more importantly, the economic status of 'respectable' women gave to their households a certain authority to define in Manenberg the content of *good* and *evil*. We can add to this the crisis of men failing to realise their roles as *masculine* figures, as beings in a position to exercise their roles as *good* fathers, as husbands, as partners. We noticed earlier how, on the Devcom reading of dysfunctionality, this 'pathology' did not simply follow from unemployment. It resulted, instead, from some vaguely defined notion of 'disintegrating' families. There is some merit in this thinking. Given the economic marginality of many Coloured men, it may be that alcoholism, family violence and so on are symptoms of the fact that many men were/are not in a position to realise their *social* 'manhood'. Economic marginality or unemployment act as castration. I will return to this in the conclusion. Now, even if this 'moral economy' is in terminal crisis there are still residues of its pre-eminence. In her ethnographic study of Sharien, a twenty-five-year-old mother of two girls, Salo recounts the story of her 'impending downfall'.

At the age of fifteen Sharien was made pregnant by a young man named Spookie from a 'respectable' household in Manenberg. Even though she was forced to leave school, Salo reports that, at the time, she was not concerned about her future. Spookie was securely employed, had formally asked to marry her, had apologised to her mother for 'spoiling' her and had assumed economic responsibility for his children. Later she was able to find a job through the process of '*ingebring*' discussed above. At about that time she heard rumours that Spookie had fathered a child with another woman. He subsequently deserted her. Sharien had in the meanwhile lost her job for staying away from work during Spookie's rape trial. As a result she became dependent on a welfare grant to support her and her two children; as well as sporadic maintenance payments from Spookie. Salo remarks: 'She was deeply concerned about the economic impact her retrenchment would have on the household income', and continues by recounting the following conversation:

> I told Tammy's father (Spookie) that she needs new shoes for Christmas. But everyone's talking about him and that woman. They're showing off their baby at the Junction [the local mall]. Where am I to find the money to buy the kids some Christmas clothes? Glen is unemployed and Brinley has only just begun looking for casual employment [her brothers that live at home]. My father gives my mother a measly R200 to pay all the bills. That's why I keep away from the house these days.[18]

What finally threatened her reputation, her 'respectability', that is, was her alleged relation with a gangster from the Dixie boys – one of the Manenberg gangs. Sharien's

---

[17] E. Salo (2000) 'Race Laws, Gender Tactics: on becoming respectable mothers during the Apartheid era', draft version of Chapter Three of her doctoral thesis.

[18] Ibid. The discussion took place in Afrikaans. The translation is provided by Salo herself.

'decline' begins, therefore, the moment she is no longer able to perform her role as a *good* mother *honourably*; when, that is, she resorts to the support of gangsters to meet her children's needs.

In the ethnography above, Sharien lost her job for quite personal reasons. But, in this respect, her story is atypical. There is growing, critical unemployment in Manenberg for reasons associated with shifts in the regional and global economy. According to a discussion document released by the Unicity Commission (2000) there are some 'alarming' economic trends in the Cape Town metropolitan area.

> Cape Town has an economy that has grown significantly faster than other metropolitan areas during the 1990s. It is also based on a relatively diverse range of sectors with strong growth potential in knowledge, information and service sectors (especially tourism). The City has strong IT, financial and communications infrastructure in a sound framework of legislation, intellectual property rights and trade agreements.

But the report adds:

> At the same time there are major negative trends that reinforce social divisions and inequality and act as a substantial brake on the economy. These include:
>
> A decline in traditional manufacturing services, which are in need of substantial restructuring to be competitive in the global market place;
>
> High unemployment, which is likely to increase as manufacturing sectors decline and the major growth sectors largely require skilled labour and capital-intensive investment;
>
> A critical skills gap between the demands of the new growth sectors and the skills of the labour force. In a global economy that is becoming increasingly knowledge based, only 15% of the people between 18 and 65 have more than a matric.

A consequence of these trends, the report concludes: 'is the growth of a substantial informal economy currently comprising some 18% of economically active population as well as growing inequality'.

The reasons for the decline of the manufacturing industry and especially of the textiles industry are numerous. We can mention, however, the lower costs of production in Asia. These are related to the frequent use of child labour, the breakup of trade unions and hence the weak bargaining position of workers, indeed, the general availability of much cheaper labour elsewhere. Contrast this with a labour market in South Africa regulated by hard-won workers' rights. What the report also correctly points out is that the vast majority of Coloureds and Africans are in no position to participate in the growing sectors of the economy. We have already heard that less than 7 per cent of residents in Manenberg have a matric and/or post-matric qualification. The figures are even lower in African areas. Most disturbing, finally, is the last remark. More and more residents are dependent on the informal economy. We know already that in Manenberg there is nothing romantic about this economy. It is not about street vendors hawking vegetables or meats, or flower sellers on street corners. It is more and more a drugs–robbery–arms trade economy mediated by gangs. For our purposes, it means that the space for households to sustain themselves *respectably* through *virtuous* activities is fast decreasing.

We can say, therefore, that the crisis in Manenberg is not simply one of unemployment. It is a crisis of households to sustain themselves *respectably*. We have seen that this last term was defined by a class of female breadwinners capable of exercising a certain moral authority in the area. There is strong evidence to suggest that, with the declining economic status of such women, there are important shifts in the 'moral economy' as well. If 'respectability' was strongly informed by religious notions of modesty and decency, what is the social impact of gangs more and more able to exercise economic control in Manenberg? Already officials in the Development Facilitation Unit in the City of Cape Town complain that residents are dissatisfied with RDP-style matchbox houses when compared to those of gangsters. Is there a new conception of 'proper living' emerging in Manenberg? To what extent is it informed by those values that govern the relationships between and within gangs?

What does it mean, therefore, to assist residents in Manenberg to meet their social and economic needs sustainably? Once we admit that such reproduction is always and without exception informed by a certain vision of life, what we have here are at least three competing imaginaries: that of the state (functionality), that of 'moral' households (respectability) and that of various gangs. Now, it is far from clear that 'functionality' and 'respectability' are mere synonyms for each other. A functional household was one where the integrity of the nuclear unit was high and where alcoholism, abuse and family violence were non-existent. Now it is likely, although this is merely a hypothesis, that the cost of living 'respectably' may have been exactly *male* 'dysfunctionality'. If, that is, respectability referred to the capacity of households to exercise a 'mothering' function (both to their off-spring and the 'community' at large) and social value was attached to such a female figure, what space did this leave for men to exercise a 'manly' function? I am assuming here that what it meant to be a 'man' drew heavily from patriarchal conceptions of authority. If 'development', therefore, presupposes 'functionality', then it is not simply about assisting residents to survive any old how. It is about ordering, arranging and creating them according to an image of the *ethical* being. It is about producing them as moral citizens. Once we admit this we acknowledge too the radical import of 'development'. It implies necessarily a normative register, an imaginary of what 'better living' is, of what a 'good life' might be. 'Development', therefore, is that process whereby the state tries to capture residents into a host of relationships (contracts through service provision and mortgages, social ties through public participation and community organisations) to compel them to act according to what it defines as functional/social/ethical behaviour. We can say too that such assistance is not simply about helping residents exercise their rights as citizens; it is about producing them as citizens in the first place. There is no evidence to suggest that the delivery of houses, of health services and of community services has gone anywhere towards achieving this goal. Indeed, there is much evidence to suggest the contrary.

The community development approach

The measure of a 'dysfunctionality'
There is a certain ambiguity within the Department of Community Development concerning the definition of 'dysfunctionality'. It is sometimes associated with certain phenomena and sometimes with others (violence and trauma, tuberculosis, alcoholism,

substance abuse and so on). At other times 'dysfunctionality' is written and spoken about as a host of social practices (crime, gangs, unemployment) that produce undesirable consequences and/or even a state of mind.

Without too much improvisation, however, we can hazard the following hypothesis: the Manenberg community is 'dysfunctional' because family units tend towards disintegration and are thus incapable of socialising (interpellating would be theoretically more precise) their youth into adulthood. As a result young men and women are raised in and through gang structures that replace the function of the nuclear household. These attach little importance to education and to the acquisition of the skills necessary to participate in the formal economy. This, in turn, compounds the dependency of residents on the informal economy, which is more and more characterised by the drugs trade and other criminal activities. Gangs, moreover, are prone to violence, producing, as a result, high levels of stress and violence-induced trauma. They are involved in sexual practices that encourage teenage pregnancy and HIV/AIDS. They control the informal economy and hence deepen the dependency of families and residents on criminality. It follows, therefore, that 'treating' dysfunctionality to make possible *appropriate* sustainable development is a question not simply of trauma counselling, Alcoholics Anonymous, better policing and so on, but of measures that a) build and/or consolidate the integrity of nuclear families[19] in the face of growing formal unemployment and b) provide youth in unstable families social outlets other than gangs. Now, it is precisely this hypothesis that is manifest in Devcom's *practice* in Manenberg and elsewhere. What are these measures and what 'good' development are they supposed to make possible?

We have considered until now the *theoretical* limits of a developmental role. We have seen that development presupposes a certain ethical norm both in how residents conduct themselves as citizens and how they sustain themselves socially and economically. In considering the work of Devcom, we have seen that the limit to development arises, in part, from the distance between how residents in Manenberg actually live and conduct themselves and the figure of the ethical citizen. That, of course, is not a theoretical limit, merely a disjuncture between the concept and circumstances on the ground (the so-called *real*). It says nothing, that is, about the internal consistency of the concept itself; merely about its match with reality. A conceptual limit is one produced either by a contradiction or an inconsistency in the way the concept is defined. What we have discussed is the way that development as outlined in the White Paper presupposes a certain ethical figure. In other words, the conditions of the citizen are not merely processes (CDFs, LDFs, mechanisms for public participation *à la* MSB) through which residents may exercise their rights. It assumes a certain standard of conduct in the way that such rights are exercised and, moreover, in the way these rights are realised. Yet, in asking what are the conditions for development, when this means the development of the *citizen*, the White Paper, the MSB and all other policy documents, legislation, etc. fail to address the conditions of such *ethical* development. But we know already that not any development

[19] The term 'dysfunctional', as it is used in Cape Town, refers in particular to Coloured working-class families on the Flats. Problems associated with African families are deemed more a product of poverty than phenomena arising from a crisis at the very heart of the family form itself. Even if the extended African family is deemed problematic from the point of view of property rights and succession, it is not deemed in and of itself a problem. This is not the case with the Coloured family.

will do: it must be 'honest', 'legal', that is, virtuous. What this means is that in Cape Town and elsewhere, the institutional design of the municipality and the resources made available are referenced only to the delivery of a range of products deemed, in and of themselves, developmental. In other words, the conditions of citizenship are said to be met when residents can exercise their rights to a house and serviced site, health facilities, libraries and so on. What is not addressed is how these products might assist residents to become ethical citizens in a position to sustain themselves virtuously. We can say, in other words, that the institutional limit to development arises from this theoretical blind spot.

An example, for clarification: in Manenberg virtuous development is deemed the economic and social sustainability of *nuclear household* services, building homes and improving health conditions to the extent to which these interventions a) help improve the integrity of nuclear families in Manenberg and b) enable such families to sustain themselves economically and socially, *in the right way*. We might say that the stability of the nuclear household is deemed the condition of ethical citizenship, where the exercise of right to a house, a serviced site, etc. deemed the conditions of *good* sustainability.

What implications does this have for the way that local government is structured?

Institutional transformation
It is not the place here to provide a history of local government changes in South Africa as a whole, or in Cape Town specifically. What is important, however, is to understand how changes in institutional design have been informed by changing notions of local governments' function and how, therefore, the organisation has been configured and resourced to achieve this mandate.

Following the local government elections in 1995, municipalities throughout the country began to implement the provisions of the Local Government Transition Act (LGTA) of 1993. What this involved primarily was the establishment of Transitional Metropolitan Councils (TMCs) in large urban conurbations, including their respective Metropolitan Substructures (MSSs), Transitional Local Councils (TLCs) in other urban areas and Transitional Rural Councils (TRCs) and Transitional Rural Representative Councils (TRRCs) elsewhere. In December 1996 in Cape Town this resulted in the constitution of the Cape Metropolitan Authority, including the establishment of six substructures (the Cape Town Metropolitan Council, the Helderberg MC, the Eastern MC, the Northern MC, the Southern MC and the Tygerberg MC). At a planning workshop held in October 1996, in preparation for the final agreement in respect of the allocation of powers, duties and functions between the CMA and its substructures, participants agreed that the City (the CMA and its six substructures) had five principal roles:

• To provide and maintain the basic municipal infrastructure and services
• To enable or facilitate development
• To regulate and build relationships between individuals, groups and institutions
• To lead social transformation, to lead the community and to administer resources
• To be an international player.[20]

---

[20] *Report on the Strategic Planning Worksession* (10 October 1996), a report compiled by Nico Mclachlan of Gouws Woods and Partners and Elna Trautman of the Department of Human Resources on the Worksession held at the Cape Town Municipality Training Centre on the 5 October 1996.

What is important to note is the distinction above between 'service delivery' and 'development'. In the way that the new council was structured, these functions were located in separate departments responsible for different activities. What may at first glance seem like a conceptual distinction was in fact nothing of the sort.

What did inform the distinction between the directorate of Community Development and Municipal Services was the idea that the provision of health, housing and community services, on the one hand, required high levels of *resident participation*, whereas that of roads, water, electricity, on the other, did not. These last-mentioned functions were believed to be technical-administrative services that required scientific knowledge and were thus most effectively managed when left to officials and engineers. Indeed, the efficient and cost-effective provision of these services was deemed a question of how best to manage these functions within the administration. In contrast, the health of residents, their accommodation and the social facilities they wanted were questions that more obviously required mechanisms to involve them in the very delivery of these services.

The location of health and other services in the department of Community Development had nothing to do, therefore, with the fact that they were somehow deemed more developmental than other municipal products. When Ahmedi Vawda became Executive Director of Devcom in 1997 he inherited a department mandated to ensure the provision of services through community participation. That is what community development meant. How the provision of these services ensured social and economic sustainability had never been addressed. Moreover, Vawda's arms had been partly tied. Not only was he not in a position to ask what public resources might best achieve development, but he was obliged to work with the resources and staff delegated to him. In other words, he had to work *as if* health, housing and community services were the most appropriate interventions through which to ensure the sustainability of households.

The work of the Department of Community Development
We have discussed so far a fundamental ambiguity concerning the way that 'development' is construed in South Africa generally and in Cape Town more especially. On the one hand, it is *practised* as the provision of a range of municipal products deemed in and of themselves developmental. On the other hand, it is conceptualised as measures to ensure the social and economic sustainability of citizens. In the first case, development is posed as an institutional-administrative question: how to deliver a range of products efficiently and cost-effectively. In the second, development begs a host of political and social questions: what would it take to assist residents in this particular area, organised in such and such a manner, afflicted with these or those problems, to sustain themselves? This difference has been too easily concealed by the lazy use of terms. Take for instance the notion of integrated development. It refers to the coordination of government departments and other agencies to deliver municipal services. Yet, depending on the definition of 'development' to which it is attached, what these services are may vary. They can either be defined generally and in advance; or they will depend on the specific *conditions* of economic and social sustainability from one area to the next. It is precisely this ambiguity that constrains the work of Devcom. The department was designed according to the first definition but tries to function according to the second. In this regard, Ahmedi Vawda has implemented a range of systems within Devcom to provide for area by area interventions.

This is intended to enable the directorate to provide for what are deemed the *conditions* of sustainability on a district basis. And yet, as we shall see in the case of Manenberg, it is far from evident how the provision of health, housing and community services will accomplish the task at hand. This tension is adequately captured by the 1998/1999 Business Plan. Here the core business of the Department of Community Development was defined as follows:

> To create an enabling environment for the management of the delivery of essential social development services (health, housing and community services – which include libraries, parks and bathing, civic amenities and buildings, art and culture and sport and recreation) that stimulates the re-building of communities.[21]

Now, we have already seen that the conditions of sustainability were defined as functional communities, where in Manenberg this referred to the stability of the nuclear family. We can ask, in other words, to what extent interventions in the fields of health, housing and community services are the conditions of such functionality? Devcom's approach, in this regard, is captured by the following strategic vision:

• establish health as a base to the city's developmental approach
• establish housing as the socio-economic driver
• establish community facilities and programmes as an instrument for social development and cohesion.[22]

Nowhere have these elements been coherently reconciled either in writing or in departmental planning sessions. Indeed, this is one of the profound criticisms made of the Executive Director by departmental staff: 'how do these concepts translate into action plans?' they ask. I will, nonetheless, attempt to propose some form of synthesis by drawing from my interviews with various officials. We can say that *in concept*, if not in practice, these elements are reconciled in the following manner: by making housing subsidies available to families and by launching an intensive campaign of building, Devcom intends to release public funds a) to create employment amongst those with basic skills and b) to consolidate the family as the core social unit in the areas in question. If housing subsidies are granted to parents, that is, it is believed that this will go some way to re-establishing their authority over the family unit. Moreover, once granted ownership of their homes it is said that households will be more inclined to look after both them and their surrounding areas (parks, streets), presumably to protect their values in an anticipated housing market. In this way, families will exercise greater control over public and social spaces to prevent or reduce crime and gang-fighting. Moreover, in providing work opportunities in a kind of housing-driven public works programme, residents will be in a position to generate an income outside the criminal economy. Given that gangs are said to supplant the family unit, enabling residents (and especially the youth) to sustain themselves elsewhere will help re-establish the integrity of the nuclear household. The strategic accomplice of this initiative is an intensive health campaign. The principle that drives it is that of *primary health care*. The emphasis, therefore, is not on the establishment of a medical infrastructure to treat various ailments and pathologies (tuberculosis, HIV, medical problems arising from alcoholism and so on) but to treat the *conditions* of these illnesses. We have already seen that for Devcom many of these problems relate to the disintegration

---

[21] *Draft Business Plan for 1998/99* (City of Cape Town, Department of Community Development, 1999).
[22] Power Point presentation (nd) on the developmental approach of the Department of Community Development.

of the family. As a result a health strategy implies addressing the causes of such family disintegration, but also treating actual illnesses so that residents can return to their families as healthy, that is, functional members.

The third element, that of community services, is deemed a way of removing residents from the influence of a gang-based culture that values violence and crime, where irresponsible sexual practices are the norm and where rape is condoned. By providing social facilities (libraries, sports fields, art and culture centres) residents can play, learn and meet through activities that are deemed conducive to social cohesion and *good* community values. Participation in such activities, that is, is deemed a way of inculcating in residents a host of social values (tolerance, fair play) that will help make of them responsible citizens. Devcom's vision for community services does not end there. Take for example the anticipated benefits of libraries. Ahmedi Vawda wants them not simply to be places of reading and learning, but places where young men and women can acquire information-based skills through access to computers and the Internet. In this way, he proposes to help 'leapfrog' residents into the information age so that their chances of entry into the formal economy are vastly improved.

If the objective here is to produce functional sustainable households, then the extent to which there is development follows from this goal. We can say with regard to housing, for example, that the measure of development is not simply how many houses have been built or maintained. The indicator would rather be the degree to which such a programme reinforced parental control, the degree to which families better maintained their assets and the degree to which they tried to exercise care over surrounding areas. In the same way, a community facility could only be said to be developmental to the extent that it helped produce more community cohesion and so on. And so on with health. It is surprising, therefore, to find none of these sorts of measures amongst the performance indicators for departmental directors and managers. What we find instead are measures relating to the extent to which certain products have been *delivered*! This despite a rigorous planning session, using what is called a 'logical framework methodology', to identify the core business of each function, the concrete activities that follow from this and the indicators to measure performance. Let us consider a typical example.

The core business of housing was defined as follows:

To promote, support and expand the role of housing in the overall economic and social well-being of Cape Town.[23]

And yet for the year 1999/2000 the performance of the department of housing was gauged by its success in:

- establish[ing] an effective and efficient management structure for existing housing stock
- provid[ing] an efficient and effective support service in regard of [*sic*] ... rented stock and new housing projects ...
- establish[ing] a cost effective and efficient maintenance service for Council letting schemes
- manag[ing] the housing delivery program for the city in line with ... strategic priorities
- prevent[ing] the occupation of ... vacant land and control[ling]/monitor[ing] existing illegal settlements

[23] *Business Plan 1998/99* op. cit.

- creat[ing] where necessary and maintain[ing] proper administration prodecures ....[24]

With few exceptions indicators refer to administrative measures to deliver, maintain and manage existing and new houses. The 'social' targets mentioned above simply concern the access of more people to housing subsidies, or they are too vague to be meaningful. What, for example, does 'redressing and enhancing the socio-economic status of previously disadvantaged communities' anticipate concretely? What is not addressed is the relationship between housing stock and the 'functionality' of the household. Now it might well be argued that, even if the delivery of housing is intended ultimately to produce the 'social and economic well-being' of residents of Cape Town, these goods still need to be supplied. Indeed, Devcom maintains that its social ambitions are long-term goals and that in the short and medium terms the emphasis must be on delivery. Indeed, if we consider briefly the work of the Directorate of Housing this is precisely what is happening. We have seen that according to the hypothesis above the functionality of nuclear families is said to be improved when they *own* a house or a flat. Devcom's housing strategy is thus to build new houses for ownership and to convert existing rented stock into privately owned property.

On the 11 December 1997 the City of Cape Town adopted a new, integrated housing policy to establish a uniform set of operational procedures across the city. Prior to this, housing policy and practice had been fragmented according to the practices of former apartheid-era councils. The then Cape Town City Council, for example, had not been responsible for hostels, only Cape Town and the former Black Local Authority of Ikapa had managed rental stock, there was no uniform policy on waiting lists and so on. According to City officials

> these differences, coupled with the breakdown of effective management of the stock over the past few years, allowed for ruthless people to take advantage of the housing stock, for many residents to be exploited, and left many poor and disadvantaged people with no protection from the City. In short, these conditions led to a situation of basic unfairness in housing in Cape Town.[25]

Here 'unfair' practices often referred to the control exercised by 'third parties' over the existing housing stock. The financial crises to which BLAs were structurally prone, together with resultant rent boycotts and political opposition, for example, effectively crippled their capacity to manage rental stock or build new homes. As a result a host of other bodies (civics, residents associations, street committees) governed access to buildings and determined and collected rents. By the time the City of Cape Town was established in 1996, the municipality 'could not register a new client without passing through one of these parties'.[26] Access to homes and the conditions of residence were determined, therefore, not by how long a family had been waiting for a house or flat and/or what they could afford. It was more a question of their political relationship to one of these parties. Realising 'fairness in housing' required, therefore, breaking the hold of these parties over the actual management of stock. Indeed, the directorate has tried to redefine the role of civics *et al.* to that of conceptualising *policy*, as in its 1998 document.

---

[24] Performance Measurement indicators developed for the Directorate of Housing within the Department of Community Development (internal document, 2000).

[25] *Housing Department Operational Procedures Manual: Managing Public Rental Stock, Home Ownership Procedures and Hostels*, City of Cape Town, 30 April 1998.

[26] Interview with Joel Mkunqwane, acting Director of Housing, Civic Centre: Cape Town, 31/8/2000.

The directorate has also been preoccupied by disputes arising from the extended nature of many African households. In the case of rented stock, the death or the departure of the lease-holder usually saw the tenancy rights, and later property rights, claimed by the remaining family members. Yet according to council policy the house or flat in question was to be allocated to the person next highest on a waiting list. In such cases it was usual for affected households to turn to street committees, who would oppose evictions. More complicated was the question of a surviving spouse where there were children from a former marriage. According to the law (outside 'traditional' areas) tenancy rights followed the normal process of intestate succession. Here the right to ownership was automatically granted to the surviving wife. Yet, in terms of the rights of primogeniture, a practice widespread in African households, rights went not to the surviving spouse but to the eldest son. In such cases children from the former marriage often refuse to recognise the rights of the second wife. They often go so far as to physically threaten court sheriffs and others who come to execute eviction orders. When this arose in the former Ikapa Black Local Authority, officials would accept the right of family members to decide amongst themselves to whom these rights should accrue. Yet such agreements were usually informal and lacked legal authority. When they were challenged in court they were frequently overturned. Hence Devcom has sought to grant to these agreements proper legal weight by routing them through a formal administrative process.

Most of the time of the directorate is thus involved in crisis management to overcome obstacles to housing delivery: responding to land invasions, evictions, installing effective management systems to deal with waiting lists, accessing provincial housing subsidies. Despite these problems the directorate claims to have succeeded in transferring 12 000 units into private ownership.

The moment we ask to what extent the delivery of housing and/or the transfer of ownership has begun to meet the developmental goals discussed above there is an alarming silence amongst officials. Or, rather, they revert to vague statements about 'meeting needs' and 'providing development in impoverished areas'. They speak of how new housing is creating markets that provide families with financial assets, how 'formalisation' encourages investment from other government departments. And yet when they begin to be more specific they admit that many people cannot afford their bonds, or the costs of improved services. They admit too that property markets are only phenomena of 'middle-class' areas. And for our purposes, most interestingly, they acknowledge finally that many residents are forced to rely, either partly or in whole, on the 'informal' economy to meet their payments.

This was acutely evident in Manenberg after a tornado destroyed numerous apartment blocks and houses. The City of Cape Town saw in the devastation a chance to 'fast-track' its housing programme by tying beneficiaries of the new accommodation into mortgages rather than tenure relationships. Remember that property ownership was deemed a way of building the integrity of the nuclear household. Given that many residents were failing to meet even their rental costs and that the new bond payments will be even higher, a council official asked if Devcom was 'not just giving people a rope to hang themselves'.[27] At the time of writing these measures had been fiercely resisted by residents; building sites had

[27] Interview with Russel Dudley, Senior Social Development Facilitator, Development Facilitation Unit City of Cape Town, 24/8/2000.

been destroyed and there had been several demonstrations at the Civic Centre in Cape Town. What this suggests is that it is not simply a question of time before interventions through housing, health and community services have the desired effects. Nor is it a question of the way in which these services are provided. I do not want to enter here into a debate about whether there is state capacity (financial and administrative) rather to provide affordable *rental* stock to the poor, or for that matter to use and train local contractors more intensively. The question, rather, is whether the obstacles to development are simply removed by the efficient, effective and affordable delivery of such products.

Conclusion

We have suggested that the notion of 'development' is haunted by a certain imprecision concerning the citizen. A resident is deemed a citizen to the extent that she is able to exercise her rights to a sustainable livelihood. We have argued, however, that such a definition betrays the ethical imaginary that it presumes. We have argued that the citizen is a moral-ethical figure, that citizenship implies a certain norm of social conduct, and, therefore, implies a certain *good* way of living together *in community*. The development of the citizen means, therefore, capturing and holding residents in relations deemed conducive to *ethical* conduct so that they may live '*properly*'. Once we admit that the standard of 'good' behaviour is given by the figure of the citizen we arrive at a rather curious inversion. If the citizen is above all a moral figure, if development means assisting residents to meet their needs sustainably, then the development of the citizen means assisting residents to reproduce themselves *morally*. Development, therefore, is not simply about meeting the needs of citizens. It is about capturing residents to a life-ethic defined by the state *so that they can be citizens*! It is about making *ethical* beings. It is about holding people in relations that make them governable by the state. Now, things get even stranger. If the development of the citizen implies an ethical norm, then development is about assisting residents to meet their needs in a *good* way, an *honest* way, a *moral* way. We can say, indeed, that producing *good* ways to meet their needs is a fundamental condition of the citizen. What might these be? Somewhat ironically, in South Africa today, the answer pertains singularly to participation in the capitalist economy. Since the demonstrations in Seattle against the International Monetary Fund and the World Bank, even CNN has started to use this term. Now, capitalist firms have proven themselves able to produce and reproduce themselves on the basis of a host of social and familial forms (migrant labour that reproduced kinship structures, slavery, child-labour, gangsterism, nuclear families and so on and on). In other words, capitalism does not *necessarily* make people in the image of the citizen; to believe so is merely a version of Marxist economism. But, even if there was an automatic identity between employment in the 'formal' economy and the citizen, there is mounting evidence that this option is not likely in South Africa. Shifts in the domestic economy towards sectors requiring skilled, educated labour mean that, for millions of South Africans, economic and social survival is increasingly dependent on the informal sector. This last term is somewhat of a misnomer; it is not some 'well-cohered and coterminous domain of economic activities'. It is rather a complex of diverse activities, referring to diverse regulatory frameworks, conditions of work, tax structures, and local and national environments (see AbdouMaliq, n.d.). Informality in Europe and America is not the same thing as it is in South Africa and/or other former colonial societies. There it tends to speak of the growing precariousness of formal employment, the growing numbers of people juggling more than one job at a time, the rising numbers of people working without Medi-care or pension schemes. In South Africa it means quite different things. Despite huge divergences across the country (in the Transkei it refers to an economy increasingly dependent on growing marijuana, in Manenberg on one that is more and more dependent on the acquisition and sale of hard drugs, in the Johannesburg CBD it means street vending and/or begging and so on) it refers increasingly to a domain of activities barely or not at all regulated by the state. Some of these are certainly capitalist in nature. They operate for profit in a market place or are sometimes monopolies, and rely on a wage-earning class of workers. They are regarded as informal, nonetheless, because their actions are either illegal (robbery, drugs, hijacking), or deemed inappropriate (prostitution) or not formally registered. Once we acknowledge this we admit several things at once: firstly that growth in the capitalist economy is not simply growth in the formal sector; secondly, that the capitalist economy is supported by a range of practices and institutions only some of which may be thought of as 'virtuous' from the point of view of the state. We can say, therefore, that the accomplice of the crisis in the formal economy and the growth of the informal economy is the social and economic sustainability of associations, gangs, syndicates, family types, not all of which are conducive to *citizenship*. They are not conducive, that is, to the production of *moral* beings of the type required by the national state. What can we conclude from this? Firstly, in the same way that capitalist relations of production do not automatically throw up a revolutionary working class, or even a working class conscious of itself as a class, nor is economic growth (whether it be formal or informal) *necessarily* a way of producing citizens. Indeed, this is precisely the critique of Marxism that economic liberals and others have never learnt – precisely because it was often a critique made from the *inside*. What we have from the World Bank, the International Monetary Fund, the South African government is a modern version of economic determinism, this time given a positive spin. But once we acknowledge that the 'ideological superstructure' is not an instance of the 'economic base' we need to look elsewhere for the conditions of the citizen.

We can credit the designers of the Reconstruction and Development Programme with having understood this, even if implicitly. The RDP was a developmental model designed to initiate economic growth according to political as opposed to simply economic criteria. Not trusting the market to do anything other than reproduce racial inequality, the RDP was intended to encourage economic growth through 'meeting the needs' of the (mostly African) poor. Where the RDP went wrong was in assuming that such needs were mostly known (give or take geographic variation) in advance. What it assumed, that is, was that the standard of '*proper living*' was given and that South Africans were already *ethical* citizens. What was never registered is that 'development' is necessarily a normative-repressive intervention intended to produce, capture and hold subjects in the image of a state ideal. As a result it misrecognised the conditions of the citizen.

The moment we admit that 'development' is not simply about ensuring that citizens meet their needs sustainably, but is about the making of citizens in the first place, we need to ask: what are the conditions of the citizen? We have seen that in Devcom's reading of 'dysfunctionality' a host of social pathologies were derived from the disintegration of the *nuclear* family. This accords with a vast theoretical and sociological literature on the importance of such families for the integrity of the *nation*-state (see, for example, Althusser 1980; Donzelot 1980). In the South African context we can note an excellent article by Andreas Bertoldi and Susan van Zyl (1998) on the relationship between crime and the impossibility of consolidating nuclear households under apartheid. The nuclear family forms only one pole of what Louis Althusser described as the family–school dyad. In other words, the production of ethical citizens depends as much on the insertion and holding of residents in certain types of family structures as it does on capturing them to the school system. This is not simply important for the *content* of the education they receive as much as it is for the relations of discipline and authority to which pupils are subjected. Let us note, finally, that these are the conditions of *national* citizens.[28] They are the conditions, that is, of making residents in the image of a national ideal of 'proper living' and of 'good', 'ethical' behaviour. This is so, not because the democratic citizen is somehow not a normative figure, but because very different sorts of 'ethics' are involved. The national citizen is a figure whose very soul has been captured by the state (he lives in a certain way, works in a certain way, practices sex in a certain way, loves in a certain way and so on). The accomplice of this is 'nation-building', the production of a South African people. In contrast, the democratic citizen is a figure without any particular features (no particular culture, gender, sexual orientation and so on). All that is expected of her is that she behaves democratically in the public domain.

References

Abdoulmaliq, S.T. (n.d.) 'On Informality and Considerations for Policy', *Dark Roast Occasional Paper Series*, Vol 1. No. 3, Cape Town: Isandla Institute.

Althusser, L. (1980), 'Ideology and Ideological State Apparatuses (Notes Towards an Investigation)', in Slavoj Žižek (ed.), *Mapping Ideology*, London and New York: Verso.

Bertoldi, A. and S. van Zyl (1998), 'Psychoanalysis and the Study of Culture: the Case of South Africa', paper presented at international conference on Change: Psychoanalytic Perspectives, hosted by the South African Psychoanalysis Trust, Cape Town, 2–5 April 1998.

Chipkin, Ivor (1997a), 'Democracy, Cities and Space: South African Conceptions of Local Government', Master's dissertation, Johannesburg: University of Witwatersrand, Department of Political Studies.

—— (ed.), (1997b) *A Developmental Role for Local Government*, Pretoria: Department of Constitutional Development. Also available at http://www.local.gov.za/DCD/dcdindexhtml

Donzelot, J. (1980), *Policing of Families*, London: Hutchinson.

Fitzgerald, Patrick (1995), 'Towards a Developmental Public Administration Paradigm', in P. Fitzgerald, A. McLennan and B. Munslow (eds), *Managing Sustainable Development in South Africa*, Cape Town: Oxford University Press.

Gordham, Pravin (1998), *The White Paper on Local Government*, Pretoria: Ministry for Provincial and Constitutional Affairs.

Osbourne, David and Ted Gaebler (1992), *Reinventing Government: How the Entrepreneurial Spirit is Transforming the Public Sector*, Reading, MA, and Wokingham, UK: Addison Wesley.

Unicity Commission (2000), 'Towards a Service Delivery and Institutional Strategy for the Unicity Council', discussion document, Cape Town, 8 June 2000.

[28] Althusser himself misrecognised the family–school dyad as the necessary conditions of proleterianisation, of making people available to the capitalist economy. Now, this rested on a reading of the state that saw it ultimately in the service of capitalism. What the apartheid experience teaches us is that capitalism does not automatically require subjects captured through the nuclear family and the school system. Instead, the family–school dyad is necessary for the production of the nation.

8

Mediating Manenberg
in the post-Apartheid Public Sphere
Media, Democracy & Citizenship in South Africa[1]

SEAN JACOBS & RON KRABILL

Introduction

The task of rethinking citizenship and coming to terms with the limits of liberation in post-apartheid South Africa takes place in many different arenas of social life. As this volume has shown, the contestation of competing claims and the challenging of liberal democracy's shortcomings have proven to be an amalgamation of ongoing processes which involve many people in a wide variety of settings. Mass media provide an important point of common contact in the midst of these processes, for it is often through mass media that the day-to-day restructuring of social and political life is given some sense of collective shape and meaning. Mass media's role includes not only the explicit communication of issues of policy and transformation, but more importantly (though also more difficult to identify) the delineation of who is a full member of the polity in question. In other words, understanding the implicit and structural – as well as explicit and intentional – ways in which mass media help define the physical and human geography of the public sphere is essential if we wish to comprehend changing notions of citizenship after apartheid.

Much of the current work on mass media in South Africa is largely concerned with the political economy of restructuring broadcasting services or changes to the public sphere. These treatments assume a kind of consistency to the normative boundaries of the public sphere, which is taken to be national and all-inclusive in scope. In light of the now common critiques of the concept of the public sphere as overly idealised and monolithic, we recognise a multiplicity of public spheres which operate within differing relationships of power with one another. This chapter thus takes the post-apartheid public sphere not as a normative concept to be recovered or protected, but rather as the ever-shifting boundaries of constant contestation over who is allowed to make valid citizenship claims on the South African political system.

[1] Previous versions of this chapter have been presented at conferences at the New School for Social Research, University of Natal-Durban, University of the Witswatersrand, and African Studies Association. Thanks for comments, at various times, by (in no particular order): Roger Friedman, Irvin 'Che' Kinnes and Elaine Salo, Jessica Blatt and Daniel Reed. Sibulele Gqada, an Idasa intern, assisted in researching articles for this chapter. The conclusions are, however, our own.

We therefore engage with the deeply political role of mass media in line with some more recent work on South African mass media (see Boloka and Krabill 2000; Duncan 2000; Horwitz 2000). Critical of the neo-liberal, capitalist-inspired moment of urban governance and development that characterises local government after 1994, we undertake a detailed analysis of media coverage of the impacts of a heavy rainstorm in Cape Town in 1999. The 'Manenberg Tornado' provides an entry point for studying the social construction of township residents as mediated through the imaginary of Manenberg and how that process impacts citizenship claims made by township residents.

Contemporary South African (democratic) politics – like elsewhere – are characterised by profound changes in the very nature of those politics. Without overstating the pervasiveness of such changes, one could argue that current politics are characterised mainly by *five* elements. The first element is the gradual but important sea change in the nature of political organisation: mass parties and mass organisations more or less decline to operate at the time of elections or to perform a disciplining function in the political sphere (Swanson and Mancini 1996). A second characteristic is that the place of mass political parties is taken by indirect forms of politics, such as 'civil society' as well as interest groups that focus on specific issues or adopt a radical or liberal stance (Desai 2002; Neocosmos 2002).[2] Third, mass media have come to substitute for and resemble the public sphere to a large degree (Page 1996; Steenveld and Strelitz 1998), hence the importance of a close analysis of how mass media treat citizenship claims from varied individuals and groups. Four, the content of politics is distinguished by the hegemony (although not outright dominance) of neo-liberal economic policies followed by governments – egged on by 'objective' think tanks, private business interests, and the major financial lending institutions and government debt agencies – and reinforced through the public sphere by mass media (Bond 2000; Marais 1998; Peet 2002). Within cities this change is reflected in the focus on a public policy discourse of 'world class' cities, ring-fencing, and the transformation of citizens to consumers (see McDonald and Smith 2001). Finally, our research is also a comment on the development of a re-racialised, class-based public sphere operating under 'democratic' conditions which perpetuate apartheid's divisions and inequalities and its consequences for poor people (the majority) to cope with and resist their economically depressed status.

The chapter takes as its entry point a series of rainstorms that visited the Cape Town metropolitan area on 29 August 1999, accompanied by very strong winds. These rainstorms are not unusual in Cape Town, as every winter the storms leave hundreds of people homeless in the squatter camps and overcrowded housing districts of the Cape Flats. However, this time the damage was more severe and acute, with the townships of Manenberg, Surrey Estate, Guguletu and Tambo Square, as well as the KTC squatter camp (all part of the Cape Town metropolitan area, or 'Unicity'), particularly affected. Local and international media subsequently began to refer to the storm as a 'tornado'.

[2] In South Africa, groups operating within the confines of the representative parliamentary sphere include groups as diverse as the constitutional rights organisation, Institute for Democracy in South Africa (Idasa), the trade-union federation Cosatu (Congress of South African Trade Unions), the business lobby group South African Chamber of Business (Sacob) Parliamentary Office, or the social welfare group, the Black Sash. Extra-parliamentary groups engaging the state include groups working on HIV/AIDS (such as the Treatment Action Campaign), energy (e.g. Soweto Electricity Crisis Committee) or housing and evictions (Tafelsig Anti-Eviction Committee).

Emergency responses by local authorities were immediate, but by the end of the first day it became clear that the damage to homes, businesses and schools ran into millions of Rands.[3] A total of 2,850 families were affected by the storm, while 825 families were left homeless. The area most affected was a part of Manenberg, where 285 Council-owned rented units were destroyed together with 80 backyard shacks and the homes of 80 sub-tenants.[4]

In the days following the storm, media coverage of the windstorm began to focus exclusively on Manenberg, while coverage of the damage in the surrounding area declined.[5] Subsequently, Manenberg became synonymous with the windstorm and the majority of news reports referred to it as the 'Manenberg Tornado'. For us, this focus on Manenberg stemmed from two sources, the first obvious and expected, the second a more complicated and important one for understanding mass mediation after apartheid. On the one hand one would expect news media to follow the action in Manenberg due to the extent of the damage there. However, a simplistic understanding of news production explains only part of the story, which is made clear by the lack of attention paid to neighbouring townships, which also suffered following the windstorm but received far less coverage. Why did the storm become the Manenberg Tornado, rather than the Cape Flats Tornado, or the Guguletu Windstorm? The answer lies in the representational force carried by evoking the name of Manenberg, not as a very real neighbourhood of equally real people, but rather as a symbolic stand-in for a range of townships. Manenberg the township no longer means only (or even primarily) the geographic location in the Cape Flats, but also and more significantly township life for working-class black people in Cape Town and, to an extent, townships across South Africa as a whole. The 'Manenberg Tornado' is only one of the more recent examples of the way in which that township has been consistently portrayed as the so-called heart of the Cape Flats, and thereby used as a substitute for a wide variety of issues impacting both residents of the Flats and (mis)understandings of them outside of the Flats. As a result, the physical space of Manenberg competes with the mediated space of Manenberg for both attention and resources in the post-apartheid public sphere. The storm exposed the minimal, or at best piecemeal, response by the state and local authorities to housing demands and struggles in that township.

We argue further that the mediation of Manenberg exposes a much more essential trend in the post-apartheid public sphere. If the restructuring of political discourse in South Africa is to continue on its current neo-liberal path, it requires that the social construction of township life diverts public policy questions away from the socio-economic rights of those left behind in the transition. The social construction of Manenberg through mass media is concerned not with the residents of the physical space called Manenberg, but rather with ensuring that the mediated space of Manenberg makes

---

[3] Rand is the local currency. At the time of writing the exchange rate was approximately $1 = R10.

[4] Information supplied by the Cape Town City Council Disaster Management Unit.

[5] Only Guguletu (a working-class 'African' neighbourhood of row houses and squatter camps) and Surrey Estate (a built-up, coloured, working-class neighbourhood) continued to receive minimal coverage, and then only when South African President Thabo Mbeki visited the areas. Most newspaper and radio news reports mentioned these two neighbourhoods only in relation to assessments of Mbeki's popularity and his leadership capabilities. In a solitary report in the *Cape Argus* on 1 September 1999, comments by Guguletu residents over perceptions of being neglected by the relief agencies and the media reflected racial tensions between Africans and coloureds. Nomsa Dlakhulu, a resident, was quoted in the article, 'Since the storm, nobody has come to visit us and offer assistance, but on the other side of the railway line we could see help was streaming in.'

sense within a nascent neo-liberal hegemony. Residents of the township were allowed to make only limited claims for emergency assistance as virtuous citizens in the immediate aftermath of the storm; when residents argued for long-term, structural change in the provision of housing and other needs after the immediate crisis created by the storm had passed, they were dismissed as ungrateful social parasites. In other words, their claims to socio-economic rights as citizens were denied.

In the post-apartheid city, the citizen–subject division is recast within a highly unequal public sphere. Although Mahmood Mamdani's (1996) original formulation of the urban/rural split remains vital to understanding the country as a whole, a parallel split is establishing itself within the urban areas of democratic South Africa. This split is developing primarily along class-based lines, between those who are viewed as citizens – with the rights and responsibilities therein – at all times, and those who are understood as citizens only in times of crisis, such as the windstorm, and even then as unequal citizens. The racialised, class-based public sphere of apartheid is thus being reinvented under democracy, with the appearance of non-racialism maintained through a small but growing black elite and middle class active in politics and cultural production. This reinvention is accompanied and reinforced through a range of other processes that unfold parallel to changes in the public sphere and its corresponding definitions of citizenship.

At a macro-economic policy level, the South African government's market-friendly blueprint for social development, the Growth, Employment and Redistribution Programme (GEAR), as well as the state's conscious withdrawal from many elements of social policy, is central to these processes (see Johnson 2000; Marais 1998). Changing notions of economic growth within the city mirror these shifts in the public sphere. Since 1994, Cape Town has been recast as 'internationally competitive' and its spin doctors, policy advisers and consultants emphasise tourism and financial services – in line with developments worldwide – as catalysts for economic growth. Communities such as Manenberg who are believed to undermine these sources of growth, or who are suspected of hurting the city's 'reputation' in attracting investment or tourism, are either excluded from this growth or their issues are only superficially addressed in order to protect that reputation. Likewise, the restructuring of municipal services through large-scale privatisation calls for a new conceptualisation of citizenship, under which the state operates like a business and citizens are reduced, without choice, to 'consumers' (McDonald and Smith 2001; Robins 2001). When citizenship becomes synonymous with consumption, many of the previous rights of the citizen suddenly disappear, replaced only by an opportunity to pay the market rate for essential services. The majority of South Africans who were denied decent services under apartheid – mainly poor and black – are particularly affected by this change; when these residents cannot afford to pay, they are forced to forfeit services. While both the poor and the affluent maintain citizenship status in theory, the former find their primary engagement with the state becoming focused more and more exclusively on their ability – or, more crucially, their lack of ability – to pay for basic services.

These same residents, when victimised by a 'natural disaster' such as the windstorm, may be viewed as full citizens deserving of state assistance for the very brief period immediately following the event, when media coverage is at its peak. But this momentary citizenship evaporates after the one-off distribution of emergency materials and the departure of sympathetic media treatments. Justification for limiting ongoing economic assistance to areas such as Manenberg necessitates that widespread crime, the inability to pay for services, the need for public housing, etc., is ascribed to social pathologies or behavioural traits; the sustained negative impact of a range of social, political and economic systems on these people's lives is conveniently downplayed. Without the wholesale attribution of dysfunction to South Africa's urban poor, the struggle of poor people for socio-economic rights would become a valid citizenship claim challenging the government's policies. Hence the stakes surrounding the mass mediation of Manenberg as a site of social pathology are greatly raised.

Changing notions of the city

In the last decade, particularly in the seven years since the first fully democratic elections in South Africa, Cape Town as a city[6] has undergone dramatic changes. At the core of these changes is a massive restructuring of local government into non-racial structures in the 1990s and the creation of new political units (from five substructures or councils to a single metropolitan council, or the Unicity). The restructuring has taken place in two stages and has involved a massive reorganisation of some 35,000 employees, and the introduction of new political objectives geared to poverty relief, democratic representation and participatory decision-making. However, these positive changes are also accompanied by major failures, most notably in service delivery to the poor, continuing racism and discrimination, and the reluctance on the part of some bureaucrats and politicians to adhere to the new principles of democratic reform. As two close observers of these processes have noted:

> Hidden among these demographic and organizational changes is a fundamental ideological shift in the way the city is governed. Gone are the days of race-based social engineering, but so too is the statist model of social engineering more broadly. From the highly subsidized, state-sponsored service delivery models of the past, service delivery has become much more 'neo-liberal' in its orientation – defined here by policies of ring-fencing, cost-recovery, corporatization and privatization. In short the city is now run like a business. (McDonald and Smith, 2001: 1)

There is an ideological battle for control in local and central government decision-making circles in Cape Town, including among public and elected officials, as well as among those groups with power to influence decision-making in the city such as mass media. However, these are simply different shades of a fundamentally new neo-liberal policy paradigm in Cape Town. This ideology has become pervasive and directly affects the delivery of basic municipal services like water, sanitation, electricity and housing. In such a context, the public policy discourse is dominated by a rightward shift where local government acts as service enablers rather than service providers, making citizens now consumers. An inevitable consequence is that people get cut off from services if they cannot *afford* to pay – a policy that is already being implemented in Cape Town in a significant way. Indeed, in a three-year period since the first round of post-apartheid restructuring in 1996, close to 35,000 households in the metropolitan area have had their

---

[6] We are here referring here to the larger metropolitan area of Cape Town, not the more narrowly defined city limits.

water supply cut off for varying lengths of time. As McDonald and Smith note in a study of water restructuring:

> Assuming five people per household in lower-income areas, this means that over 170,000 individuals in the Cape metro area have been denied their constitutional right to a basic water supply as a result of these cost-recovery policies – a practice that would no doubt be exacerbated by full-scale ring-fencing and corporation. (2001: 8)

These changes mirror the ascendancy of neo-liberalism as a broader policy blueprint at a national level since the early 1990s through today (see Bond 2000; Marais 1998). The Cape Town city council's response in Manenberg is consistent with this shift in national politics (see Robins 2001).

Popular constructions of contemporary Cape Town usually present the city as '… the acceptable face of South Africa, a haven of liberalism, a hedonistic lotus eaters' city in a gorgeous Mediterranean setting… Cape Town on the lush, narrow ledge between Table Mountain and the Atlantic Ocean, is a White City, the first and the last in Africa…' (Reed 1993: 139). The city's poorer sections are presented as a 'sinister edge'. Journalist and documentary film-maker, Daniel Reed, captured it in this way:

> The Cape Flats, vast, poor and violent, are a *purgatory* to the Mother's City's paradise. The Flats are reached via the Hell Run, the stretch of motorway between White Cape Town and the squatter metropolis of Crossroads-Khayelitsha. The army has a permanent presence on the Hell Run, but has failed to prevent youths from stoning the traffic. A wall is being built to isolate the motorway from the shacklands on either side. In the wide buffer zone between the Georgian villas of Cape Town and the set of tiny Black shanties, lie the coloured estates and gangland of the Cape Flats. (1993: 139)

Anthropologist Suren Pillay (2003) has pointed out that this kind of representation is repeated in academic writing in a way that reproduces stereotypes and disempowers citizens of poorer neighbourhoods. Criminologist Don Pinnock, who built a career on his study of gang culture in Cape Town, portrayed the 'Cape Flats' as the geographic space in which gangsterism emerges:

> It is here that one finds squatters, the overcrowding and the poverty of Africa. Most people on the Cape Flats do not own property or capital, and the majority are unskilled or semi-skilled laborers. (Pinnock 1984: 3; quoted in Pillay 2003: 285)

Pinnock paints a picture of the Cape Flats as a vast expanse of belts, rows and columns of dull, grey concrete 'compounds' in which 'on any day of the week the most noticeable feature is the many young people on the streets' (Pinnock 1984: 4; quoted in Pillay 2003: 285). These young people, as a result of the torn social fabric ripped apart by the Group Areas-inspired dislocation, mutate into the vicious street gangs that stalk the Cape Flats. Pinnock notes that 'ganging is primarily a survival technique, and it is obvious that as long as the city is part of a socio-economic system which reproduces poverty, no amount of policing will stop the ghetto brotherhoods' (Pinnock 1984: 99; quoted in Pillay 2003: 285). Following this argument, the answer would therefore lie in solving the socio-economic problems of South African society. Give people jobs, and they won't rob and steal and they won't sell drugs.

Pillay argues that this picture may contain a considerable degree of validity, but it also obscures quite a bit. The Cape Flats is not just full of unemployed youth that live in a 'working-class culture', which is presented as a homogeneous, coherent set of shared patterns of interactions. The 'Cape Flats' is delineated by a range of important cleavages that may be regional, religious, class-oriented, linguistic, ethnic or gendered, with shifting combinations of these at different moments.[7]

One-dimensional views of the Cape Flats also permeate the election documents of the main political protagonists in the city, the African National Congress and the rival Democratic Alliance (DA). McDonald and Smith (2001) have pointed to the convergence between the two major political parties contesting political power in Cape Town on notions of the responsibility of the state to citizens.

The Democratic Alliance (DA)[8] election documents for the November 2000 local elections, for example, make it clear that 'local government must create enabling environments to develop world-class cities and towns and locally competitive and viable municipalities.' To do so, the DA proposed 'local enterprise zones offering rates holidays and subsidized infrastructure development aimed at targeted investment' (Democratic Alliance 2000: 11). When the DA argues about who will gain from investment, they make clear their distinction between citizens based on their ability to pay for services through taxation. In a section titled 'City improvement districts', the party promised that they will promote the idea of geographic segregation of service delivery and promise that 'levies raised from property owners will be spent only in the CBD [Central Business District] and only on the priorities identified by the local residents and businesses' (Democratic Alliance 2000: 11). The DA further states, not at odds with their behaviour prior to the alliance's recent split, that they would.

> create a culture of payment for all services consumed above the lifeline level, inter alia by strictly collecting all arrears and debt. DA municipalities will also clamp down on people stealing municipal services like water and electricity. Towards this aim we will institute improved controls and monitoring, including more effective metering systems. (Democratic Alliance 2000: 25)

The African National Congress (ANC) position on privatisation, its view of Cape Town and its distinctions between citizens is less clear and more difficult to decipher than the DA. At best, the ANC leaves the issue of privatising public services ambiguous. At worst, the party is disingenuous in its policy position, using the language of public sector service provision when it needs to score political points but then opening the doors to private sector participation when it comes to writing legislation (McDonald and Smith, 2001). The ANC's track record as the governing party of Cape Town from 1996 until they were voted out in November 2000 points to this ambiguity. The ANC local government actively drove a privatisation and corporatisation agenda. During this time, the City of Cape Town introduced the first city improvement districts (CIDs) in the metropolitan area. The first of these came on stream in November 2000 in the central business district of Cape Town

---

[7] Although race, class, religion, language and gender feature, the reductive tendency to assert the primacy of the economic is nonetheless maintained in these analyses, according to Pillay (2003: 286)).

[8] The Democratic Alliance, formed to contest the November 2000 local government elections, consisted of the liberal, pro-free market Democratic Party and the New National Party (the renamed party of apartheid; it had governed South Africa 1948-94). Between them, they controlled a majority of the seats in the council.

with much fanfare from the city council and local business associations. As McDonald and Smith (2001) point out, the council released a multi-paged, colour broadsheet announcing the benefits of the CID with two of the ANC's top councillors and a senior administrator pictured on the front page striding confidently across an intersection in the centre of the city.

A second CID was operationalised in December 2000 in Claremont (a secondary but growing business node in a predominantly white suburb of Cape Town). This came with promises of many more CIDs to come (up to 60 of them over the next few years according to a newspaper article written by the director of the private firm responsible for developing these initiatives). The two CIDs in operation include private sector policing, video monitoring, increased private sector cleansing (with disinfectants for the sidewalks and streets) and stated policies of removing vagrants and informal parking attendants from the CID areas. Promotional material for the Claremont CID even included a full front-page advertisement in a local community newspaper with the CID's puppet mascot, Clarie, carrying a large police club in its hand.

ANC-controlled councils were also responsible for massive cut-offs for non-payment of services. By 1999, approximately 16,200 households had their water cut off by these two councils for non-payment or non-compliance. This translates to approximately 81,000 people in the Cape Town and Tygerberg substructures having to go without water for varying lengths of time during the ANC's tenure (McDonald and Smith 2001). The ANC also failed to implement any major rates or tariff reforms in the municipalities that they governed in the interim period, bowing instead to pressures from ratepayer associations in historically white areas to keep local tax increases to a minimum. Efforts are under way to create market value assessments on properties (some of which have not been valued since the 1970s) and efforts were made to introduce across-the-board rates in middle- and upper-income areas, but these increases were a far cry from the more radical 'one city, one tax-base' redistributive slogan of the ANC in the early 1990s. Similarly, tariff increases on water and electricity have been minimal and provided little in the way of cross-subsidisation to poor areas.

Changing notions of the public sphere

These changes in notions of the city and citizenship are accompanied by profound transformations of the mainstream public sphere and its political discourse. Democratisation in South Africa has brought with it intense debates over the very nature of that democracy. In the 1980s, within the anti-apartheid, liberation context, the dialogue on democracy was conducted between the ANC and the people organised under distinct, independent, politicised organisations. With the initiation of the negotiated transition to democracy in the early 1990s, this dialogue has shifted to being held between the ANC and representatives of white capital and the white bourgeoisie.

The dialogue has thus been transformed from a material debate among the masses into a seemingly ideological (though no less material) debate among political and economic elite. It is increasingly dominated by technical-legal questions of rights and individual freedoms with the result that ordinary people are largely bypassed by the debates and excluded from determining the nature of political and economic developments (Johnson 2000: 1). What has begun to emerge is an 'elite-pacted democracy' in which government becomes increasingly detached from the people and systematically aims to neutralise the scope of and organisational capacity of popular movements (see Blake 1998; Johnson 2000).

Abstract, ideological debates are attempting to maintain the status quo by replacing material debates on the substantive outcomes of democracy (Johnson and Jacobs 2004). The uproar among political and economic elite over important 'liberal democratic' rights issues such as equality and freedom of expression is ironically accompanied by a deafening silence on socio-economic rights, particularly as they affect the poor.

The structure and operation of post-apartheid South African media both influence and are influenced by these changes in the public sphere. Prior to 1994, most forms of mass media held little or no legitimacy in the eyes of the majority of South Africans; however, many South Africans hoped for and granted greater legitimacy to media following the democratic elections. Yet mass media, the government and business share many of the same conservative views outlined above, particularly regarding socio-economic policy.

The political leadership often attempts to remind media that they are on the same side of these debates, in spite of the press's claim on the title of fourth estate. Nelson Mandela, as early as 1992, was warning a journalist interviewing him, 'we are sitting on a time bomb ... their enemy is now you and me, people who drive a car and have a house. It's order, anything that relates to order [that's the target], and it's a very grave situation' (Saul 2002: 41). At other times, South African media could hardly be more enthusiastic for government's conservative economic agenda. In May 2000, for example, the Johannesburg business news weekly, the *Financial Mail*, reported that President Mbeki 'has lost patience with the Congress of South African Trade Unions (COSATU) and the SA Communist Party's opposition to government's market-friendly policy', with the unions' national strike 'against spiraling unemployment and grinding poverty [being] the last straw for the President' (*Financial Mail* 2000). 'What irks Mbeki most', the *Financial Mail* writer suggested at the time, 'is the COSATU/SACP contention that his free-market economic policy mix is to blame for rising unemployment and poverty.' This evident convergence of political and economic interests raises the question of media's roles in shaping democratic debate and public policy, and returns us to our entry point: mediated Manenberg and its citizens.

Mediating Manenberg past and present

Since its inception, the geographic and political space of Manenberg, as well as its people, has been the subject of ceaseless mediation by mass media, including such genres as music, documentary film and news reporting. Starting with the construction of this council estate on Cape Town's flatlands in the late 1960s, Manenberg's residents have served as the referential frame for the Cape Flats among outsiders. The coded descriptions discussed above of the Cape Flats in general and Manenberg in particular were reflected in the ideological divisions of the news media under apartheid. Manenberg's inhabitants were unfortunate victims to the 'liberal' white, English-language press, while to the Afrikaans press and the state-controlled radio service (and television following its introduction in 1976) the township represented the culmination of an apartheid-ordered, managed and segregated reality.

In the 1970s, jazz pianist Abdullah Ibrahim's song 'Manenberg, Is Where it's Happening' celebrated the defiant spirit of Manenberg's residents against apartheid's social, economic and political excesses. This image of Manenberg was also immortalised in a documentary on Ibrahim's life.[9] Manenberg serves as a symbol of apartheid oppression and of resistance to the system in Ibrahim's composition. Progressive journalists throughout the 1980s continued this reference to Manenberg's defiant spirit in writings, both at home and abroad; one such example is found in William Finnegan's essay in the UK *Granta* magazine's special Africa edition, 'The Silent Majority of Cape Town' (1994). Manenberg also serves increasingly as the archetypal case-study of the identity politics of Cape Town as manifested by ethnicity and the impact of the political transition on poor, working-class communities and economies of desperation.[10]

In spite of its lionised history, Manenberg currently serves the public sphere as a space of social pathology that is reproduced through media images of daily violence and gang killings. This image gained particular prominence in media reports during the early 1990s (cf. Pillay 2003; Reed 1993: 154).

The most well-known example among recent media treatments of the township is Daniel Reed's documentary, 'Cape of Fear'. Focused on the Hard Livings gang, whose headquarters are located in Manenberg, this film was one attempt at breaking with the usual portrayal of the township. Reed spent over a year doing field research and filming around Manenberg with the support of community activists, who saw his film as part of a campaign to focus attention on the politico-economic crises faced by poor communities on the Cape Flats (Kinnes 1999, personal communication). Reed made his film, however, to be shown in the United Kingdom; it was commissioned by the British Broadcasting Corporation (BBC) and was part of a series of six documentaries filmed during 1993. The documentary itself was shown on British television for the first time in 1993.[11]

'Cape of Fear' followed the stories of three central characters in Manenberg – two self-confessed gang leaders (Rashied and Rashaad Staggie) and an ANC-aligned community activist (Irvin Kinnes). Through the film, Reed sought to highlight the political and economic origins of the crime economy and how the residents (including the Staggies, who dominate the narrative) cope with or struggle against this reality.[12] However, when bootleg copies of the film reached South Africa and subsequently featured in police attempts to arrest the Staggies, the film gained cult status among gang members (Kinnes 1999). Much later a heavily edited version of the film was screened on public television in South Africa and created a great deal of public debate, even spawning a whole genre of 'gang documentaries' by SABC TV news analysis programmes.

The film and subsequent media spotlight did indeed bring attention to the socio-political problems in Manenberg. It was therefore not surprising when Nelson Mandela,

---

[9] 'Abdullah Ibrahim. A Brother with Perfect Timing', C. Austin (dir.), 90 minutes, VHS/PAL, 1986.

[10] Elaine Salo-Miller (in her doctoral dissertation) and Irvin Kinnes (both as an activist and in his published work) have explored these identities in post-apartheid Manenberg in their work.

[11] Reed also wrote a companion text to the series of films (of which this documentary formed a part) that contained a few chapters on Manenberg (Reed 1993).

[12] Personal communication with Daniel Reed.

campaigning to become the country's first democratic President during the 1994 election campaign, felt it necessary to tour Manenberg. While there, he told a crowd of mainly ANC supporters:

> Your community and its problems have been very much in the news and I have been deeply concerned to hear of the gangsterism and crime that daily threatens your lives; of the fear in which you live. (Mandela, 1994)

However, subsequent media attention on the film had the opposite effect from what Reed intended; instead of focusing debate on the socio-economic roots of struggle in Manenberg, the film cemented the image of social pathology in Manenberg and its residents.

This one-dimensional rendering of Manenberg as a high crime area continued unabated after the 1994 elections. Gang warfare in Manenberg evolved into a seemingly endless round of Chicago-style drive-by shootings, assassinations and ambushes. Hundreds of innocent bystanders were killed or maimed in the crossfire. Manenberg acquired a reputation for viciousness unmatched on the Cape Flats. The area was nicknamed Murdererberg and Kill Me Quick Town. The area also featured prominently in the attacks on suspected drug houses and gangsters by the controversial vigilante group, People Against Gangsterism and Drugs (PAGAD), throughout the late 1990s (see Pillay 2003).

By the year 2000, this mediated reputation of Manenberg as the Petri dish of South African social pathology resulted in the City of Cape Town municipality planners, policy makers and senior managers identifying the township as a 'zone of poverty' that required 'special treatment' (Robins 2001: 2). Since the advent of democracy, Manenberg has taken on poster child status for social, political and economic dysfunction, even at the national level. Yet this dysfunction is ironically but consistently portrayed as separate from the public policies which directly impact residents of Manenberg and other townships in the Cape Flats. Coverage of the windstorm highlights this disjuncture, in that, unlike issues of crime and unemployment, no existing media narratives of a natural disaster like the windstorm could explain away the tragedy as the fault of Manenberg's residents themselves. Yet mainstream media nonetheless managed to deflect coverage away from substantive policy issues – whether preventative or responsive – raised by the windstorm.

'Act of God' or act of media?

An analysis of local media coverage of the windstorm shows that damage to houses in Manenberg (and surrounding areas) was reported as a 'natural crisis' by both the press and the government. Using Internet-based search engines and looking at hard copies of specific editions, we sampled twenty-two news articles and editorials in the South African media, with the bulk coming from the two main English-language newspapers in Cape Town – the *Cape Times* (www.iol.co.za) and the *Cape Argus* (www.argus.co.za). Other articles were also considered from the *Sunday Times* (www.suntimes.co.za) – which is published in Johannesburg but has a 'Cape Edition' – and the smaller circulation but important weekly *Mail and Guardian*.[13] While a localised news event would normally be

---

[13] The *Mail and Guardian* carried only two articles and proved the exception to the trends we identified: 'Cape Town A Tale of Three Cities', 9 October 1999; and 'Anatomy of a Wind Event', 3 September 1999.

the focus of just a handful of articles, the fact that the 'Manenberg Tornado' generated more than twenty articles over the following year is a clear indication of its significance as a local event.

We have focused on an analysis of the Cape Town press's coverage of the 'tornado' due to its geographic proximity to Manenberg and because these papers claim the largest circulation among newspapers read by the city's inhabitants – across class and race lines. Articles were surveyed over specific periods: (1) in the immediate aftermath of the windstorm, that is from 29 August to 5 September 1999; (2) two weeks later; (3) two months later; and (4) one year after the windstorm took place. We also looked at news reports from the public broadcaster's SABC News Web Site (www.sabc.co.za) and a range of reports by the municipal services section, including a City of Cape Town briefing to the country's President.

Our analysis found that references to the political and historical context of housing in Manenberg barely made the news. For most of the media, in editorial and news columns, this was a 'natural' crisis and it was treated as such.[14] Almost no reference was made to the fact that such natural weather events become *crises* as a direct result of social policies and neglect.

To those familiar with the physical space of Manenberg, the windstorm exposed acute housing shortages on the Cape Flats, the unsafe and overcrowded conditions in Manenberg, and the structural defects of housing in the area. A team of international engineers – knowledgeable about the impact of wind on housing construction – argued at the time that:

> The occurrence of wind damage to the roofs and sometimes even the walls of houses during severe storms are common and there is a tendency to dismiss it as an act of God for which neither the designer nor builder can be held responsible. However, it is believed that in many cases the failure [*sic*] are due to faulty design and construction rather than to the wind speeds exceeding the generally accepted values prescribed in building regulations and codes of practice.[15]

In spite of the report above, and the work of the University of Cape Town's Disaster Mitigation Unit, frighteningly little attention was paid to the possibility that the damaged housing itself was substandard, thus leading to the disproportionate impact of the storm on impoverished areas of Cape Town.

The surveyed articles illustrate, firstly, an obsession with reference to the windstorm as a tornado in headlines as well as in the content of articles. As pointed out earlier, this is at odds with scientific descriptions of the storm. At a political level, though, calling the windstorm a tornado served the needs of authorities by allowing them to treat the poor as victims and the storm as a natural crisis, rather than as a physical breakdown in the provision of housing.

Thus the residents of Manenberg only periodically enter the world of citizens, and then

---

[14] For example, see '2 Die in Cape Town' (*Cape Argus*, 29 August 1999) and 'Too Calm After the Storm' (*Sunday Times*, 3 September 1999), which referred to the storm as a 'freak tornado'.

[15] Joint Research Project sponsored by German Science Foundation and German Association for Technical Cooperation, 'Study into the Impact of Wind on Design of Low-Rise Buildings'. URL: http://www.aib.ruhr-uni-bochum.de/wwsi/germany/mp1.html.

only as victims of natural disaster and/or social pathology. The solution, therefore, was to give them blankets and food baskets, as opposed to addressing substandard housing throughout the Cape Flats. So-called disasters that affect poor people are hence treated as extraordinary, despite the fact that they repeat themselves in 'floods' every winter in Cape Town. In the case of the windstorm in Manenberg, there was still little information available one week after the damage from the local authorities – or enquiries from journalists to those authorities – regarding how and where the thousands of affected people would be housed.

Secondly, the majority of the articles display an emphasis on the political competition between the elites represented by political parties and formal political institutions.[16] The articles reported the political squabbles over who should claim credit for relief work in the aftermath of the disaster. To some extent this was justified. The ANC-dominated Cape Town City Council and the New National Party-dominated provincial administration set up their own disaster funds amid claims the other had violated protocol and procedures. The Western Cape government announced a R500 payment to each of the affected families from the social welfare budget as council officials were still assessing the extent of the damage.

The political squabbling first erupted hours after the disaster. The first major dispute, a day after the storm, was about where the Western Cape Premier Gerald Morkel would be sitting during a media briefing by city officials in the yard of the Manenberg police station. The then provincial minister for social services Peter Marais loudly objected to the premier being left out. A number of newspaper reports focused extensively on this 'snub' (see footnote 16). The failure of city officials to show up at a provincial planning meeting and their apparent resistance to pressure from the Cape Metropolitan Council to take over the disaster management did not ease tensions.

Thirdly, when residents of these areas did speak directly – devoid of the ample social capital possessed by their more affluent white counterparts – they were depicted as 'ungrateful' or 'unfortunate' victims by local media. A related theme was a focus on crime allegedly connected to the windstorm. Sixty-three per cent of the articles focused on crimes taking place in Manenberg after the storm, blaming the community-based 'Manenberg Disaster Committee' (MDC). The MDC had emerged in the aftermath of the disaster among residents of the affected area and was engaged in a public dispute with the City Council over the reconstruction of the area, the type of replacement housing and who would benefit from rehabilitation of the area. For example, the council wanted to exclude certain classes of sub-tenants from qualifying for replacement housing. While most of the articles could not prove that the MDC was responsible for the stealing and looting, it nonetheless made a direct link between acts of crime and the MDC and demonised the efforts of the MDC. There were no reports, either in the immediate aftermath of the storm or in the months following, of any of the crimes being solved or even investigated. This line of reporting clearly buttressed the theme of the affected residents as ungrateful for the assistance they received.[17]

---

[16] For example, see 'Politicians bicker over storm relief' (*Cape Times*, 30 August 1999) and 'Storm over tornado aid blows hot' (*Cape Argus*, 2 September 1999).

[17] For example, see 'Housing rebels tear into tornado homes' (*Cape Argus*, 31 August 2000) and 'Tornado victims ask where is the money' (*Cape Argus*, 19 October 1999).

Our fourth and final observation regarding media reports of the storm reflects the racialised and exclusionist nature of Cape Town politics held over from the apartheid era, which refuses to see Africans as 'natural' inhabitants of city politics. Media reports concentrated almost exclusively on 'Area 1' – which is part of Manenberg – while nearly ignoring damage in Guguletu and other areas of Manenberg and the surrounding townships. This is partly due to the fact that Area 1 was the only area in which houses were demolished and rebuilt, or new housing was constructed. This was also the only area – as reported – where the council was having problems with the MDC committees.

However, the media focus on Area 1 also displays the racialised response of both the council and mass media, as informed by the history of mediation in Manenberg. This focus is exacerbated by the lack of journalists among the mainstream press with proficiency in Xhosa and other African languages apart from Afrikaans, paralleled by the dearth of mass media products in these languages. Reporting in Afrikaans or English thus eases journalists' efforts – particularly in the rush of meeting a deadline – in reporting parallel events in Manenberg (where Afrikaans is the primary language) instead of Guguletu (where Xhosa is the most spoken language). The result is a flattened view of the entire Cape Flats, which erases the differences and even the similarities between various townships and their residents within the Flats, in much the same way Pillay pointed out in his analysis of academic writing on Manenberg.[18]

These four trends in coverage of the so-called Manenberg Tornado – deflecting the issue of substandard housing by calling the storm a tornado, focusing on political infighting around relief efforts, emphasising criminal actions, and a racialised reporting of the event – all combine to perpetuate a view of Manenberg and its residents as mired in a social pathology which is somehow removed from the beautiful city of Cape Town. This is confirmed, through shifts in the media narrative, over time. In the first week following the windstorm, the media stressed the goodwill of Cape Town citizens while including affected residents as victims and the indecisiveness of government on how to deal with the issue. Months following the disaster, the concentration shifted to the infighting between the council and the MDC, particularly alleged corruption by the MDC in the process of allocating emergency housing and the inconsistency of the City Council and the government as a whole. One year later, coverage was dominated by reports that the council was taking the 'sleazy', 'ungrateful' victims to court.

Conclusion: mediated citizens

The analysis above can be understood in two ways. The first is a simple, and perhaps easily anticipated, outcome: poor people have less access and little say in their own representation within mass media. This is hardly a new or unique conclusion, though it is no less important an observation as a result. The failure to give residents of Manenberg direct voice in making meaning regarding the windstorm, and by association regarding their

---

[18] Thanks to Roger Friedman, former *Cape Argus* news journalist and former *Cape Times* news editor, for this insight. Friedman, along with photographer Benny Gool, covered Manenberg full-time throughout the 1990s, providing in-depth and valuable reportage of developments in the neighbourhood.

homes and lives, is an egregious though common oversight on the part of mass media which threatens to erase township residents from meaningful engagement in the public sphere.

In response to this erasure, however, Manenberg residents have always created meaning from their own lives that refuses to simply mimic their portrayal within mass media. At times, Manenberg's people have even attempted to seize production of media portrayals of themselves, from Ibrahim's composition to today. As Elaine Salo-Miller (1998), Irvin Kinnes (1999) and others have pointed out, Manenberg's denizens are not simply victims objectified by mass media representations of their lives.[19]

The second and more significant reading of this analysis, then, is that coverage of the 'Manenberg Tornado' shows us just one instance of Manenberg's symbolic role in making sense of the continuities and contradictions between apartheid and post-apartheid South African politics and notions of citizenship. This mediation also takes place when the government, roused by editorials in the mainstream press, responds to the rise of violent crime and gangsterism in Manenberg by increasing the presence of police in the area – but only until media attention subsides again. Every year local authorities call on volunteer organisations to provide people subjected to flood damage with blankets and food parcels, or to make repairs to the drainage system, without providing official leadership to ensure these projects' success. Discussion of the structural and political factors that contribute to mass homelessness remains mostly outside the mainstream public sphere. Residents of Manenberg are treated at best as unfortunate victims, if not ungrateful criminals, without ever addressing their more profound claims for structural change, made as citizens. The social construction of Manenberg and similar locations across the nation through comparable processes thus plays a crucial role in deflecting wider systemic issues of socio-economic rights by discrediting the citizenship claims of township residents, thereby narrowing the acceptable scope of democratic discourse and limiting the shape and size of the post-apartheid public sphere.

---

[19] In fact, a whole new scholarship and journalism have emerged documenting the struggles of ordinary citizens and grassroots organisations pushing for socio-economic rights under the new democratic dispensation (Desai 2002). Indications are that South Africa's poor majority is increasingly using their democratic citizenship, especially through the courts and on the streets, to challenge non-delivery of services and public policies. If this trend continues, it will surely bring about a very different level of debate on which rights and whose rights are fundamental to democracy.

Biliography

Blake, M. (1998), 'Are the Poor Being Heard?' in C. Barberton, H. Kotze and M. Blake (eds), *Creating Action Space. The Challenge of Poverty and Democracy in South Africa*, Cape Town: David Philip and Idasa.

Boloka, G and R. Krabill (2000), 'Calling the Glass Half Full: A Response to Berger's 'Towards an Analysis of the South African Media and Transformation, 1994–1999', *Transformation*, 43: 74–85.

Bond, P. (2000), *Elite Transition*, Pietermaritzburg: University of Natal Press.

Democratic Alliance (2000), *Election Manifesto for Cape Town. Cape Town: Democratic Alliance*. Cape Town: National Office.

Desai, A. (2002), *We are the Poors. Community Struggles in Post-apartheid South Africa*, New York: Monthly Review Press.

Duncan, J. (2000), 'Talk Left, Act Right: What Constitutes Transformation in South African Media', *Communication Law in Transition Newsletter*, 1(6) June 10. http://pcmlp.socleg.ox.ac.uk/transition/issue06/ duncan.htm.

Farquharson, K. (1999), 'Racialised Media Discourses in the "New" South Africa: The Makgoba Controversy', *Research in Politics and Society*, 6: 175–94.

Finnegan, W. (1994), 'The Silent Majority of Cape Town', *Granta* (48), 239–49.

Glaser, D. (2001), *Politics and Society in South Africa. A Critical Introduction*, London: Sage Publications.

Harber, A. (2002), 'Journalism in the Age of the Market', *Harold Wolpe Lecture*, 26 September, Centre for Civil Society, University of Natal-Durban.

Hofmeyr, J. (2002), 'Trusting the Messenger: An Analysis of Public and Elite Confidence in the South African Print Media', Unpublished Paper. Centre for International and Comparative Politics, Department of Political Science, University of Stellenbosch, South Africa.

Horwitz, R. (2000), *Communication and Democratic Reform in South Africa*, Cambridge: Cambridge University Press.

Howarth, D. (1998), 'Paradigms Gained? A Critique of Theories and Explanations of Democratic Transition in South Africa', in D. Howarth and A. Norval (eds), *South Africa in Transition. New Theoretical Perspectives*, London: Macmillan Press.

Jacobs, S. (2000a), 'Is the Media Democratic?' *Mail and Guardian*, 22 October, 32

—— (2000b), 'Mass Media for Minorities', *Mail and Guardian*, 14 January, 26.

Johnson, K. (2000), 'The Trade-Offs Between Distributive Equity and Democratic Process: The Case of Child-Welfare Reform in South Africa', *African Studies Review*, 43(3): 19–38.

Johnson, K. and S. Jacobs (2004), 'Democratization and the Rhetoric of Rights: Contradictions and Debate in Post-Apartheid South Africa', in Harri Englund and Francis B. Nyamnjoh (eds), *Rights and the Politics of Recognition in Africa*, London: Zed Books.

Kinnes, I. (1999), 'The Hard Livings: The Impact of the Political and Social Transition to Democracy in South Africa on the Gang in Manenberg'. Unpublished Masters dissertation, London School of Economics.

Mamdani, M. (1996), *Citizen and Subject: Contemporary Africa and the Legacy of Late Colonialism*, New Brunswick: Princeton University Press.

Mandela, N. (1994), 'Nelson Mandela's Election Speech in Manenberg', retrieved from <htpp://www.anc.org.za/ancdocs/speeches/1994/sp940400a.html>

Marais, H. (1998), *South Africa – Limits to Change: The Political Economy of Transition*, London: Zed Books.

McDonald, D., and L. Smith (2001), 'Privatizing Cape Town: From Apartheid to Neoliberalism in the Mother City', Unpublished Paper, Municipal Service Project, University of Witswatersrand.

Neocosmos, M. (2002), 'The Construction of a State-Consensus in South Africa: Authoritarian Nationalism, the Depoliticisation of Politics and the Exclusion of Popular Democratic Discourse', paper presented at the International Conference on 'Reconceptualising Democracy and Liberation in Southern Africa', 11–13 July 2002. Windhoek, Namibia: Nordic Africa Institute/Namibia Institute for Democracy/Legal Assistance Centre.

Page, B. (1996), *Who Deliberates: Mass Media in Modern Democracy*. Chicago: University of Chicago Press.

Peet, R. (2000), 'Ideology, Discourse, and Geography of Hegemony: From Socialism to Neo-Liberalist Development in South Africa', *Antipode*, 58–90.

Pillay, S. (2003), 'Experts, Terrorists and Gangsters: Problematising Public Discourse on a Post-Apartheid Showdown' in Herman Wüsserman and Sean Jacobs (eds), *Shifting Selves: Post-Apartheid Essays on Mass Media, Culture and Identity*, Cape Town: Kwela Books and South Africa History Online.

Pinnock, Don (1984), *The Brotherhoods*, Cape Town: David Philip.

Reed, D. (1993), *The Beloved Country*, London: BBC Books.

Robins, S. (2001), 'Housing Citizens and Planning Urban Futures', paper delivered at Southern African Research, Information and Publications Service Workshop on Political Culture in Southern Africa, Harare, Zimbabwe, 13–15 June.

Roselle, L. (2002), 'The Role of Political Communication in the Diffusion of Ideas: Soviet Television and New Thinking In International Security, 1985–1991', paper presented at the 2002 meeting of the American Political Science Association, Boston, Massachusetts.

Salo-Miller, E. (1998), 'Personhood, Space, Violence in Manenberg', paper presented to the Annual Meeting of the African Studies Association, November, Chicago, Il.

Saul, J. (2002), 'Cry for the Beloved Country: The Post-1994 Denouement', in Sean Jacobs and Richard Calland (eds), *Thabo Mbeki's World: The Ideology and Politics of the South African President*, Pietermaritzburg: University of Natal Press; London: Zed Books.

Swanson, D. and P. Mancini (eds) (1996), *Politics, Media and Modern Democracy: An International Study of Innovations in Electoral Campaigning and Their Consequences*, London: Praeger.

Steenveld, L. and L. Strelitz (1998), 'The 1995 Rugby World Cup and the Politics of Nation-building in South Africa', *Media, Culture and Society*, 20: 609–29.

III
Cultural Plurality & Cultural Politics after Apartheid

9

Negotiating Gender & Personhood in the New South Africa*
Adolescent Women & Gangsters in Manenberg Township on the Cape Flats

ELAINE SALO

Introduction: reading the global in the local space

It was one of my regular afternoon visits to Grande Street, in Manenberg, and I sat in Mareldia's small sitting room with six adolescent women. They stretched out languidly on the small faux Victorian living room suite, each taking turns to draw on a single cigarette that was passed around. The door was shut to prevent the unwelcome intrusion of any of the older female neighbours. We were watching a youth programme on Simunye,[1] the national TV Channel One, whose signature tune repeated the phrase *We are One*. Soon the room's humble furnishings faded from view as we were engrossed in the images projected from the TV screen. The two young people presenting the programme, a male and a female were both black, very well groomed and fashionably dressed. He sported a cool set of dred-locks, was dressed in baggy pants and sweatshirt, accessorised with a Nike swatch and Sketcher shoes. Her hair was well slicked back and tied in a ponytail. She was fashionably thin, and wore a shoestring top. They both addressed their viewers in English, which they spoke with private school accents, sometimes interspersing their speech with an isi-Zulu word or phrase. They were reading letters and comments from viewers. 'She's well dressed, I like her', Claudette says. 'Is he wearing Nikes?' Nazli asks. 'My mother said that she would buy me a pair like that at Edgars,' she says. I wondered about the price of Nikes at the popular department store. 'Nielie has a pair exactly like that. When she wears them with her Levis she really looks sharp,' Tessa commented. Turning to me she asked, 'When are you going to buy me a pair like that?' Tessa then said, 'One doesn't see coloured people on TV. It's only Black or White. Look at the TV announcers and the kids on Cody and Dub.'[2] 'But there are coloured kids on Yo TV' I retorted. 'They all speak English', she replied.

* This article first appeared in the *European Journal of Cultural Studies*, 6 (3), August 2003.
[1] Simunye is the name for Channel One on the South African Broadcasting Corporation's television system. The term, meaning togetherness, is invented from the Xhosa prefix *Si-* (meaning 'we') and *kunye* ('to be together'). It signifies the broadcast media's efforts at nation-building after 1994.
[2] A South African children's television programme, aimed at viewers aged seven to approximately thirteen years.

There were a number of TV continuity announcers as well as adolescents on the youth programmes who resembled the coloured people in Manenberg. As the youth programme ended with a musical video featuring African-American singer Monica, I departed, my thoughts awhirl with the issues my adolescent friends have raised about television role models, brand name clothes, language and accents that are racially and economically codified. These youth seemed to imply that the TV personalities did not resemble people from their own community, because they spoke English or appeared to be better off. At the same time, these young women were learning that the broadcasting media and the English language were not the exclusive possessions of whites any longer; that South Africans from diverse racial and ethnic backgrounds could now claim the language and the media as their own; that brand name clothing and fashionable dress styles were not necessarily markers of race or that fashionable dress codes did not necessarily signify an individual's moral values or socio-economic class.

The study presented here is part of a broader ethnographic research project conducted between 1998 and 2000, in which I examined the shifts in identity in young men and women's identity in Manenberg, a predominantly coloured, Afrikaans-speaking township in Cape Town, South Africa. In this chapter I examine how male and female youth recreate racial and gendered identity firstly in relation to local histories, repertoires and ideals of masculinity and femininity and secondly in relation to global cultural forces. First, I examine how local residents asserted an alternative, positive, resistant notion of personhood in the local Manenberg context, in an apartheid context where they were officially defined as inferior persons on the basis of race. I argue that the local residents utilised the coloureds' official place in the spatial, social and economic apartheid land-scape and creatively inverted the official meanings of colouredness to reclaim a positive sense of identity, rooted within the moral sphere. I then examine how young women and men destabilise the local notion of personhood in the post-apartheid era, by marshalling the cultural capital offered to them via the imagery of femininity and masculinity offered in American soap operas, rap music and international brand name clothing.

Global cultural flows, local meanings

Many proponents of cultural globalisation argue that cultural flows are from the North to the South and lead to Northern hegemony and local cultural destruction (Zeleza 2002). These proponents contend that these flows lead to cultural hybridisation (see Nuttall and Michael 2000), or to cultural hegemonisation and homogenisation (Ake 1997, quoted in Zeleza 2002). Naomi Klein (2001) argues that the same hegemonising processes occur as marketing processes located in urban centres and usurp the cultural forms of the ghettoised peripheries in the North. She examines how multinational clothing and shoe companies assume control over youth subcultural forms such as Black ghetto music and dress codes in the urban peripheries of North America through branding. Klein maintains that companies like Nike neutralise the unique critical local meanings of these cultural forms through their branding process. She also assumes that the youthful customers who purchase products such as Nike sports shoes take on the same cultural meanings that the brand name company executives ascribed to these goods.

Theorists such as Klein (2001) and Claude Ake (1997, quoted in Zeleza 2002) assume that cultural globalisation is teleological and propagates Northern imperialism. Ake contends that it is through the consumption of Northern-produced goods that local difference is obliterated, creating cultural homogenisation. The arrival of Northern popular culture (usually American) would foreshadow the destruction of local cultural practices, the markers of cultural difference.

In contrast to these perspectives Paul Zeleza (ibid.) and Daniel Miller (1995) argue that cultural globalisation does not necessarily lead to 'generic Westernization' (Miller 1995: 5). Zeleza draws our attention to the meanings that consumption of global cultural forms and goods take on as it occurs in, and is shaped by, specific local histories and cultural contexts, when he argues that:

> When people of the South consume the imported products and seductive images, their pleasures and meanings are processed and perceived through the complex filters and registers of their own culture. In other words, 'local cultures' ... are far more resilient and adaptable than the champions or critics of cultural globalisation often allow, and people, even poor ones, are not passive receptacles of alien cultural products. (Zeleza, 2002: 14)

Zeleza's argument suggests that, far from homogenising the variety of cultural styles and identities found in local contexts in the South, cultural flows of music, dress styles and technological gadgetry emanating from the North are incorporated into local values and practices and given new meaning. Far from dislocating identities from the local context, the creative uses of these cultural practices and products frequently resonate with local social divisions and struggles around race, gender and class and the struggles about the meanings of local identities. Similarly Miller argues that even when the 'locals' outside the cosmopolitan centres consume imported cultural ideas, goods and practices their identities are not necessarily subsumed by the dominant meanings associated with these factors in the metropolis. He renovates and then applies the theoretical notion of differential consumption of global forms to understand the rise of novel identities in local contexts beyond the Northern based metropolitan centres. He argues that consumption, as the quintessential act of modernity, is shaped by local histories of modernity, and local forms of social stratification that are rooted within the rupture from tradition. This peculiar interlinkage leads to an *a posteriori* difference and the rise of novel identities in the local context. I would add that these novel identities are at once rooted in, and ruptured from those that are considered to be more traditional.

The following South African study is informed by Zeleza's and Miller's view that the meanings associated with the consumption of global cultural ideas, practices and products in the local context cannot be assumed to signify the same identities and/or spaces in which these features originate.

Urban marginalisation and the social construction of race

Many contemporary historical studies and museum exhibitions in post-apartheid South Africa have focused on the previously marginalised black[3] population's memories of their

---

[3] I use black in the generic sense here to refer to people classified as coloured, Indian or African in the South African context.

communities prior to the forced removals experienced under apartheid (see Field 2001; Rassool and Prosalendis 2001). These works recoup the memories of these communities as social and economic vibrant places that apartheid obliterated. They do not indicate that, in the forty years since the first removals, social webs have been painstakingly re-spun in these old dumping-grounds. Furthermore, few have reflected upon the manner in which these spaces have acquired multiple new meanings since resettlement.

The physical boundaries that apartheid architecture set in place to anchor and constrain artificially created racial communities in the urban landscape still endure in the post-apartheid context. Until the 1980s, the most courageous efforts to challenge the imposed physical and social separation of people ultimately collapsed in the face of stringent laws. The implementation of apartheid legislation over 46 years has profoundly influenced South Africans' definition of communities and of persons especially in the local township settings. Legislation such as the Population Registration Act[4] forcibly classified people into racial categories, and the Group Areas Act compelled them to live in racial ghettoes like Manenberg, a township situated on the grey, sandy Cape Flats, north of the green belt of leafy suburbs that runs along the perimeter of Table Mountain. The township is one of numerous identical housing projects that were constructed in the 1960s and 1970s for those classified coloured, who were forcibly removed from areas proclaimed white by the Group Areas Act.[5] These new townships imbued the racial category 'coloured' with unique physical, spatial and socio-economic meanings. Whilst legislative acts such as the Population Registration Act of 1950 defined who the coloureds were, the Group Areas Act of 1950 designated where they could live. Legislation such as the Coloured Labour Preference policy[6] simultaneously created a hierarchy of deprivation in the Western Cape, in which coloureds were given job preference over Africans, and ensured a cheap labour force for the Western Cape textile and farming industries. The social welfare and housing policies also defined coloureds as an intercalary racial group. Within the hierarchy of black deprivation, coloureds were given preferential access to social welfare grants and housing over Africans (Salo 2004; West 1984).

Gendering race: apartheid welfare and the economy of the Western Cape

Coloureds' place in the urban landscape was entrenched by the group's relocation to the Cape Flats. Likewise the racial category was gendered through the implementation of welfare and housing policies that located adult coloured women in a unique relation to the apartheid bureaucracy.

[4] In terms of the Population Registration Act, South Africans were categorised into different racial groups, namely white, Indian, African and coloured. Coloureds and Africans were divided into a number of sub-groups. Africans were divided into ethnic sub-categories that were based upon linguistic differences. 'Coloureds' were defined as 'those who cannot be defined as either white or African' (Wilson and Ramphele 1989; Western, 1996). Yet, despite this negative definition, the category was subdivided into seven sub-categories that included group designations such as 'Cape Coloured' and 'Other Coloured'.

[5] The Group Areas Act legislated race-based residential segregation in 1950 and caused the forced removal of approximately 750,000 people in urban areas between the 1960s and 1980s.

[6] The Coloured Labour Preference Policy legislated that coloured labour be given work preference over Africans in the Western Cape. In this way Africans were denied residence in the Western Cape and the urbanisation of Africans was contained (Goldin 1987) until 1985, when the pass laws were removed from the statute books.

This gendering process occurred in two ways, namely through the bureaucratic assumptions about family formation that shaped the welfare and housing programmes, and secondly through the specific feminisation of the industrial workforce in the Western Cape urban economy (ibid.). In the first case, the apartheid state assumed that all households conformed to the Westernised two-parent family norm where fathers and mothers fulfilled stereotyped gendered roles. Consequently child welfare grants were only payable to women as mothers and public housing was only provided to families with wives and children. Secondly, within the economic sphere, the feminisation of the labour force in the textile industry, together with the impact of the Coloured Labour Preference policy in the Western Cape, defined coloured women as preferential workers. Until recently, adult women held relatively powerful economic statuses within these townships as the conduits to scarce economic resources or to shelter. They embodied the bridge between the coloureds' social location as an inferior race during apartheid, and the positive identity that was produced in social relations and within the spaces of the township.

Defining community in the local context

Manenberg township endures forty years after the first removals. Its existence is due to state repression, the severe housing shortages in the city as well as the township residents' ability to refashion social communities over time. Over this period, residents have creatively reconstituted the township's physical and racial boundaries, using these borders as the physical and cultural capital to fashion an alternative, positive notion of personhood and community. The township's physical and social density also influenced its residents' perceptions of community, and differentially fashioned their social interactions with others within the supposedly homogeneous racial area. In Manenberg, the densest housing is found in the central zone and consists of a core of apartment blocks locally referred to as '*die korre*' or the courts. These apartment blocks are so densely constructed that the spatial boundaries between the street and domestic space are blurred, reconfiguring the distinctions between private and public space.

The physical density is matched by population density. Approximately 80,000 people live in this township (Koen 1997). Informal housing suggests that the figure is higher. A vast network of informal housing settlements called *hokke* or shacks crowd into small yards to provide extra living and work space. This physical and social density ensures that residents are in constant social contact. As I will show later, this social and physical density is important in shaping motherhood as the epitome of femininity in this context. The population is impoverished and, at the time of my research, unemployment was unofficially estimated to be at least 50 per cent. In the face of widespread economic need, those who had access to a steady income exercised enormous social and cultural power. In the majority of households, the welfare payments that women received to support their children were the only source of income, emphasising adult women's importance in their roles as mothers.

Within the local community these women's relatively privileged economic status was reconfigured to emphasise their social and moral obligation to their own and other households. They mediated the local residents' relationship with the state through their frequent entreaties in the offices of the welfare, housing, education and prisons adminis-tration. In doing so, they ensured the community's economic and social existence. These adult women epitomised local respectability and morality in Manenberg, through the efflorescence of their mothering role beyond the private domain. Finally they policed the individual's moral standing within the community, by monitoring young men's and women's dress, activities and behavioural codes in public. The adult women's power could only be asserted in the context of a small, intimate community, where reputation was shaped through intimacy, gossip and visible performance. I argue that, whilst women's economic activities and moral judgements imbued 'colouredness' with gendered meaning in the local context, the men defined the boundaries of the local community in which these meanings mattered.

Defining community - gendered boundaries, gendered persons

For the outsider Manenberg appeared to be a homogeneous racial township, a single geographic and social unit. However, for the township residents, socio-spatial boundaries criss-crossed this geographic unit, dividing it into multiple small communities. Persons were produced and identified within these small communities through young men's boundary-making activities and adult women's actions as mothers of the community. These women identified and nurtured persons through the economic and social assistance that they offered, and the judgements they made about individuals' moral standing in the com-munity. The young men embodied and defined the social and spatial boundaries of the community wherein the adult women's actions were meaningful. Local communities were limited to a single street, or consisted of a number of courts. The young men produced the boundaries of the local community through ganging practices and aesthetics. Through this process, they negated the legitimacy of state-imposed borders and in so doing reclaimed their gendered agency in the local context. Eleven male gangs existed in Manenberg, each associated with its own particular turf. The gang turfs were identified and marked off by gang graffiti that were daubed on every available outer building wall and street sign. These turf boundaries also represent the physical, social and moral limitations of the local community. When young men committed crimes such as theft, or break any social rules outside their gang turf, adult women within their community actively denied these youths' criminal behaviour. In these contexts, only the young men's actual or fictive kin relationship to respected adult women and their location within a respectable local household mattered.

Male youths' criminal actions or social misdemeanours within their gang turf, the moral space of the local community, were another matter. Adult women pressured the gang leader to identify and punish the offender severely. Punishments took the form of severe physical beatings. Men also marked the boundaries of the local social and moral community onto their bodies by means of tattoos representing the gang insignia. The tattoo enabled gang members to identify other men as enemies located outside the boundaries of the local communities, who were perceived as threatening strangers. Within the boundaries of the local community the tattoos were hidden under clothing and went unacknowledged.

In the local community young men were assessed as eligible marriage partners and fathers by virtue of their statuses as adult women's sons and as members of a respectable household, and not primarily as breadwinners. Young women, in contrast, were judged in terms of the local ideology of domesticity. Motherhood and women's domestic responsibilities were regarded as the ideals of femininity. Consequently young women were expected to confine their mobility to the domestic space, where they spent their time completing household chores or caring for younger household members. When they were seen on the street, the senior women would enquire about their reasons for being out on the street while scrutinising their dress to assess whether it was suitably modest or not. During these encounters the young women respectfully lowered their gaze as they spoke with their elders. They were required to restrict their mobility to the limits of the local community, unless they were accompanied by a group of friends or an older woman. A daughter's display of modest behaviour or dress reflected a woman's ability to raise her children well and to run a respectable household. The following example indicates how senior women manipulated the norms and expectations associated with ideology of domesticity to coerce young women into expected modes of femininity.

Lindsey had introduced me to 'Sister' Vonna during my initial visits to Rio Street. She was regarded with much respect in Rio Street. When I first met her, she was seated on an upturned milk crate outside her gate chatting with a few older women while watching locals going about their daily business in the street. Vonna was modestly dressed in a housecoat that covered a knee-length skirt and blouse. She also wore the customary head-scarf, like the other senior women.

One afternoon she expressed great concern for twenty-year-old Lindsey's growing notoriety. Mothers publicly announced that they preferred their daughters to date young men whom they knew, from '*ordentlike*' or respectable households within their own communities. Local gossip networks had spread the word that Lindsey was dating a notorious gang member from another community, in defiance of the local social norms. She was also seen in a shebeen[7] located in the adjacent community, drinking beers with her new partner. Her dalliance with a gangster in a disreputable space placed her own, her mother's and her household's respectable reputation at risk and threatened their valuable links to the local networks of assistance. Lindsey's mother was chronically ill and relied on the young woman to run the household. The younger woman, in turn, relied heavily upon women like Vonna to obtain advice about the maze of state bureaucracies she had to negotiate in order to obtain assistance for her disabled parent and her two children.

I was concerned about the local women's account of my friend's behaviour. Still, Lindsey's reputation could still be rescued. She had not yet been written off as '*sleg*' or bad, even though the women expressed concern about her perceived moral decline. Vonna asked me to help swing the current, ambivalent opinion about Lindsey's reputation, by requesting her to visit the older woman's home. When I arrived at Lindsey's home, she answered my knock on the door and let me in. Her eyes were bloodshot, her face blotchy and swollen, possibly from weeping.

'Where have you been? I've come to fetch you,' I said. 'We're sitting at Vonna's house. Come along.' She refused, shaking her head vehemently. After I pleaded with her for a while Lindsey reluctantly decided to accompany me. 'Wait then, while I change my pants,'

---

[7] Shebeens are informal bars or pubs that are a central feature of the urban black townships in South Africa. They often operate without an official licence to serve alcohol and have been historically associated with urban black protests against the apartheid state.

she replied, sighing heavily. She removed a skirt from the small wardrobe and proceeded to change into it. Then she tied her hair in the customary *doek* or headscarf that most women wore here as part of their everyday attire. This was the first time in as many days that Lindsey would be appearing in public on the street and she intended to use the opportunity to silence those who claimed that she was bad. She was intent on asserting her respectability to all and sundry gossipers, by dressing in the modest attire associated with the ideal femininity. Our short stroll to Vonna's home occurred under the watchful eyes of a clutch of older women, who were seated on their upturned milk crates outside their doorways. During our 'visit', Vonna lectured Lindsey about the threat she posed to her reputation by dating a gangster, and requested her to spend more time at home 'looking after herself' and her mother. A week after our visit, Lindsey broke off her relationship with the young man.

The physical boundaries of the community also became its social and moral boundaries, where the individual's willingness to live by the local code of modesty, interdependence and self-sacrifice earned him or her the respect accorded to worthy persons. The local moral community was considered to be a sphere of purity. It defined the social group where moral and social obligations to others took precedence over economic instrumentalism, and where values such as modesty, loyalty, mutual respect, self-sacrifice, interdependence and assistance were valorised. Young people like Lindsey learned that, even during intense personal crises, they had to display the practices and aesthetics associated with these values to earn the respect of the senior women. The adult women identified and ultimately controlled the ideological means whereby young men and women became persons within the community. However, with the demise of apartheid, the power that these adult women exercised in the local moral economy had begun to wane. Their prominent social position was being eroded by the changes in the structural socio-economic factors and the male and female youth's innovative leisurely practices.

The local reinserted in the global – unravelling the economic scaffolding of local personhood

Since apartheid legislation such as the Group Areas Act and the Population Registration Act were removed from the statutes in the1990s, the dominant as well as the alternative meanings ascribed to the apartheid racial categories and landscape have changed. In the post-apartheid era, the effects of racialised and gendered policies are being systematically dismantled, undermining the dominant meanings attached to racial and ethnic categories, language and physical landscapes. These changes also steadily chip away at the notions of personhood that have been produced from the accretions of social interaction and ideologies within the local context of the coloured township, and that are based on, but constituted in resistance to, the imposed racial exclusivity of apartheid policies.

In Rio Street, Manenberg, the local moral economy relied upon and was articulated by a racially based political economy that favoured coloured women's statuses as mothers and workers. However, the racial hierarchy of deprivation has been done away with, along with coloured women's privileged access to the child welfare grants. The monetary value of these has been sharply reduced by national welfare budget cuts as well as by the state's desire to spread welfare resources more equally throughout the population. At the same time the textile and canning industries in the Western Cape have been downsized due to the effects of trade liberalisation (Clofed 2002; International Labour Resources and Information Group, 2002). Approximately 30,000 people lost their jobs in the industry during the 1990s (SAIRR 2000), most of them coloured women. Their status as mothers and their hold over economic and moral power that ensured the physical survival of their communities have waned. This uncertainty has undermined the senior adult women's power to define the key features of the moral economy. Community members' adherence to the dictates of this ideology does not automatically guarantee economic and material survival any longer or, for some, even respect. Accordingly, the moral economy's purchase over residents in Manenberg is slipping, together with its notion of personhood and the associated modes of behaviour and dress styles. However, this delinkage has created a space for the renovation or the transformation of personhood in the local context. This process in Manenberg communities such as Rio Street is expressed increasingly in the lives of the youth who are coming into adulthood in the current post-apartheid context.

The old, exclusively white spaces and institutions, which were better resourced in the past, have become sought-after spaces to occupy, work or reside in for South Africans of all races. These spaces have taken on new meaning as national cosmopolitan spaces of cultural, racial and ethnic diversity. The youth from contexts like Rio Street also desire to inhabit these spaces, where they can learn the norms, practices and codes of the new South Africans. However, access is only made available to those with the requisite economic resources. Housing prices and schools fees in these privileged areas increased enormously after the Group Areas and Separate Amenities Acts were rescinded in the early 1990s. Such changes restrict access to those who were economically well off and reflect the increased demand for these residences and services. For those who continue to live in the poorer, racially homogeneous townships, such as Manenberg, the media such as television or radio become the alternative means to access these cosmopolitan spaces, albeit through vicarious consumption of soap operas and popular music, while public transportation provided for brief visits to popular city nightspots.

As the young men and women in Rio Street accessed these cosmopolitan spaces, they transgressed the locally imposed social and physical boundaries and reinvented the meaning of local public and private spaces. Through their transgressive and trans-formative practices, they were acquiring the cultural capital that facilitated their ability to occupy or imagine themselves as part of the national spaces of cultural, racial and ethnic diversity. In doing so, they actively destabilised their own identities, prising them apart from the apartheid-imposed socio-economic, spatial, moral or linguistic markers of gender, class and race. Their increased ability to transcend the racial, linguistic and spatial limits imposed by the old apartheid policies, and their growing familiarity with the wide range of cosmopolitan South African styles, languages, spaces and social customs became the defining characteristics of an emerging personhood in the local context. This in turn diminished the mothers' ability to produce and nurture social persons within the bounded-off local contexts, as the central aspect of identity.

Television programmes – remaking race, remaking the nation

Since television was introduced in South Africa in January 1976, the content of entertainment and news programmes and the bodies that inhabit this virtual world have reflected the national political policies and trends. Accordingly, during the apartheid era television programmes broadcast on the single TV channel reflected apartheid racial policies, and the belief that white, and specifically Afrikaner nationalist, culture was superior. Until the late 1970s, TV broadcasters and news anchors were exclusively white. Later, more TV channels were introduced to broadcast programmes that were geared to support the Bantustan[8] policy and its associated cultural essentialism. After the broadcasting services were restructured in 1993, the three SABC channels broadcast in all languages, (although English dominates), while news anchors and TV presenters represent the racial, ethnic and gender diversity of the population (Barnes 2003).

TV channels such as Simunye or Channel One were popular among the young women in Rio Street for good reason. The channel targeted young viewers and its programmes were devoted to popular music videos, fashion or game shows. These young women were able to watch their favourite youth programmes in the afternoons and early evenings from their living rooms, while still remaining within the quintessential feminine domestic spaces. However, the messages that these programmes conveyed about romance, sexuality and heterosexual relations, as well as the young women's discussions about these issues, transformed these domestic locales into transgressive, hybrid spaces from which the new ideas and practices of divergent, new feminine identities emerged.

Two of the most popular shows among the Rio Street women were the locally produced dating game show *Buzz* broadcast on Channel One and the soap opera *Backstage* screened on e-TV, the independently owned station. The imagery as well as the dialogue contained in these two programmes conveyed different notions of romance, femininity and masculinity from those which existed in Manenberg, generating a creative dissonance for the adolescent viewers, and producing intense discussion on these issues.

Buzz was a popular show based upon a dating game for teenagers whilst *Backstage* was a locally produced soap opera about youthful students who attend a media and drama school. *Buzz* was presented by a fashionably thin, well-dressed young woman. In this popular dating game show, adolescents had to select a prospective date and then, together with their new partner, compete with another couple for a night on the town in a chauffeured limousine and new, designer-label clothes. Youthful competitors hid behind a screen so they were invisible to their prospective dating partner. Each competitor then marketed him or herself to the prospective partner in the hope that s/he would be selected as the desirable date. The prospective dating partner had to select the date who s/he

---

[8] According to this policy, each of the nine ethnic groups that constituted the African population was an emerging nation, with its own territory, language and culture. According to Afrikaner nationalists, the Afrikaners, the most advanced nation, had to nurture these nations into independence. The Bantustan Act of 1970 provided the legislation for the creation of independent Bantustans. The Transkei, the Xhosa 'homeland', was the first Bantustan to be given 'independence' in 1975. Bophuthatswana followed shortly after, in 1977, as the 'independent' Bantustan for the Tswana-speaking people. These Bantustans deprived millions of black South Africans of their rights to South African citizenship (see Lye and Murray 1980).

thought was the most compatible. In the final contest for the grand prize, the two remaining couples were tested on the degree of compatibility between the partners, in areas such as TV viewing choices, food tastes, etc. The two partners who possessed the greatest degree of compatibility were the ultimate winners. In shows such as *Buzz*, individual image and the ability to market oneself were the only qualities that mattered. A person's physical or social roots were not traceable except by accent and language. Competitors were able to present themselves and choose a favourite, free from the gaze of adult women, the local notions of morality and the gossip that distinguished the good girl or boy from the 'slut' or the gangster in the local context.

One evening after I had watched this programme with a few of the Rio Street girls, we began discussing the gendered expectations in relationships. Sixteen-year-old Rozelda commented on the fact that the successful couple deserved to win, because the young man proved that he could treat a young woman with respect. 'Not like this guy I'm seeing now,' she said. 'He slaps me if I refuse to go out with him, or if I don't tell him where I've been.' 'How can you tell that the young man in the show would not beat up his partner?' I asked. 'Because he paid a compliment to the girl about her dress, and he let her speak first when they were asked whether they looked forward to their date. He didn't speak on her behalf. That's the way a girl should be treated – with respect, not slapped around. That's the way I want to be treated,' she replied. Earlier, Rozelda had told us about her partner, 22 year old Nazir, who had punched and slapped her when he discovered that she had spent the weekend visiting her cousin in another township, without his permission. 'He thought that I had met another guy there, and so he beat me. Why can't I go where I want, without having to tell him?' she said in frustration. Her critical comments resonated with the others' concerns about the high levels of interpersonal gender-based violence amongst the youth in their community. Through this TV programme they were able to envision an alternative image of dating relationships that allowed young women to express their opinions without the fear of incurring their partner's wrath. Their comments challenged the local notions of gender roles in heterosexual relations, in which physical violence went unnoticed and was often tolerated. Ultimately, however, the young women did not comment on the fact that none of the players selected partners of another race group or that for the most part, the show's participants reinforced rather than challenged the dominant gender stereotypes about dating behaviour.

In the other popular soap opera, *Backstage*, the storyline revolved around a group of young adults who attend a local college of performing arts and who hope to become radio DJs, beauty queens, jazz musicians, Kwaito[9] artists or R 'n' B singers with recording contracts. The protagonists, who were drawn from diverse ethnic or racial backgrounds live in a commune and seemed to have the available economic resources to lead independent lifestyles away from parents, parochial local communities or other family members. During their free time they frequented a small nightclub where fashionable dress, anxious conversation about winning a recording contract or a beauty contest and cellular telephones were *de rigueur*. The characters and the narrative in *Backstage* prised apart the old notions that South Africans should live and mix only within racially homogenous

---

[9] Kwaito is a popular South African music genre that originated in the Black townships in the 1990s. It incorporates African – American rap styles with indigenous urban slang, to produce a unique musical form.

communities or that Blackness automatically signified poverty. However, the show still reinforced South African gender stereotypes quite powerfully.

The young female characters were portrayed as modern, fashionably thin, feminine yet independent, career women. However, this modern, gendered stereotype was merely a veneer on the age-old, dualistic archetypes of the virtuous, self-sacrificial woman and the egoistical, gold-digging harridan that informed the protagonists' actions. Male characters, in contrast were portrayed either as ambitious, young performing artists or streetwise rogues, looking for easy, often illegal means to enrich themselves. Like the women in the show, all embodied the height of fashion. All the men attempted to woo over partners through classical romantic gestures, such as extravagant attention or expensive gifts. However, in spite of reinforcing gender stereotypes, it portrayed young men and women sharing friendships and dating across the colour line.

Interracial dating was also discussed intensely among the young women viewers in Rio Street. After we had watched the latest episode of *Backstage*, sixteen-year-old Nazli expressed distaste for dating men who were not coloured. 'I've heard that these African guys usually want to marry more than one woman,' she said, expressing a commonly held racial stereotype that all African men were practising polygamists. 'Well, I would date or marry an African guy, if he's smartly dressed and can provide me with a good home and provide for my children. The point is not what colour the guy is, but whether he can provide for you and treat you with respect!' Tessa responded hotly. Nazli looked at Tessa uncertainly, but then agreed that 'If he can provide for you and remain loyal, then colour wouldn't matter.' Through these discussions about the protagonists in shows like *Backstage*, the young women were questioning the entrenched racial boundaries in the local context, and, in so doing, imagining gender relationships beyond the narrow choices that their mothers prescribed. At the same time they were writing themselves into a national, racially diverse community beyond the boundaries of Rio Street.

In shows such as *Buzz* or *Backstage*, the most important audience were the actors' peers, who were imagined to be located everywhere, unmarked by the signifiers of economic, social or moral status except the dress styles and accents that were associated with an imagined cosmopolitan South African youth culture. Here, the old sexual, moral, spatial and economic signifiers of race were being unravelled. In addition, race was represented as a free-floating, empty category, whose meanings were recreated through the individual's actions.

Access to new cultural capital through television programmes freed the young women, at least temporarily, from the stifling constraints of the local social and moral norms. These Rio Street adolescents' transformation and renovation of the local domestic and public spaces through their consumption of TV programmes and popular music often inspired the more adventurous few to find their way across the city to the cosmopolitan nightclubs or trendy beachfront neighbourhoods. However, their physical and social journey into these spaces was bedevilled by the gap between their know-how of the South African cosmopolitan style and spaces and their lack of the material resources required to actually inhabit this world. These Rio Street adolescents lacked the necessary economic resources to purchase the expensive designer items, and sometimes their attempts to move into the trendy, new spaces set them up against the constraints of personhood in the local context. This was especially true for the courageous young women who pushed the envelope of locally imposed norms of femininity. The most potent threat that a parent held over all adolescents who transgressed local norms was that of eviction from the household. The intergenerational tension that emerged from the contestation about femininity and modesty surfaced in the identity of the Taxi Queen.

I met seventeen-year-old Chantal about a week after she returned home to Rio Street. She had been living in Sea Point, a trendy neighbourhood on the Atlantic seaboard for the past five months. When I met her, she was dressed in tight-fitting black jeans, figure-hugging black sweater and a pair of high-heeled, open-back mules. Her peroxided blonde hair was cut extremely short in the style that was fashionable among black Kwaito stars and she sported a set of perfectly manicured fingernails. Her sister, nineteen-year-old Patricia, appeared quite unsophisticated in comparison, in her loose-fitting sweatpants and plain white T-shirt. We were seated in their living room, watching Patricia feed her four-month-old son. 'Everyone expected me to be the one to fall pregnant,' Chantal said. 'Every old woman in this road gossiped about the way I dress and they had a fat lot to say about me going to the clubs in the city with Gavin, the taxi driver. And look who brought the baby home – Patricia, the quiet one, who did as she was told, and spent all her time indoors. Not me, the one they called the Taxi Queen. They think, because I went to the clubs, I was doing it (sex) with all the men. I was just having fun, meeting all these interesting people from everywhere.' Patricia listened quietly to her sister's tirade.

Chantal said that her father, who ruled their home with an iron hand since their mother's death, had banned them from going out after sunset. He also refused to provide them with any pocket money for outings or for new clothes. She said that 'a friend took me to the clubs in Long Street, and I had a great time. So I used to sneak out every Friday night to go. They think that I do it with Gavin so that he can drive me to the city. They can't imagine that we're just friends.' Her father had evicted her after he had learned that she was hitching rides to the city from the local minibus taxi drivers. Therafter, Gavin took her to a house in Sea Point that was owned by Roshan, the leader of the HL$ gang,[10] who used it to distribute illicit drugs. She said an older woman ran the house, and that a few other teenagers from Manenberg lived there too. The teenagers were expected to cut blocks of crack into smaller pieces of 'rock' for sale on the street. In return they were given free accommodation and R800 (US$80) per week to spend. She said that they enjoyed shopping for clothes at the stores in the popular Victoria and Alfred Waterfront. She said that she had learned to dress in a more fashionable manner from Mina, the housekeeper, and from watching the other young women in the club. Mina had also taught her about contraception and that's why she was able to avoid getting trapped in Patricia's situation. She had befriended some of the young white women she had met at the clubs and had learned that they too used contraceptives. 'They're not bad, even though I know that the old women here would think that they had loose morals,' she said.

The police raided the house in Sea Point one evening. That day the group of teenagers did not cut up any crack and were all watching a video when the police arrived. All the young people were legal minors and so they were let off with a severe warning. Thereafter they were escorted to their homes in Manenberg. Chantal said that her father had given her a severe beating. 'But I'll find my way back there once the heat has died down,' she

---

[10] Gang graffiti abbreviated gang names in this manner to mark the gang turfs. The $ signs was used to indicate the plural form as well as the gangs' preoccupation with material acquisitions such as cash, jewellery or cars.

said. 'He can't keep me prisoner here.'

In order to market themselves individually, unmarked by their place of origin in Manenberg, these young men and women needed access to the resources such as the expensive brand name clothes or the cosmopolitan, hybrid spaces that enabled them to break out from the socio-economic and physical constraints of the township. In the context of township poverty, young women like Chantal could only access these items or places through the friendships they formed with relatively better off taxi drivers or powerful gangsters. While these friendships provided them with individual agency and the possibility of carving a different life-path for themselves beyond Manenberg's boundaries, they also presented them with new constraints.

Like the young Berber women who desired Western-style negligees and lingerie in Abu-Lughod's study (1990), adolescents like Chantal were written into new, gendered and economic relations of power that may subjugate them in novel ways. These relations opened up new, diverse vistas of existence that they could desire or attain, and that would free them from local generational and gendered constraints. And, for a very few, the meaningful and lasting friendships or relationships that they developed with young, better-off men whom they met in these nightspots may mean the difference between a life of poverty in Manenberg and a qualitatively better one in the city's middle-class suburbs. However, these young women were the exception and often their ability to break free permanently from the impoverished lifestyle in Manenberg was based on their prior educational training, their adeptness at switching linguistic codes, and their acquisition of the necessary social skills and personal style associated with their better-off peers.

More often the girls' relations with the taxi drivers and the gangsters from similar socio-economic backgrounds implicated them in activities that pushed them back into the very impoverishment they sought to escape, or new relations of gender subordination that were life-threatening. They were also publicly renounced by their local peers – and sometimes found themselves outside the networks that they had to rely on for their material and social well-being.

Reconfiguring the masculine meanings of space in the local context

Like the young women who reconfigured the meanings of domestic, living-room spaces, youthful male counterparts carved out an alternative public space for themselves, in the form of the 'hok' or cage where they too were able to engage in activities and conversation beyond the reaches of the older generation. According to the local residents, hokke were first constructed in Manenberg in the late 1980s as some men sought to create self-employment opportunities and meet the local demand for housing. The large hokke were glamorous multi-roomed sites that served as the local nightclub and discotheque. They also served as the headquarters for the powerful gangs and were used as meeting places where gang activities were discussed. In contrast, smaller hokke were humbler, one-roomed spaces that doubled up as the corner shop and the meeting place for the smaller, less powerful gangs.

The hok or shack in Rio Street fell into the latter category. It was a lean-to, constructed out of a few corrugated iron sheets secured against the side-wall of the apartment block. The owner operated a small shop from a little apartment window that opened onto the *hok*. A small speaker was suspended from the roof with wires connected to a radio somewhere in the apartment and belted out the latest tunes on Radio Good Hope, the station that broadcast the local news and the latest international R & B and rap artists. The music was interspersed with DJ chatter about popular Cape Town clubs such as Dockside and the Galaxy. Since 1994, local radio stations have broadcast more news and discussions about local events on the Cape Flats and provided detailed reports about gang practices and attacks during periods of local unrest. In this way, gang activities that were shrouded in secrecy in the past, or that went unreported have become part of the public domain, and gangs acquired greater notoriety.

A few arcade game machines filled the small *hok*, where young men were engrossed in the game flashing on the small screens. Other young men stood around in a conversational group, sharing a cigarette or taking a swig from an illicit bottle of cheap wine. They were discussing the most notorious gang, the Hard Livings and their activities intensely, often expressing admiration for the gang's defiance and its members' ability to avoid arrest. The TV music videos and radio broadcasts of African American rap artists such as Tupac Shakur and Dr D.R.E were extremely popular in the *hokke* of Manenberg in 1998. Tupac's lyrics about Black men's ganging practices in American inner city neighbourhoods resonated with these young men's experiences. Invariably someone would play a tape recording of his music in the Rio Street *hok*, to which everyone would sing along. Tupac's song 'Strictly for my N.I.G.G.A.Z.' was by far the most popular. The lyrics described his defiant stance in the face of an unnamed opponent, describing a confrontation that many local men faced. They began to refer to each other as niggaz rather than 'broer' or 'brother'. Gang members also competed with each other as they flashed the hand signals, gold jewellery and the phrases that these performers used. The most powerful gang in Manenberg, the Hard Livings (HL$), had renamed their turf 'West Side' and painted a huge mural of Tupac Shakur on a building wall, thereby appropriating this powerful cultural image to assert their own dominance in the area, and to gain the respect of the smaller, less powerful gangs like the Young Dixie Boys of Rio Street.

The *hok*'s dual function, as corner shop and as a male hang-out where gang activities were openly discussed, provided a visible masculine place within the local public space. The young men's actions and conversations in this space moved gangs' activities from the peripheries of the local community to its centre. The gangs' secret rites of passage became part of the public domain through the radio talk shows, and increased their notoriety. The young men of Rio Street, who had few opportunities to obtain employment, openly talked of alliance with and membership of the more powerful gangs as the sole means to obtain respect in the local context. In doing so, they were locating men's status as gangsters at the heart of masculine personhood. In the process they challenged the senior women's power to define the public spaces as a moral sphere and destabilised their roles as the sole arbiters of personhood in the community. At the same time, they appropriated the international symbols of the rap music industry and reconstituted the gangster image to denote glamour and allure within the community rather than unfamiliarity and danger.

Conclusion

In this essay I have argued that male and female youth in Manenberg have renovated and reconfigured the local meanings of personhood in Manenberg through their engagement with specific aspects of global youth culture. Consumer culture has enabled youth to assert their membership of the new South African nation and to erase their apartheid township roots as well as the negative meanings attached to race. The emergent notions of personhood emphasised the individual's familiarity with the cosmopolitan styles and spaces of the new South Africans whose bodies were no longer anchored in specific racialised spaces or marked with ethnic accents and dress codes. In the innovative practices of this emergent personhood, the individual aimed to develop a consummate skill to manipulate space, linguistic codes, accents, dress style and attitude, so that they were able to route and reroute their roots as they consumed the image of the new South African. In this process these youth appeared to break free from archaic, racist apartheid notions of personhood in the national context, as well as moral notions of personhood in the local context. Yet, whilst this emergent construction of personhood enabled individual men and women to learn the skills, attitude and styles that freed them from racial ghettoes, and cross boundaries of race and class with ease, freedom could only be had through ready access to material assets such as financial resources or transportation. The less well-off male and female youth from Manenberg formed liaisons with powerful male gangsters in their struggle to obtain the material resources that allow them to break free from the constraints that are imposed in the local community. In doing so they wrote themselves into new configurations of gendered power relations.

References

Abu-Lughod, L. (1990), 'The Romance of Resistance: Tracing Transformations of Power through Bedouin Women', *American Ethnologist* 17(1): 41–55.

Barnes, T. (2003), 'Days and Bold: The Fascination of Soap Operas for Black Students at the University of the Western Cape, South Africa', in Paul Tiyambe Zeleza and Cassandra Rachel Veney (eds), *Leisure in Urban Africa*, Trenton, NJ: Africa World Press.

Clofed (2002) www.clofed.co.za/stats.htm

Field, S. (ed.) (2001), *Lost Communities, Living Memories. Remembering Forced Removals in Cape Town*, Cape Town: David Philip.

Goldin, I. (1987), *Making Race. The Politics and Economics of Coloured Identity in South Africa*, London: Longman.

International Labour Resources and Information Group (2002), *An Alternative View of Gender and Globalisation* Irig Globalisation Series No. 6, Cape Town: International Resource and Information Group.

Klein, N. (2001), *No Logo No Space, No Choice, No Jobs*, London: Flamingo.

Koen, C. (1997), A Socio-demographic Profile of Manenberg Residents and Summary of Key Problems the Community Face, Unpublished manuscript, University of the Western Cape.

Lye, W. and C. Murray (1980), *Transformations on the Highveld. The Tswana and Southern Sotho*, Cape Town: David Philip.

Miller, D. (1995), 'Introduction: Anthropology, Modernity and Consumption', in Daniel Miller (ed.), *Worlds Apart. Modernity through the Prism of the Local*, London: Routledge.

Nuttall, S and C.A. Michael (eds) (2000), *Senses of Culture. South African Cultural Studies*, Oxford: Oxford University Press.

Rassool C. and S. Prosalendis (eds) (2001), *Recalling Community in Cape Town. Creating and Curating the*

District Six Museum, Cape Town: District Six Museum.

SAIRR (2000), *South Africa Survey 2000*, Johannesburg: South African Institute of Race Relations.

Salo, E. (2003), 'Race Laws, Gender Tactics. "Coloured" Women and Welfare in Manenberg, South Africa', unpublished paper delivered to the Anthropology Dept, University of Western Cape.

West, M. (1984), *Influx Control. The 1983 Statistics*, Cape Town: South African Institute of Race Relations Cape Western Region.

Western, J. (1996), *Outcast Cape Town*, Minneapolis: Minnesota University Press.

Wilson, F. and M. Ramphele (1989), *Uprooting Poverty. The South African Challenge. Report for the Second Carnegie Inquiry into Poverty and Development in Southern Africa*, Cape Town: David Philip.

Zeleza, P.T. (2002), 'Rethinking Africa's Gender and Globalization Dynamics', unpublished paper, presented at the Women's Worlds Congress, the 8th International Interdisciplinary Congress on Women, Makerere University, Kampala, Uganda, 21–26 July 2002.

10

Refracting an Elusive South African Urban Citizenship
Problems with Tracking Spaza[1]

ANDREW SPIEGEL

Introduction

Two recently completed studies of aspects of urban African living arrangements in South Africa have, from quite different perspectives, come to a conclusion that there is a strong popular sense of what is proper for South African millennial urban life – particularly as regards domestic material culture. Helen Meintjes (2000) studied domestic appliance ownership patterns in three distinct areas in and around Soweto, Gauteng province. She showed that people there strive to possess and display a variety of modern electrical appliances in their homes. They do so to demonstrate, as much to domestic visitors as to themselves as householders, that they are part of the modern world through being fully connected into its commodity circuits.[2] Nontobeko Yose (1999) considered the implications of a shack to formal house upgrade in an area of Cape Town. She found that, at the very moment that they removed to their new formal houses, many people elected to dispose of their old furniture and go into debt to purchase new items that they considered to be the only kind appropriate for urban living. The old furniture and the shacks in which they had been living were seen as too 'rural' – as were the multilateral relationships of generalised reciprocity that, through connecting them locally but not into world-wide commodity circuits, had enabled them to survive the vicissitudes of life in the city.

Although neither Meintjes nor Yose states it quite that way, their findings suggest a popular sense that being a 'proper' urban citizen in contemporary South Africa means that one must simultaneously be and feel oneself to be tied into modern commodity circuits; and that one must be able to demonstrate one's connectedness into and in those circuits

---

[1] An earlier version of this chapter was published under a different title (Spiegel 2002). My thanks to Constance Nontobeko Yose, who first alerted me to a meaning of *spaza* other than as the adjective in *spaza* shop. Also to Raj Mesthrie and Kay McCormick for their comments on my efforts, to participants in a seminar in the Department of Social Anthropology, UCT, and to the various individuals cited below as having contributed through their personal communications with me. I of course accept sole responsibility for any errors or other shortcomings.

[2] In that respect their persistent desire to ensure connectedness resonates with the concerns of contemporary urban Zambians over their connectedness to the wider economic world (Ferguson 1999).

through the items of domestic material culture that one possesses and displays. For Meintjes, this is supported by her comment that 'By consuming various items, objects and appliances considered to be contemporary and "properly" modern ... residents in Soweto and [nearby] Lusaka City marked, performed, ... demanded their participation in, rather than exclusion from the modern world' (2000: 125).

Establishing and maintaining similar connectedness are an explicated aim of the dominant paradigm of globalisation, as reflected in the following extracts from a statement from the G8's July 2001 Genoa meeting: 'We are determined to make globalisation work for all our *citizens* and especially for the world's poor... Drawing the poorest countries into the global economy is the surest way to address their fundamental aspirations' (quoted in *Cape Times*, 23 July 2001; emphasis added). Given that aim, it appears that, at least at the level of material aspirations, but also probably at the level of what constitutes contemporary citizenship, there is significant convergence between globalisation strategists and South Africa's urban poor.

Fiona Ross (see Ross and Spiegel 2000) offers further data that seem to reinforce the conclusion about a popular sense of the importance for South Africa's urban poor of connectedness to a modern world that can specify what is proper. Reflecting on the impact of another shanty upgrade process in the Western Cape, she reveals a tendency, led by leaders of the shanty-town community, towards a reconstitution of domestic social relationships that suggests an imposed acceptance of a set of norms often associated with bourgeois conventionality. It is as if those leaders, and many of their followers, have come to an understanding that to live in a formal house means to be a fully-fledged urban citizen who subscribes to and lives by a set of 'proper' relational norms. They include formal marriage and maintenance of nuclear-type family arrangements.[3]

The present chapter takes a critical stance on the proposition that urban citizenship in contemporary South Africa is closely intertwined in the popular imagination with a sense of propriety that comes from material connectedness and commodity exchange relations. My approach here is from the perspective of a set of data that focus on a distinct ambiguity in popular notions of contemporary propriety and that suggests a much more elusive and fluid popular understanding of urban citizenship than that suggested by my reading of Meintjes (2000) and Yose (1999). Those data reveal that attempts to define neatly what constitutes urban (or indeed any) citizenship in contemporary South Africa is fraught if that definition is linked to simple notions of what constitutes modernity whether in form or function – what Gaonkar (1999) calls modernity's social transformational moment, a moment that would carry the world along a teleological trajectory of development towards uniformity for the supposed sake of higher living standards; a moment that thus seems to overwhelm quotidian agency through a Foucauldian process of normalising and standard-ising, and thereby disenchants the world and makes it meaningless.

The chapter focuses attention on a linguistic term, *spaza*, rather than directly on material culture and socio-economic relationships, to show the elusiveness of urban citizenship as a concept, at least as refracted through that linguistic term. Before doing

---

[3] F. Ross (pers. comm.) has said that acceptance of these norms by some has led to further marginalisation of others in the shanty population, and has resulted in greater vulnerabilities to domestic violence. If domestic violence is regarded as being unacceptable among those who desire a formal house, reports of its occurrence can lead to disqualification from the right to claim such a house.

that, however, we need to come to grips with the term and its multiple and ever-changing meanings. The polyvalency of the term is, of course, familiar to many (but by no means all) of those who use it. But it has remained hidden particularly from non-African language speakers and from non-lumpen portions of the South African population. Indeed, as I show below, the hidden nature of that polyvalency is one of its strengths.[4]

Spaza shops and their history

It has become commonplace in contemporary South Africa to refer to very small-scale retail outlets situated in township[5] people's homes, whence neighbours can obtain basic groceries and other domestic essentials, as *spaza* shops. It was thus with some confusion that I listened to Nontobeko Yose tell me that all the houses in the shack area of Marconi Beam where she was working in 1997 were *spaza* houses. How, I wondered, could every house in the settlement be a *spaza* shop? Given that the settlement was not situated on a main thoroughfare, if everyone was selling the same small range of domestic essentials, who, I asked, was buying them? 'No,' replied Ms Yose. 'I didn't say they were all *spaza* shops. I said they were all *spaza* houses.' Clearly the term *spaza* had meanings beyond those I already knew. As Ms Yose went on to explain, *spaza* can be used to describe something not contextually proper or normal, a simulacrum in the sense of an unsatisfactory alternative. The shacks in Marconi Beam were *spaza* houses because they did not meet the standards accepted for urban living, just as an old broken bag would be *spaza* for a young aspirant student such as she, as would a person's strange gait.

Intrigued by polyvalency of meaning, as anthropologists should be, I immediately wondered about the derivation of the word *spaza*. But Ms Yose was unable to assist. She knew it as used to described *spaza* shops and things not quite right and proper – even, she added, artificial. But she was unable to tell me where it came from or why that word in particular was used to signify those meanings. And so I began to turn to other students for help.

As already indicated, a common understanding of *spaza* shops is that they are micro enterprises operated by black people from within the confines of their residences. Yet, I was reminded, there were no *spaza* shops in the townships before the mid to late 1970s. True, people attempted to operate small retail outlets – particularly shebeens[6] – for selling

---

[4] I have elsewhere discussed some of the ethics of exposing the popularly hidden set of ideas embedded in the word *spaza* (Spiegel 2003).

[5] The term 'township' is used quite specifically in South Africa to refer to densely settled residential areas that, during the apartheid years, were established for black people on the outskirts of cities and towns (*Dictionary of South African English* 1996: 730). Despite its use internationally to describe a small town or village forming part of a larger whole, the term's use in South Africa has not been so general. The name Soweto, for example, is an acronym deriving from South Western Townships, an aggregation of contiguous areas planned for exclusive residential occupation by people classified as African. For discussion of the apartheid system of population classification by racial and other characteristics see West (1988).

[6] Shebeen (originally an Anglo-Irish word) describes an illegal (unlicensed) liquor outlet. Given the fact of legislated prohibition of sale (and indeed gifts too) of commercially produced alcohol to Africans in South Africa until 1962 (Rogerson 1992: 332), production and distribution of various home-brewed alcoholic beverages has long been a significant source of income for African women in South Africa's cities (see Hellmann, 1948; van Onselen 1982). Descriptions of illicit liquor outlets as shebeens date back to at least 1900 (*Dictionary of South African English* 1996: 634).

liquor – from their township homes. But for the most part, other than the shebeens, such outlets seem not to have been as common as they have become in the past twenty-plus years. Why the growth?

The year 1976 saw the start of a major popular uprising of African people against the injustices and inequities of apartheid that were increasingly undermining their sense of citizenship. The uprising was sparked off in Soweto by resistance of schoolchildren to the apartheid state's imposition of Afrikaans as a medium of instruction in schools for African people. But it was not simply against that one rather blundering educational policy decision. The policy's propagation and implementation provided opportunity for expressions of deep-seated resistance that had long been welling up, but had been relatively submerged since the banning a decade and a half earlier of the African National Congress (ANC), Pan-Africanist Congress (PAC) and related resistance/liberation organisations.

One product of the uprising was the beginning of rapid attempts to reform aspects of the apartheid system. Another was increasingly widespread black activism against the institutions of apartheid, oppression and exploitation. Such activism, suppressed and forced underground during the 1960s, had become quite visibly virulent already in the early 1970s. An increasingly powerful and vocal trade union movement arose, and a new Black Consciousness movement developed among activists, who managed, for a short while, to sidestep the bans that had been imposed early in the 1960s on the ANC and PAC and the dissemination of their materials.

Among the methods of resistance adopted by such activists was a consumer boycott of formal economic retail outlets, particularly those that were associated with repressive actions against workers and their newly revived unions. But the principle of consumer boycott was not limited to worker and union support. Indeed, it increasingly became a weapon against a range of political institutions and state agencies – local government agencies in particular. When aimed at the private sector, it was often adopted with the intention that popular pressure on white-owned business might speed up the process whereby business might feel coerced to demand reform (and hopefully eventual capitulation) by the apartheid regime.

Spaza shops, students told me, arose as a feature of the township landscape, in the shadow of these kinds of boycotts. They arose in a context in which it was increasingly difficult to enforce apartheid legislation that had aimed to restrict African people's trading opportunities in the cities and their associated townships – allowing only select individuals a maximum of a single formal licence to trade in town (Southall 1980). The apartheid state's objective was that aspirant traders should remove to the Bantustans[7] to trade there – although restrictive regulations undermined opportunities for entrepreneurial growth there too and the objective was not often attained (e.g. Bank 1991, 1997). But our concern here is not only the fact that consumer boycotts of formal economic enterprises offered opportunity for informal trade to grow. It is the nature of the new informal enterprises, as part of an institution of resistance, that is of interest; for it provides a window onto some popular understandings of the origins of the idea of *spaza* and onto the etymology of the

---

[7] Bantustans were areas of land set aside for exclusive African occupation, where systems of governance were meant to follow 'traditional' African ways and where regimes of African collaborators were established as formal leaders. In time all were supposed to have become fully independent states. Only four of the designated ten achieved that status, which was never recognised beyond the borders of South Africa (also see *Dictionary of South African English* 1996: 47).

word *spaza*.

The *Dictionary of South African English* (1996: 670) quotes various sources – all dating from the late 1980s onwards – that reflect the idea that *spaza* shops grew from entrepreneurial efforts to engage in illicit informal trade. The *Dictionary* quotes K. Ngwenya's 1989 article in *Drum* magazine: 'The word [*spaza*] describes the way traders were forced to operate underground because they usually broke all rules and regulations…' (ibid.). But it offers no etymology.

Why, I asked the various quite separate groups of students, were they called *spaza* shops? Where does that word *spaza* come from? Among the first responses I obtained were those from various Zulu first-language speakers, who explained that it comes from the Zulu verb *ukuphazama* (or, more precisely, from its derivative noun *isiphazamisa* – see below for translations). These same respondents went on to offer reasons why it came to be used in the late 1970s to describe the retail outlets now widely described as *spaza* shops. The reasons, as I shall now show, were directly linked to the very history of consumer boycotts outlined above.

Various respondents explained that when small 'tuck shops' began to operate from people's homes in African townships (probably, they said, in the late 1970s), they were supported in part because they offered a way to purchase one's daily essentials without patronising formal white-owned shops. By engaging in such transactions, I was told, both the 'tuck shop' proprietors and their customers were said to be disturbing and hindering the operation of formal enterprises. A 'tuck shop' thus constituted an *isiphazamisa* (Zulu), in other words a hindrance, impediment and disturbance, to formal stores and implicitly to the whole formal economy (and political-economic system) that they were understood to represent. The element of resistance that *spaza* shops represented was thus constituted immediately in the original word used to describe them. Although in an elided (clipped[8]) form, *spaza* reflects the action of resistance to apartheid-imposed laws through its apparent derivation from *isiphazamisa* (that which causes hindrance or annoyance – Zulu; Xhosa = *isiphazamiso*).[9]

Etymological tracking

To support this explanation, it seemed evident I would need to consider some classical dictionaries' translations of words I was told were those from which *spaza* derived. These were words such as *–phazama* and their derivatives or sound-shift equivalents in cognate languages. I began with the Zulu from which I had first been told the term *spaza* derives

---

[8] My thanks to Linda van Huyssteen, who has pointed me towards the term 'clipping', though I have yet to work with the socio-linguistic and linguistic literature on such processes.

[9] Gerald Stone (pers. comm. 4 October 2001) suggests that *spaza* is a prison-gang-inspired Afrikanerisation of the Zulu word *isifiphazo*, a noun which Doke, Malcolm and Sikakana (1988: 62) translate as 'deceit, cunning'. *Isifiphazo* derives from *ukufiphaza* ('v. tr. 1. obscure, darken. 2. deceive, ibid.). This is a variation I have not pursued as closely as I have what follows because of the greater difficulty I perceive in 'clipping' *isifiphazo* than *isiphazamisa* to form *spaza* (or *sphaza*). *Fipha* is recorded as an ideophone that in Zulu is '1. of dullness, obscurity, darkness. 2. of wincing, flinching. 3. of deceiving. 4. of frowning, scowling. 5. of dizziness' (ibid.) and in Sesotho 'to become extinguished at once; to be very dark' with a derivative verb *hofiphatsa* meaning 'to prevent from seeing well, to deceive' (Mabille *et al.* 1974: 83). It is interesting, nonetheless, that both *ukuphazamisa* and *ukufiphaza* entail a process of reducing clarity of vision and understanding.

(although it seems almost as likely that it derives from Xhosa). In their *English and Zulu Dictionary,* Doke *et al.* (1988: 243; see also Doke *et al.* 1990: 651; Doke and Vilakazi 1948: 651) offer the following as English equivalents for the Zulu verb *(uku-)phazama*: '[to] be disturbed; blunder; interrupt; disturb' and they translate the noun *–phazamo (umphazamo, imi-*[pl.]*)* as 'disturbance, interference'. Kropf and Godfrey's (1915: 326) classic Xhosa dictionary corroborates with a translation of the Xhosa version of the verb *(uku-)phazama* as 'to fail to act through neglect or inability; to be unsteady, thoughtless, inconsiderate; to make a mistake, but not on purpose; to be interrupted, disturbed, hindered'. The more accessible *English–Xhosa Xhosa–English Dictionary* published by Via Afrika (n.d.: 67) translates *(uku-)phazama* as to 'be mistaken, be misled, be confused, blunder, fail' and *(uku-)phazamisa* as to 'mislead, confuse, cause to blunder; hinder, obstruct; interrupt'. Fischer's (1985: 385) *English–Xhosa Dictionary* suggests a slight variation on the verb *(uku)-phazama*, which it offers as a translation for the active voice English verb 'to mistake' (both in transitive and intransitive forms), rather than the passive voice forms offered by Kropf and Godfrey (1915). Various Xhosa-speaking informants have suggested that the active voice usage reflects contemporary everyday usage (but see the Zulu dictionary translations that continue to reflect a passive voice form even in its most recent (Doke *et al.*, 1990) edition. Fischer (1985: 167, 276) offers the causative Xhosa verb *(uku)-phazamisa* for the English 'to distract and to disturb'.

But it is the noun form of the causative verb, *isiphazamisa (isiphazamiso)*, that my informants had suggested was the source from which the clipped term *spaza* derives – because of the way that the prefix *isi-* is often elided in the spoken form to be spoken as just an *'s'* sound.[10] The word *isiphazamisa* is a derivative noun from the verb *-phazama* with the addition of a causative suffix. Thus, although none of Doke *et al.*'s Zulu dictionary editions (1948, 1988, 1990) lists that specific noun, we can readily recognise that its causative suffix leads to its meaning 'that which causes disturbance or blunder'.

Indeed Kropf and Godfrey (1915: 327) offer that kind of explanation for the Xhosa *isiphazamiso*, which they translate as 'that which causes detention, hindrance, confusion, difficulty, interruption'. Again they are corroborated both by Via Afrika's *English–Xhosa Xhosa–English Dictionary* (n.d.: 67), which offers a translation of the noun *-phazamiso (isiphazamiso)* as 'something causing blunders, misleading thing; obstacle, hindrance; interruption', and by Fischer (1985: 167, 276), who translates each of the English nouns 'distraction', 'disturbance' and 'hindrance' as the Xhosa word *isiphazamiso*.

Importantly, if we are to be able to claim legitimacy for the above etymology, we need to establish whether there are similar constructions in cognate languages. I have been able to find them in SiNdebele, SeSotho and Shona, although in the latter two instances one has to allow for sound shifts. SiNdebele, having only very recently branched from what became Zulu, unsurprisingly has almost identical words (with only the aspirating 'h' being absent). Elliot (n.d.: 163) translates the verbs *-pazama* as 'make a blunder (being disturbed)' and *-pazamisa* as 'cause to blunder, disturb, confuse'. There is no derivative

---

[10] Why the aspirated *ph* should be lost (at least in written form) to the plosive *p* is less obvious, except that neither English nor Afrikaans differentiates the two and the written form may simply be being treated as part of an English/Afrikaans lexicon. This switch in the written form reflects similar kinds of uninformed spellings that one sees in earlier dictionaries (e.g. Kropf and Godfrey 1915), where 'p' is used interchangeably for both the plosive and aspirated forms.

noun *isipazamisa*, but, as in Zulu, it is an acceptable form for something that causes blundering, disturbance or confusion.

For Sesotho (Southern Sotho), Mabille *et al.* (1974: 371) offer 'to be annoyed' as a translation of the verb *(ho-)phatsama*; and they translate its derivative causative *(ho-) phatsamisa* as 'to annoy; to bother'. Although not listed by Mabille *et al*, the noun form, *sephatsamiso* (a conventional extension) implies something annoying, bothering, disturbing, etc.

Making allowances for further sound shifts, there is also a clear equivalent in Shona, as listed in Hannan (1974: 539), where the intransitive verb *-potsa* is translated as to 'Miss. Make a mistake. Blunder. 2. Throw at and miss. 3. Take a shot at. 4. Bewitch by means of harmful "medicine"'; and the transitive verb *-potsanisa* is translated as 'Confuse, put things in the wrong order'. While the noun derivative form *chipatsaniso* (or *zvipatsaniso*) is not listed, it would follow logically in terms of the same conventions of language construction as apply in the other languages cited, and would carry the meaning of 'something that confuses or puts out of order'.[11]

The very fact that there are equivalents in cognate languages suggests that there is strong reason to accept the etymology offered me by my various sources. But, as we shall see below – and for me a great disappointment when I realised it – the evidence about its direct link to 1970s political activism, albeit very persuasive, is much more difficult to demonstrate as fully or compellingly.[12] The popular understanding that *spaza* shops arose as institutions of resistance is indeed supported by the argument that, at least in one sense, the term *spaza* reflects precisely that resistance. In circumstances of increasing boycott and other forms of resistance to the apartheid state and the white-dominated institutions that supported it, forms of trade that had the effect of disrupting and disturbing formal economic enterprise were part of the struggle against apartheid. But the further fact that the word was already in use in the 1960s, as I soon came to discover, undermines the easy link between its use and political resistance in the 1970s.

Spaza dissembling

Seeking confirmation of the etymology I had been offered by my student respondents, I turned for help to Cliff Dikeni, then a lecturer in African Languages at the University of Cape Town. He was able to refer me to various sources that indeed confirmed my new understanding of the meaning and construction of the words *isiphazamisa* and *isiphazamiso*. But he stunned me when he explained that he remembered the word *spaza* being used, as an adjective to mean 'imitation', in Johannesburg of the 1960s (29

[11] My colleague Owen Sichone (pers comm., 18 April 2000) has said that the verb *uku-pusa* in Nwamanga and in Bemba (both spoken in Zambia) means: 'to miss when throwing, shooting' (a stone, spear, bow, rifle, etc.). He has added that the causative form *uku-pusya* carries connotations of disruption and hindering – sometimes by supernatural means – the skills of a hunter or warrior for whom the ability to throw or shoot is crucial: 'you miss because someone does something to prevent you succeeding'. The noun form *chipusya* is 'that thing or influence that causes you to miss.' Sichone also referred to a Bemba proverb *umukulu apusa akawe, ta pusa akewo* (lit: Elders miss (the mark) with a stone but do not miss with words = Elders may no longer be technically skilled, but mark their words for the wisdom they reveal).

[12] Don Mattera (pers. comm., 15 April 2000) adamantly refutes any such derivation or the link to political activism. The evidence seems compelling to me nonetheless.

February 2000, pers. comm.). At the time, he says, one could obtain copies of a popular brand of sneakers that went under the brand name 'Tenderfoot'. Those copies were described as *spaza tackies*[13] because they were not the real thing – a phrase that resonated immediately with Ms Yose's comment that first drew my interest. It also continues to be common today among some parents who, unable to afford the demands of their children for expensive footwear, buy cheap shoes to tide them over:

> ... if your child's pair of shoes has just been worn out and you don't have sufficient money to buy the right thing, so you go to buy the R20.99[14] pair of tackies, and you call that a *spaza*. 'I've just bought this pair of *spazas* until I've got the money to buy the Nikes that you want.' He can use them in the meantime so that he is not walking barefoot. (Ntombizodumo Ngxabi, pers. comm., 26 October 2000)

Other people too have since explained to me that one can describe various items of apparel, such as a piece of clothing, as *spaza* when the item referred to is regarded as cheap and of poor quality. It is as if what some people described as South African street language (*Tsotsitaal*[15]) has developed its own word for ersatz: as leading poet, journalist and ex-Sophiatown[16] sage, Don Mattera, explained (pers. comm., 15 April 2000), 'If you ask me "Is that for real?" I will answer "That is no *spaza*" [i.e. it is indeed for real] ... Something *spaza* is not the real McCoy.'[17] Similarly, students such as Nontobeko Yose explained that actions can be described as *spaza*, so that one may say that a person (for example) walks *spaza* when one means that the person has a strange or unusual gait.[18] And yet others have explained the use of *spaza* as an adjective to describe a stupid and incompetent person – otherwise signified by a wave of the right hand across the face from right side forehead to left side chin, palm facing towards the face. In the instances where I was offered this explanation, the gesture was used to explain the meaning, and sometimes linked to pejorative descriptions of recent arrivals in town who lacked the supposed niceties of urban mannerisms – those who had not (yet?) learned to be proper urban citizens.

Interestingly, despite its lack of etymology, the *Dictionary of South African English*

[13] *Tackies* (pl.; sing. = *tackie*) is a common word in South African English that is used to describe rubber-soled canvas shoes (sneakers; sandshoes) (*Dictionary of South African English* 1996: 705). One possible etymology for *tackies* is the Scottish-English dialect term 'tacky' to describe 'cheap, rubbishy' (ibid.). The idea of a cheap imitation of something rubbishy begins to beggar the imagination. But that Tenderfoots were indeed popular at the time is confirmed by John Comaroff, who says he too wore that brand of sneakers as a South African youngster in the mid-1960s.

[14] At the time of the interview, the South African Rand was worth about US$0.138. By July 2001 it had fallen to US$0.122, and by December that year hit an all-time low of US$0.0769, after which there has been a mild recovery.

[15] *Tsotsitaal* is a patois used and developed differently across the country that derives from a mix of various African languages, Afrikaans and English (*Dictionary of South African English* 1996: 743). It has been said to have been a 'clever' language 'spoken first mainly by criminals, partly as a means of avoiding being understood by others within earshot' (ibid.). Another description is *Flytaal*, 'An urban (especially township) argot', so described because it is a language (*taal* in Afrikaans) that is 'fly' (in the English sense of 'knowing; wide awake') (*Dictionary of South African English* 1996: 231).

[16] A 'mixed-race' suburb in Johannesburg, demolished in the 1950s as part of the apartheid government's efforts to create racially segregated residential areas. Sophiatown was also very significant for being a locus of much interracial activity – particularly around music – and is sometimes seen as the font of persistent urban African cultural forms.

[17] The term has also been used in that way in a recent TV show, where a bogus traditional healer is described as *spaza*, implying a complete fraud (*Going Up*, SABC TV1, 1 March 2000). My thanks to Pam Maseko for this reference.)

[18] One first-language English-speaking student has suggested that there may be a link between this usage and the colloquial (South African and British English) English-language insult that someone's behaviour is '*spaz*'

recognises these same kinds of meanings. Its first entry (alphabetically arranged: adjective before noun and verb) against the word *spaza*, the *Dictionary* offers 'camouflaged, dummy' as translations of the adjective *spaza* (1996: 670). As that use corresponds with a series of sources I have begun to assemble from discussions with various other informants, I now turn in that direction.

Continuing my enquiries, I entered discussions with a range of people, both men and women and ranging in age from their early thirties to their mid-sixties, in the Western Cape and Gauteng provinces. Most confirmed the use of the word *spaza* as imitation by offering explanations that something is *spaza* when it is unreal or artificial. Jim Buthelezi, whose early childhood was spent in Sophiatown in the 1940s, explained (pers. comm., 31 March 2000): 'we used to rub a farthing against some silver paper to make a *spaza tickie*' (small silver threepenny coin – *Dictionary of South African English* 1996: 718–9).[19] And the words and gestures of Nomangesi Mbobosi Mzamo, a teacher trainer in Cape Town, provide another illustration. When asked about the meaning of the word *spaza* she derisorily waved her hand and arm and contemptuously extended the 'ee' sound at the end of the phrase as she exclaimed: 'It [that 'nonsense thing'] is *spaza-nje* (lit: merely *spaza*[20])' (pers. comm., 11 April 2000). One Free State woman who came to Johannesburg in the early 1970s as a domestic worker (a SeSotho first-language speaker) and another who arrived around the same time from Gazankulu (a ChiTsonga first-language speaker) both said they had first learned the term *spaza* to mean fake, unreal, etc. when they had come to the city, and had not heard or used it before that. But another, a paediatric nurse originally from the Eastern Cape but then at Soweto's Baragwanath Hospital[21] in the early 1980s and later in Edendale in KwaZulu-Natal in the early 1990s, explained that her first exposure to the word was when it was used by rural traditionalist Zulu mothers to refer to a dummy (pacifier) for their babies.

> *Isiphaza(miso)* is a word used to describe a baby's dummy – one of those things that you give to a child but it has no milk in it. I first heard the word used to describe a dummy when I was working as a nurse in Baragwanath Hospital in 1982, when I was in a paediatric ward. I heard it from a woman from KwaZulu – a (child) patient's mother who was wearing one of those Zulu traditional headdresses, as many of them did. She said '*animnikeni isphazamiso leso sake*' (give her that dummy of hers). … I think this *sphaza* is a Zulu word. Zulu people don't have dummies. But they looked at how it works – the baby thinks it's eating something, and the baby is just being *phazamisa*-ed. To *phazamisa* someone is to disturb or distract that person. … I also heard it used by a woman from the area next to Greytown where people were killing each other – Msinga – in 1991/2/3. It was in an orthopaedic children's ward in Edendale. Also talking about a dummy. Whenever a lodger-mother[22] in hospital feels it's not yet time to feed the child she

---

[18] (cont.) (probably derived from spastic) when it is ungainly, unusual, unacceptable or silly. Although the idea of a convergence of Zulu-*Tsotsitaal* and (South African) colloquial English is appealing, I have no evidence at all to support such an argument.

[19] Joe Mafela, screen-play writer (with Roberta Durant) and sitcom actor, was born in Sophiatown and grew up in Kliptown. He too associates the word *spaza* with something that is 'not genuine, a look-alike' (pers. comm., 9 January 2002).

[20] Kropf and Godfrey's (1915: 272) entry for the terminal adverb *-nje* offers four translations, the third of which is most telling here: 'expressing contempt: *bangabantu-nje*, they are just common, ordinary people; *umgumntu-nje-na?* are you just a common man? *uteta-nje* you just talk; *nje-kodwa* without reason, merely, simply'.

[21] Now Chris Hani-Baragwanath Hospital.

[22] Refers to the mothers who live in the hospital while their babies and children are being treated.

would call for a *sphaza* for the baby. They sometimes say *sphazamiso* or *isiphazamiso*. Others then shorten it to *sphaza*. (Ntombizodumo Ngxabi pers. comm., 26 October 2000)[23]

Significantly, various respondents added to their explanations that the verb *ukuphazamisa* can be used to describe teasing, harassing or even tormenting through offering a false or misleading picture or story that is then described as *spaza* – one that is not simply and only fake but also intended to dissemble and thereby to confuse, discompose and bewilder.

And so I turned to the 'experts' for further advice, starting with Sizwe Satyo, Professor of African Languages at the University of Cape Town (pers. comm., 17 April 2000), Aggrey Klaaste, editor-in-chief of New Africa Publications (pers. comm., 13 April 2000) and Don Mattera, poet, playright and writer (pers. comm., 15 April 2000). All three confirmed the above meanings of *spaza*. They also all indicated that the word *spaza* can be used in the form of a verb, to mean much the same as what I have above explained *ukuphazamisa* to mean. Satyo said that, as a verb, *spaza* means 'to show off; to be pretentious and not genuine'. In Klaaste's words, 'If I *spaza* you, I am making a fool of you; pulling the wool over your eyes.' And in Mattera's much more richly flavoured version:

> *Spaza* is a Sophiatown word; *Tsotsitaal* ... You are only playing the fool: *Ek spaza net* [I just *spaza*]. *Net 'n negro-in-die-tien*.[24] It's a form of speech. Beating about the bush. [*Ek*] *spaza maar net* [(I) am just kidding] ... *Ag man, die Boere* are giving us trouble, *maar 'snet die spaza* [Oh, man, the police are troubling us, but it's just a ploy]. *Hulle spaza maar net met die gaai* [They are simply fooling around with the guy]. You can also use *spaza* to mean 'eyeblind' the authorities. Think about Bezwoda:[25] *hy't 'n spaza geslaan met'ie Amerikans* (lit: he hit a *spaza* with the Americans; he pulled a fast one with the Americans).

The notion of *spaza* as something intended to bewilder ('eyeblind' in Mattera's terms) is evident in two other reports I gathered about its use. Both of their contexts again suggest that the term may have anti-apartheid political roots, albeit this time dating from the 1960s – although, having just made the comment about 'eyeblinding the authorities', Mattera, supported by colleague Sidney Mahlangu, who was with him for part of the time of our discussion, was adamant *spaza* has no direct political connotations. Nonetheless, and like Mattera's reference to the *Boere* (police), the targets of efforts to dissemble and confuse in the two instances I have recorded are indeed the police, rather than friends, kin and neighbours engaged in banter and teasing.

The first example comes from my discussion with a small group of first-language Xhosa-speaking women in the Western Cape. One among them was Nomangesi Mbobosi Mzamo (pers. comm., 14 March 2000). During that first discussion, Ms Mzamo was initially unable (or unwilling) to offer me any etymology of the term *spaza*. All she did, almost as if to put me off the track and *spaza* (or *phazamisa*) me, was to agree with another member of the group who said simply: '*spaza* comes from *Tsotsitaal*' – as if saying that

---

[23] I have here recorded the term as *sphaza* as Ms Ngxabi was very clear in her aspirated pronunciation – just as I have also heard from various others (see note 9).

[24] Mattera carefully spelled this phrase out for me, but did not offer me a translation. I can only guess it is another way of saying 'it's ersatz', though the derivation of the phrase itself cries out for explanation.

[25] A reference to Dr Werner Bezwoda, a Johannesburg oncologist who has allegedly faked breast-cancer chemotherapy trial results (*Mail and Guardian*, 14–20 April 2000).

meant it would have no further etymology because it derived from a language other than her mother-tongue Xhosa. Yet, when I suggested, in response, that I'd gathered from other sources that it might be an abbreviated version of the Xhosa word *isiphazamiso*, Ms Mzamo elatedly confirmed that that was quite right.

She then went on to explain that one could use the term to describe activities such as concerts and church services. For example, she explained, she had grown up in the Western Cape town of Wellington and, during 1964, had seen church-type gatherings held at the edges of wooded areas near the town. But these were not real church services. Rather they were gatherings called during times when meetings of the ANC and PAC, then necessarily underground because both organisations were officially banned, were held deep within those forests. Described locally as *spaza* services, the church-style gatherings were called to provide decoys in order to confuse (*ukuphazamisa*) the police and put them off the scent. They were not 'real' church services, just imitations of the real thing.

Similarly, Steven Mosela, a first-language Sesotho-speaking worker in Johannesburg who was born in Sophiatown in 1942 and moved with his parents to Evaton near Vereeneging ten years later, recalled decoy concerts being held outside people's Gauteng homes in which political meetings were held in the early 1960s. And he added that they were described by the term *spaza* (pers. comm., 31 March 2000).

But, tempting as it is to accept the simple argument that *spaza* is a term developed in the process of resistance to apartheid, evidence from Steven Mosela and his colleagues who grew up in and around Sophiatown, and from various others, undermines that argument. For Jim Buthelezi, a first-language Zulu-speaking worker born in Sophiatown in 1938 and bred in Pimville (now part of Soweto), the idea of *spaza* as fake, a copy, not the real thing, was something he learned as part of the process of being socialised in the world where he grew up: 'it just came to us from the old days' and did not arise only in the 1960s (pers. comm., 31 March 2000). For Khampe Khampe, a first-language Tswana speaker who is now a member of the SA National Commission for UNESCO, 'it was something I learned on the soccer field in Rustenburg where I grew up' (pers. comm., 31 March 2000).

Similarly, poet and writer Don Mattera, born in 1935 and whose earliest memories are of and from Sophiatown, places his first memory of the word in the early 1940s to mean not real, as does Joe Mafela, scriptwriter (with Roberta Durant) and popular sitcom actor who was also born in Sophiatown, albeit somewhat later than Mattera. Both Mattera and, later, Joe Mafela adamantly rejected my suggestion that *spaza* might derive from the Zulu *isiphazamisa* (*isiphazamiso* in Xhosa).[26] Both did so on the basis of a perceived clear distinction between the rural and the urban. As Mattera said, 'The word [*spaza*] has its origins in urban culture. It has no origins in rural things' (which 'things' implicitly include uses of the Zulu word *isiphazamisa*). Implicitly for Mattera, at this point the idea of a

---

[26] Mattera suggested that it might be based on a Latin root as is (he suggested) the Afrikaans word *spaar* (the English 'spare' derives from Old English and is of Germanic origin – *Concise Oxford Dictionary* 1999: 1375). As Sizwe Satyo (pers. comm., 17 April 2000) has pointed out, the politics of language construction is such that people claim ownership of words and their derivation that often denies other possible etymologies. In both Mattera's and Mafela's cases, as recognised sources of knowledge about *Tsotsitaal* and its Sophiatown (and 'colloquial') origins, the notion of urban distinctiveness is as important for claiming such authority as Yose (1999) and especially Meintjes (2000) show it is for demonstrating where propriety's boundaries are located. Interestingly, various other people have suggested that there may be a link between *spaza* and the name Spar used by a Netherlands-based chain of franchised convenience stores. Again Satyo's comment is pertinent: those

propriety that marks off urban citizenship was more important than finding an etymological continuity between urban and rural. Yet, earlier in our conversation, and without any prompting from me, he had commented that *spaza* is not a Zulu word – almost as if he was wondering out loud about its likely Zulu (and therefore 'rural') origins. Joe Mafela (pers. comm., 9 January 2002) confirmed the sense of a clearly distinctive category of urban (township) life as the source of what he called 'colloquial' terms when he said: 'It [*spaza*] is colloquial, and that's straightforward. It's not from anywhere except the townships.'

That said, and bearing in mind Satyo's, Klaaste's and Mattera's use of the word *spaza* as a verb (to 'eyeblind'), let us return to the meaning of the verb *ukuphazamisa* as 'to dissemble and thereby to bewilder and mislead'; in Mattera's words: 'to upset plans, to push aside, to cause an impediment'. Yet they are suggested by various informants and carry the implication that the derivative Zulu noun *isiphazamisa* (Xhosa = *isiphazamiso*) refers to those actions intended to or having the effect of dissembling and impeding and thereby bewildering and misleading.

Spaza as trickster type

We can, I think, link those translations to the wide range of passive and hidden forms of resistance – detailed in the literature on resistance to colonialism in general, to apartheid in particular and to the exploitative nature of industrial labour – that were less directed towards upending the imposed status quo than towards disrupting its operations and confusing its agents (e.g. van Onselen 1976, 1982; see also Scott 1985). Indeed, Gerald Stone, who is presently compiling a lexicon of prison and ('coloured') township gang slang, suggests (pers. comm., 4 October 2001) that the term *spaza* first came into use amongst members of the Regiment of the Hills, a gang of outlaw migrants during the last decade of the nineteenth century in and on the outskirts of the gold-mining centre that formed around what is now Johannesburg (van Onselen 1982).[27] I have no further evidence to support such an argument or to be able to fix the moment when the clipped form *spaza* (or *sphaza*) began to prevail. Yet it seems more than likely that the terms *ukuphazamisa* and *isiphazamisa* have a long history of use: to describe those very actions, and their manifestations, in southern African struggles against colonialism in general and its particular form of apartheid, as well as against the constraints of industrial labour relations and relationships. I realise that it may not be possible to find proof for such a claim, because of the limited range of written vernacular records in which the evidence would have to be found. Yet I make the suggestion as a hypothesis and on the basis of the contemporary evidence about use, described above, of both the terms *ukuphazamisa* and *spaza* to suggest the intention to bewilder, both in everyday banter and in various contexts of a need to confuse, discompose and impede those who exercise power through the state. If that is indeed a persistent use of the terms *ukuphazamisa* and *isiphazamisa*, my

---

[26] (cont.) who see *spaza* as first and foremost an adjective to describe a kind of shop will be inclined to make that kind of linguistic association.

[27] Stone adds that the word *spaza* is now in currency in South Africa's prison gangs and means 'a deceit; an appearance calculated to deceive' and that 'its verb form means to deceive'. *Spaza* shops, he says, are therefore 'shops disguised as homes' (pers. comm., 4 October 2001).

argument about the struggle roots of *spaza* can hold, albeit without a neatly specified date of origin of the abbreviated version or of the context in which it was coined.

Rosaldo (1989: 190ff) has pointed to the fact that humour is often used as what he calls a 'weapon of subaltern consciousness'. He goes on (ibid.: 206ff) to remind us that, when that occurs, we ethnographers are often blind to how that humour is being used by the subjects of our attentions to convey their perceptions of us as agents of the very processes that subordinate them: processes that include our recording and codifying their practices and meanings. Rosaldo's aim is to emphasise the importance of recognising, in ethnographic analysis, 'a relational form of understanding in which both parties actively engage in "the interpretation of cultures"' (ibid.: 206–7).

My aim here is to indicate that, through recognising the relational nature of my efforts to establish an etymology of *spaza*, I seem to have fallen upon a kind of trickster trope in the word *spaza*. As indicated above, the poet Don Materra and the actor Joe Mafela were both insistent, during our quite separate discussions, that I was wrong to presume either a Zulu or Xhosa source for the word *spaza*, or (in Mattera's case) that it had any political connotations. And, having just explained to me that to *spaza* is (simply) to fool around and tease or confound, Mattera quickly asked whether I was sure that I had not been *spaza-ed* by those who had led me to those presumptions. Thus did he make fun of our discussion and simultaneously attempt to *spaza* me through playing upon the irony in the trope, all the while to bewilder me and my efforts to 'capture' and record the nature of its trickery.

Looking back, then, on Nomangesi Mbobosi Mzamo's initial unwillingness, some weeks earlier, to let me into the subterfuge of *spaza* until I had demonstrated some prior understanding, I came to realise the nature of the trope as trick intended to bewilder and dissemble – as if in an effort to undermine the hegemony of modernity, at least in what Gaonkar (1999) describes as its social transformational moment. As I have pursued the meanings and the etymology of *spaza*, I have thus had increasingly to recognise when attempts were being made to divert my interest and attention – by various exercises in deception – precisely because my informants did not want me to recognise the creative subterfuge and deceptions that are what constitute *spaza*. In that sense, then, *spaza* constitutes a trope of deception used to keep at bay the Weberian disenchantment and meaninglessness, the Foucaldian routinisation and standardisation, of modernity.

Spaza as simulacrum of modernity

But, as Gaonkar (1999) points out in his reflections on the work of Baudelaire, one can also envision modernity, indeed see modernity being manifested, as a cultural modernity in which imagination and innovativeness are celebrated, where 'modernity is the transient, the fleeting, the contingent...' (Baudelaire 1972 quoted in Gaonkar 1999: 4). Modernity, at least in its cultural moment – which is as important to us here as it is to Perlas (2000) in his argument for the development of a robust global civil society that draws its strength from 'cultural power' – thus implies transience, disruption and disturbance.

Looked at from this perspective, *spaza* is more than just a trope of resistance to modernity. It is, in and of itself, a practice of an alternative modernity – a simulacrum of modernity in its cultural mode. It is a creative means to disturb and disrupt those parts of the (social-transformational) modernist project that would and do routinise and disenchant. Just as that aspect of the modernist project has striven, through the colonial and now the top-down (elite) globalising moment,[28] to disrupt and disturb social and cultural vitality by imposing a new-found order of rationality, so does *spaza* do the same to that very process. It does so by creating and promoting, indeed by privileging, an adversary culture of instability that is as much modern as the social transformational project itself. But it is not, and cannot be, hegemonic. Spivak (1993: 79) points out that the subaltern subject is 'irretrievably heterogeneous'. So, I would argue, is the adversary culture onto which *spaza* offers a window. As a cultural creation of criticality and questioning, a 'form of discourse that interrogates the present' (Gaonkar 1999: 13), it is therefore at once supremely (culturally) modernist and yet necessarily clandestine, for it is practised in arenas of power that privilege routinisation and standardisation. Its creative criticality appears therefore as suspicion that derives from its state of being embattled by a hegemonic attitude and its determination to destabilise. Its deceptiveness and drive to bewilder – its irony – is thus its strength: both for defining its modernity in terms of its own transience and disturbance – its creativity and fleeting imaginativeness – and for its efficacy in providing a sense of autonomy from the depravations of social-transformational modernity concerned only with the political and economic.

Autonomy and fluid urban citizenship

What then of the issue of urban citizenship and its relation to propriety and modernist connectedness in a global world? I indicated at the outset of this chapter that various recent studies have begun to demonstrate a growing hegemony among South Africa's urban poor of the social transformational aspects of modernity. I also suggested that that hegemony is, in turn, producing a sense that urban citizenship is increasingly defined in terms of a set of material and political behavioural norms that reflect the impulses of elite globalisation strategists. Yet, as I have attempted to argue here, we need to realise that there is also a creative culture-based counter discourse of urban citizenship in the popular South African air. It is one that can be seen reflected in the various transient meanings of the word *spaza*, with their implications of fleeting disturbances and subtle criticality of neatly ordered categorisations – including those implicit in attempts to define neatly what constitutes both urbanity and citizenship. The modernist connected-ness through commodity circuits – the millennial capitalist milieu of which Comaroff and Comaroff (2000) write so eloquently – has its ironic parallel in another exchange circuit of creativity and transience in constructions of meaning, as the case of *spaza* demon-strates. It is a circuit in which the imaginativeness of what is exchanged, and of the very cultural processes of their exchange, enables it to remain aloof of the hegemony of

<hr/>

[28] Appadurai (2000) has an important new take on globalisation from below that recognises the extent to which small-scale local civil-society imperatives have increasingly used the technologies of modern communication to transform themselves into global movements. Appadurai's argument resonates strongly with that of Filipino activist Perlas (2000), who champions the cause of a global civil-society movement that must, he argues, assume custodianship of 'cultural power' and thereby reconstitute globalisation as an imperative for realising comprehensive sustainable development that serves the best interests of all.

commodity exchanges. It is also a circuit of exchange that, by offering a vision of a socially experienced and culturally practised alternative modernity, obliges us to rethink our notions of citizenship as definable simply in terms of the hegemonic principles that are located in the political and economic domains. The counter discourse uses its culture-based and creative criticality to disturb simple statist notions of citizenship. And it offers at least some citizens a sense of their ability to retain a degree of autonomy from institutions that constrain them through normalising practices, and a means to challenge the definitions whereby citizenship is conventionally constituted (see Ellison 1999: 70–71 in Jones and Gaventa 2002: 16). It is thus a discourse that enables citizenship – at least for some contemporary urban South Africans – to be practised and understood as creatively fluid, and of often fleeting and discordant allegiances, characteristics that are critically necessary when much urban development policy fails to recognise the fluidity that constitutes people's everyday lives.

References

Appadurai, Arjun (2000), 'Grassroots Globalization and the Research Imagination', *Public Culture* 12(1): 1–19.
Bank, Leslie (1991), 'A Culture of Violence: The Migrant Taxi Trade in Qwaqwa 1980–90', in Eleanor Preston-Whyte and Chris Rogerson (eds), *South Africa's Informal Economy*, Cape Town: Oxford University Press.
—— (1997), 'Of Livestock and Deadstock: Entrepreneurship and Tradition on the South African Highveld', in Deborach Fahy Bryceson and Vali Jamal (eds), *Farewell to Farms: De-agrarianisation and Employment in Africa*, Leiden: African Studies Centre.
Comaroff, J. and J.L. Comaroff (2000), 'Millennial Capitalism: First Thoughts on a Second Coming', *Public Culture*, 12(2): 291–343.
Concise Oxford Dictionary (1999), Oxford: Oxford University Press.
Dictionary of South African English (1996), New York: Oxford University Press.
Doke, C.M. and B.W. Vilakazi (1948), *Zulu–English Dictionary*, Johannesburg: Witwatersrand University Press.
Doke, C.M., D.M. Malcolm and J.M.A. Sikakana (1988), *English and Zulu Dictionary*, Johannesburg: Witwatersrand University Press.
Doke, C.M., D.M. Malcolm, J.M.A. Sikakana and B.W. Vilakazi (1990), *English–Zulu Zulu–English Dictionary*. Johannesburg: Witwatersrand University Press.
Elliot, W.A. (n.d.), *Notes for a Sindebele Dictionary and Grammar*, 2nd edition, Bristol: Sindebele Publishing Co.
Ellison, N. (1999), 'Beyond Universalism and Particularism: Rethinking Contemporary Welfare Theory', *Critical Social Policy*, 19(1): 57–83.
English–Xhosa Xhosa–English Dictionary (n.d.) Cape Town: Via Afrika Publishers.
Ferguson, James (1999), *Expectations of Modernity: Myth and Meanings of Urban Life on the Zambian Copper-belt*, Berkeley: University of California Press.
Fischer, A. (1985), *English–Xhosa Dictionary*, Cape Town: Oxford University Press.
Gaonkar, Dilip Parameshwar (1999), 'On Alternative Modernities', *Public Culture*, 11(1): 1–18.
Hannan, M. (1974), *Standard Shona Dictionary*, 2nd edition, Salisbury and Bulawayo, Rhodesia Literature Bureau.
Hellmann, Ellen (1948), *Rooiyard: A Sociological Survey of a Native Slumyard*, Northern Rhodesia: Charles Livingstone Institute: Rhodes Livingstone Papers No. 30.
Jones, Emma and John Gaventa (2002), *Concepts of Citizenship: a Review*, Brighton: Institute of Development Studies, Development Bibliography 19.
Kropf, Albert and R. Godfrey (1915), *Kafir–English Dictionary*, Lovedale: Lovedale Mission Press.
Mabille, A., H. Dieterlen and R.A. Paroz (1974), *Southern Sotho-English Dictionary*, Morija: Morija Sesuto Book Depot.
Meintjes, Helen (2000) 'Poverty, Possessions and Proper Living: Constructing and Contesting Propriety in Soweto and Lusaka City', unpublished Masters dissertation, University of Cape Town.
Perlas, Nicanor (2000), *Shaping Globalization: Civil Society, Cultural Power and Threefolding*, Quezon City, Philippines: Centre for Alternative Development Initiatives.

Rogerson, Christian (1992), 'Drinking, Apartheid and the Removal of Beerhalls in Johannesburg 1939–1962', in Jonathan Crush and Charles Ambler (eds), *Liquor and Labour in Southern Africa*, Athens: Ohio University Press, pp. 306–38.

Rosaldo, Renato (1989), *Culture and Truth: The Remaking of Social Analysis*, London: Routledge.

Ross, Fiona and Andrew Spiegel (2000), 'Diversity and Fluidity Amongst Poor Households in Cape Town and the Heterogeneity of Domestic Consolidation Practices', *Tanzanian Journal of Population and Development* 7(2): 147–69.

Scott, James (1985), *Weapons of the Weak: Everyday Forms of Peasant Resistance*, New Haven: Yale University Press.

Southall, Roger (1980), 'African Capitalism in Contemporary South Africa', *Journal of Southern African Studies*, 7, pp. 38–70.

Spiegel, Andrew (2002), 'Is it for real? Notes on the Meanings and Etymology of *Spaza* in South African Popular Culture', in R. Gordon and D. Lebeau (eds), *Challenges for Anthroplogy in the African Renaissance*, pp. 282–94.

—— (2003), 'Revealing a Popular South African Deceit: The Ethical Challenges of an Etymological Exercise', in Pat Caplan (ed.), *The Ethics of Anthropology*, London: Routledge.

Spivak, Giyatri (1993), 'Can the Subaltern Speak?', in P. Williams and L. Chrisman (eds), *Colonial Discourse and Post-Colonial Theory*, Hemel Hempstead: Harvester Wheatsheaf, pp. 66–111.

van Onselen, Charles (1976), *Chibaro*, Johannesburg: Ravan.

—— (1982), *Studies in the Social and Economic History of the Witwatersrand* (2 vols), Harlow: Longman.

West, Martin (1988), 'Confusing Categories: Population Groups, National States and Citizenship', in E Boonzaier and J. Sharp (eds), *South African Keywords*, Cape Town: David Philip, pp. 100–10.

Yose, Constance Nontobeko (1999), 'From Shacks to Houses: Space Usage and Social Change in a Western Cape Shanty Town', unpublished Masters dissertation, University of Cape Town.

11

Coloureds don't Toyi-Toyi
Gesture, Constraint & Identity in Cape Town

SHANNON JACKSON

During the transitional post-apartheid era (the mid-to-late 1990s) many individuals and groups capitalised on the liminality of the moment to openly express and explore newly invigorated boundaries of identity, ethnicity and cultural difference. As Crawford Young reminds us, 'social change tends to produce stronger communal identities' (1994: 4), so various nascent and sublimated forms of collective association began to effervesce to the political surface. South Africa's coloured[1] population, for example, began to utilise the recently democratised public sphere to debate vigorously the meaning of their own group origins, their general alienation from both white and black/African politics, and their own distinct visions of non-racial and multiracial governance. The subject of a racially or ethnically distinct coloured identity would not have even been so comfortably discussed ten years ago. Some of these shifts inspired broad and occasionally nervous attention to their resemblance to incendiary sites of ethnic nationalism occurring in other parts of the globe.

During the decades of active anti-apartheid resistance, the ambiguous codification of a separate 'mixed-race' population left room for a wide variety of political and cultural alliances between coloureds and other South Africans. The outcome of this was that collective boundaries rarely coalesced around the coloured position as a specific source or site of opposition. The symbolic and practical contours of this complex category, however, began to undergo pronounced changes in the early 1990s. In a seemingly atavistic move, in fact, coloureds in the Western Cape gave the National Party their vote in 1994, preventing the African National Congress from taking the Cape in the national

---

[1] According to South Africa's Population Registration Act (No. 30, 1950), a 'Coloured' person is one who is not a European and not a Bantu (indigenous African). During the apartheid era, they were generally understood as a residual statutory population, classified more by what they were not, than what they were. The term 'coloured' came to acquire pejorative connotation, and many used so-called Coloured, or simply Black when referring to themselves. Their genealogical heritage can be traced to the late eighteenth, early nineteenth century when a variety of European groups colonised the Western Cape region, introducing contact between slaves (from India, Indonesia, Madagascar), indigenous Khoisan and Bushmen and themselves. This resulted in a 'mixed-race' group who came to occupy the interstices of colonial boundaries. Today, they are the most complex element of the South African 'rainbow' and defy tidy cultural or racial reification.

election. This drew the 'Coloured Question' to the surface of political debate – this is the question of where authentic coloured group boundaries lie, and how best to invoke or identify these without committing the original sin of racial reification. Coloureds, for the first time, were openly examining a set of associations and experiences that felt distinctly their own, that felt 'real', even historically suppressed, culminating in a search for the content or substance of 'colouredness'.

At the level of academic enquiry at the time, broad debates about ethnic pluralism were also unfolding. A series of academic conferences and discussion forums, as well as a broad body of literature (both popular and academic), surfaced in the early 1990s that engaged ethnicity as both a cultural and political phenomenon. A certain prescriptive urgency informed these discussions in light of the need to craft a constitution and electoral process that would include recognition of cultural difference without eroding the expansion of civil society. I will argue that much of this debate failed to offer heuristic perspectives or frameworks for either encapsulating or explaining the appearance of the unique set of experiences expressed as 'colouredness'.

One of the most significant conferences that emerged out of this period was held at Rhodes University, Grahamstown, in April 1993, entitled 'Ethnicity, Identity, and Nationalism in South Africa: Past, Present, Future'. A pattern or theme to the papers presented at the conference was a consistent effort, particularly by means of the tools of deconstruction, to deflate the salience of ethnic nationalism by illustrating its fictional qualities. Participating anthropologists Edwin Wilmsen, Saul Dubow and John Sharp point out that 'deconstruction certainly robs ethnicity of the mythic sense of timelessness on which it thrives, but to say that ethnicity is artificially constructed does not enable us to dismiss it as illegitimate' (1994: 348). They further assert that 'The intellectual and political task, therefore, is to find a vocabulary that recognises … forms of ethnic identification that are flexible and polyvalent…' (ibid.). A category that gained currency in light of this 'intellectual and political' task was that of instrumentalism.

In a policy paper circulated in Cape Town at this time, political scientist Crawford Young indicates that 'Recent debate about ethnicity suggests that there are three interactive dimensions: primordial, instrumental, and socially constructed' (1994: 8). In essence, a sort of compromise was established from amongst the three options Young presented – that of instrumentalism and a rational, instrumental model of the subject. This is a model in which ethnicity is understood as one among many identity positions that can be consciously invoked by the subject under specific historical-political circumstances. For a special issue of *Indicator South Africa*, Patrick McAllister and John Sharp provide an overview of the April 1993 conference papers. Drawing from Jan Nederveen Pieterse's contribution they stress the point that 'Ethnic identities are formed…when people who share one or more cultural traits become conscious of internal cohesion and difference from others' (1993: 9). This focus on the substance and degree of consciousness of the political actor and the need for flexibility on the part of the political theorist helps deconstruct part of the naturalist alibi often hidden in ethnic rhetoric.

This approach also relies on an idealist model of the subject – a model in which mind and body are essentially separate. In the words of John Comaroff, it is a valorisation of heroic human agency (1996). Politics becomes a product of consciousness and consciousness can be changed. The 'realness' of ethnicity can in a sense be challenged by limiting its 'reality' to the domain of a specific model of consciousness – it is only real so long as it is believed to be real, so proper consciousness is that which is capable of ironic distance from itself. The value of this broad intellectual exercise for the South African context was that it allowed academics the comfort of engaging 'the ethnic taboo' (McAllister and Sharp 1993) while keeping ethnicity discursively alive as a historical and therefore constructed category. But it also reified a particular subject position – that of the subject as instrumental, rational and capable of conscious distance from its own body – a body which, by extension, is knowable, controllable.

John Sharp and Emile Boonzaier presented one of the few conference papers which specifically addressed coloured identity. They examine the revitalisation of Nama ethnicity in the coloured rural reserves, and push the instrumental model to its extreme by suggesting that both the broader coloured and the more specific Nama positions have to be understood as forms of highly conscientious performance. Those who revive traditional associations with Nama culture 'do so with a conviction that is tempered by a self-conscious reflexivity' similar to acting on a stage (1994: 416). This puts Nama and coloured identity into the privileged position of representing model forms of reflexivity. John Sharp, in a separate essay, even refers to such conscious navigation as intrinsically ironic.

> Ordinary coloured people may well derive a sense of satisfaction and dignity from a new assertion of an autonomous coloured identity; given past history, however, they will not forget, *of their own volition*, that the boundaries of such an identity will *always* be provisional and subject to context. (1996: 101; my emphasis)

In a more comprehensive and recent publication, Courtney Jung offers a similar analysis of Zulu, Afrikaner and coloured political identities. She incorporates the papers presented at the 1993 conference into her own analysis to challenge the notion that South Africa is an inherently divided society. She argues instead that all of these identity positions are the products of conscious manipulation, and are therefore quite flexible. She states that 'Political identity must be self-conscious' (2000: 20) and then goes so far as to assert that identities 'held in cultural, linguistic, or religious domains are not relevant to identities held in the political domain unless and until they are infused with political content' (22). This eliminates all the centripetal pull of cultural crystallisation and language interference from analytical view. She expounds on coloured identity through statistical data that indicate more educated, urban and therefore more conscientious coloureds tended to vote for the ANC in national and local elections and exhibited more secular, cross-cutting group associations (ibid.: 245). She is further suggesting, then, that socio-economic mobility and education, i.e. rationality and participation in civil society, magically reduce the tendency for groups to politically operationalise separate racial and regional identities. But, as I will demonstrate, coloureds have been participating in civil society and all its bourgeois virtues for over a century, yet they still manifest ambiguous and occasionally primordialist political affiliations.

Though I support the contribution made by these discussions and value their various positions as a way of discursively crafting political models and further challenging ethnicity as ideology, I want to propose that the tendency to rely on an instrumentalist model whereby political identity becomes analytically separate from 'cultural, linguistic, or religious domains' oversimplifies the relationship between politics and culture and therefore between mind and body. It also fails to offer theoretical account for what is deemed a proper form of consciousness. I would argue that, in the effort to lend prescriptive force to the conscious, rational and voluntary bedrock of civil society, instrumentalism occludes the body as a site or source of political meaning altogether.

The tendency amongst many of these theorists methodologically and analytically to rely on data sources such as voting practices, voluntary behaviour and verbally expressed political positions, particularly amongst elites, also valorises the relevance of consciousness and consciously volunteered information at the expense of more tacit and diffuse domains of meaning. Courtney Jung herself states that she does not include participant observation in her study; she relies strictly on surveys, interviews with political elites and voting statistics to draw her conclusions. Her specific analysis of coloured identity politics in the 1990s therefore reads like a thin description of the ways in which national political parties (primarily the ANC and NP) were able or unable to manipulate coloured constituents into accepting or rejecting their 'colouredness'. Such an approach overlooks some of the contradictory behaviour of coloureds who would, in my own experience, voice conscious rejection of a separate coloured identity in one context and then unreflexively channel their energies into separate coloured cultural affiliations in another. Instrumentalism also fails to offer any insight into why particular qualities of 'colouredness' became meaningful in the 1990s and how these express a sense of continuity with highly selective elements of the past.

This chapter will explore a particular reading of contemporary expressions of coloured identity as a way to contribute a more balanced interpretation of ethnic identity to that larger discussion begun in 1993. This interpretation will focus on the role of the phenomenological body as both a material and imaginative site for the negotiation of those lived boundaries which are structured across time and space. This will include an exploration of some of the historical and ethnographic clues that can be assembled from participant observation, open-ended interviews and casual conversations to demonstrate that instrumentalist and rationalist theories of ethnicity and identity make it difficult to include contradictory behaviour and to consider the role of more latent sources of meaning. Political behaviour, in essence, is too narrowly defined by such theorists. The role of the body and its spatial-semantic associations needs to be included as an essential variable in expressions of racial and ethnic pluralism if both the conditions and the meaning of such expressions are to be fully understood.

The politics of gesture

According to Henri Lefebvre, 'Gestural systems connect representations of space with representational spaces…. Gestures are also closely bound up with the objects which fill space…' (1991: 215). So, when a South African who refers to him/herself as coloured makes the statement, 'Coloureds don't toyi-toyi',[2] he/she is consciously rejecting a gesture

---

[2] Toyi-toyiing is a demonstration of uniform political dissatisfaction. It is an embodied form of resistance popularised in South Africa in the early 1980s amidst a Defiance Campaign, waged to render the country ungovernable. It can be summarised as an up-and-down thrusting of the body to a beat which seems to emanate

along with the spatial objects, signs and signals assembled through such a gesture. There is also, within this rejection, a set of semantic and unconscious associations being made between the representational space of the body and its archive of experience. In 1996–7, I conducted ethnographic fieldwork in Cape Town where I focused on the political beliefs and ideologies of an increasingly vocal group of coloured intellectuals, students and activists expressing dissent and disappointment with the ANC-led transition to post-apartheid governance. I found that many of these intellectuals were establishing distance in various ways from what was understood as a knowable and in some respects overdetermined body. On occasion, the body they were seeking distance from would be described in terms such as 'unpredictable', 'violent', 'shameful', or more politely as a sort of unstable, Manichaean body torn between traditional and secular loyalties.

The University of the Western Cape,[3] historically a coloured university, experienced profound demographic changes in its student population in the mid-1990s. This contributed to expanding tensions between coloured and African students and faculty, particularly during the run-up and aftermath of the 1994 elections. It therefore offered a valuable context to observe and document public expressions of group difference. During the 1995 school year, I found many coloured students as well as faculty making periodic reference to the undisciplined and violent nature of African student protests occurring on the campus. General fear was expressed around the prevalence of disgruntled students toyi-toyiing into classrooms and onto desks while the more 'respectable' (i.e. coloured) students stayed passively seated. Coloureds, under such circumstances, were expressing something about the 'locatedness of identity' by means of the controlled and individualistic education of their own bodies. Borrowing the words of Marcel Mauss, theirs has been an 'education in composure' (1973: 86). Mauss describes composure in a similar rhetoric of primitivism.

> [It is] a retarding mechanism, a mechanism inhibiting disorderly movements; this retardation subsequently allows a co-ordinated response of co-ordinated movements setting off in the direction of a chosen goal. This resistance to emotional seizure is something fundamental in social and mental life. It separates out, it even classifies the so-called primitive societies; according to whether they display more brutal, unreflected, unconscious reaction or on the contrary more isolated, precise actions governed by a clear consciousness. (ibid.)

When I first heard the statement 'Coloureds don't toyi-toyi' made by a professor at UWC I began to explore the meaning of toyi-toyiing, and found that it can be interpreted as a pre-modern or tradition-bound connection between the body and its surface as a site of political expression. This suggests, on the part of those who distance themselves from such connections, explicit identification with a modern rather than traditional body. The ideological and philosophical boundaries separating tradition and modernity, in fact,

---

[2] (cont.) from within; it is often accompanied by chants, raised fists, and sometimes weapons. Like the menacing movement of a military regiment, it is a demonstration of strength in unity, but, unlike the regiment, it is spontaneous and unrehearsed, intended to signify resistance rather than conformity.

[3] The University of the Western Cape, located in the Cape Flats, which circumscribe the more habitable areas of Cape Town, was built in 1959 as part of the Bantu Education System. This system was designed to provide separate institutions for separately defined populations, so coloureds, as a statutory group, were given UWC as their own. Its history, therefore, is intimately tied to the struggle to both deconstruct and celebrate 'colouredness' as a cultural and political category. In 1995 UWC became one of the primary sites for discussion and debate about the meaning and significance of 'colouredness.'

became particularly salient during the initial stages of the post-apartheid transition. The difficult separation between the two was a popular theme amongst those debating the role and significance of ethnicity to the implementation of either non-racial or multiracial democratic governance in South Africa (Horowitz 1991). Where many Africans looked to this transitional phase in nation-building to express, entrench and legitimate African culture and identity, others, particularly coloureds, felt alienated and even threatened by such prospects.

In the run-up to the April 1994 national election, the Nationalist (Apartheid) Party capitalised on the tensions between Africans and coloureds by perpetuating fear that an African-led ANC victory would threaten the middle-class values and aspirations many coloureds had come to espouse (Jung 2000). This invigorated a regionalist (Western Cape) coloured identity which effervesced in the wake of the general Africanisation of the public sphere as well as Nationalist Party campaign tactics, but was not simply a conscious response to the tactics of party and political elites. In a conversation with a coloured political activist and UWC history instructor, I was told that, for many coloureds who participated in the anti-apartheid struggle, 'African' simply meant wearing dashikis, growing dreadlocks and feeling a transcendent solidarity with those who were black and African first, South African second. 'We believed in an idealised version of the ANC. Ours was an ethnic sublimation performed at a cost – a truer self was being silenced.' He told me that at the close of clandestine ANC meetings in the townships of Cape Town, when it was time to walk home, he would head for Bonteheuwel (a coloured suburb) and his black 'comrades' would head for Langa (an African township). And though the two areas are in close proximity, he pointed out 'they are culturally a world apart'. The sense of alienation from Africans that coloureds feel therefore occurs at more than the political level. This individual was expressing a sense that his political mind was Africanised, but that his body was following a divergent path. There is more to identity here than its political trappings and surface expressions; coloureds and Africans have come to incorporate very different relationships to space and to embodied boundaries.

Elaine Scarry once wrote that 'power is in its fraudulent as in its legitimate forms always based on distance from the body' (1985: 46), partly because 'to have a body is to be describable, creatable, alterable, and woundable' (206). The statement 'Coloureds don't toyi-toyi' in some ways establishes conscious distance from one idea of the body, but unconscious affiliation and association with another. The statement was made to me on several separate occasions, and always by coloured individuals commenting, either sarcastically or sincerely, on the way they distinguish themselves from those they had begun, at the time, to isomorphically refer to as 'African'. One individual said to me, as we witnessed large groups of African students toyi-toyiing across a courtyard on the UWC campus: 'that's not the way *we* handle *our* problems' – as if to toyi-toyi is really an African thing and, since coloureds don't toyi-toyi, they must not by extension consider themselves African. To make such a statement or draw such a distinction is therefore a complex declaration of embodied difference. At a conscious level, the body is understood as a trap – a political dead end, so to use the body as an instrument of resistance is to remain locked in the past. But, at another level, this reflexivity translates into the belief that coloureds are, by their very embodied difference, capable of more secular, civic and therefore moral expressions of political conviction. In some respects, then, the assertion that coloureds respond to primordialism with ironic and reflexive distance is correct (Sharp and Boonzaier 1994; Sharp 1996), but the content of such consciousness has to be historically accounted for, otherwise it comes to resemble the same *sui generis* qualities as that of primordialism. The content of such consciousness is also inconsistent and contradictory – if coloureds are uniquely civic-minded, then we still have to account for lapses and lacunae in such consciousness.

Making room for contradiction

Throughout the mid-to-late1990s, various elements of Cape Town's coloured community initiated projects and events which invoked and even revived their own distinct relationships to embodied space, time and practice, i.e. to the boundaries of their own contested identity. During a rally held at the annex to the National Gallery in Cape Town in March of 1997, a young man circulated throughout the gathered crowd wearing a T-shirt emblazoned with the words *liewer Khoi-Khoi as toyi-toyi* (rather Khoi-Khoi than toyi-toyi). This rally was initiated by various Western Cape coloured community leaders, including Peter Marais (Western Cape MEC for Local Government), who wanted to express their convictions regarding the repatriation of the remains of an indigenous Khoisan woman they consider their collective ancestor.[4] Peter Marais had been interviewed by Mark Gevisser for a regular column in the local *Mail and Guardian* in 1995, where he reinforced many of the themes that subsequently inspired this large gathering, one of which was the desire to legitimate a separate coloured history, linked autochthonously to the Western Cape and distinguished by the celebration of a heroine who was a victim of racial discrimination rather than an aggressive leader of violent rebellion.

> There has never been a real close affinity between blacks and coloureds down here in the Cape. Right now fear still channels most of the decisions that people make. Fear of the unknown. And what we see happening all around us – the murders, the assaults, the disrespect for authority and conventions – that doesn't help bring us any closer. We also have our skollie [criminal] elements, but we frown on them. We never carry them on our shoulders like heroes. When you see a man dying in the street with a tyre around his neck while the people around him are dancing [toyi-toyiing], that's foreign, man! Its foreign to us! Its got nothing to do with race. It has to do with behavioral patterns. With norms. With standards. With preferences. (15/22 June 1995)

The statement on the young man's T-shirt also signifies a contradiction. It establishes African and indigenous (Khoi-Khoi) affiliations amongst a community which rejects or distances itself from the contemporary African communities in its midst. The simultaneous reference to the symbolic gesture of toyi-toyiing indicates that coloured identity

---

[4] Saartje Baartman has become, in the words of Marilyn Martin (director of the National Gallery), 'an icon … in fractious post-apartheid coloured politics' (1996: 9). Saartje was an indigenous Khoisan woman who was sent to Europe in the early nineteenth century; she became a living specimen, employed by entrepreneur Hendric Cezar to satisfy growing popular and scientific curiosity about the nature of African primitives and human genetic diversity (Gould 1981; Gilman 1986; Fabian 1987; Skotnes 1996; Abrahams 1997). She died in 1815. Her remains were dissected and preserved by renowned naturalist George Cuvier, and eventually housed in the Musée de l'Homme in Paris. Various coloured communities have been focused on repatriating her remains, claiming her as an icon in their own nation-building process (Wicomb 1998).

can be organised around the rejection of a conspicuous body, which is then replaced with that of an indigenous Khoisan. On one level this adds legitimacy to the boundaries of collective association, on another level it brings contradiction directly to the surface of political expression. In some respects, this rally was an instrumental and political use of the rhetoric of ethnicity in vogue in post-apartheid South Africa at the time. In other respects, it illustrates a tension or contradiction between reified notions of ethnicity and a conscious embrace of a modern body characterised by composure and discipline – a body that doesn't toyi-toyi.

The contemporary use of Khoisan identity as a binding trope for contemporary struggles over coloured identity can, in some respects, be interpreted as recalling the theme of concupiscence and contamination[5] that hovers around discussions of coloured history. By claiming indigenous origins, coloureds combat some of the negative connotations of having a 'mixed-race' heritage, but thwart a full embrace of modern and bourgeois subjectivity. The unequivocal statement 'Coloureds don't toyi-toyi', followed by the rallying cry *'liewer Khoi Khoi as toyi-toyi'*, then, suggests the habituation of a spatial semantics associated with public constraint, self-governance and a desire to selectively claim particular aspects of history. It is a desire to gain distance from the body, but an indication of the impossibility of actually or fully transcending it.

Some of the power inhering in this contradiction lies in the role it has played in organising space and spatial meaning in Cape Town since the late eighteenth, early nineteenth centuries. Other aspects of its enduring power lie in the fact that coloureds have incorporated or been forced to incorporate a set of historically unrealisable values. Frantz Fanon describes a similar set of conditions for former slaves in the Antilles where one becomes an 'anxious man who cannot escape his body' (1967: 65). This is not to suggest that abstracted and representational space, even that of the body, has agency outside or above the social, but rather that because space is itself made possible by the fact of the practical, phenomenal body (Lefebvre 1991), it is something that cannot be consciously or magically willed away. It also offers an analytical frame for ethnographic explorations of political difference, particularly those that do not translate into tidy or coherent models of instrumental possibility.

Re-membering the coloured body

The archive of embodied experience is something imbued with a highly localised set of constraints, contradictions and values which unintentionally unfolds over time like 'the hidden persuasion of an implicit pedagogy' (Bourdieu 1977: 94). In what ways, then, have coloureds come to embody, at both the conscious and unconscious level, the contradictions inherent in the promises of bourgeois liberation? The ideals of self-governance and self-control historically propagated by the bourgeois public sphere have had profound influences on Cape culture; the organisation and meaning of urban space in Cape Town has historically reinforced, particularly amongst the working classes, the value attached

---

[5] Zoë Wicomb comments on the use of Saartje Baartman as an icon of coloured identity. According to Wicomb, she 'exemplifies the body as a site of shame, a body bound up with the politics of location. I adopt her as icon precisely because of the nasty, unspoken question of concupiscence that haunts coloured identity…' (1996: 93).

to symbols of bourgeois status recognition. For coloureds, however, the conditions of their own liberation were embedded in a liberal system of governance premised on achieved and secular forms of status which could never be fully realised. This means that the habituation of these liberal ideals through the combined control of the individual body, the built environment and the abstracted domains of civic life has left today's coloureds suspended in a kind of permanently tensed hypervigilance about public representations of their own interiority. This is a group, therefore, which has been wilfully drawn into the transcendent associations of universal subjectivity, but has been materially unable to enjoy its promises.

Coloureds, whose domestic spaces and dense urban communities were 'sterilised' by the forced removals of the apartheid regime's Group Areas Act, have had to rebuild their communities away from the city centre in the Cape Flats. The genealogy and significance of the perceived threat of contamination of racial as well as health boundaries posed by the mere existence of a coloured community in the city centre have been well documented in the South African literature (Coetzee 1980; February 1981; Holmes 1995; Wicomb 1998). In Cape Town, particularly in the late nineteenth, early twentieth century, primary sources of contamination, both cultural and biological, were assumed to be the racially mixed inhabitants of ghettoes like District Six, and the bodies that were cast as the most degenerate were those of coloured women. Coloured women, of course, were the ones who most betrayed the proper separation of private and public spheres enforced by liberal reformers and upset a gender as well as racial order understood to be both natural and necessary to the health of urban society.

In an interesting analysis of the relationship between gender and disorder in the modern city, Elizabeth Wilson concludes: 'To the extent that it released women from the patriarchal family, the nineteenth-century city could be viewed as "unnatural"; and ideas about nature and the natural shaded into metaphors of disease' (1991: 34). Contemporary research into struggles over maintaining boundaries of respectability therefore focuses on women in the coloured townships and suburbs (Salo, this volume). These are the satellite spaces which were created in the twentieth century as a way to reduce the proximity of coloured bodies to the city centre.

Are there ways in which the contradictions embedded in conscious contemporary actions unconsciously suggest embodied or tacit recollections of this history, of the need and ultimate inability of individuals in cities to control for the dangerous contact that proliferated between/among bodies? Since space, according to Lefebvre, is simultaneously a product and a means of production, it is useful to address the production of the coloured category in its experiential as well as representational dimensions, as part and parcel with the production of the spaces which coexisted with its inception. 'Itself the outcome of past action, social space is what permits fresh actions to occur, while suggesting others and prohibiting yet others' (Lefebvre 1991: 73). In this regard, the coloured experience can be analytically linked to spatial practice and, since its genealogy, in a sense, begins with the onset of urbanisation, the passage from one mode of production to another, and the reform efforts which were specifically applied to this group in Cape Town, its current boundaries can be interpreted as recalling this history.

It is certainly true that in observing and documenting the process of ethnographic self-fashioning in the moment, themes that recur in the effort to narrate coloured history are the spatial significance of the Western Cape, specifically Cape Town, the juridical significance of the moment of emancipation from slavery, and the embodied significance of discipline, containment and distance from boundaries associated with liminality and disorder. These factors became particularly salient to me while attending a meeting put together by a group of coloured activists and intellectuals in August of 1996. A group of about fifteen community leaders gathered in the Planned Parenthood Conference Center in Observatory, a historically grey, or 'mixed-race', neighbourhood just outside of Cape Town's central business district. This group came together to express their frustrations with the treatment of coloureds by local ANC officials, and to brainstorm about alternative forms of organisation which would allow them to express 'cultural' rather than 'political' difference. One participant expressed his views of the task at hand:

> ...There is a particular experience out there that needs to be linked to [a larger debate about nation-states and ethnic difference].... We don't disregard the colonial experience that took place and we don't want to disregard the period of new colonialism, but we need to say that within that colonial period ... a group of people emerged because of that colonial experience. A particular pride and experience needs to be located. But, I still argue that whatever comes out of this, it mustn't be removed from the particular mainstream thing that is happening out there.... If we start a Coloured political [rather than cultural] party, it will be political suicide. (3 August 1996)

Much of this meeting revolved around narrating 'that colonial experience' and came to rest on the significance of slavery to the way coloureds understand themselves as a distinct group. One participant stated: 'What we need is a cultural moment, such as the holocaust, which allowed young Jews to conceptualise their own experience.' Another participant responded: 'Our alienation, like that of the African American, has its roots in slavery, slavery tried to take away our identity and it succeeded.'

It was decided that, in addition to a cultural moment, the group needed a cultural hero, one who would help galvanise nostalgia for the distinct traditions and values they wanted to reinforce. One participant, an Anglican priest, had just finished reading local historian Bill Nasson's account of the South African War (1899–1902), titled *Abraham Esau's War* (1991), so he suggested Abraham Esau as one such hero. This led to a discussion of Esau's biography and the significance that his life holds for rural coloured communities in the Western Cape. Esau had been a blacksmith living in Calvinia during the War, and became an informant for British intelligence. In retaliation for his spying and organised resistance, Esau was imprisoned and then savagely killed by Boer Commandos in 1901. An Esau Memorial Chapel was erected in Calvinia after Union was established in 1910, but it was subsequently torn down in the 1960s by the apartheid regime. According to Nasson,

> Esau's sacrifice and suffering had been in defense of a natural triangular political symbiosis between 'civilised' men, the rights and protections of Cape constitutionalism and the British empire. The harnessing of citizenship 'rights' and 'freedoms' to the imperial interest could scarcely have been more explicit....Significantly, this recognition of Esau's British identity was also how many of Calvinia's Coloured populace chose to see it. And their identification was not simply a passive acting out of imperialist values prescribed from above; it was a means of promoting class pride, dignity and a tenacious sense of local independence. (1991: 132)

Esau therefore embodies, for rural communities, as well as urban groups such as the one that gathered in August of 1997, the values associated with Cape liberalism. He also, more interestingly, represents the ambiguous position of the coloureds who fought on behalf of the British Empire during the South African War, but were betrayed when the Empire promised to include them as full citizens and did not. The betrayal of the coloureds on the part of the British is still remembered by residents of the Coloured Rural Reserves. In a conversation with an activist in Leliefontein (a small rural town north of Cape Town – an area known as Namaqualand), he pointed out to me that Namaqualanders are still waiting for the rewards they were promised in return for their loyalty to the British. He compared their betrayal to the forty acres and a mule promised, but never delivered, to North America's former slaves.

The group that gathered in 1997 decided to call itself the December First Movement – the emancipation of slavery for the Cape Colony was declared on 1 December 1834. And it was agreed that their ritual public inauguration would occur the following December at a site on Spin Street, downtown Cape Town, known as an area where slave auctions were conducted in the eighteenth and nineteenth centuries. Emancipation as a moment of origin, and Abraham Esau as a collective hero, allowed this group to establish conscious links to what Nasson describes as 'a profound respect for a stable "British" law and order; a consciousness of inherited rights in citizenship, customary freedoms and constitutional liberties underwritten by a sense of natural justice...' (1991: 122). The group also consciously rejected the channelling of their interests into political platforms. This means that their in-group affiliations, which translated into subsequent political rejection of the ANC, were sustained in the more tacit domain of what the group itself referred to as a 'cultural' organisation. Their liberal and civic associations ironically became a conscious means for rejecting an ANC which had become the most inclusive, non-racial and secular political party at the time.

Emancipation and Englishness

Another limitation of the instrumentalist position is that it channels analytical focus onto the spontaneity of the moment. Ethnicity, as a product of rational ends–means calcula- tions, occurs for actors navigating information that is drawn from immediate experience. But to understand why one set of boundaries or symbols is chosen to express ethnicity over another requires an exploration of cultural, rather than specifically political, meaning. Meaning, then, has to be analysed from within the constraints of history, structure and the phenomenological processes by which bodies establish comfort across time and space. The relationship between boundaries of identity and the evolution of the built environment is one such way to explore embodied meaning.

In the early nineteenth century, South Africa's slave- and household-based VOC (Dutch East India Company) economy was replaced by an industrialising and market-based economy. The built environment and the domain of social reproduction, by extension, came to reflect a blend of new possibilities as well as old constraints. A particular model was gaining currency in this transition – that of the nuclear family and its corresponding domain of consumption, the private household. But, for ancestors to today's coloureds, the old constraints of patriarchal hierarchy and ascribed status established under the Dutch continued, albeit in different form, endured alongside the new freedoms of individuation and market exchange. Ultimately the tensions between old and new forms of racial distinction fostered contradictory and/or partially liberated bodies and spaces in Cape Town. The genealogy of the coloured category is itself inscribed against a background of economic transition and liminality, objectified by the laws of private property and rules of public propriety, yet restricted and frustrated by the proliferation of various forms of racial ordering, class distinction and spatial segregation.

Architectural and archaeological evidence of the earlier Dutch colonial period (seventeenth to eighteenth centuries) suggests that the spatial organisation of Cape Town was not explicitly segregated according to class or ethnic distinction (Malan 1993, 1998; Worden 1998–9). The primary distinctions at the time would have been between free and slave labour, and Christian and non-Christian status. The arrival of the British in the late eighteenth century brought a more explicit focus to the meaningful content of achieved, publicly expressed status. British liberalism, 'with its increasingly explicit rejection of slavery, fractured the hegemony of slaveowner paternalism and gave the slaves the psychological and intellectual freedom to begin more openly to affirm a new sense of what was and what might be' (Mason 1994: 47). Ordinance 50 (1828) was passed so that indigenous Khoisan could own property and sell their labour freely as individuals (Marais 1968; Sales 1975; Elphick and Giliomee 1989). In other words, the British looked at former slaves and indigenous Khoisan as potential citizens, capable of full participation in the production of modern colonial society.

The permissive and diversifying atmosphere of the nineteenth-century South African city, and the increasingly blurred distinction between city, village and farmstead (Marks and Bezzoli 2000: 265), however, challenged the ability of the entrenched elite in Cape Town to control public displays of status and wealth, particularly where consumption had become, in a sense, 'a substitute for virtue' (Wilson 1991: 59). So Robert Ross, in his most recent historical analysis of the Cape Colony, uses body language and physical-spatial posture as a way of plotting the status distinctions that endured and even expanded during the height of British urbanisation (1999). Emancipation, then, would have introduced the lifting of prior restraints in terms of ascribed status, but would have introduced the possibility for new restraints in terms of regulating social-spatial order. This era of reform, a time when the meaning of individual freedom was being ideologically embraced with alacrity, was also, therefore, a period marked by the rise of modern racism and segregation (Bickford-Smith 1989; Worden and Crais 1994).

Part of the dual rhetoric of emancipation and colonisation was attention to privacy and intimacy as means of cultivating moral community. The private domestic sphere became morally ordered by a larger logic of conjugal intimacy, patriarchal gender distinctions and the amplification of market relations (Comaroff and Comaroff 1992). Elizabeth Wilson describes a nostalgia that persists in London for an era marked by the safety of bourgeois boundaries, nostalgia for a 'pervasive English privacy' characterised by 'lives veiled by lace curtains, of a prim respectability hiding strange secrets' behind respectable facades (1991: 4). The emancipated ancestors of today's coloureds, be they slaves or indentured Khoi labourers, were the explicit targets of the kind of liberatory legislation designed to make particular models of family, intimacy and therefore respectability possible.

According to historian Wayne Dooling, 'One of the most important elements of [amelioration] legislation, therefore, was the promotion of stable family units by allowing slaves to marry and by forbidding the sale in separate lots of husbands, wives and children under the age of ten years' (1994: 30). It was no accident, then, that the Cape of Good Hope Philanthropic Society would only apprentice young female slaves in the effort to integrate former slaves into society.

> Funds will be best employed by emancipating female children between three and ten years to be apprenticed until sixteen years.... during the period of Apprenticeship, such children may be induced to acquire habits of industry and skill in domestic or other useful Employments, which shall enable them to earn their future livelihood. (Meeting Minutes of the CGHPS, 24 July 1830)

By focusing their attention on young girls, they positioned women as the primary means of literally reproducing private households, and therefore private individuals. *Family*, consequently, became the most expressed trope in emancipation discourse in Cape Town (Shell 1989, 1994).

Mission stations, like Bethelsdorp and Genadendaal, located east of Cape Town, created specifically for Khoisan (then referred to as Hottentots) and freed slaves, were primary sites for the inculcation of habits of proper domesticity (Sales 1975). The primitive reed huts and wattle and daub structures of the indigenous Khoisan living on mission stations were the constant target of derision and malign comment as these were associated with the uncivilised nature of the frontier in general, and therefore had to be transformed. 'These huts are as unfavorable to industry, as they are to health' (Philip 1969 [1828]: 209). The Reverend John Philip further observed that the lack of privacy in these spaces meant bodies slept in close proximity, and were therefore doubly jeopardised by the disease and degeneracy that accompanied such a lack of decency. 'When men and women are huddled together in a place not more than six or eight feet square, delicacy is impossible. Modesty has been defined as the outwork of virtue; and we can do very little for a people in the scale of morals, if we do not succeed in imparting this virtue to females' (Philip 1969 [1828]: 211).

The transformation of bodies by means of the moral ordering of space meant privatising space in a way that would privatise the interior (moral source) of the body. This meant positioning women, the 'natural' facilitators of domestic privacy, at the gateway between the public and the private in all its spatial-symbolic expressions. But this involved relieving women of public labour and building expensive houses with doors, windows and separate rooms. The mission stations had difficulty sustaining the levels of productivity necessary to supply the need for cash they were themselves cultivating (Sales 1975). In order to make the improvements on their 'much maligned reed houses', mission station residents had to bring in enough money to purchase materials and engage in collective public labour – this took away from the time spent earning the money necessary to make the improvements in the first place. 'Once a "need" for clothing, better houses, tools and wagons, and so forth, became established, the need was for more money than was ever available, even in the best years' (Sales 1975: 89). Ironically, it was the pressure among missionaries and government officials to create settled modes of existence which actually led many to migrate away from the areas set up to establish such settlement. Migration was usually to cities – the centres of disorder and degeneracy. The age of 'Englishness' (Bickford-Smith 1995; Ross 1999), as this period has been described, was therefore one of propagating the values of privacy and private property, without necessarily expanding the material conditions which made their realisation possible.

As the British began to implement their own system of governance alongside the expansion of market-based production, they also began to systematically withdraw the rights and freedoms rhetorically offered former slaves and indigenous Khoisan. This was made possible by means of the codification of all non-European labour contracts. The Masters and Servants Ordinances established to regulate 'non-European' labour in the Cape actually facilitated continuity with the patriarchal slave-based household (Scully 1994, 1997; Shell 1994). One of the primary targets of these Ordinances was the labor contract itself. As the new liberal constitution under the British established all subject-citizens equal before the law, labour contracts had to be distinguished as binding only when they were between men (Scully 1997). The hiring of freed black males brought the added bonus of his dependents. It was the labour of dependants which facilitated the survival of nucleated households. This translated into a general continuity in labour relations between former slaveholders and former slaves. 'Married women lost their abilities to be free agents because, through marriage, they became subject to the law of coverture which prevented women from making contracts' (Scully 1997: 86).

Another aspect of the transition from a slave-based economy to a market system was the diversification of trade and the expansion of a commercial bourgeoisie in Cape Town. This is where social relationships began to assume the form of exchange relationships. Private property ownership became more widely available, internal sources of capital were stimulated, and the overall economy began to flourish with abolition (Meltzer 1994), but for whom? Despite the expansion of the economy, slaves, once they were free, had very few opportunities to participate fully in the expanding market economy. After 1838 only 4 per cent of the former slave population settled independently on public land. Of the some 25,000 slaves freed in 1838, some 3,000 went to live on mission stations, which became one of the primary options in escaping farm labour (Scully 1997), but did not allow them the means to own land.

Historian Pamela Scully further points out, 'after 1838 both freed women and men contributed to the household by working for money – women were not confined to the private sphere in the same way as their settler counterparts' (1997: 74–5). This left them vulnerable, in ways similar to working-class women in Europe, to the prevailing circular rationale that women, as the moral foundations of society, should be shielded from the contaminations of public life in order to provide it with its moral foundation. So women who worked were considered morally suspect, and basically all coloured women worked. Recent statistics even indicate that coloured women continue to dominate the workforce in Cape Town (Van der Merwe and Van der Merwe, 2000). In the words of Elizabeth Wilson, 'Women in cities' therefore came to be 'perceived as the objects of both regulation *and* banishment' (1991: 46).

Family, as a conjunctive site of social reproduction, and its spatial counterpart, the private household, became organising themes in the transition from one legal and economic model of society to another. The domestic domain, according to the Comaroffs, 'connoted a social group (the family) whose interrelated roles, duly sanctified and naturalized, composed the division of labor at the core of "civilized" economy and society and … presupposed a physical space (the "private" house), that was, in principle, clearly marked and bounded' (1992: 272). Where it was once the primary means of economic and social production under Dutch rule, the household became, under the British, a site of social and economic *re*production. It was evolving into a foundational institution separate and abstracted in its boundaries from civil society, economy and the state. The emotional ties of a nuclear (heterosexual) family, held constant in time and space by the household structure, established the interior boundaries of intimacy and the individuated privacy necessary to the expression of civic public exchange, such as that demanded by the emergence of a market economy. It was believed that the family and participation in its spatial and relational boundaries, as autonomous from those of the state and economy, ensured the reproduction of private individuals who could behave outwardly as if they were inwardly free (Habermas 1991). In other words, the household became part of the naturalising alibi essential to the magical production and reproduction of civic consciousness (McClintock 1995).

Contamination and the proxemics of constraint

For the late nineteenth and early twentieth centuries, coloured artisans and labourers settled in Cape Town in emerging working-class neighborhoods like District Six, which, because of its proximity to the city and to commercial centres offered viable opportunities for the production of private households. A contemporary resident who was forcibly removed in the 1960s expresses the psychological benefit of being able to return home to District Six at the end of a workday:[6] 'District Six was my refuge – a place to feel safe and happy, it was wonderful to come home at night and be with all my people' (Adams and Suttner 1988: 55). District Six (originally called District Twelve) had evolved, by the late nineteenth century, into a cosmopolitan, architecturally complex, mixed community or ghetto, depending on your point of view. In the words of sociologist Don Pinnock, it

> was originally farmland. It was first settled by whites attached to the Dutch East India Company. Then in the early-nineteenth century it expanded rapidly when members of the city's growing middle class began to build modest homes for themselves within easy reach of the central area.... The houses were unpretentious, mostly two-storied, and built in terraces in a style which has come to be accepted as typical of the Cape under Georgian and Victorian rule. Narrow blocks were laid out parallel to Hanover Street, and small semi-detached houses with long service lanes were built. (Pinnock 1984: 19)

Eventually, however, the respectable layer of District Six expanded inward, proliferating a dimension of the community's space that was inaccessible from the public sphere of the street. A built layer, in essence, was added and hidden from public view: 'Behind the respectable facades ... [emerged] a grid of streets of jerry-built row housing in which the poor lived in overcrowded conditions' (Marks and Bezzoli 2000: 266). This practice proliferated as the space was taken over by predominantly low-income coloured as well as immigrant European families seeking cheap housing in close proximity to other family members and centres of industrial production. As a result, District Six became crowded and dense, drawing all sectors of South Africa's population into close proximity. Shamil

---

[6] District Six was destroyed in 1960, its residents were relocated to specifically coloured townships on the Cape Flats, and nothing was ever built in its place. One of the primary complaints among those who were relocated into the council flats and housing complexes which characterised these areas was the distance that had to be travelled in order to get to their places of work.

Jeppie captures the inward retreat of families by means of a reordering of space in his description of domestic intimacy in District Six of the 1950s:

> Houses were compact places. Given that they were mainly single-story semi-detached houses or double-story row houses, they were long and narrow rather than square and spacious, giving them a sense of depth from the stoep or front entrance. A net curtain was very often hung at the end of the lobby, cutting off either the kitchen or the sitting room from the street. The curtain represented an internal frontier between private and public. It symbolically protected the intimate domestic space and kept the world at bay. Behind it, women could be less concerned with their appearance, a family's real class – in the colloquial sense – could be hidden or revealed, and arguments settled without the rest of the neighborhood watching. (1998: G4)

It is with the persistent outbreak of disease in the late nineteenth century (first smallpox, and then bubonic plague) that this condensed overcrowded layer, obscured behind polite facades, becomes exposed to public scrutiny. The very first forced removals in Cape Town occurred in 1901 with the outbreak of plague.[7] Eventually, District Six became one of the primary targets of sanitation rhetoric and drew the concern of apartheid urban planners to the fact that it was dangerous and in need of 'surgical' excision (Pinnock 1984, 1989). The built environment and the surface of the body become continuously conflated where urban pathology is associated with overcrowding and the condensed contact that proliferates among specific bodies. Statistics for 1995 and 1996, in fact, indicate that, of all the population groups in South Africa (Asian, black, coloured, white), coloureds have the highest number of persons per household in urban areas and one of the lowest in rural areas (Van der Merwe and Van der Merwe 2000). Part of the official (apartheid) perception that coloureds exhibit inherent criminal proclivities comes from the observation that they live in too close contact with each other.

Such official perception has its own continuity, however; it does not emerge strictly out of the apartheid architect's imagination. Overcrowding, by the late nineteenth century, was an indication to the public, particularly Cape Town's Municipality, that inner city coloured residents were incapable of the 'proper' use of space. 'As far back as 1867 District Six was considered overcrowded, and for the next hundred years migration into the area continued almost unabated' (Pinnock 1984: 20). Public discourse generated around periodic out-breaks of epidemics between the late nineteenth and early twentieth centuries in Cape Town indicates an ongoing concern about the ways in which coloureds, particularly Malays, governed their own bodies. The following quotes suggest the broader sentiment of the period:

> Sirs – The Malays refuse to be vaccinated, and, as a matter of course, are being decimated by the smallpox. Serve 'em right say I. But I wish to know if the Mohammedan Malays who won't adopt the only precaution which can check the spread of a foul disease, are to be at liberty to go about communicating to the European Christians the disease in question. Looking into a Wynberg omnibus this afternoon, I found it occupied by six dirty, greasy, fat, old Malay women. (*Cape Argus*, 26 October 1858)
>
> Kindly inform me and the public at large as to the best method of disinfecting washing, etc. There is a grave danger attached to the sending out of wash clothes, for in the majority of cases they are taken to the dwelling-houses of the Malays.... (*Cape Times*, 6 March 1901)
>
> The habits and manner of living of both Native and Coloured people favor the spread of

---

[7] Africans were forced out of the center of the city and onto the Cape Flats into areas like Ndabeni. This was one of the first efforts to separate African and Coloured residents of the city.

disease.... If such [contaminated] persons could be segregated it would do much to reduce the number of [diseased] patients. (*Municipal Journal*, September 1918)

With the forced removal of Africans in 1901, Cape municipal attention became focused on intervention into the habits of working-class coloureds, particularly in the domains of cleanliness, spatial organisation of households and child-rearing practices (see Records of the Medical Officer of Health, Cape Archives). Such scrutiny brought the gaze of scientific experts directly into the private domains of coloured households.

Contamination can therefore be understood as another spatial component of the categorical association between particular bodies, their own interior qualities and the spaces they occupy. The fact that the area many coloureds currently associate themselves with is District Six, where the rigid boundary distinctions of Victorian society were challenged in many ways, indicates the emotional energy that prevails in the ambiguous links established by the difficulty many households experienced in preserving privacy. Because District Six became publicly associated with crime, poverty and unhealthy living conditions, its predominantly coloured residents also became associated with these qualities. It was decided that District Six posed a health risk and therefore had to be systematically sterilised, resulting in its total demolition the early 1960s.

Expectations that emancipated slaves and free blacks would automatically establish the kinds of habits and households that would allow them to participate in the benefits of full citizenship under the British have prevailed into the twentieth century. These habits were initially inculcated by missionaries and then by the nurses and teachers trained and deployed by urban municipal officials. But, the proliferation of epidemic disease and eventually crime and overcrowding meant that coloureds who lived in the city's centre and satellite suburbs were assumed incapable of the control and discipline necessary to the enjoyment of the fruits of a civilised status.

Conclusion

Consciousness, considered the wellspring of civil society, becomes a magical and *sui generis* quality for those espousing instrumentalist interpretations of political action. Civic-mindedness is something that has to be historically accounted for, and in South Africa such a history begins with the valorisation of gendered households, private property and a built environment which unequivocally separates public virtue from private vice. To understand the embrace, reification and occasional contradiction of such qualities of consciousness by contemporary coloureds requires an understanding of the incomplete inculcation of such habits of mind by those coloureds consciously and unconsciously constrained by the limits of their own liberation.

References

Abrahams, Yvette (1997), 'The Great Long National Insult: "Science", Sexuality and the Khoisan in the 18th and Early 19th Century', *Agenda*, 32: 34–48.
Adams, Hettie and Suttner, Hermione (1988), *William Street, District Six*, Diep River: Chameleon Press.
Bickford-Smith, V. (1989), 'A "Special Tradition of Multi-Racialism?" Segregation in Cape Town in the Late

Nineteenth and Early Twentieth Centuries', in W. James and M. Simons (eds), *The Angry Divide*, Cape Town: David Philip.

—— (1995), *Ethnic Pride and Racial Prejudice in Victorian Cape Town*, Johannesburg: Witwatersrand University Press.

Bourdieu, Pierre (1977), *Outline of a Theory of Practice*, Cambridge: Cambridge University Press.

Coetzee, J.M. (1980), 'Blood, Flaw, Taint, Degeneration: The Case of Sarah Gertrude Millin', *English Studies in Africa*, 23(1): 41–58.

Comaroff, John (1996), 'Ethnicity, Nationalism, and the Politics of Difference in an Age of Revolution', in E. Wilmsen and P. McAllister (eds), *The Politics of Difference*, Chicago: University of Chicago Press.

Comaroff, John and Jean Comaroff (1992), *Ethnography and the Historical Imagination*, Boulder: Westview Press.

Dooling, Wayne (1994), '"The Good Opinion of Others": Law, Slavery, and Community in the Cape Colony, *c.*1760–1830', in N. Worden and C. Crais (eds), *Breaking the Chains*, Johannesburg: Witwatersrand University Press.

Elphick, R. and H. Giliomee, (eds) (1989), *The Shaping of South African Society, 1652–1840*, Middletown: Wesleyan University Press.

Fabian, Johannes (1987), 'Hindsight: Thoughts on Anthropology Upon Reading Francis Galton's Narrative of an Explorer in Tropical South Africa (1853)', *Critique of Anthropology*, 7(2): 37–49.

Fanon, Frantz (1967), *Black Skin White Masks*, New York: Grove Weidenfeld.

February, V.A. (1981), *Mind Your Colour*. London: Kegan Paul International.

Gilman, Sander (1986), 'Black Bodies, White Bodies: Toward an Iconography of Female Sexuality in Late Nineteenth-Century Art, Medicine, and Literature', in Henry Louis Gates, Jr (ed.), *'Race', Writing, and Difference*, Chicago: Univerisity of Chicago Press.

Gould, Stephen Jay (1981), *The Mismeasure of Man*, New York: Norton.

Habermas, Jürgen (1991), *The Structural Transformation of the Public Sphere*, Cambridge: MIT Press.

Holmes, Rachel (1995), '"White Rapists Made Coloureds (and Homosexuals)"', in M. Gevisser and E. Cameron (eds), *Defiant Desire*, London: Routledge.

Horowitz, Donald (1991), *A Democratic South Africa? Constitutional Engineering in a Divided Society*, Berkeley: University of California Press.

Jeppie, Shamil (1998), 'Interiors, District Six, c. 1950', in H. Judin and I. Vladislavic (eds), *Architecture, Apartheid and After*, Rotterdam: Netherlands Architectural Institute.

Jung, Courtney (2000), *Then I Was Black: South African Political Identities in Transition*, New Haven: Yale University Press.

Lefebvre, Henri (1991), *The Production of Space*, Oxford: Blackwell Publishers.

McAllister, Patrick and Sharp, John (1993), 'The Ethnic Taboo', *Indicator South Africa*, 10(3): 7–10.

McClintock, Anne (1995), *Imperial Leather: Race, Gender and Sexuality in the Colonial Contest*, New York: Routledge.

Malan, Antonia (1993), 'Households of the Cape, 1750 to 1850 Inventories of the Archaeological Record', Ph.D. Thesis, University of Cape Town.

—— (1998) 'Beneath the Surface – Behind the Doors. Historical Archaeology of Households in Mid-Eighteenth Century Cape Town', *Social Dynamics*, 24(1): 88–118.

Marais, J.S. (1968), *The Cape Coloured People*, Johannesburg: Witwatersrand University Press.

Marks, Rafael and Bezzoli, Marco (2000), 'The Urbanism of District Six, Cape Town', in D. Anderson and R. Rathbone (eds), *Africa's Urban Past*, Oxford: James Currey.

Martin, Marilyn (1996), 'Forward', in Pippa Skotnes (ed.), *Miscast: Negotiating the Presence of the Bushmen*, Cape Town: University of Cape Town Press.

Mason, John (1994), 'Paternalism Under Siege: Slavery in Theory and Practice During the Era of Reform, *c.* 1825 Through Emancipation', in N. Worden and C. Crais (eds), *Breaking the Chains*, Johannesburg: Witwatersrand University Press.

Mauss, Marcel (1973), 'Techniques of the Body', *Economy and Society*, 2(1): 70–88.

Meltzer, Lalou (1994), 'Emancipation, Commerce and the Role of John Fairbairn's *Advertiser*', in N. Worden and C. Crais (eds), *Breaking the Chains*, Johannesburg: Witwatersrand University Press.

Nasson, Bill (1991), *Abraham Esau's War*, Cambridge: Cambridge University Press.

Philip, John (1969 [1828]), *Researches in South Africa*, reprint, New York: Negro University Press, Vols I and II.

Pinnock, Don (1984), *The Brotherhoods*, Cape Town: David Philip.

—— (1989) 'Ideology and Urban Planning: Blueprints of a Garrison City', in W. James and M. Simons (eds), *The Angry Divide*, Cape Town: David Philip.

Ross, Robert (1999), *Status and Respectability in the Cape Colony, 1750–1870*, Cambridge: Cambridge University Press.

Sales, Jane (1975), *Mission Stations and the Coloured Community of the Eastern Cape 1800–1852*, Cape Town:

A.A. Balkema.

Scarry, Elaine (1985), *The Body in Pain*, New York: Oxford University Press.

Scully, Pamela (1994), 'Private and Public Worlds of Emancipation in the Rural Western Cape, *c*. 1830–42', in N. Worden and C. Crais (eds), *Breaking the Chains*, Johannesburg: Witwatersrand University Press.

—— (1997), *Liberating the Family? Gender and British Slave Emancipation in the Rural Western Cape, South Africa, 1823–1853*, Portsmouth: Heinemann.

Sharp, John (1996), 'Ethnogenesis and Ethnic Mobilization: A Comparative Perspective on a South African Dilemma', in E. Wilmsen and P. McAllister (eds), *The Politics of Difference*, Chicago: University of Chicago Press.

Sharp, John and Boonzaier, Emile (1994), 'Ethnic Identity as Performance: Lessons from Namaqualand', *Journal of Southern African Studies*, 20(3): 405–16.

Shell, Robert (1989), 'The Family and Slavery at the Cape, 1680–1808', in W. James and M. Simons (eds), *The Angry Divide*, Cape Town: David Philip.

—— (1994), *Children of Bondage*, Johannesburg: Witwatersrand University Press.

Skotnes, Pippa (ed.) (1996), *Miscast: Negotiating the Presence of the Bushmen*, Cape Town: University of Cape Town Press.

Van der Merwe, Hannes and Izak Van der Merwe (2000), 'Population: Structure and Dynamics in Crowded World', in R. Fox and K. Rowntree (eds), *The Geography of South Africa in a Changing World*, Oxford: Oxford University Press.

Wicomb, Zoë (1996), Keynote Address, African University English Teachers Association Annual Meeting, University of the Western Cape, 4 July.

—— (1998), 'Shame and Identity: the Case of the Coloured in South Africa', in D. Attridge and R. Jolly (eds), *Writing South Africa*, Cambridge: Cambridge University Press.

Wilmsen, Edwin, Saul Dubow and John Sharp (1994), 'Introduction: Identity and Nationalism in Southern Africa', *Journal of Southern African Studies*, 20(3): 347–53.

Wilson, Elizabeth (1991), *The Sphinx in the City: Urban Life, the Control of Disorder, and Women.* Berkeley: University of California Press.

Worden, Nigel (1998–9), 'Space and Identity in VOC Cape Town', *Kronos*, 25: 72–87.

Worden, Nigel and Clifton Crais (eds) (1994), *Breaking the Chains*, Johannesburg: Witwatersrand University Press.

Young, Crawford (1994), 'Ethnic Diversity and Public Policy: An Overview', Unpublished Manuscript.

12

Palaces of Desire
Century City & the Ambiguities of Development [1]

RAFAEL MARKS

Following in the wake of international urban trends, South African cities are rapidly transforming into archetypal postmodern cities. Just as the 'apartheid city' developed through a combination of racist ideologies and Modernist functionalism, so our new urban spaces are shaped through the articulation of local conditions with global economic and cultural forces. Released from the grip of state control, our cities are now at the mercy of that most nebulous of conceits – the free market. Not so much freedom of the city, as freedom to profit.

Through its sheer scale and bravado, the rapidly developing Century City symbolises this new South African urban condition. A postmodern phoenix rising from a vast tract of alien vegetation from the late 1990s onwards, this is not just another development in the city, it is a city in itself. Combining retail, leisure, offices, residential and ecological components under one proverbial roof, Century City represents the ultimate commodification of urban space and services. There are no low-cost housing projects here, or public schools or libraries, only those aspects of urban life that can be conveniently repackaged, reprocessed and reimaged. One can live, work and shop within the same complex without having to leave the 'City's' gates, inhabiting a fictitious space, insulated from the troubles beyond its borders. Constructing a fantasy pre-modern urbanism in the centre of post-apartheid Cape Town it is the ultimate real fake. Yet its ramifications are anything but fake.

This chapter explores some of the urgent theoretical and practical questions that Century City raises. Three main themes are explored. The first locates Century City in the global phenomenon of market-led urban development that has overtaken Cape Town. It is within the contradiction between public rhetoric promoting urban equity and economic development, and the reality of market forces that Century City has been able to develop. The relevance of such developments in this city remains arguable and calls into question the ability or political will of local and other government authorities to influence

---

[1] An earlier version of this paper, written in collaboration with Marco Bezzoli, was presented to the Urban Futures conference, held in Johannesburg, July 2000.

225

them. The second theme is the loss of the public realm. It explores the implications of the new private city, a space of minority privilege and majority exclusion, with its consequent implications for urban citizenship. The third theme to be explored is that of urban identity and local heritage. With a cacophony of bastardised architectural 'styles', the development is a postmodern simulacrum, the ultimate 'hyperreal' experience. Yet if the city is serious about inclusive forms of urban development, about instilling a sense of civic pride and meaningful public spaces, we need to move beyond the wave of nostalgic pastiche that currently grips the city.

Century City occupies an ambiguous position in the development of the city. While celebrated in the media, it represents a serious missed opportunity to restructure the city through democratic and progressive urban regeneration, through a genuine reinvigoration of the public realm, and by instilling a common vision and identity to the city. The question left hanging is who is in control of Cape Town's urban development and what form should it take?

Postmodern geographies

The global phenomena of urban polarisation and restructuring have been well documented in the cities of the West, most famously in urban studies of Los Angeles, where the condition of postmodern urbanisation has been most clearly sketched out. Edward Soja (1995) identifies six 'geographies' which define this condition. The first is a restructuring of the economic base of urbanisation, from Fordist to post-Fordist modes of production. In other words, the shift from the tight organisation of mass production and mass consumption to more flexible production systems, vertically disintegrated but geographically clustered in 'new industrial spaces'.

The second geography is the internationalisation and the global expansion of capital with greater interconnectedness to other world cities, through shifts in economic conditions as well as culture and population movement. The third 'geography' can be described as a radical restructuring of urban form and of the conventional language used to describe cities. From megacity to edge city, from technoburb to exopolis, a great number of neologisms describe the opposing tendencies that have resulted in the 'city simultaneously being turned inside out and outside in' (ibid.: 131).

The fourth and fifth geographies describe the consequences of increasing privatisation of the public realm and the changing social structure of urbanism: marked increases in social, economic and cultural inequalities and increasing fortification and wallification of the various aspects of urban life. The last geography represents a radical shift in the 'urban imaginary, the way in which we relate our images of what is real to empirical reality itself' (ibid.: 134). In many ways this is the most pertinent aspect of the postmodern condition, involving the intrusion and growing power of an urban hyperreality, of simulations and simulacra – exact replicas of originals that never existed. Our urban spaces have become an alternative Sim City, a 'hypersimulation that confounds and reorders the traditional ways we have been able to distinguish between what is real and what is imagined' (ibid.: 135).

Fragmented development

Cape Town displays many of those qualities described above. Continuing along a trajectory set many years ago, the city is undergoing a rapid transformation along two predominant lines. Released from the grips of the apartheid state, the 'free market' has been set loose on existing inequitable urban conditions, consolidating our cities into ever more divided and segregated spaces. No longer only along race but along class lines as well. While the influx of rural migrants continues to swell the informal settlements daily, so the city's edges are continually eaten up by the virulent spread of *arriviste* suburbia. And while billions of rands pour into these suburbs, so the poorer areas continue to languish, recipients of a fraction of this investment.

This divergent development has a clear geographical pattern. The vast majority of the poor live in the south-east region – Khayelitsha, Nyanga, Phillipi, where social conditions are poor, infrastructure absent or inadequate and the communities are spatially removed from economic opportunities (CMC 1998). By contrast, areas such as Bellville and Durbanville to the north have a well-developed transport infrastructure, a diverse range of land uses, including commercial development, employment opportunities, high-quality educational facilities, and development space and good service provision (ibid.).

Apartheid policies of decentralisation, combined with modernist ideologies and subsequent free market economics, have led to an urban development characterised by the hybridisation of the periphery and centre (GUST 1999), where the outskirts of the city have adopted many of the characteristics of the classic city and blown out to the scale of the motor car. While this pattern is uneven it is clearly articulated in areas such as Tygerberg/ Durbanville and Claremont, which have become major contenders for the position of primary economic generators in the region. The largest new developments also tend to focus on the periphery, from the R3.5 billion Capricorn Technology and Industrial Park and R1.5 billion Westlake Business Park near Muizenberg, to the R7 billion Saldhana Steel plant to the north. The Waterfront remains the only significant development in the city centre.

These and other major developments, including Century City and the recently completed SunWest Casino in Goodwood, illustrate a further characteristic of the city's fragmentation, that of urban discontinuities and urban voids. Invariably zones of commodified public space and thematised developments, these areas of privilege represent pockets of investment at the expense of the surrounding areas. While official discourse seeks the transformation of Cape Town into a more equitable and integrated city, the reality is marked by inadequate investment to alleviate the legacy of apartheid, while commercial development capitalises on the globalisation of Cape Town. The contrast between the flourishing private sector and the deepening poverty of the Western Cape could not be starker. In 1999, private non-residential investment in the Western Cape amounted to over R10 billion, or 66 per cent of total investment. By contrast, government investment amounted to less than 1.5 billion, or 9.4 per cent of total investment, while Provincial Administration's housing and local government budget for 1999/2000 was only R85.5 million. Concurrently, housing subsidies to the Western Cape were cut in 2000 by 32 per cent to R238 million (*Cape Times* 2000). As Christine Boyer (1992) argues in another context, in a city of fragmented development 'increasing spatial

Photo 1: The new public realm – anyplace, anytime, anywhere (© Marco Bezzoli)

differentiation results, and the gap looms larger between neglected land and revalued places, between the poor that the market ignores and the well-to-do that it privileges'.

Meanwhile the CBD suffers a flight of capital. With little available land and no private/ public partnership funding, the city centre is fighting a losing battle with the competing pressures for development and funding in the decentralised 'CBDs' of Khayelitsha, Phillippi, Durbanville and Claremont. A tension exists between the need to develop the periphery, where the vast majority of the city's population live, and the need to maintain the 'historical centre' of the city as an economically and socially viable CBD. Things have got so bad in the centre that business leaders and local government have got together to form the Cape Town (Central City) Partnership, reminiscent of the Business Improvement Districts (BIDs) of America, where businesses and property owners tax themselves voluntarily in order to maintain, improve and control parts of the city centre (Zukin 1995: 33). Utilising a 'managing into the street approach' to properties under their control, the Partnership aims to revitalise the city centre by managing, developing and promoting it as a leading centre for retail, commercial, residential, cultural, entertainment, educational, tourism and leisure activities (*Financial Mail*, 27 August 1999). One property specialist has suggested that the only way the CBD will survive is by managing it like a supranational shopping centre.

Globalising Cape Town

The expansion of globalised capital, though still largely concentrated in the First World, has major ramifications for South African cities. The increasing importance of regional trade blocs and the massive spread of electronic commerce have blurred national boundaries. Cities have become more like city states, no longer tied to local or national borders but linked into an international network of urban economies and cultures. And the cities themselves are splintering into a multitude of semi-autonomous zones, creating murky regions of private/public partnerships and commercial interest.

Nationally, the government treads a delicate line between the global imperative of GEAR policies and the national rhetoric of poverty alleviation and social justice. At the metropolitan level, the authorities recognise the dual challenge of promoting Cape Town as a global city and tourist destination while providing access to basic urban infra-structure and services at an affordable rate in the marginalised areas. As one document authored by the now defunct Cape Metropolitan Council noted, 'the core business of local government [is to reduce] poverty to enhance global competitiveness and improve living standards of the poor' (CMC no date).

The Provincial Administration similarly promotes the Western Cape, and Cape Town in particular, as a world city. As part of this globalising vision, eight core sectors are being promoted in order to achieve a 'desired growth pattern'. These include tourism, hi-tech industry, film and TV production, and craft production, as well as financial services and medical services, research and equipment (WESGRO 1999a). In order to achieve this, Province places special emphasis on the upgrading of transport facilities, particularly the airport and port; putting Cape Town in the fast lane of the information superhighway; expanding the Western Cape's professional services sector; and developing a strong private equity and venture capital sector (WESGRO 2000). The amount spent by the Provincial Administration on business promotion and tourism rose from R24.3 million to R143.9 million between 1998 and 2000. At 1.4 per cent of the overall Provincial budget, this figure is nearly double that allocated to housing and local government (WESGRO 1998/9). Some of the effort would appear to be paying off. Financial and business services, though employing only 5.9 per cent of the region's workforce, contributes nearly 16.4 per cent of the Western Cape's gross regional product, second only to manufacturing (ibid.).

At the time of Century City's inception and main period of construction, Cape Town's six local municipalities operated in a state of flux. They were caught in the contradiction of being given greater responsibilities to provide urban services to an increasing population with decreasing public funds. With diminishing intergovernmental transfers of funds, they became increasingly dependent on their rates base for funding. Mandated through Integrated Development Plans to identify key service delivery objectives and mechanisms for addressing basic needs in the area, they also had to link planning to budgeting and implementation processes. Yet the pressure to attract investment pitted each council against the other and the absence of effective metropolitan coordination led to a winner-takes-all situation. Each Municipality sold itself to the market in glossy brochures promoting investment and development opportunities. With only 4.6 per cent of the Metropolitan region's population, Blauberg Municipality, Century City's authority of

Photo 2: Palaces of desire – Century City from the N1 (© Marco Bezzoli)

Photo 3: The walk to work – the Century City's 'convenience and accessibility' is only for those with cars (© Marco Bezzoli)

Photo 4: The privatised road system – Century City emphasises security and the car

(© Marco Bezzoli)

Photo 5: Disneyfication of the city – thematisation of public and private life

(© Marco Bezzoli)

choice, visioned itself to be 'the most preferred location in South Africa ... where ordinary people strive to settle; entrepreneurs want to invest; South Africans choose to spend their holidays; and foreign tourists insist on visiting' (WESGRO September 1999b). The newly formed Unicity, combining the Cape Metropolitan Council and the six municipalities into an overarching authority, may go some way towards rectifying this intra-urban rivalry, while at the same time attempting to make the city more efficient and effective in the global competition for investment.

The MSDF (Metropolitan Spatial Development Framework)

The commodification and marginalisation of local government responsibilities has also seen the role of local authority planners become increasingly privatised. Two different sets of rules have come to govern the practice of planning. Planners who act as agents of the state bureaucracies, claiming to act in the 'public interest', and those who are agents of private capital, responsible ultimately to the bottom line of profitability (Dear 1989: 450). There is a constant flow of professionals gaining experience in the public sector moving into the private sector, where they can exert greater influence. Property developers have already developed an analogous planning apparatus, whereby they employ their own experts to navigate and influence the bureaucratic maze (ibid.). Concurrently, public planners have been convinced by the rhetoric of a corporatist-style planning, in which the rules of the development game have been conceded in advance (ibid.). At the end of the day, the role of planners has been reduced to the exigencies of rezoning.

One exception to this tendency is the recently completed and well-publicised Metropolitan Spatial Development Framework (MSDF), commissioned by the CMC. This comprehensive document seeks to guide the form and location of physical development in the Cape Metropolitan Region through policy and legislation. Through the definition and delineation of 'structuring elements' – sub-metropolitan nodes, activity corridors and activity streets, Metropolitan Open Space Systems and Urban Edges, the MSDF seeks to ensure a more sustainable, higher density, more equitable and integrated urban development, while containing urban sprawl and developing 'quality urban environments' (CMC 1999).

While attempting to replace the discredited metropolitan guide plans, for all its good intentions, the MSDF represents a further attempt to control urban development through spatial planning. Yet in an economic climate in which the developer is king and the role of planning marginal, the effectiveness of the MSDF is questionable. Despite a comprehensive spatial strategy for the region, local authorities woo capital seeking land for profit, regardless of the larger spatial picture. Focusing on humanistic concepts of 'good city form' and spatial organisation, the MSDF fails to account for the new 'mega projects' mushrooming all over Cape Town.

These developments, of which Century City is but one, seek huge tracts of empty land, easily accessible and easily serviced, more often than not located on the periphery. The developers, Monex, themselves explicitly highlight the problem. In South Africa, where investment is crucial but limited, they state that 'there is an imperative to adopt a flexible approach to investment projects ... the interpretation of the MSDF is arguably less important than the recognition of market forces' (Planning Partnership 1999: 137). Indeed, Century City sits smack in the void between two run-down strips, Koeberg Road and Voortrekker Road, identified in the MSDF as potential 'activity corridors'. In so doing, it contributes neither much needed investment nor economic or transport linkages into either. Instead, it positions itself as a regional supra-regional development, located on a far superior connector – the N1 freeway, itself developing into a new kind of freeway strip development between Century City and Durbanville.

'City of the millennium'

Century City is big. With R2 billion worth of development ranged across 250 ha of relatively centrally located land, it is the third largest (private or public) development in the Western Cape and by far the biggest single commercial development in the region. The area of the land alone is almost the same size as the CBD. As Monex proudly claims, 'this vote of confidence in the city combines leisure, retail, offices and residential components on a scale never before undertaken in Africa'. Its scale, range of facilities and future cultural and economic impact on the rest of the city lend credence to claims that it is 'a city for the millennium' (*Cape Times*, 24 November 1999).

The history behind the site is clouded in controversy. Originally acquired by housing developers Ilco Homes in 1989 on an overdraft loan from the Boland Bank, the land was destined as an extension to the neighbouring Summer Greens, a low-rise, middle-income suburban residential area. With mounting debts and a planning authority that took three years to approve the rezoning application, Ilco Homes found themselves in financial trouble and the land lay empty for years. In March 1995, at the instruction of the Boland Bank, a major supporter of the then National Party, Ilco Homes was instructed to sign over control to a company nominated by the bank. Enter Monex Developers, in whom Boland Bank has a substantial interest.

Buoyant with the success of Tygervalley Shopping Centre, the first 'shoppertainment' complex in Cape Town, they had been working on the Century City project for two years and made several overseas trips to market it internationally. They had also been talking to the then Milnerton Planning Department for at least a year, which perhaps explains why the rezoning application for the new development was passed by the newly formed Nat-controlled Blauberg Municipality in less than three weeks (*Noseweek*, Issue 13, August 1995).

The vision began to materialise in the form of a General Development Plan approved by the planning authorities a few months later. Less a vision for development than a series of conjectures, the plan identified portions of the site for future possible precincts – office park, theme park, shopping centre, casino. The proposals illustrated a hybrid mix of pedestrian-scaled mixed-use urbanity and suburban development, all connected by a sub-urban ring road and separated by acres of parking. As with all city plans, the plan remains in a constant state of flux, subject to market forces and changing economic fortunes. With so much media hype, it is difficult to keep track of what is fact and what is fiction.

At the heart of the development lies the 'retail component', completed in 2000. Like everything at Century City, size is everything when it comes to the shopping centre. Not only is it the largest in the country with some 121,000 m² of retail space, 460 shops and 45 restaurants, it also houses the largest cinema complex – a 21-screen multiplex cinema seating 4,500 people, the biggest interactive science centre in South Africa – the R40 million MTN Science Centre – and 9400 m² of lettable office area in two eight-storey blocks.

More than just a shopping centre, visitors are provided with 'an extension of a lifestyle' and a series of fourteen micro shopping environments each with its own identity and each tapping into different segments of the market: not so much shopping as 'shoppertainment', where the boundaries between retail, culture and education have become irreversibly blurred. 'The vision for the centre is not to create just another shopping mall, but an exciting holistic experience in an environment that will be pleasing to everyone while catering for most lifestyle groups,' says managing director Martin Wragge (*Cape Times*, 24 November 1999). Explicitly aimed at capturing the tourist market, the shopping centre boasts drop-off and collection areas for coaches, welcome lounges and 'a host of guest services not provided at any other shopping centre in South Africa'.

Perhaps the most high-profile feature of the development is the R350 million Ratanga Junction theme park. Subtitled 'the wildest place in Africa', and offering 'unparalleled entertainment for the whole family', it consists essentially of a series of rides through the nether regions of the African jungle. Hosted by a series of fantastical characters such as Felix the Belgian scientist and Cherub – part crocodile, part monkey, part bird – visitors are transported into a land of 'fantasy and adventure'. Rides include Crocodile Gorge, where one encounters a 'remnant of a stilt village belonging to an ancient tribe of hunter gatherers' and a crashed 'Ratanga Air Transportation Service Dakota', and the Diamond Devil Run, where visitors hurtle 'in and out of the old original and dilapidated mine shaft built by the Diamond Devil Mining Co. at the turn of the century'. Ratanga reconstructs a fictitious African identity and history, most explicitly in the mould of Disneyland.

Adjacent to the Ratanga complex is the R50 million Dockside [*sic*] nightclub and entertainment centre, capitalising on Cape Town's entry into the globalised and commodified culture of big-name concerts and international club nights.

To the south of the shopping complex lies the office park. Seeking to attract high-tech companies and professional services that connect into the global economy, it has been developed as an 'intelligent city', providing 'the physical and technological infrastructure to meet tenants' and residents' requirements in the future'. Geared initially to large corporate offices, there is an increasing demand from small and medium businesses who want to be near the 'intense commercial activity' that Century City is generating (*Saturday Argus*, 11 March 2000).

The office park is Century City's major drawcard, capitalising on the flight of business from the city centre towards the northern suburbs. At least seven corporate regional headquarters have already been built, housing the offices of Nashua, PQ Africa, Discovery Health and Telkom, and more recently PricewaterhouseCooper, Nashua and Vodacom. Says the MD of Vodacom, 'the central location of Century City on the N1 midway between Cape Town and Bellville had been a major consideration' in relocating there (*Saturday Argus*, ibid.). Despite their 'intelligence', the buildings are dressed up in pastiche neoclassical (read: neocolonial) clothing, an architectural and urban design language intended to distinguish this precinct 'as something special and worthy of patronage' (Planning Partnership 1999: 22).

Even before the final finial had been placed on the boundary fences, another 'mixed use precinct' was under way. Described in the planning documents as a 'highly visible and accessible' mixed-use activity corridor and intended to have a more urban character than the office parks alongside the N1, it is in fact destined to be a heady concoction of Disneyesque fantasy even further removed from the pre-industrial Europe that the rest of the development is intended to evoke.

On the periphery of the main development lies Century Place, a 'walled security village'. Offering 'stylish architecture', 'elegant lifestyle' and an 'unparalleled invest-ment', this small development is safely hidden behind a camera-controlled access barrier. Houses are presently selling for between R375,000 and R2 million (Century City 2003). A second similar development, Century View, is also about to start on site, with up to 2,500 houses of different types in different enclaves, including a couple of retirement villages, The Grange and Heritage Close (ibid.).

In the centre of the development is a 16 ha wetlands conservation area, containing a permanent waterbody and a seasonal one. The former drains the canals from the development, while the latter forms part of a sensitive ecosystem that had been disturbed by the development of the Summer Greens housing development to the north. Renamed 'Intaka Island' (from the previous Afrikaans Blouvlei), the creation of this conservation area was a precondition of the Provincial Administration in granting Century City development rights.

In addition to the completed or near-completed projects, Century City proposes a water park, a 'Lifestyle Retail and Motor Precinct' with 27,000 m^2 of lettable space for home, lifestyle and motor showroom retailing (ibid.), a further office precinct called Waterford Mews for small and medium-sized businesses, hotels and a conference centre. Previous press releases have also promised a R120 million theatre for blockbuster musicals such as *Les Misérables* and a R100 million superdome to seat 12,000.

'A city within a city'

The loss of the 'traditional' public realm is a much commented on and much lamented phenomenon, both here and abroad. Although the distinction between pubic and private space has always been ambiguous, today the boundaries have become increasingly blurred. In using the term 'collective space', the Spanish architectural critic Sola-Morales describes 'public spaces that are used for private activities or private spaces allowing a collective usage' (GUST 1999). Shopping centres and theme parks are these new spaces – safe, clean, predictable yet full of hidden promise. The centre of suburban life, they provide a common consumer focus for the amorphous suburbs (Crawford 1992: 22). Sealed from the realities of everyday life, these escapist cocoons, palaces of desire, have become the new public realm, racially mixed meeting places of the new South African middle classes. As Zukin (1995: 54) points out, visual culture, spatial control and private management make shopping centres an ideal type of new public space: 'Cities have never been able to control space so effectively as does corporate culture.'

In South Africa the concept of a 'public realm' has always been more socially and racially fractured than in the West and, in the paranoid social body, controlled secure environments have found a growing market. Visible security is seen as a vital part of the successful marketing of any major commercial or residential development in this country and the fragmented urban landscape has become pockmarked with these privatised public spaces. From 'gated residential communities' to office parks, from 'Technology Parks' to 'Business Parks', from shopping centres to theme parks, these developments reflect an increasing obsession with security and control. As Mike Davis (1990: 233) argued ten years ago in Los Angeles, the 'obsession with physical security systems, and collaterally, with the architectural policing of social boundaries, has become a zeitgeist of urban restructuring, a master narrative in the emerging building environment of the 1990s ... on the bad edge of postmodernity, one observes an unprecedented tendency to merge urban design, architecture and the police apparatus into a single, comprehensive security effort'.

Century City epitomises this 'carceral' city. It is, in effect, a new city state within a city. In a postmodern inversion of medieval urban morphology, the city walls have been brought into the interior. No longer defining and protecting an urban collective, these new city walls exclude and privilege, insulating its inhabitants from the crime and grime beyond its boundaries. With the connivance of the public authorities, Century City has diminished, rather than enhanced, the public realm of the city. Needless to say, this has profound implications for urban citizenship and public rights.

Urban segregation

The private city enhances urban segregation and exclusivity by privileging the wealthy while effectively marginalising the poor. It achieves this in three main ways. The first is through its emphasis on mobility for the car. By locating itself on the N1, Century City is explicitly orienting itself to the car and individualised transport. As Martin Wragge explains, the key to the shopping centre is convenience and accessibility. Century City will have the first shopping centre in the country where visitors can drive directly off the freeway 'without crossing a single traffic light or stop street, straight into the parking lot from the front door' (*Cape Times*, 24 November 1999). The ramp alone has cost R34m and there is space for 9,200 cars, excluding the 3,500 parking bays for Ratanga Junction and the many hundreds of spaces for the office park. Meanwhile, the metropolitan public transport system remains underfunded and the majority of the population cannot afford cars.

The second way of maintaining exclusion is through private security. Even once within the outer walls and control barriers, a further set of gates prevent uncontrolled access into the individual developments. These are all manned by private security guards. The relationship between private transport and individual security is highlighted by Wragge, who stated that 'greater emphasis is being placed on creating an easily accessible and consumer-friendly environment with state of the art parking management technology and high level security through CCTV' (*Cape Times*, 24 November 1999). Indeed, 'enhanced personal security is one of the founding principles of development at Century City' (POA no date). In addition to private security guards patrolling the grounds and a specially set up SWAT team, both funded by all members of the Property Owners Association, Century

City contracts out a contingent of the South African Police, for whom it has provided a special police station in the precinct.

The layers of internal security have developed through an insidious process of privatisation of the internal road network, a process jointly engineered by Monex and the Municipality. Originally developed as the primary access road within the development, Century Boulevard was constructed as a public road by Monex to standards laid down by the Municipality, then vested with the council. In the so-called interests of public safety, Monex subsequently applied to proclaim and lease two sites straddling Century Boulevard. Through a standard legal process called 'closure procedure', the road was deproclaimed as a public road and converted into a publicly owned 'erf' with a private road built on it. Monex could then lease the land from the municipality, which remains responsible for the maintenance of the road and services. Through this process, legal obstacles to the erection of access control booms were removed. Further control points have subsequently been erected at other points along the road.

The third method of ensuring exclusivity of the development is by default – the all-encompassing commodification of the urban realm. The whole emphasis of the development is on the facilitation of consumption, the production of desire and fantasy that can be bought and sold. Substituting a genuine public realm with a simulated fiction, Century City inextricably links shopping with diversion and pleasure. The urban experience is ultimately reduced to a moment of commercial exchange, reserved only for those with money to spare.

Urban governance

The private city also has major implications for urban governance. With no community participation and little public notification of the development prior to the rezoning approval, this major piece of city land has been removed from the hands of the local authority, and hence the public domain. Control of the development remains firmly in Monex's hands. Retaining ownership of Ratanga Junction, the shopping centre and the wetland, it services, subdivides and sells the remaining land according to the General Development Plan. All new owners are obliged to join a Property Owners Association, to which they also pay regular levies.

This form of 'shadow government' (Garreau 1988: 187) is not uncommon in South Africa. Body corporates, homeowners' associations, public/private partnerships, quasi-public institutions and other essentially private regimes have filled the vacuum left by the retreating state. And, as Joel Garreau (ibid.) points out, they are usually organised like corporations and given names that do not begin to hint at their power – they have the power to tax, the power to legislate and the power to coerce. The objective of these organisations is to 'privatise or dismantle public spaces and services and to implant zoning regulations which in effect keep the undesired out' (Holston and Appadurai 1996: 191). Century City's POA is precisely one of those bodies. It ensures that all new developments conform to a set of development rules and regulations, it maintains an aesthetic architectural code (a neocolonial style stipulated by the directors of Monex), and is responsible for internal security, maintenance and general matters pertaining to the upkeep of Century City.

Yet while all land remains ultimately owned or controlled by Monex, the construction of feeder roads and services was subsidised by government. The rezoning and development of the site was made conditional on a financial agreement between council and the developer with regard to partnerships in services provision and construction of roads. The council was responsible for the capital contribution for financing and providing all external engineering services, with an obligation from Monex to provide a contribution to this cost in the form of a development levy, as well as financing of all internal services. This former is to be made in a series of tranche payments totalling R14.275m over a ten-year period and is intended to pay for all future external services necessitated by Century City, such as stormwater and transport routes. And half the cost of Sable Way, a slip road off the N1 providing the main access into the complex, was paid for by the public authorities, a sum of money representing nearly one-quarter of the Province's total housing and local government budget.

Described in one report as an 'innovative public–private partnership in fast tracking infrastructure and services provision' (Department of Constitutional Development, no date: 44), the long-term effects are somewhat different. In paying the services development levy, Monex is absolved of any responsibility for future contributions. Yet now that the services have been built there appears to be no clarity in maintenance responsibilities since the Municipality is ultimately responsible for the major stormwater and electrical reticulation running through the site and which serve the rest of the city. A similar confusion exists with the road network. One of the major constrictions of the over-all development is the accessibility of the site. As the development increases, so will the demand for greater accessibility. Falling outside the dominion of Monex, pressure will no doubt be brought to bear on the Municipality to provide the additional services and roads.

This dilemma is highlighted by Monex themselves in their Revised Development Scenario. In a veiled threat, they claim that

> if the current bulk limitations are enforced on the site in perpetuity, it will choke off vibrant economic growth.... If Monex hit a ceiling of development rights, and had to turn away prospective investors, it would have a negative effect on the region as well as the project. There are many indications which suggest that investors are attracted to particular sites or opportunities, and if these are closed to them, they may not necessarily find a suitable alternative in the city, which means that the investment could be lost entirely. (Planning Partnership 1999: 62)

Developers fully understand the need for planned infrastructure to support their projects, and are quite willing to manipulate government for their purposes. The withdrawal of the state from investment in the public realm supports this shift of fiscal resources to corporate-defined redevelopment priorities (Dear 1996).

The Disneyfication of Cape Town

The privatisation of the urban realm goes hand in hand with the thematisation of public space. While malls assume the status of ersatz cities, the city centre increasingly presents itself more and more as a great open-air shopping mall. In the competitive location game in which cities and regions market themselves, imageability has become a new selling point. This is true both to encourage capital investment and to attract tourists. Spatial design codes and architectural pattern languages become increasingly important in selling the look of an upbeat environment. Lifestyle and liveability, visualised and represented in spaces of conspicuous consumption, become important assets that cities proudly display (Boyer 1992: 201). Simulated landscapes of exotic and imaginary terrains, cleverly combining the fantastic with the real, become the ideal background props for our contemporary acts of consumption (ibid.: 200). As American developer James Rouse once said, 'profit is the thing that hauls dreams into focus' (Crawford 1992: 17).

Century City itself is a carefully constructed fiction of pre-modern European urbanity, evoking a city of bygone days, before the age of monopoly capitalism and mass transport. Four visions presented in Century City's General Development Plan propose a mixed bag of references. The first hints at a sort of 'Edwardian London meets the canals of Amsterdam'. A wrought iron bridge spans the canal, located on an axis with a squat obelisk marking a major traffic turning circle. A triumphal arch marks a main entrance gate into the development, while a 'pleasure boat' in the foreground eagerly awaits non-existent passengers. Various other street furniture and paraphernalia drip with an aesthetic soaked in nostalgia.

The second image, rather less detailed, suggests Venice turned Disneyland. A gondolier and his gondola drift into view, heading for a shopping centre, while a remnant of Rome's forum threatens to collapse under the shear weightlessness of the concept. A third image tries for 'medieval Italy meets nineteenth-century European neoclassicism', Schinkel awash in Tuscany. Heavy monumental architecture flanks inane stone structures. Finally, the last image shows a 'typical pedestrian street' in one of the residential quarters, inspired by 'San Gimignano, Siena, Lucca, Florence-Tuscany'. Potted plants in oversized containers, water fountains, wrought iron street lights, balconies overlooking the street transport an imagined piece of Italy to the flats of Cape Town.

Images such as these are intended to conjure up emotionally satisfying visions of bygone times, a nostalgia for the traditional city when it was a 'coherent place of intimate streets, lined with small-scale facades and shopping arcades, ornamented with signs, punctuated by open spaces, trees, lampposts and benches' (Boyer 1992: 202). They are designed for inattentive viewers, tourists or city travellers who browse these real-life stage-sets, scarcely aware of how the relics of the past have been indexed, framed and scaled. These curious mixtures of reconstituted styles-of-life and fashionable environments have proved effective tourist attractions worldwide. They have become 'culinary and ornamental landscapes through which tourists – the new public of the late twentieth century – graze, celebrating the consumption of place and architecture, and the taste of history and food' (ibid.).

This is not the densified, integrated, equitable city of the MSDF seeking to rebuild the post-apartheid city with meaningful public spaces and a reconstructed urban fabric. Rather, it is a carefully constructed fiction, where, cut off from the realities of the city beyond, the pleasure of the viewer suspends critical judgement. It is not so much densification as disneyfication. As one writer has cogently argued, these developments contribute to the decline of civil society by rendering poverty, homelessness and minority cultures invisible (McNamara 1999: 188). Yet if, as Zukin (1995: 59) argues, theme parks are a tightly structured discourse about society, representing a fictive narrative of social identity, then what does it say about the future direction of our cities? Despite official discourses about integrated development plans and economic and development planning, the reality is that we are witnessing increasing divisions between those who participate in the 'narrative of global corporate culture' (ibid.: 61) and the rest of the population who continue to suffer the legacies of apartheid and poverty.

Public spaces are the primary sites of public culture, windows into the city's soul. They are an important means of framing a vision of social life in the city, a vision both for those who live there and for those who visit. They are also important because they are physical and metaphorical spaces of negotiation, continually mediating the boundaries and markers of human society. Yet the specificity of Cape Town is rapidly becoming replaced by a generic urbanism inflected only by appliqué, in which urban design 'is almost wholly preoccupied with reproduction, [and] the creation of urbane disguises... at pains to assert its ties to the kind of city life it is in the process of obliterating' (Sorkin 1992: xiv). The experience of post-apartheid Cape Town, with its lost sense of community that never was, and increasing crime, segregation and marginalisation, resonates with that of Los Angeles, where social experiences of church, school and ethnicity are not universally shared and 'Disney motifs constitute a common culture, a kind of civil religion of happy endings, worry-free consumption, technological optimism and nostalgia for the good old days...participation without embarrassment' (Weinstein 1996: 31).

Which city is this century in?

Hanging on the wall of the National Gallery in Cape Town is a painting by James Ford entitled 'Holiday time in Cape Town'. Painted in 1904, it presents a panoply of imperial Victorian imagery such as London's Albert Memorial, Garnier's Opera from Paris, a miniature Eiffel Tower, fountains and statues, all fronting a Venetian waterfront with gondolas and pleasure boats. All of Cape Town's multicultural society is out on the promenade participating in a show of civic pageantry. Behind the dense city, with its mix of oriental and European spires, lie verdant farms and forests on the slopes of Table Mountain, embraced by a rainbow. Steam trains take passengers into the nether regions of the mountain, while the mountain itself looms large and ever present, a rugged presence behind the urbane and civilised city.

Both a fantasy of imperial utopia and a celebration of the British empire, much of the imagery embraced in this painting has found its way into Cape Town's contemporary urban environment. Century City itself is James Ford's painting made incarnate, updated and commodified, a city of hyperreality where fiction and fact become indistinguishable. Not so much a reproduction of a past reality, but a simulacrum of a future that never was. Indeed, the only reality at Century City is the cruel logic of the market. In a city so obsessed with pseudo-neocolonial architecture, based on a cleansed and dehistoricised past, the question begged is which century is this city in? Or which city is this century in?

This chapter has stressed the contradiction between public discourses on urban integration and equitable development and the reality of hard-edged global capitalism. In the absence of adequate political will and public funds, pressure is continuously brought to bear on local authorities to approve and subsidise commercial developments such as Century City. The city is beholden to private developers and democratic planning processes have been marginalised. Far from attempting to rectify the inequalities and spatial patterns of the apartheid city, the free market has intensified existing divisions. The rich retreat into their well-serviced laagers, protected by fences, private security and nostalgic fantasy, while the poor are locked outside, battling with decreasing public services. The apartheid legacy of (urban) segregation continues to intensify with differing access to goods and services.

Although South Africa is ostensibly a democratic society with 'free and fair' elections every five years, this national democracy has done little for expanding notions of citizenship at an urban and local level. Citizenship concerns more than the right to participate in politics, 'it also includes other kinds of rights in the public sphere, namely civil, socio-economic, and cultural' (Holston and Appadurai 1996: 200). Cities have traditionally been the strategic arena for the development of citizenship where the concentrations of the non-local, the strange, the mixed and the public catalyse process which expand the rules, meanings and practices of citizenship (ibid.: 188). Indeed, it was in the cities that the fight against apartheid was often the strongest. Yet developments such as Century City undermine attempts to transform and expand notions of citizenship, precisely through its divisive tactics of segregation, its manipulation of public funds, its denial of local culture and history, and perhaps most saliently through the commodification of public services and urban space.

Already we are seeing the ways in which people's identity and cultural allegiance are defined through the market, concerned less with a shared social imaginary than with the latest branded goods. Yet, despite the polarising and disempowering tendencies of the free market, the remaining public spaces of the city may still be the most important sites through which citizenship may be rethought. There may be something irreducible and non-transferable, necessary if not quite sufficient, about the public street and square for the realisation of a meaningfully democratic citizenship (ibid.: 202). For as Michael Sorkin (1992: xv) argues,

> the privatised city … is a lie, simulating its connections, obliterating the power of its citizens either to act alone or to act together…. The theme park presents its happy regulated vision of pleasure … as a substitute for the democratic public realm, and it does so appealingly by stripping troubled urbanity of its sting, of the presence of the poor, of crime, of dirt, of work. In the 'public' spaces of the theme park or the shopping mall, speech itself is restricted: there are no demonstrations in Disneyland. The effort to reclaim the city is the struggle of democracy itself.

References

Boyer, Christine M. (1992), 'Cities for Sale', in Michael Sorkin (ed.), *Variations on a Theme Park*, New York: Noonday Press.

Cape Metropolitan Council (CMC) (1998), 'Levels of Living', report, Cape Town.

Cape Metropolitan Council (1999), 'Metropolitan Spatial Development Framework' report, Cape Town.

Cape Metropolitan Council (CMC) (no date), 'A Poverty Reduction Framework for Local Government in the Cape Metropolitan Area', report, Cape Town.

Century City (2003), official website, centurycity.co.za.

Crawford, Margaret (1992), 'The World as a Shopping Mall', in Michael Sorkin (ed.), *Variations on a Theme Park*, New York: Noonday Press.

Davis, Mike (1990), *City of Quartz*, London: Verso Press.

Dear, M. (1989), 'Survey 16: Privatization and the Rhetoric of Planning Practice', *Environment and Planning D:*

Society and Space, 7.

—— (1996), 'Intentionality and Urbanism in Los Angeles, 1781–1991', in Allen J. Scott and Edward W. Soja (eds), *The City – Los Angeles and Urban Theory at the End of the Twentieth Century*, Los Angeles: University of California Press.

Department of Constitutional Development (no date), 'Local Authorities Role in Local Economic Development', report, Pretoria.

Garreau, Joel (1988), *Edge City – Life on the New Frontier*, New York: Doubleday.

GUST (Ghent Urban Studies Team) (1999), *The Urban Condition: Space, Community and the Self in the Contemporary Metropolis*, Rotterdam: 010 Publishers.

Holston, James and Arjun Appadurai (1996), 'Introduction', in James Holston (ed.), *Cities and Citizenship*, Durham and London: Duke University Press.

McNamara, Kevin R. (1999), 'CityWalk: Los(t) Angeles in the Shape of a Mall', in GUST (1999).

Planning Partnership (1999), 'Century City: Revised Development Scenario and Macro Traffic Impact Assessment', Cape Town; document submitted to Blaauberg Municipality for approval, 2 September 1999.

POA (no date), Century City's Property Owners Association regulations.

Soja, Edward W. (1995), 'Postmodern Urbanisation', in Sophie Watson and Katherine Gibson (eds), *Postmodern Cities and Spaces*, Oxford: Blackwell.

Sorkin, M. (ed.) (1992), *Variations on a Theme Park*, New York: Noonday Press.

Weinstein, Richard S. (1996), 'The First American City', in Allen J. Scott and Edward W. Soja (eds), *The City – Los Angeles and Urban Theory at the End of the Twentieth Century*, Los Angeles: University of California Press.

WESGRO. (1998/9), Annual Report, Cape Town.

—— (1999a), 'Western Cape Economic Monitor', Cape Town, 2nd Issue.

—— (1999b), 'Investment and Development Opportunities: Blaauwberg', Cape Town, September.

—— (2000), 'Western Cape Economic Monitor', Cape Town, January.

Zukin, Sharon (1995), *The Cultures of Cities*, Oxford: Blackwell Publishers.

Index